Fodor

The Himalayan Countries

Kathleen Cox

Fodor's Travel Publications, Inc.
New York and London

Fodor's The Himalayan Countries

Editor: Stephanie Woodard
Art Director: Fabrizio La Rocca
Map Editor: Suzanne Brown
Cartographer: David Lindroth
Illustrator: Karl Tanner
Cover Photograph: Andy Selters/Viesti Associates

Design: Vignelli Associates

About the Author

Kathleen Cox, a contributing writer for *Fodor's India*, writes about the subcontinent for numerous American and Indian publications, including *Travel & Leisure, Harper's Bazaar, Vogue, Indrama,* and *World of India.* She is a featured correspondent for *Indian Express*, India's most widely read newspaper. A former columnist for the *Village Voice* and *Playboy*, she was the co-writer and coproducer of the documentary comedy film, *Gizmo!*

Special Sales

Fodor's Travel Publications are available at special discounts for bulk purchases (100 copies or more) for sales promotions or premiums. Special editions, including personalized covers, excerpts of existing guides, and corporate imprints, can be created in large quantities for special needs. For more information write to Special Marketing, Fodor's Travel Publications, 201 East 50th St., New York, NY 10022. Inquiries from the United Kingdom should be sent to Fodor's Travel Publications, 20 Vauxhall Bridge Rd., London SWV 2SA.

Contents

7 Tibet *302*

Maps and Plans

Foreword

Fodor's Himalayan Countries, the first guide to cover this area exclusively, gives you the information you need to create an *adventure*, which is what a vacation to this part of the world should mean. With this new publication, Fodor's recognizes the importance of creating a *responsible* guidebook. As new destinations open up to tourism, the sudden presence of the foreigner creates a lasting impact, not just on the fragile Himalayan ecosystem, but on the lives of the people for whom these mountains and valleys are home.

This is an exciting time for Fodor's, as we continue our ambitious program to rewrite, reformat, and redesign all 140 of our guides. Here are just a few of the new features:

★ Brand-new computer-generated maps

★ A unique system of numbers and legends to help readers move effortlessly between text and maps

★ A new star rating system for hotels and restaurants

★ Stamped, self-addressed postcards, bound into every guide, to give readers a chance to help evaluate hotels and restaurants

★ Complete page redesign for instant retrieval of information

★ FODOR'S CHOICE—Our favorite adventures, romantic hideaways, festivals, and more

★ HIGHLIGHTS—An insider's look at the most important developments in tourism during the past year

★ TIME OUT—The best and most convenient lunch stops along exploring routes

★ Exclusive background essays to create a powerful portrait of each destination

★ A mini-journal for travelers to keep track of their own itineraries and addresses

The author wishes to express her gratitude to the following government officers for their invaluable assistance: Mr. S. K. Misra, Secretary of Tourism for the Government of India, Mr. B. K. Goswami, Director General of Tourism and Additional Secretary of Tourism for the Government of India, Mrs. Leela Nadhan and Mrs. Sudha Kothary, officers in the Government of India Tourist Office abroad; Mr. Chudasama at Air India; Mr. Mansoor Suhail, Press Attaché for the Pakistan Mission to the United Nations; and Mr. Pervaiz Butt, Managing Director of Pakistan Tourism Development Corporation.

Officers from state tourist departments and corporations in India were also especially helpful: Mr. S. K. Verma, Managing Director of Himachal Pradesh Tourism Development Corporation; Mr. B. R. Singh, Secretary-Commissioner of Tourism, Mr. Mohiuddin Shah, Director of Tourism, and Urgain Loondup Goba, Tourist Officer, Jammu and Kashmir; Mr. Surendra Mohan, Secretary of Tourism, Uttar Pradesh; Mr. Anil Baruah, Director of Tourism, and Ms. Leena Barua, Tourist Officer, Assam; Mr. A. Didar Singh, Secretary of Tourism,

Meghalaya; Mr. K. C. Pradhan, Secretary of Tourism, Ms. Aungi Namgyal, Joint Secretary of Tourism, and Ms. Choki Namgyal, Tourist Officer, Sikkim; Mr. J. Sanyal, Secretary of Tourism, West Bengal; Mr. S. P. Dutt, Manager Tourism, Air India; and Commander Jogindar Singh at Vayudoot and Secretary of the Indian Mountaineering Foundation.

In Pakistan, the following private guides were indispensible: Mr. Fayyaz Ul Hassan, Mr. Asif Zaidi, and Mr. Abdul Shakoor. In Nepal, Mr. Bishnu Subedi, Secretary of the Nepal Association of Travel Agents, provided appreciated assistance. Finally, thanks to Sir Edmund Hillary for his gracious contribution.

While every care has been taken to ensure the accuracy of the information in this guide, the passage of time will always bring change and, consequently, the publisher cannot accept responsibility for errors that may occur.

All prices and opening times quoted here are based on information available to us at press time. Hours and admission fees may change, however, and the prudent traveler will avoid inconvenience by calling ahead.

Fodor's wants to hear about your travel experiences, both pleasant and unpleasant. When a hotel or restaurant fails to live up to its billing, let us know and we will investigate the complaint and revise our entries where the facts warrant it.

Send your letters to the editors of Fodor's Travel Publications, 201 E. 50th Street, New York, NY 10022.

Highlights and Fodor's Choice

Highlights

In the Himalayan countries, the most promising development in 1990 is the increase in vacation options. Trekking is not the only alternative today. Skiing or heliskiing, golfing, fishing, wildlife safaris, hang gliding, mountain biking, reclining in hot springs—they're now happening in the Himalayas.

For travelers heading to Nepal, north India, or north Pakistan, there's more good news. At press time, a favorable exchange rate continued to stretch the dollar's value, and the cost of the fanciest accommodations, most lavish meals, most expensive transportation remained far less than in Europe or the United States. Bhutan, however, which is determined to hold down its number of tourists, recently increased its obligatory daily charges to $110–$250, depending on the time of year and the type of trip (trekking is the cheapest way to visit this country). Group travel to Tibet is also expensive.

Here are the latest tourism developments that can affect your trip.

Bhutan A heavy influx of travelers during the spring and fall has led to chronic overbooking of Bhutan's limited accommodations and a shortage of trustworthy vehicles for in-country sightseeing. To encourage trips during off-peak months, Bhutan's tourist department now offers tours from November to March to the eastern half of the kingdom—renowned for it's world-class weavers—and a series of winter treks, each under a week in duration. Visitors from March to June and September to November can also join a new five-day nature trek. All trips can be booked through Bhutan Travel in New York.

At press time, Bhutan's small 12- and 14-seat national aircraft were out of commission. All flights into the country now use an 80-seat jet.

Nepal In 1989 Nepal and India became embroiled in a serious trade dispute, which shut down numerous border crossings between the two countries and has led to fuel and food shortages in Nepal. The central issues are complex; but at press time, both parties were determined to find a solution. On a brighter note, Nepal recently inaugurated its new international terminal at Tribhuvan Airport in Kathmandu, which should help alleviate airport congestion. As of 1990, visitors can also visit the newly opened former kingdom of Dolpo in the northwest or trek new routes around Mt. Kanchenjunga in the northeast.

India Because of internal political disputes, foreigners planning to visit the state of Assam in the northeast or Srinagar and Leh in Jammu and Kashmir (including Ladakh) are advised to check with the Indian Tourist Department before booking their trip. On the positive side, India offers many new adventures and destinations. In 1990 the northeastern states of Sikkim, Meghalaya, and Assam are no longer completely off-limits. Entrance is still tricky—you must get a special permit and travel with a government approved agency.

Darjeeling in northern West Bengal was closed in 1988 because of political problems, but the disputing factions signed an agreement and once again the Queen of the Hill Stations is receiving guests. Under certain situations a special permit is also required. Travelers bound for Darjeeling can also plan to take the delightful "Toy Train," shut down due to track problems until 1989 (*see* Arriving and Departing, Northern West Bengal in Chapter 5: North India).

In northwestern India, a new road is passable by jeep from Manali in Himachal Pradesh through Ladakh's Zanskar Valley to Leh, Ladakh's district headquarters—a rugged drive through lunar landscapes and an ancient Buddhist realm. The road is open only in summer and you must be part of a group arranged by an approved travel agency.

Pakistan With the election of Benazir Bhutto as prime minister in 1988, Pakistan has joined the democratic community. Thanks to a sympathetic press, there has been an increase in the number of annual visitors.

New accommodations have been built, and additional hotels are planned for the hill station of Murray, north of Islamabad, and Gilgit in the Federally Administered Northern Areas (FANA).

Great new adventures also await visitors to Pakistan in 1990. One of the best is a five-day yak ride to the village of Shimshal in FANA near the border of China. And while everyone has heard of the Karakoram Highway, two lesser known highways to FANA get rave reviews for spectacular vistas and thrills: the recently completed Skardu–Gilgit Road and the Punial Highway, which connects the frontier towns of Gilgit and Chitral. The Punial is still under construction, but don't let that deter you.

Tibet Given the recent problems in China and the ongoing struggle for autonomy in Tibet, the section on this former kingdom has been abridged in this first edition. Tibet remains a destination where visits by foreigners demand thoughtful consideration. At press time, group travel and flights into Lhasa have resumed, but entry into Tibet will still be subject to the mercy of the Chinese authorities.

Fodor's Choice

No two people will agree on what makes a perfect vacation, but it's fun and helpful to know what others think. We hope you'll have a chance to experience some of Fodor's Choices yourself while visiting the Himalayan countries. For detailed information about each entry, refer to the appropriate chapters within this guidebook.

Lodgings

Nepal *Kathmandu:* Yak and Yeti Hotel *(Very Expensive);* Dhulikhel Mountain Resort, Dhulikhel *(Expensive);* Dwarika's Kathmandu Village Hotel *(Moderate)*

The Terai: Tiger Tops Jungle Camps at Royal Chitwan National Park and Royal Bardia Wildlife Reserve *(Very Expensive)*

North India *Himachal Pradesh:* Chapslee, Shimla *(Expensive);* Woodville Palace Hotel, Shimla *(Expensive);* May Flower Guest House, Manali *(Moderate)*

Kashmir: Houseboats on Nagin Lake, Srinagar *(Moderate);* Lake Isle Resort, Srinagar *(Moderate)*

Ladakh: Hotel Lha-Ri-Mo, Leh *(Moderate)*

Northern Uttar Pradesh: Carlton's Hotel Plaisance, Mussoorie *(Moderate);* The Savoy, Mussoorie *(Moderate)*

Assam: Tourist Lodge I, Kaziranga National Park *(Inexpensive)*

Meghalaya: Hotel Pinewood Ashok, Shillong *(Moderate–Inexpensive)*

Northern West Bengal: Himalayan Hotel, Kalimpong *(Moderate):* Windamere Hotel, Darjeeling *(Moderate)*

North Pakistan *Nathiagali:* Hotel Pines *(Inexpensive)*

Karakoram Highway, Part I: PTDC Motel and Campsites, Naran *(Moderate–Inexpensive)*

Federally Administered Northern Areas: Shangrila Tourist Resort, Skardu *(Expensive);* NAWO Rest House, Phandar *(Inexpensive)*

North West Frontier Province: Pearl Continental Hotel, Peshawar *(Expensive);* Swat Serena Hotel, Saidu Sharif *(Moderate);* Chitral Mountain Inn, Chitral *(Inexpensive);* Madyan Hotel, Madyan *(Inexpensive)*

Dining Experiences

Nepal *Kathmandu:* Naachghar *(Expensive);* Fuji Restaurant *(Moderate–Inexpensive);* Rumdoodle *(Moderate–Inexpensive)*

North India *Himachal Pradesh:* Chapslee, Shimla *(Expensive–Moderate)*

Ladakh: Punjabi vegetarian roadside stand, Khalsi *(Inexpensive)*

Northern Uttar Pradesh: The Savoy, Mussoorie *(Expensive)*

Assam: Paradise, Guwahati *(Inexpensive)*

Meghalaya: Pinecone Restaurant, Shillong *(Moderate)*

Northern West Bengal: Glenary's, Darjeeling *(Moderate)*

Sikkim: Blue Poppy, Gangtok *(Inexpensive)*

North Pakistan *Lahore:* Abbott Road food stalls *(Inexpensive)*

Nathiagali: Hotel Pines *(Inexpensive)*

Federally Administered Northern Areas: Shangrila Tourist Resort, Skardu *(Expensive–Moderate)*

North West Frontier Province: Swat Serena Hotel, Saidu Sharif *(Moderate);* Salateen Restaurant, Peshawar *(Inexpensive);* Pathan-burger roadside stall, Khawazakhela *(Inexpensive)*

Journeys

Nepal *Kathmandu:* Drive to Lhasa, Tibet

North India *Himachal Pradesh, Ladakh:* Drive from Manali to Leh

Ladakh: Drive from Kargil to Zanskar

Northern Uttar Pradesh: Drive from Mussoorie to the Char Dhams

Meghalaya: Drive from Shillong to Garo Hills

Himachal Pradesh: Toy Train ride from Kalka to Shimla

Northern West Bengal: Toy Train ride from Bagdogra to Darjeeling

North Pakistan *Federally Administered Northern Areas:* Drive along the Punial Highway; drive along the Karakoram Highway; drive along the Skardu-Gilgit Highway

North West Frontier Province: Drive from Peshawar to Darra-Adam Khel

Tibet Drive from Lhasa to Lake Mansarovar and Mt. Kalash

Outdoor Adventures

Bhutan   *Thimphu:* Trek to Lunana

Eastern Bhutan: Trek to Mera and Sakteng valleys

Nepal   *Kathmandu:* Rafting the Sunkosi

Pokhara: New trek to the ancient kingdom of Dolpo; horseback riding

The Terai: Wildlife safaris, Royal Chitwan National Park

Mt. Everest: Walk-in trek from Jiri; new trek in northeast Nepal to Mt. Kanchenjunga

Jumla: Trek and rafting run to Royal Bhardia Wildlife Reserve

North India   *Himachal Pradesh:* Hang gliding, Kangra Valley; rafting, Sutlej River; trek, Manali to Ladakh

Kashmir: Skiing and golfing, Gulmarg; trek, Kishtwar to Srinagar; trout fishing

Ladakh: Rafting, Zanskar River; trek from Padam to Leh

Northern Uttar Pradesh: Biking, near Corbett National Park; trek, Gangotri Temple to Kedarnath Temple

Assam: wildlife safaris, Manas Tiger Reserve or Kaziranga National Park

Sikkim: Winter trek

North Pakistan   *Karakoram Highway, Part I:* Horseback riding, Balakot to Chilas

Federally Administered Northern Areas: Biking, Karakoram Highway to Khunjerab Pass; trek, Baltoro Glacier to Concordia K2; yak safari, Passu to Shimshal villages

North West Frontier Province: Trek through the Kafir-Kalash villages

Tibet   Trek to Eastern face of Mt. Everest; trek to Mt. Namche Barwa

---

Lazy Thrills

Nepal   *Kathmandu:* Flight over Mt. Everest

North India   *Gangtok:* Helicopter flight around Mt. Kanchenjunga

Delhi: Himalayan Mountain Flight

North Pakistan   *Federally Administered Northern Areas:* Polo match at Shandur Pass or Gilgit

Karakoram Highway, Part I: Pakistan Disco Bus ride, Kaghan Valley

Festivals

Bhutan	*Paro:* Paro Festival
	Thimphu: Thimphu Festival
Nepal	*Kathmandu:* Indra Jatra; Durga Puja; Red Macchendra-natha Jatra
North India	*Himachal Pradesh:* Dussehra in Kulu Valley
	Ladakh: Hemis Festival
	Northern Uttar Pradesh: Daily Arti in Haridwar
	Assam: Rongali and Durga Puja
	Meghalaya: Shillong Tourist Festival; Wangala
North Pakistan	*North West Frontier Province:* Chitral Festival; Jashn-E-Khyber Festival, Peshawar; Kafir-Kalash festivals

Pilgrimages

North India	*Himachal Pradesh:* Lake Manimahesh
	Kashmir: Amar Nath
Tibet	Mt. Kailash and Lake Mansarovar

Cultural and Religious Sites

Nepal	*Kathmandu:* Temples and monuments in Old Kathmandu, Lalitpur, and Bhaktapur
North India	*Himachal Pradesh:* Bhimakali Temple, Sarahan
	Kashmir: Nishat Bagh and other Moghul gardens, Srinagar
	Ladakh: Alchi and other Ladakhi monasteries
	Northern Uttar Pradesh: Ashrams in Haridwar; Kedarnath and Badrinath Temples
	Assam: Kamakhya Temple, Guwahati
	Sikkim: Rumtek and Pemayangtse monasteries
North Pakistan	*Lahore:* Old city
	North West Frontier Province: Old city of Peshawar
Tibet	Jokhang Temple and Potala Palace, Lhasa; Barkor Bazaar, Lhasa; Kumbum Monastery, Gyantse; Tashilhunpo Monastery, Shigatse

Tribal Peoples

Bhutan	*Eastern Bhutan:* People of Mera and Sakteng valleys
North India	*Himachal Pradesh:* The Malanas and the Gaddi
	Meghalaya: The Garo

North Pakistan   *Karakoram Highway, Part I:* The Gujjar, Kaghan Valley
North West Frontier Province: The Kafir-Kalash near
Chitral; the Pathans

Nature's Greatest Display

Pakistan   *Federally Administered Northern Areas:* The Karakorams
and their glaciers

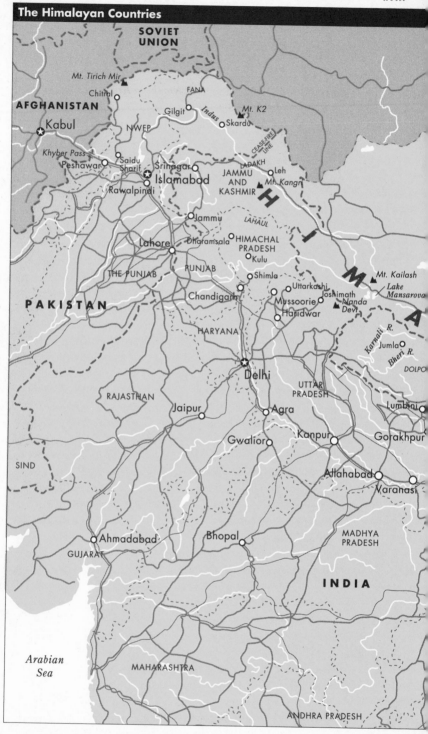

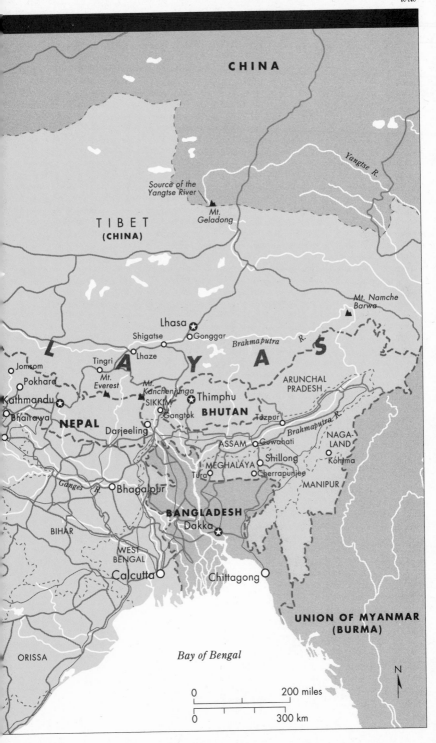

World Time Zones

Numbers below vertical bands relate each zone to Greenwich Mean Time (0 hrs.).
Local times may differ, as indicated by lightface numbers on the map.

Algiers, **29**

Anchorage, **3**

Athens, **41**

Auckland, **1**

Baghdad, **46**

Bangkok, **50**

Beijing, **54**

Berlin, **34**

Bogotá, **19**

Budapest, **37**

Buenos Aires, **24**

Caracas, **22**

Chicago, **9**

Copenhagen, **33**

Dallas, **10**

Delhi, **48**

Denver, **8**

Djakarta, **53**

Dublin, **26**

Edmonton, **7**

Hong Kong, **56**

Honolulu, **2**

Istanbul, **40**

Jerusalem, **42**

Johannesburg, **44**

Lima, **20**

Lisbon, **28**

London (Greenwich), **27**

Los Angeles, **6**

Madrid, **38**

Manila, **57**

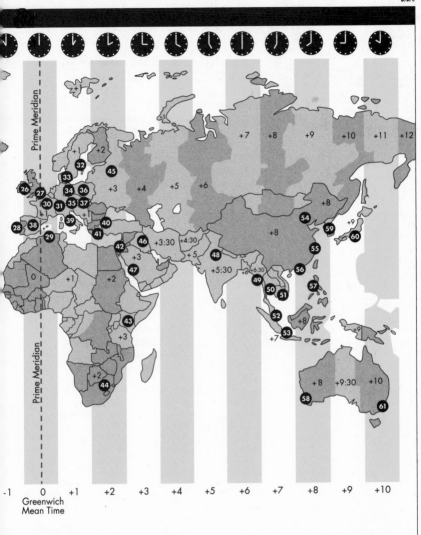

Prime Meridian

+1 +2 +3 +4 +5 +6 +7 +8 +9 +10 +11 +12

+3:30 +4:30 +5:30 +6:30

0 +1 +2 +3

-1   0   +1   +2   +3   +4   +5   +6   +7   +8   +9   +10
Greenwich
Mean Time

Introduction

by Sir Edmund Hillary

Currently the New Zealand ambassador to India, Sir Edmund Hillary is best known for his 1953 climb with Tenzing Norgay of Mt. Everest, the first successful climb of the world's highest peak.

I was first introduced to the mountains of New Zealand when I was 16 years old and went with a high school party to the volcanic peaks 240 miles south of Auckland. Our train arrived at midnight, and there was snow everywhere—on the railway platform, on the forest trees, and covering the great peaks that were outlined clearly against the bright moonlit sky. I had never seen snow before, and the impact was tremendous—I believe this was the initial inspiration that started the love of mountains that has dominated my life for more than half a century.

For many years, I climbed energetically in the New Zealand Alps, gaining in experience and skill and overcoming a series of new and challenging first ascents and new routes. I read voraciously books on the Himalayas by great climbers, such as Smythe and Shipton, and developed the hope that I, too, might someday have the opportunity to attempt the world's highest summits.

I have always been physically robust, though I regarded myself as only adequate rather than highly expert in technical skill. But one characteristic I did seem to possess—if I made up my mind to undertake some difficult challenge, I usually found ways and means to carry it out.

In 1951, three New Zealand companions and I pooled our modest finances, assembled our ordinary Alpine climbing equipment (we couldn't afford sophisticated high-altitude gear), and traveled by aircraft and ocean liner to Colombo in Sri Lanka. For days, we traveled by train through India—past Madras and Calcutta, up the valley of the Ganga River, and finally into the Himalayan foothills. We drove up the steep winding road to the hill station of Ranikhet and then, to our great excitement, saw the mighty Himalayan peaks lining the horizon.

We had arranged for four Sherpa porters to meet us there—redoubtable figures we had read about and learned to admire secondhand. They proved to be all we had expected—tough, cheerful, and loyal—and we commenced a friendship that has lasted nearly 40 years.

We headed north through the Himalayan foothills, over high passes and deep valleys, and up to the holy temple of Badrinath, with the sharp and beautiful summit of Nilkanta towering above. We moved north even farther to Mana Pass on the Tibetan border and then for a couple of months climbed and explored in regions that had rarely, if ever, been visited by foreigners. We made six first ascents of peaks ranging from 6,000 to more than 7,000 meters (20,000 to more than 23,000 feet) and reveled in our sense of freedom in this remote area.

Our enthusiasm for the Himalayas was firmly established, and when two of us were invited to join Eric Shipton's first reconnaissance of the south face of Mt. Everest, we were eager to go. We chased after the British team through Nepal's heavy monsoon rains, fording fast-flowing streams and crossing the great Arun River in shaky dugout canoes. In the village of Dingla, high on a hillside, we caught up to our companions, and I met Eric Shipton for the first time— someone whom I had always greatly admired. We struggled in damp conditions over high ridges and mountain passes and then forced our way up the valley of the Dudh Kosi River and climbed up into the Khumbu region—the major home of the Sherpa people. On every side loomed fantastic mountains—some of the most spectacular in the world—Mt. Amadablam, Mt. Kangtega, and Mt. Tamserku—all peaks that my expeditions were later to climb for the first time.

I became a close friend of Eric Shipton, and mostly we worked together as a team. From a nearby high ridge, Eric and I had a look into the great Western Cwm on the south side of Everest and realized for the first time that a demanding but feasible route did, in fact, exist up this side of the mountain. Our team forced a hazardous route up the great shattered icefall to the lip of the Western Cwm—but that was as far as we were equipped to go, and we returned back down the mountain and across country to Kathmandu.

In 1952, two strong Swiss expeditions continued up our route. One, in the premonsoon season, reached 8,500 meters (28,000 feet), a height that had been achieved a number of times on the Tibetan side of the mountain. Their second attempt in the postmonsoon season was buffeted by strong winds and cold temperatures, and they were forced to retreat below 8,200 meters (27,000 feet). But they had made a mighty effort! Our turn came in 1953. Our team was experienced and strongly motivated. Slowly, we forced a route upward, and on May 29, 1953, Tenzing Norgay and I set foot on the summit of Mt. Everest for the first time.

But the Himalayas are not only mountain summits—superb though these may be. There are also great ridges and deep valleys, beautiful flowers, and the deep green of the monsoon season. There are a multitude of tiny villages with cheerful, friendly people and Buddhist monasteries perched in lonely beauty on steep mountain faces with great peaks above.

I had built up a deep affection and respect for the Sherpas and spent much time in their homes with their wives and children. It was impossible not to realize that they lacked many of the things that we in the West took for granted—in particular, schools and medical facilities. For a long time, I thought about it and did nothing. I'd return to a familiar village only to find that a child I had held on my knee had died— nobody knew why. I sat around a meager fire with a group of Sherpa friends and suddenly asked them, "If there is something I could do for you and your families, what should it be?" The response was immediate: Urkein, my chief Sherpa guide spoke without hesitation, "More than anything, we need a school in our village of Khumjung. Can you help us?"

For the first time, my attitude changed from concern to action. I raised the necessary funds from friends in the United States, and in 1961 we set to work and constructed the Khumjung School, the first permanent school in all the Khumbu area. Initially only 40 children attended, but the number rapidly grew to more than 300 students. Petitions were being presented from everywhere. Thami village wrote, "Our children have eyes yet they are blind!" Who could refuse such a request?

For 30 years now, I have been involved in these projects— 25 schools, 2 hospitals, 10 medical clinics, many bridges and freshwater pipelines, a reforestation project, and even a couple of mountain airfields.

I have learned to admire not only my original friends, the Sherpas, but many other of the varied people of Nepal—the Rais, the Tamangs, the Chhatris, and the Gurungs—and have undertaken projects with many of them.

Those of us in the developed countries find it easy to enjoy the mountain people of Nepal. They are small in size but physically tough and can carry enormous loads far beyond our own capacity. But more than anything, they have a great sense of humor and are generous and hospitable. They treat us with respect, but as equals. To us, they are gentle and kind, yet we know they are mighty warriors as the famous Gurkha Brigades have clearly displayed.

The Himalayas are a fascinating mixture of mountains and rivers, of brilliantly flowering trees and gorgeous alpine blossoms, of great glaciers and deep remote valleys, of people with a great variety of cultures and religions. Once you have been there, you will never forget the experience—and most of us who have feel the urge to return again and again.

1 Essential Information

Before You Go

Government Tourist Offices

Only India has internationally based tourist offices (*see* Before You Go in Chapter 5).

Tour Groups

The following companies stay up to date on the latest developments in the Himalayas, have knowledgeable guides, and provide responsible service. The traveler who wants to be doubly careful can call the American Society of Travel Agents, Consumer Affairs Department (tel. 703/739–2789), to check on any American-based company.

In addition to this list, some excellent Western tour operators specialize in a particular destination. Some companies have overseas representatives or offices. For companies and tour operators in the West that specialize in one area, check those listed in each destination chapter. Himalayas-based tour operators also offer high-quality trips, at a lower cost.

Most companies offer two price structures, one with and one without airfare from the West. If you choose a package based exclusively on land costs, you can arrive or depart according to your own schedule. With all recommended companies, you can join a fixed departure tour, or you can ask for a more expensive, custom-designed trip. Those travelers who don't like group travel should consider a minitour that lasts for a week or less. This is one way to get into destinations that have group travel requirements.

Finally, ask tour operators about expenses covered in the tour cost, such as supplementary insurance coverage. If your trip involves physical exertion, ask about the degree of difficulty and prior experience required.

General-Interest Tours
From the U.S. and Canada

Abercrombie & Kent International (1420 Kensington Rd., Oak Park, IL 60521, tel. 312/954–2944 or 800/323–7308) is the granddaddy of the travel business, offering excellent cultural tours throughout the region.

Above the Clouds Trekking (Box 398, Worcester, MA 01602, tel. 617/799–4499 or 800/233–4499), also based in Nepal, sponsors Nepalese family treks, biking trips, photography workshops, health-related treks offering university credits, and an international mountaineering camp. It also offers treks in Tibet, Bhutan, and India and a jeep excursion from Kathmandu in Nepal to Lhasa in Tibet.

Distant Horizons (679 Tremont St., Boston, MA 02118, tel. 617/267–5343 or 800/333–1240) offers excellent cultural tours with some of the best Asian authorities as guides.

Indoculture Tours (Suite 272, 5601 W. Slauson Ave., Culver City, CA 90230, tel. 213/649–0424 or 800/234–4085) sponsors theme-oriented tours based around festivals, visits to monasteries, and excellent pilgrimages in India, Nepal, and Tibet. It also offers trips to Pakistan.

InnerAsia Expeditions (2627 Lombard St., San Francisco, CA 94123, tel. 415/922–0448 or 800/551–1769) offers a variety of vehicular tours and treks, many with cultural emphases, in

Nepal, Bhutan, India, Pakistan, and Tibet. It also sponsors excellent rafting trips and safaris in Nepal and mountain climbing in Bhutan, Nepal, and Tibet.

Lute Jerstad Adventures (Box 19537, Portland, OR 97219, tel. 503/244–6075), a small concern run by a Himalayan scholar, offers rafting and jungle safaris, as well as excellent culture and nature tours, including a snow-leopard nature camp in Ladakh and an overland trip from Tibet to Pakistan. It also sponsors good treks in India, Pakistan, Nepal, and Tibet.

Journeys (4011 Jackson Rd., Ann Arbor, MI 48103, tel. 313/665 –4407 or 800/255–8735) promotes active participation in foreign cultures. You plant trees, pick up garbage, go on a medical trek to a poor village in Nepal, or help restore a monastery in Ladakh. The company also offers theme-oriented treks and rafting and jungle safaris.

Lindblad Travel, Inc. (Box 912, Westport, CT 06881, tel. 203/ 226–8531 or 800/243–5657) offers classy general tours in Tibet, Bhutan, Nepal, and India and wildlife safaris in India and Nepal. It is not an outdoor adventure specialist.

Mountain Travel (6420 Fairmount Ave., El Cerrito, CA 94530, tel. 415/527–8100 or 800/227–2384) is a pioneer in outdoor adventure in the Himalayas, offering numerous mountain climbing, rafting, and jungle treks in Nepal, India, Bhutan, Tibet, and Pakistan. It sponsors rugged cultural tours by jeep from Nepal to Tibet, around Pakistan, and into China.

Odyssey Tours, Inc. (1821 Wilshire Blvd., Santa Monica, CA 90403, tel. 213/453–1042 or 800/654–7975) offers numerous cultural theme tours, including home stays, festivals, pilgrimages, and study tours focusing on traditional medicine in India, Nepal, Bhutan, and Tibet.

Overseas Adventure Travel (349 Broadway, Cambridge, MA 02139, tel. 617/876–0533 or 800/221–0814) offers treks in India, Bhutan, Tibet, Pakistan, and Nepal that teach mountaineering or combine rafting and jungle safaris. A percentage of the trekking fee is donated to the protection of the trails.

Tiger Tops International (2627 Lombard St., San Francisco, CA 94123, tel. 415/346–3402), which has offices in Nepal and India, has pioneered many of the best treks and mountain expeditions in Tibet and Nepal. The company offers Indian treks and runs Nepalese rafting excursions, some with jungle safaris in idyllic game-park retreats.

Wilderness Travel (801 Allston Way, Berkeley, CA 94710, tel. 415/548–0420 or 800/247–6700) offers numerous treks in India; rafting, jungle safaris, and mountain climbing in Nepal; and vehicular excursions in Pakistan and Tibet.

From the U. K.   **Abercrombie & Kent International** (Sloane Square House, Holbein Pl., London SW1W 8NS, tel. 01/730–9600) is the British-based office of this excellent company mentioned above.

ExplorAsia (13 Chapter St., London SW1P 4NY, tel. 01/630– 7102) serves as a liaison for Tiger Tops and its subsidiaries— arranging treks, rafting, or safaris to the Tiger Tops Wildlife Resorts.

Karakoram Experience (Trekkers Lodge, 32 Lake Rd., Keswick, Cumbria CA12 5DQ, tel. 07687/73966, 72267) is one of the pioneers in outdoor Pakistani adventures: treks, mountaineering, and biking. It also offers excellent treks in India, Nepal, and Tibet.

Special-Interest **Archaeological Tours** (Suite 1202, 30 E. 42nd St., New York,
Tours NY 10017, tel. 212/986–3054) sponsors excellent scholar-led
From the U.S. tours in Tibet, India, Nepal, and Bhutan.
and Canada **King Bird Tours** (Box 196, Planetarium Station, New York, NY
10024, 212/866–7923) sponsors in-depth bird-watching tours in
Bhutan, India, Nepal, and Tibet.
Nature Expeditions International (474 Willamette St., Box
11496, Eugene, OR 97440, tel. 503/484–6529) sponsors nature
and culture tours led by anthropologists and biologists in Tibet,
Nepal, India.
Questers: Worldwide Nature Tours (257 Park Ave. S, New York,
NY 10010, tel. 212/673–3120) offers tours led by naturalists in
India, Bhutan, Nepal, and Tibet.

Special Tours for **Evergreen Travel Service** (19505L 44th Ave. W, Lynnwood, WA
Special Needs 98036, tel. 206/776–1184 or 800/435–2288) creates customized
skiing and rafting trips and generalized tours for the handicapped traveler. Trekking is currently under study. No matter
how severe your handicap, this well-run organization will find
the way for you to enjoy the Himalayas.

When to Go

If you want a vacation away from crowds of tourists, avoid
trekking in Nepal's Annapurna circuit in autumn or spring.
Head instead to Nepal's northwest or northeast, go east to
India's Sikkim or into Bhutan, or go west to any part of north
Pakistan. Srinagar in Kashmir is crowded from June to Au-
gust, and Kathmandu in Nepal is popular in autumn.

If you go to a popular festival, that, too, will be crowded. Not
with tourists, but with villagers, who themselves are a fascinating part of the event. Planning your trip around a gala
occasion is a smart way to get more from your vacation. For a
complete list of events, see Festivals and Seasonal Events in
each destination chapter.

What to Pack

Clothing The Himalayas are a year-round destination. Since each area
has its own weather cycle, pick your destination, refer to the
When to Go information in the appropriate chapter, and pack
accordingly.

Travelers should realize that what is appropriate in the West
isn't necessarily appropriate in the East. Only children can get
away with short shorts. Men should dress in comfortable jeans
or long shorts. A T-shirt is not offensive, but the topless look
should be left to the wandering *sadhu* (Hindu holy man). If it's
warm, women should stick to skirts or lightweight slacks.
Though shorts are acceptable attire in the West, and many foreign women wear them in the Himalayas, women who reveal
bare legs under even a conservative pair of shorts remain a dubious curiosity to the people of the East. To enter a holy shrine,
women must wear a below-the-knee-length skirt or dress or
neat pants. To go braless is mindless. Any woman dressed in a
scooped or plunging neckline must be prepared to accept wandering eyes and unflattering remarks. Travel in a Moslem
society (Pakistan and parts of India) calls for even more discre-
tion. Women should consider wearing *shalwar kameez*, the

local long blouse and loose trousers, which are inexpensive and flattering. Bathing suits should be conservative.

The Adventure   The trick to an adventure wardrobe is triple layering. The lay-
Wardrobe   er next to your skin (long johns) should be made of polypropylene, thermax, capilene, or silk. These fabrics carry moisture away from the skin to the outer surface of the garment. Cotton sponges up perspiration and will make you wet and cold when the temperature drops. Since you're traveling to the world of the *dhobi* (launderer), not the dry cleaner, bring a supply of tops and bottoms that are washable.

For the second layer, wool, fleece, or a synthetic fabric knitted into thick pile, like Polar Plus, is best. Choose a down vest if you anticipate cold weather. Comfortable jeans or lightweight Polar Plus trousers are good choices.

For the third layer, bring a well-made, generously sized windbreaker or lightweight parka insulated with a small amount of down and made of Gore-Tex (or an equivalent fiber like Zepel or VersaTech), which not only allows for the escape of moisture but is waterproof, not merely water-repellent. Bulky down parkas are advisable only for winter excursions or a climb into the higher mountains. Bring a pair of lined Gore-Tex overpants—indispensable in the rain and cold or when you're thrashing through wet underbrush. Top-of-the-line clothes are available from Marmot or Patagonia in the United States or Rohan in Canada and Great Britain, companies that outfit Himalayan expeditions.

In the Himalayas, a hat is a necessity. In fact, two hats are best: a wool ragg cap to wear when it's cold and a hat with a wide brim to shield you from sun and rain. Remember: 70% of all lost body heat escapes through the head and neck. Also bring wool gloves.

Bring three pairs of sturdy, broken-in shoes that offer ample support: sandals, sneakers (with waffle soles), and waterproof hiking boots (with Vibram soles). The boots should fit over both polypropylene undersocks and heavy athletic socks. Be sure the boots aren't too heavy, and remember to buy an extra pair of laces.

Miscellaneous   Sleeping bag or no sleeping bag? That depends on where you're going and how. Many adventure outfits supply all the gear. If you need a sleeping bag, choose one with an outer shell that will keep you dry. As for the weight, you don't need a bag designed for an assault on Mt. Everest unless that's the trip you've planned. A down bag guaranteed to keep you warm at 15°F (a fairly cold temperature during the Himalayan trekking season) is adequate. If you don't carry a sleeping bag, bring a sleeping-bag liner; it will come in handy in rustic accommodations.

Take a small day pack that will hold a sweater, camera, and plastic quart-size water bottle (a must for excursions). Consider bringing along a good pair of binoculars, which will bring the Himalayas closer. Bring sunglasses that block out ultraviolet rays.

Electric current in the Himalayas is 220 volts, 50 cycles. If you have appliances that adapt to this voltage, bring plug converters with two-pin round-head plugs.

Also bring the following necessities: sewing kit, fold-up umbrella, cotton bandanas, lightweight absorbent towel, premoistened towelettes, pocketknife with can opener, lock and key for each duffle or bag, quart-size water bottle of rigid polyethylene, high-power impact-resistant flashlight, spare batteries (unless they're a popular size), and waterproof boot polish. Women should bring sanitary napkins or tampons— Asian brands are substandard.

Carry your passport and your money (most of it should be in traveler's checks) on your person. Keep multiple records of your checks and put a copy in each bag. Leave behind all unnecessary credit cards.

Luggage Use good-quality soft luggage or well-made duffles that are waterproof and keep them locked. Airlines will not accept untagged luggage. Indicate your destination address, with dates of arrival and departure, on luggage tags, just in case your bags go astray. Also put identification inside and remove all old tags. Though porters are available in much of the Himalayas, it is a good idea to carry two small bags rather than one, to divide the weight.

Taking Money Abroad

The Himalayan countries have strict rules against the importation of their own currency by tourists. International airports in each country have currency-exchange booths that are always open for arriving or departing overseas flights. When you change your money, remember to get a certain amount in small denominations. Also reject torn bills, especially in India. Many merchants, hotels, and restaurants won't accept worn or tattered bills, and it's a hassle to go to the *one* bank where you can exchange them.

American Express and **Thomas Cook** traveler's checks are the international drafts of choice in the Himalayas. Buy a fair percentage of them in small denominations for those times when you need instant cash and the banks are closed. Small denominations are also a convenient solution to a tricky buy-back policy. If you cash a hefty amount of money in Pakistan, Bhutan, and Tibet, you could be stuck at the end of your trip with useless paper you can't exchange for your own currency. Follow the guidelines in each destination chapter.

Along with your traveler's checks, bring a list of foreign offices where you can get refunds if they're lost or stolen. And remember, though most hotels will gladly exchange your checks, they usually give a lower rate than banks and exchange houses. In Nepal and India, you'll also be tempted to change money on the black market, which gives a better exchange but is illegal.

Getting Money from Home

Currently, the only reasonable way to get money from home is to cash a personal check with an **American Express card** or, if you're a highly placed executive, with the **Thomas Cook Carte d'Or** at these companies' respective offices.

What It Will Cost

Except for Bhutan, which charges a healthy per diem, and Tibet, where group travel is obligatory and pushes up the price of a vacation, the dollar goes a long way in the Himalayas. In India, Pakistan, and Nepal, the value of the dollar increased between 1987 and 1989. For more information, see What It Will Cost in each destination chapter.

Passports and Visas

Travel to the Himalayas requires a passport and a visa for each country you intend to visit. Visa information is discussed in the Before You Go section of each country chapter. Within certain states in India's northeastern Himalayas (Sikkim, West Bengal, Meghalaya, and Assam), you must also apply for a Restricted Area Permit. Getting this permit can take up to three months (*see* Before You Go in Chapter 5 for details).

Americans Applications for a new passport must be made in person; renewals may be obtained in person or by mail. First-time applicants should apply well in advance of their departure at a U.S. Passport Agency office in Boston, Chicago, Honolulu, Houston, Los Angeles, Miami, New Orleans, New York, Philadelphia, San Francisco, Seattle, Stamford (CT), Washington DC, or at a local county courthouse or certain post offices. Necessary documents include a completed passport application (Form DSP-11); proof of citizenship (birth certificate with raised seal or naturalization papers); proof of identity (driver's license, employee ID card, or any document with your photograph and signature); two recent, identical, two-inch-square photographs (black and white or color); and a $42 application fee for a 10-year passport (those under 18 pay $27 for a five-year passport). Passports are mailed to you in about 10 working days.

To renew your passport by mail, you'll need a completed Form DSP-82; two recent, identical passport photographs; and a check or money order for $35.

Canadians Apply in person to one of 17 regional passport offices in Edmonton, Halifax, Montreal, Toronto, Fredericton, Hamilton, London, Ottawa, Hull, Quebec, St. John's, Saskatoon, North York, Victoria, Windsor, Vancouver, or Winnipeg. You can also send a completed application (available at any post office or passport office) to the Bureau of Passports (Complexe Guy Favreau, 200 Dorchester W, Montreal, Que. H2Z 1X4). Include $25, two photographs, a guarantor, and proof of Canadian citizenship. Passports are valid for five years and are nonrenewable.

Britons Passport applications are available from travel agencies or a main post office. Send the completed form to your nearest regional passport office (locations include London, Liverpool, Newport, Peterborough, Glasgow, and Belfast). The application must be countersigned by your bank manager or by a solicitor, barrister, doctor, clergyman, or justice of the peace who knows you personally. In addition, you'll need two photographs and the £15 fee.

Customs and Duties

On Arrival Each Himalayan country has its own set of rules on what you can bring into the country; refer to each destination chapter.

On Departure
Americans U.S. residents bringing any foreign-made equipment from home, such as cameras, should carry the original receipt or register it with U.S. Customs before leaving home (Form 4457); otherwise they may pay duty upon return. U.S. residents may bring home duty-free up to $400 worth of foreign goods. Each member of a family is entitled to the same exemption, regardless of age, and exemptions can be pooled. For the next $1,000 worth of goods, a flat 10% rate is assessed; above $1,400, duties vary with the merchandise. Included for travelers 21 or older are one liter of alcohol, 100 cigars (non-Cuban), and 200 cigarettes. Only one bottle of perfume trademarked in the United States may be imported. There is no duty on antiques or art over 100 years old. Anything exceeding these limits will be taxed at the port of entry and may be taxed additionally in the traveler's home state. Gifts valued at under $50 may be mailed to friends or relatives at home duty-free, but not more than one package per day may be mailed to any one addressee and packages may not include perfumes costing more than $5, tobacco, or liquor. The United States has strict limitations on the import of food, plants, and items made from protected animal species, including ivory and most furs of wild animals.

Canadians Canadian residents have a $300 exemption and may also bring in duty-free up to 50 cigars, 200 cigarettes, two pounds of tobacco, and 40 ounces of liquor, provided these are declared in writing to customs on arrival and accompany the traveler in hand luggage or checked baggage. Personal gifts can be mailed marked "Unsolicited Gift—Value under $40." Request the Canadian Customs brochure "I Declare" for further details.

Britons British residents may import duty-free 200 cigarettes or 100 cigarillos or 50 cigars or 250 grams of tobacco (*Note:* If you live outside Europe, these allowances are doubled), plus one liter of alcoholic drinks over 22% volume or two liters of alcoholic drinks not over 22% volume or fortified or sparkling wine, plus two liters of still table wine, plus 50 grams of perfume, plus nine fluid ounces of toilet water, plus other goods to the value of £32.

In addition, no animals or pets of any kind may be brought into the United Kingdom. The penalties for doing so are severe and are strictly enforced.

Traveling with Film

Normally, five trips through modern airport scanners won't affect film; six or more trips, and the film could be damaged. In many Himalayan airports, you can avoid the scanner by showing your camera to the security-check officials. Some officials will demand that you disassemble your camera and remove the lens and all the batteries. If you don't trust scanners, bring special lined film-protection bags. Dust is a problem throughout this part of the world; buy an inexpensive skylight filter to protect your lens and keep your camera under wraps when it's not in use. You can buy film everywhere but Tibet and Bhutan.

Film prices in the region are generally low. You can also buy batteries, unless they are an obscure size.

Staying Healthy

Though immigration officials don't normally ask to see an **International Health Certificate,** this is one destination where it's smart to have one. The certificate contains invaluable information in case you need medical attention. See your doctor about obtaining one.

For an up-to-date directory of U.S. doctors who specialize in tropical illnesses, contact Dr. Leonard Marcus at the **American Society of Tropical Medicine and Hygiene** (148 Highland Ave., Newton, MA 02160). Include a 9×12 inch stamped envelope with 90¢ postage.

The **International Association for Medical Assistance to Travelers** (IAMAT) is a worldwide association offering a list of approved doctors. For their directory, contact IAMAT (417 Center St., Lewiston, NY 14092; in Canada: 188 Nicklin Rd., Guelph, Ontario N1H 7L5; in Europe: 57 Voirets, 1212 Grand-Lancy-Geneva, Switzerland).

For $4.95, the **U.S. government** offers an annual publication titled *Health Information for International Travel.* Contact the Superintendent of Documents (U.S. Government Printing Office, Washington, DC 20402, tel. 202/783–3238).

Shots and Medications
Three months before departure, talk to your doctor about protection (highly recommended) against malaria, typhoid, cholera, tetanus, polio, measles, mumps, rubella, and meningitis. At press time, protection against cholera is required to cross from India into Pakistan. If you plan to trek in remote areas of Tibet, consider protection against rabies. Dog bites are rare, but, if you're attacked, you can forget about catching the animal to see if it's rabid. To get the latest inoculation information and requirements, obtain publication (CDC) 85-8280 from the Superintendent of Documents (for address, see above).

High Altitude Sickness
This adverse reaction to low oxygen content in the air is serious. Once you reach 10,000 feet, acclimatize before you set off on a strenuous uphill journey, then climb slowly, and drink lots of fluids. If your urine turns bright yellow, you're not drinking enough. Eat foods that are high in carbohydrates and cut back on salt. High altitude sickness can be prevented if you proceed with care. Stop and rest immediately if you develop any of the following symptoms: nausea, loss of appetite, extreme headache or lightheadedness, unsteadiness, sleeplessness. If resting doesn't help, head for lower ground. This is one illness that *can* kill you.

Sun Protection
Always wear a wide-brimmed hat and sunscreen and, in sun or clouds, keep your eyes protected behind sunglasses that block ultraviolet rays. Also remember, when you're in snow, UV rays reflect from below as well.

Vermin
If you travel during or right after the monsoon (time varies from area to area), protect yourself against leeches. Cover your legs and carry salt. Don't wear sandals. When a leech clings to your clothing, dab it with a pinch of salt, and it will fall off. If itching persists, apply an antiseptic; infection rarely occurs. For bedbugs, buy a bottle of Dettol (available in the Himalayas)

or an equivalent antiseptic and mix a capful in your shower water. It relieves itching and discomfort.

Medical Kit Bring a medical kit containing mosquito repellent with at least 95% deet (N. diethyl toluamide), adhesive bandages, plastic-strip thermometer, water-purification tablets, aspirin or its equivalent, diarrhea medication, antibiotic, antiseptic skin cleanser, high-altitude pills, sunscreen with a sun protection factor of at least 24, and zinc oxide or lip balm with sun block. If you foresee needing any prescription medication, ask your doctor at home to write a prescription beforehand, using the drug's generic name.

Food and Water Precautions Eat only cooked vegetables and peel all fruit, choosing fruit with thick skins. Avoid all pork products and make certain that meat is cooked thoroughly. Eat hot foods while they're hot. Boil water and unpasteurized milk for 10 minutes before consuming. Purify water with iodine tablets to kill parasites. Avoid ice cubes and use treated water to brush your teeth. In restaurants and other public places, drink hot beverages or bottled carbonated drinks.

Insurance

Travelers may seek insurance coverage in three areas: health and accident, lost luggage, and trip cancellation. Your first step is to review your existing health and homeowner policies; some health-insurance plans cover health expenses incurred while traveling, some major medical plans cover emergency transportation, and some homeowner policies cover the theft of luggage.

Health and Accident Several companies offer coverage designed to supplement an American or Canadian traveler's ordinary health insurance:

Carefree Travel Insurance (Box 310, 120 Mineola Blvd., Mineola, NY 11501, tel. 516/294–0220 or 800/645–2424) provides coverage for medical evacuation.
Health Care Abroad, International Underwriters Group (243 Church St. W, Vienna, VA 22180, tel. 703/281–9500 or 800/237–6615) offers comprehensive medical coverage and emergency evacuation.
International SOS Insurance (Box 11568, Philadelphia, PA 19116, tel. 215/244–1500 or 800/523–8930) provides medical evacuation services.
Travel Guard International (1100 Centerpoint Dr., Stevens Point, WI 54481, tel. 715/345–0505 or 800/826–1300) offers medical insurance, with coverage for emergency evacuation.
British travelers may apply to **Europe Assistance** (252 High St., Croydon, Surrey CR0 1NF, tel. 01/680–1234), which insures against sickness and motoring mishaps.

Lost Luggage If your baggage disappears, report it to the police immediately. Airlines and many insurance companies insist that notification be made within 24 hours. Lost luggage is usually covered as part of a comprehensive travel insurance package that includes personal accident, trip cancellation, and sometimes default and bankruptcy insurance.

Several American and Canadian companies offer comprehensive policies:

Access America Inc. (Box 807, New York, NY 10163, tel. 800/284–8300) is a subsidiary of Blue Cross–Blue Shield.
Near, Inc. (1900 N. MacArthur Blvd., Suite 210, Oklahoma City, OK 73127, tel. 800/654–6700).
Travel Guard International (*see* Health and Accident, above).

The **Association of British Insurers** (Aldermary House, Queen St., London EC4N 1TT, tel. 01/248–4477) offers British Travelers comprehensive advice on all aspects of vacation insurance.

Trip Cancellation   Flight insurance is often included in the price of a ticket when paid for with American Express, Visa, and other major credit cards. It is usually included in combination travel insurance packages available from most tour operators, travel agents, and insurance agents. Most policies don't cover natural disasters, such as landslides, which can also interfere with your trip plans. Britons should contact the Association of British Insurers (*see* Lost Luggage, above).

Student and Youth Travel

Students who travel to the Himalayas should get an **International Student Identity Card,** which entitles them to student discounts on some airlines and public transportation and on entrance fees to some museums and monuments. The card includes emergency medical insurance. Apply to the **Council on International Student Exchange** or CIEE (205 E. 42nd St., New York, NY 10017, tel. 212/661–1414). In Canada, the card is available from the **Association of Student Councils** (187 College St., Toronto, Ont. M5T 1P7).

Americans   **Council Travel,** a CIEE subsidiary, is the foremost U.S. stu-
and Canadians dent travel agency, specializing in low-cost charters and other airfare bargains and tours. CIEE's 80-page *Student Travel Catalog* and "Council Charter" brochure are available for $1 from Council Travel offices in New York (address above); Berkeley, LaJolla, Long Beach, Los Angeles, San Diego, and San Francisco, CA; Chicago, IL; Amherst, Boston, and Cambridge, MA; Portland, OR; Providence, RI; Austin and Dallas, TX; and Seattle, WA.

Students who want to work abroad should contact **CIEE's Work Abroad Department** (205 E. 42nd St., New York, NY 10017). The council arranges a few paid and voluntary work experiences in the Himalayas for up to six months and publishes books of interest to the student traveler: *Work, Study, Travel Abroad: The Whole World Handbook* ($8.95 plus $1 postage); *Work Your Way Around the World* ($10.95 plus $1 postage); and *Volunteer! The Comprehensive Guide to Voluntary Service in the U.S. and Abroad* ($5.50 plus $1 postage).

U.S. students should also refer to *The Young American's Scholarship Guide to Travel and Learning Abroad* (Intravco Press, Suite 1303, 211 E. 43rd St., New York, NY 10017, tel. 212/972–1164; $14.95 including postage) for a list of programs abroad, availability of scholarships, and application procedures.

The Mountaineering Institutes in India (Himachal Pradesh, Uttar Pradesh, and West Bengal) and Nepal also offer inexpensive summer trekking and mountaineering experiences that are open to foreign youngsters (*see* Outdoor Adventures in each destination chapter).

Britons **Operation Raleigh** (Alpha Pl., Flood St., Chelsea, London SW3 5SZ, tel. 01/351–7541) offers a few work/study projects in the Himalayas for individuals aged 17 to 24.

Traveling with Children

If you have children, don't hesitate to take them to the Himalayas. Doctors are available. The food is safe if you follow all the guidelines listed in Staying Healthy, above. Make sure they have all necessary immunizations. The secret to a successful experience for them is good advance planning. If you're arranging an adventure with a tour operator, tell the company the ages of your children and their special interests, and the company can create an itinerary around the children's needs. Most operators, even those based in the Himalayas, offer family-oriented treks on which the walking is easy; they can provide ponies equipped with special saddles for the very young. You will find guides and porters are very kind and helpful with children.

Game sanctuaries are a child's delight, providing that rare opportunity to see wild animals in their natural habitat. Many rafting trips are easy. Life jackets are supplied; the equipment is excellent. Give the rafting concern time to prepare, by notifying it of the ages of your children. The concern will tell you if the trip is too risky. Ski resorts have courses designed for the young, and there are swimming pools and lakes to enjoy.

If you're planning your trip around a festival, keep in mind that many Hindu celebrations involve animal sacrifice, which may upset your child. When sacrifice is an integral part of a recommended event, it's noted under Festivals and Seasonal Events in each destination chapter. In general, regional dance performances and Buddhist celebrations, with their colorful dances, are great fun for the young. Play it safe and check with your travel agent or the local tourist departments before you attend.

Publications *Family Travel Times,* an 8- to 12-page newsletter, is published 10 times a year by Travel with Your Children (80 Greenwich Ave., New York, NY 10011, tel. 212/206–0688).

Getting There On international flights, children under age 2 not occupying a seat pay 10% of an adult fare. Various discounts apply to children aged 2–12. Reserve a seat behind the bulkhead, which offers more legroom and can usually fit a bassinet (supplied by the airline). Inquire about special children's meals or snacks offered by most airlines. The flight to the Himalayas is long. Bring a bag of dime-store amusements and surprise gifts to dole out along the way. If your child craves certain Western treats, bring them along.

Child Care Many Western-style hotels supply excellent baby-sitters.

Hints for Disabled Travelers

The Information Center for Individuals with Disabilities (20 Park Plaza, Room 330, Boston, MA 02116, tel. 617/727–5540) offers useful assistance and a list of travel agents that specialize in tours for the disabled.
Moss Rehabilitation Hospital Travel Information Service, (12th

St. and Taber Rd., Philadelphia, PA 19141, tel. 215/329–5715) provides information on sights, transportation, and accommodations in destinations around the world.

Mobility International (Box 3551, Eugene, OR 97403, tel. 503/ 343–1284) has information on accommodations and organized study around the world.

The Society for the Advancement of Travel for the Handicapped (26 Court St., Brooklyn, NY 11242, tel. 718/858–5483) offers access information.

The Itinerary (Box 1084, Bayonne, NY 07002, tel. 201/858– 3400) is a bimonthly travel magazine for the disabled.

Hints for Older Travelers

Trekkers who've seen the far side of 70 have climbed great heights in the Himalayas. Speak candidly with your travel agent or tour company about your concerns and needs.

Travel Industry and Disabled Exchange (TIDE, 5435 Donna Ave., Tarzana, CA 91356, tel. 818/343–6339) is an industry-based membership organization with a quarterly newsletter.

National Council of Senior Citizens (925 15th St. NW, Washington, DC 20005, tel. 202/347–8800) is a large nonprofit advocacy group with a monthly newsletter.

Mature Outlook (Box 1205, Glenview, IL 60025, tel. 800/336– 6330) is a travel club for people over 50, with a bimonthly newsletter.

Travel Tips for Senior Citizens (U.S. Dept. of State Publication 8970) is available for $1 from the Superintendent of Documents (U.S. Government Printing Office, Washington, DC 20402).

Further Reading

Regional *Mountains of the Gods*, by Ian Cameron, provides a good overview of the Himalayas, their people, and historic explorations. *When Men and Mountains Meet*, by John Keay, has great stories about 19th-century explorers of the western Himalayas. *The Snow Leopard*, by Peter Matthiessen, centers on an experience in Nepal, but it captures the spiritual aura of all the Himalayas. *Stones of Silence*, by the eminent scientist George Schallar, records the same adventure experienced by Matthiessen.

Bhutan *The Dragon Kingdom: Images of Bhutan*, with text by Blanche Christine Olschak and photographs by Ursula Markus-Gansser and Augusto Gansser, provides good descriptions, with an emphasis on religion and dance, and gorgeous photographs. *Bhutan: A Kingdom of the Eastern Himalayas*, with text by Françoise Pommaret-Imaeda and Yoshhiro Imaeda and photographs by Guy van Strydonck, is a reissue of an excellent assessment of contemporary Bhutan. *Dreams of the Peaceful Kingdom*, by Katie Hickman, is a personal account of a young woman's trek through Bhutan.

India *The Discovery of India*, by Jawaharlal Nehru: If you've never read Nehru, you're in for a treat. His sense of his country's history is passionate and poetic. *Freedom at Midnight*, by Larry Collins and Dominique Lapierre, is a spellbinding account of India's break from Britain. *India File*, by Trevor Fishlock, is a perceptive journalist's view of modern India. *Portrait of India*, by Ved Mehta, is an excellent contemporary study by a native son. *The Speaking Tree*, by Richard Lannoy, is a wonderful introduction to Indian culture. *The Art of Indian Asia*, by Henrich Zimmer (completed and edited by Joseph Campbell), is required reading for the art or mythology buff. *Tales of India*, by Rudyard Kipling, is light reading from one who knew India intimately. *The Raj Quartet*, by Paul Scott, will get you in the mood for your trip.

Nepal *Journey through Nepal*, by Mohamed Amin, Duncan Willetts, and Brian Tetley, gives a good overview of Nepal with eye-stopper photos. *Buddhist Himalaya*, by David Snellgrove, provides a fine analysis of the monuments in Nepal and other nearby areas. *A Guide to Trekking in Nepal*, by Stephen Beruschka, is a must for trekkers. This physician knows Nepal and the routes. He also knows how to keep you healthy. Sir Edmund Hillary has written several books on his mountain-climbing experiences in this kingdom: *High Adventure*, *Schoolhouse in the Clouds*, *High in the Thin Cold Air: The Story of the Himalayan Expedition Led by Sir Edmund Hillary* (coauthored with Desmond Doig). He's an engaging writer, and his love for Nepal shines through.

Pakistan *Daughter of Destiny*, by Benazir Bhutto, is a provocative account of the life of the new prime minister and an impassioned interpretation of Pakistan under Zia. *Passage to Peshawar*, by Richard Reeves, offers a tough assessment of contemporary Pakistan. *Journey through Pakistan*, by Mohamed Amin, Duncan Willetts, and Graham Hancock, provides a good overview of Pakistan accompanied by beautiful photographs. *To the Frontier*, by Geoffrey Moorhouse, an account of a three-month journey through Pakistan, is filled with excellent observations and insights. *A Short Walk in the Hindu Kush*, by Eric Newby, is amusing and informative—another personal account of an exploration into foreign cultures. *The Man Who Would Be King and Other Stories*, by Rudyard Kipling, has a good selection of short stories by one who lived in Peshawar and used the surrounding valleys for many of the settings and inspirations.

Tibet Three companies specialize in books on Tibet: **Snow Lion Publications** (Box 6483, Ithaca, NY 14851, tel. 607/273–8506), **Shambhala Publications** (Box 308, Boston, MA 02117, tel. 617/424–0030), and **Wisdom Tibet Publications** (23 Dering St., London W1, Great Britain, tel. 01/499–0925). **Potala Publications** (107 E. 31st St., New York, NY 10016, tel. 212/213–5011) also stocks most of the following titles.

Himalayan Pilgrimage, by David Snellgrove, records this scholar's seven-month journey through Tibet and provides a detailed introduction to its culture and religion (Shambala). *In Exile from the Land of Snows*, by John F. Avedon, provides a thorough account of the Chinese invasion and tragic aftermath. *My Land and My People: Memoirs of the Dalai Lama of Tibet* is a heartbreaker written by His Holiness in 1962. The Dalai Lama's agony, predicament, and unswerving faith are moving and compelling. *The Tibet Guide*, by Stephen Batchelor, is a travel guide that offers a complete cultural description of Tibet. (Wisdom Tibet). *Tibetan Phrasebook and Tapes* is perfect for the traveler who wants to try to speak the native language on arrival (Snow Lion).

Arriving and Departing

Getting to the Himalayas by Plane

Fly into one of four cities: Lahore (via Karachi or New Delhi) in Pakistan, New Delhi or Calcutta in India, or Kathmandu in Nepal. You could also fly into Islamabad via Karachi, but Lahore is a historic city that shouldn't be missed. From the United States or Canada, direct flights involve a stopover either in England, Europe, the Middle East, or the Far East. Numerous international carriers offer various fare structures. Pakistan International Airline (PIA) and Air India, with its domestic subsidiaries Indian Airlines and Vayudoot, frequently offer incentive travel packages. Once you select your destination, refer to Arriving and Departing for the four cities mentioned above for complete details on airlines and flight times.

Discount Flights Major airlines offer a wide range of ticket prices. As a rule, the earlier you buy the ticket, the lower the price and the greater the cancellation penalty (up to 100%).

An APEX (advance-purchase) ticket on a major airline can be a good value if you can work around the restrictions: The tickets must be bought in advance, they restrict your travel time, and they include penalties for travel changes.

Charter flights offer the lowest fares but have limited departures, poor on-time records, and strict cancellation policies. Check with a travel agency about the charter flight packager's reputation. It's particularly important to know the packager's refund policy if the flight is cancelled. One popular charter operator is **Council Charter** *(see* Student and Youth Travel, above), a division of the Council on International Educational Exchange.

Somewhat more expensive—but up to 50% less than APEX fares—are tickets purchased through consolidators that buy blocks of tickets on scheduled airlines and sell them at wholesale prices. You may lose all or most of your money if you change plans, but you will be on a scheduled flight with less risk of cancellation than a charter. Once you've made your reservation, call the airline to make sure you're confirmed. Two popular consolidators are **UniTravel** (tel. 800/325–2222) and **Access International** (250 W. 57th St., Suite 511, New York, NY 10107, tel. 212/333–7280).

You can also join a travel club that offers its members special discounts, such as **Moments Notice** (40 E. 49th St., New York, NY 10017, tel. 212/486–0503), **Discount Travel International** (114 Forrest Ave., Narberth, PA 19072, tel. 215/668–2182), and **Worldwide Discount Travel Club** (1674 Meridian Ave., Miami Beach, FL 33139, tel. 305/534–2082).

Enjoying the Flight Since the air on a plane is dry, it helps to drink a lot of nonalcoholic liquids while flying; drinking alcohol contributes to jet lag and dehydration. Some travelers also swear by a mild short-acting prescription sleeping pill to help defeat jet lag. Feet swell at high altitudes, so it's a good idea to remove your shoes. Sleepers usually prefer window seats to curl up against; those who like to move about the cabin should request aisle seats; bulkhead seats have more legroom.

Smoking FCC regulations require U.S. airlines to find seats in a nonsmoking area for all who wish them. This is not necessarily the case for foreign airlines.

Luggage Regulations Airlines allow two pieces of check-in luggage and one carry-on piece per passenger. Each piece of checked luggage cannot exceed 62 inches (length + width + height) or weigh more than 70 pounds. Carry-on luggage cannot exceed 45 inches (length + width + height) and must fit under the seat or in the overhead luggage compartment.

Luggage Insurance On international flights, airlines are responsible for lost or damaged property up to $9.07 per pound (or $20 per kilo) for checked baggage and up to $400 per passenger for unchecked baggage. In Bhutan, some flights have a 20-kilo maximum. Take valuables with you on the airplane or purchase additional lost-luggage insurance available at the check-in counter of some airlines or at airport booths operated by **Tele-Trip** (tel. 800/228–9792), a subsidiary of Mutual of Omaha. **Travelers' Insurance Co.** (1 Tower Sq., Hartford, CT 06183) will also insure checked or hand baggage. Itemize the contents of each bag in case you need to file a claim.

Labeling Luggage Be certain to put your home address on and in each piece of luggage, including hand baggage. If lost luggage is recovered, the airline must deliver it to your hotel or home, at no charge to you.

Staying in the Himalayas

Getting Around the Himalayas

Though you can travel to some Himalayan destinations by plane, many areas are accessible only by car or jeep. Without exception, traveling in remote areas should be considered part of your adventure: a chance to see spectacular scenery, visit quiet villages tucked along narrow, winding roads that are at times harrowing but always memorable. For more detailed information, refer to the Getting Around section in each destination chapter.

By Plane From Delhi, Calcutta, Lahore, or Kathmandu, you can fly to various popular destinations in the Himalayas. Most airlines in this region have a shortage of aircraft, and traffic is heavy. Try to make all flight reservations before you depart. You must also reconfirm your purchased ticket in person or through your hotel (by phone may leave you stranded) at least 72 hours ahead of flight time. Since customs in some countries may reverse family and given names, be sure you have reserved and reconfirmed under the same name. Because flights are often overbooked, arrive at the airport at least an hour in advance.

By Train A few tracks run to mountain destinations in India and Pakistan.

By Hired Car or Jeep with Driver You can travel at your own speed, go where you want, stop when you want. Transporting your car with driver across borders, however, is possible only between India and Nepal.

All roads in the mountains are at the mercy of the elements. Arrive prepared for landslides, freak snowstorms, bridge washouts, roads under water. Since the Himalayas are sensitive border areas, the military in each country is usually aware of current road conditions; check with them or the local police.

When crossing the road, travelers in the Himalayas should remember that traffic moves on the left, the reverse of Canada and the United States.

By Bicycle Bicycles are becoming a popular form of travel in the Himalayas. To find out about bike tours, consult Outdoor Adventures in each destination chapter.

Car Rental

Self-drive cars are available only in Pakistan, where there are no road signs in English. If you wish to travel by car, hire a car (or jeep) with driver, from the recommended travel agencies listed in each destination chapter.

Behavioral Dos and Don'ts

Taking Photographs Ask before you take photos of people or of religious objects, ceremonies, and festivals. Remember, too, that photography is not permitted in airports or at sensitive military sites including some bridges.

Introductions In most of the Himalayas, with men, Western etiquette usually prevails, but don't extend your hand to a woman when you meet her. If she's Hindu and married, she'll usually have a *tika* (colored dot) on her forehead: place your palms together in front of you. With a Moslem woman, who will usually be veiled, just smile and nod. If she's Buddhist, and probably wearing a long robe-style dress, put your right hand to your forehead. Throughout the Himalayas, open displays of affection are considered offensive.

Accepting Hospitality If someone offers you tea, try not to refuse. Tea is safe to drink, and the invitation can lead to a pleasant exchange with the local people. When you're welcomed into a house, try to observe the rules governing the seating. Often men sit separate from women. If in doubt, ask.

There are numerous other customs associated with food and the partaking of meals. Very often, the evening's agenda is the reverse of our own. In many Himalayan households, you arrive, sit and talk, then the food is served. After you eat, the evening is over. Don't be surprised if the woman of the house serves her guests but doesn't join the gathering. Don't protest, don't follow her into the kitchen (frequently, the kitchen is off-limits, especially in Hindu homes). Just accept her behavior as the tradition of this particular home.

When you eat, you may not be given utensils; use your right hand (the left is considered unclean). If you want second helpings or if you are buying openly displayed food, don't help yourself with your hands, especially in a Hindu society; this act pollutes the food. Your host or vendor will serve you.

Religion Visiting a religious monument demands respect. With all sects, you must remove your shoes before you enter a shrine; don't speak in a raised voice. Some structures are off-limits to visitors who don't practice the faith; don't try to bribe your way inside. With all religions, you should walk clockwise around the structure (inside and out); with Buddhism that also includes shrines such as *chortens*, *stupas*, and *mani* walls. Women should always be properly dressed. *(See* What to Pack, above.) Ask before you take photos. If you have the opportunity to meet a priest or monk, don't offer your hand. Hold your palms together in front of you and bow your head. Observe the following additional guidelines.

Hinduism Some Hindu and Sikh temples, in keeping with their philosophy of nonviolence, prohibit *all* leather products inside a shrine. Many temples also expect you to purify yourself by washing your hands and feet in a nearby tap or tank before you enter. In a Sikh *gurdwara* (temple), a woman should have her head covered, and no visitor should point his or her feet toward the sacred idol or Holy Book; nor should he or she step over anyone sitting in prayer or meditation. In general, play it safe; if you decide to sit on the floor of a Hindu or Sikh temple, sit cross-legged or with your feet tucked beneath you. In some shrines, sexes are separated. Look around before you sit, and let the situation govern what you do. At some Shiva temples, a holy man may invite you to partake in a few puffs of *ganga* (marijuana or hashish); decline. Drugs are illegal for all foreigners.

Buddhism A lot of well-meaning tourists commit the unforgivable when they visit a Buddhist monastery. You're perfectly welcome to spin any prayer wheel, but just as you must circumambulate the interior and exterior of a monastery in a clockwise direction, you must follow this rule when you spin prayer wheels. Inside the monastery, interior cushions and chairs are reserved for *lamas* (monks). Sit on the steps outside or on the floor. If you get to meet a *rimpoche* (head lama) or a respected monk, don't turn your back on him when you leave. If it's raining when you visit a Buddhist compound, you should close your umbrella out of respect. This same principle applies if you see a lama on the street. In Bhutan, you can't use an umbrella in the palace complex.

Islam To enter a mosque, remove your shoes, cover your head, and step right foot first over the threshold into the courtyard. You must now purify yourself with a ritual cleansing: washing your hands, feet, and forehead in the nearby tank or tap. If a prayer service is under way, women must observe any separation of sexes that exists. Never say "Assalam Alaikum" (welcome) to someone who's praying or to a religious leader reading the *Quran*. If you want to show your understanding of Islam, when you enter a mosque, say: "Assalamo Alaikum Ya Ahlel Qaboor." This means roughly: "God bless you, oh, people who are living in the graves" (living because though the body has died, the spirit is now free).

Tourism: Positive Beneficence

"One rupee, one pen"—a child's plea for money and a disposable pen—it's a plaintive cry heard in local languages throughout the Himalayas. For the traveler with a pocketful of just-converted currency, it's hard to resist a pair of wistful young eyes. However, these children are learning a humiliating and self-destructive way to make an income. Charity that turns children into beggers, dependent on the beneficence of foreigners, is misdirected. Travelers are encouraged to contribute to environmental-protection organizations and charities *(see* be-

low) or to visit local schools or medical clinics and make a donation to a responsible adult.

Tourists must also recognize that when they head into remote
areas, their behavior creates an impression that is hard to
erase. During your visit to the Himalayas, please follow the
behavorial dos and don'ts described above and in each destination section. This is an important and appreciated way to show
that you care.

Charities and   **Chipko Movement** (Naveevan Ashram, Post Office Silyara,
Environmental   Tehri-Garhwal, Uttar Pradesh, India) is dedicated to the envi-
Organizations   ronmental preservation of the Himalayas. **Students Edu-
cational and Cultural Movement of Ladakh** (Secmol Compound,
Karzoo, Leh, Ladakh, Kashmir, India) has worthy projects to
protect Ladakh's culture. **Indian National Trust for Art and
Cultural Heritage** (71 Lodi Estate, New Delhi, India) is work-
ing to protect India's environment and culture. **The Himalayan
Trust** (c/o Elizabeth Hawley, Box 224, Kathmandu, Nepal) is
Sir Edmund Hillary's organization, devoted to helping the
Nepalese. **Scheer Memorial Hospital of Seventh Day Adventists**
(Box 88, Kathmandu, Nepal) provides excellent medical facili-
ties for the Nepalese. Adjuncts of the Tibetan government in
exile, **Tibet Fund** (Office of Tibet, 107 E. 35th St., New York,
NY 10016) and **Tibet Foundation** (43 New Oxford St., London
WC1A 1BH, England) have excellent orphanages and provide
assistance to Tibetan refugees. **Edhi Welfare Centre** (Bolton
Market, Sarafa Bazar, Karachi-II, Pakistan) runs self-help
projects in Pakistan. **Charitable Trust Hospital** (c/o Chaudhry
Mohammad Siddiq, 14-B Main Gulberg Rd., Lahore, Pakistan)
is an excellent medical institution providing care to the destitute.

Telephones

Staying in touch is possible in major cities. For instructions on
how to make phone calls, refer to this category in each destination chapter.

Mail

In India, Nepal, and Pakistan, you can receive mail through the
American Express office. In Tibet, you can receive mail through
your **hotel**. For details, refer to this category in each destination chapter.

Tipping

Customs vary throughout the Himalayas. Check each destination section for details.

Opening and Closing Times

Hours for banks, shops, and attractions vary throughout the
Himalayas. Check each destination section for details. Hindu
temples are open round the clock. There is no admission
charge, but if you make a donation, the priest will say a prayer
on your behalf. Buddhist monasteries are the homes of their
monks; it is best to visit between sunrise and sunset. Admission
charges vary. Mosques are free of charge and open round the
clock, but some prayer services are open only to Moslems.

Shopping

Bargaining is expected and part of the fun: Offer 50% of the offered price; settle for 75%. If haggling wears you out, shop in fixed-price shops. Since each area has its own specialties, refer to each destination chapter for best buys.

Over the years, souvenir-hungry travelers have ruthlessly carted off priceless treasures. Don't buy religious antiques, even from fancy shops; chances are the original owner was cheated. Purportedly century-old *thang-kas* (Buddhist religious scrolls) are usually fake; if not, they're illegal purchases. Patronize traditional artists who produce lovely new artwork and handicrafts. Do not buy products made of endangered species.

Outdoor Adventures

The following list outlines the adventures offered by the destinations at press time. Numbers and types of adventures are increasing rapidly, so check further with the tour groups listed in Before You Go to the Himalayas, above, and in the Outdoor Adventure category in each destination chapter.

Bicycling: India, Nepal, Pakistan, Tibet.
Camping: everywhere.
Cave Exploration: India (Meghalaya).
Climbing and Mountaineering: everywhere.
Fishing: Bhutan, India, Nepal, Pakistan.
Golfing: India, Nepal, Pakistan.
Hang Gliding: India (Himachal Pradesh).
Horseback Riding: everywhere.
Ice Skating: India (Himachal Pradesh).
Hot Springs: Bhutan, India, Nepal, Pakistan.
Jeep Safaris: India, Nepal–Tibet, Tibet–Pakistan, Pakistan.
Organized Photography Expeditions: India, Nepal, Pakistan.
Polo (elephant or pony): India, Nepal, Pakistan.
Rafting: India, Nepal, Pakistan; under study in Bhutan.
Sightseeing Flights: India (Sikkim and Delhi), Nepal.
Skiing and Heliskiing: India.
Trekking: everywhere.
Ski Treks: India.
Waterskiing: India.
Wildlife Safaris and Jungle Excursions: India, Nepal, Bhutan.
Yak Safaris: India, Pakistan.

Dining

In big cities or popular destinations, expect Chinese, Continental, and vegetarian or nonvegetarian Indian, Nepali, and Pakistani cuisines. You can eat in your hotel, try local restaurants accustomed to tourists, or go local and point out interesting dishes in a purely ethnic eatery.

Once you go remote, food options decrease. Expect to eat a lot of rice, noodles, *pulses* (grains), and locally grown vegetables. Regional specialties are described in this category in each destination chapter.

Mealtimes In general, breakfast and lunch are served at times similar to our own. Dinner, however, is on the early side. Restaurants often shut down by 10:30 PM. Delhi, Calcutta, and Lahore are exceptions.

Precautions Very often the locally popular restaurant that looks worn around the edges offers the safest food. A small restaurant that can't afford refrigeration cooks food acquired that day. This isn't always true with the fancy hotel. Since electricity can be temperamental and the chef buys in bulk, the hotel's refrigerator can be a repository for more than foodstuffs.

Hotel restaurants tend to cook with a lot of oil, which can lead to an upset stomach. You can ask the restaurant to use less oil. Fried foods from stands on the street can look delicious, but check the oil. If it looks as old as the pot, it could be rancid and make you sick.

When you eat in a local restaurant, bring a handkerchief. You may end up eating without silverware, the paper napkins may be useless, the sink may have no towel. Finally, refer again to Staying Healthy in Before You Go to the Himalayas, above.

Ratings and Prices The same rating and pricing system applies throughout the Himalayas.

Highly recommended restaurants are indicated by a star ★.

Category	Cost
Very Expensive	over $15
Expensive	$10–$15
Moderate	$5–$10
Inexpensive	under $5

per person, excluding drinks, services, and taxes

Lodging

Popular destinations have hotels and inns to suit every budget. Other areas offer a limited selection, and what you find will be inexpensive, with a simple room and limited facilities. Some accommodations have only an Asian-style toilet (two thin marble slabs where you put your feet and then squat), which is easy to get used to and practical. The shower may be just a cold-water spigot; hot water is often provided by bucket. All Western-style hotels and lodgings have Western-style bathrooms unless indicated. In remote destinations, sleeping bag sheets or sleeping bags are suggested. You should also anticipate power or bathing water shortages or the absence of electricity. Candles provided by the hotel will romantically solve one difficulty; the other problem you'll have to accept.

Ratings and Prices The same rating and pricing system applies throughout the Himalayas.

Highly recommended lodgings are indicated by a star ★.

Category	Cost
Very Expensive	over $100
Expensive	$60–$100

Moderate	$25–$60
Inexpensive	under $25

*Prices are for a standard double room or a cottage, including taxes and excluding service charges.

Credit Cards

Credit cards, especially American Express, Diners Club, MasterCard, and Visa, are good in fancy shops, hotels, and restaurants in India, Nepal, and Pakistan. The following credit card abbreviations are used: AE, American Express; CB, Carte Blanche; DC, Diners Club: MC, MasterCard; V, Visa.

2 Portraits of the Himalayas

The Himalayas:
A World of Dreams

Few destinations inspire such a wealth of superlatives as the Himalayas. A region more than half the size of Europe, the Himalayas sweep across northern Pakistan, northern India, southern Tibet, Nepal, and Bhutan, creating an unforgettable landscape. Forested valleys, some tropical, lead to high peaks that stop the monsoon, creating otherworldly mountaintop deserts. Massive glaciers extend for miles; rivers, chilled with melting snow and ice, race through deep, dark gorges. Wild animals—including rare snow leopards and blue sheep—race along craggy cliffs. Brilliantly colored fauna grow abundantly.

Ancient principalities, like the fiercely independent kingdom of Bhutan or the former kingdom of Sikkim (now a part of India), flourish. Tribal peoples are to be found: the Gaddi in India, the Lo-pa in Nepal, the Kafir-Kalash and Pathans in Pakistan, all of whom swear a greater allegiance to their tribes than to the countries that now rule their lands. Buddhists and Hindus revere the Himalayas as the source of their sacred rivers and the abode of their gods.

The Himalayas are more than the largest mountain expanse, with the world's loftiest peaks and longest glaciers; they're also the world's youngest mountain range—only two or three million years old—adolescent in a geological life span. Their formation was cataclysmic. About 80 million years ago, the Earth had two vast continents that slowly divided and moved across the world's oldest body of water, the Sea of Tethys, into the positions they hold today. During this time, a section now known as India floated from the Southern Hemisphere toward the north until its hard rock slammed into the soft soil of Asia. In time, India pushed against Asia and exerted so much pressure, it swallowed up the Sea of Tethys to the north. In its place emerged the Himalayas.

The Himalayas divide into distinct regions. The Hindu Kush begins as a series of nearly treeless slopes that rise out of barren Afghanistanian hills then slowly climb until they spill into northwest Pakistan. "Hindu Kush" means "Hindu killer." In the 14th century, Indian slaves, herded over the snowy passes to distant Arab masters, perished in the cold.

The Karakoram Range, which lies to the west of the Hindu Kush, is a formidable chain boasting the world's greatest concentration of massive peaks and gigantic glaciers, including the world's longest nonpolar glacier and K-2, (the K is short for Karakoram), which rises to 8,618 meters (28,268 feet), second only to Everest. Until recently, this austere region was difficult to visit; but in 1978, the Karakoram Highway that links Pakistan to China was completed, and jeeps now bring in tourists who witness firsthand this grand interplay of granite and ice.

Three chains of mountains form the Great Himalayas, a nearly 1,500-mile (2,400-kilometer) expanse from northeast Pakistan to northern India, southern Tibet, and all Nepal and Bhutan. The Siwaliks, extending from the Brahmaputra River in the east to the Indus River in the west, is the southernmost range, with foothills averaging 600 meters (2,000 feet) in height. The Terai, a wide forested tract, borders the Siwaliks on the north and leads to the Lesser Himalayas, where peaks extend to 6,000 meters (20,000 feet).

The Lesser Himalayas are blessed with abundant flora and fauna and receive a generous snowfall and a heavy monsoon that unleashes annually 120 inches of rain in the east. Earthquakes and landslides rearrange the hillsides and trigger flash floods, suddenly shifting the course of powerful rivers and ripping open new gorges. No wonder Hindus claim this is the abode of Shiva, their god of destruction.

To the north are the Greater Himalayas, or Trans-Himalayas, a crescendo of peaks that stretch more than 1,500 miles (2,400 kilometers) from Nanga Parbat, altitude 8,131 meters (26,660 feet), in northwest Kashmir to Namcha Barwa, altitude 7,760 meters (25,445 feet), which straddles Tibet and Bhutan. On the Tibetan and Nepalese border, you find the king of kings, Mt. Everest, at 8,877 meters (29,108 feet).

Any peak can be the setting for the drama in which climbers and, more recently, skiers, rafters, hang gliders, and balloonists battle nature and their own limitations. Success or failure, it hardly matters, as long as the body survives and the soul finds meaning. The Himalayas, the abode of the gods, is the abode of the adventurer—a rare place where all of us can soar to new heights.

The Abode of Gods: Religions of the Himalayas

Throughout the Himalayas, faith is expressed in art and architecture, in festivals, and in daily activities.

Buddhism

Siddhartha Gautama was born into a princely family in Lumbini along the Indian and Nepalese border around 563 BC. He renounced his privileged status—an act called the Great Renunciation—lived as an ascetic, then entered a lengthy meditation, which led to his Great Enlightenment.

Transformed, Siddhartha went to Sarnath, near Varanasi in India, and preached his revolutionary sermon on the *dharma* (truth), also called "The Setting in Motion of the Wheel of Truth or Law." His discourse set forth his Four Noble Truths, which define the essence of Buddhism: (1) Life is connected to suffering, (2) a suffering that arises from greed, insatiable desires, and man's self-centered nature; (3) once man understands the cause of his suffering, he can overcome it by following (4) the Eightfold Path.

The Eightfold Path includes right views and right aspirations, which lead to wisdom. Right speech, right behavior, right means of livelihood, and right efforts to follow the path to salvation relate to proper and intelligent conduct. Right meditation and right contemplation bring *nirvana* (supreme bliss).

Siddhartha Gautama became the Buddha (Enlightened One) or Sakyamuni (Lion of the Sakyamuni clan); and his faith became Theravada Buddhism, a religion of compassion and reason that did not worship idols. His followers did not consider Sakyamuni the founder of Buddhism, but simply the historic Buddha of their time.

In the 1st century AD, a second school, Mahayana Buddhism, was formed and introduced the concept of the *bodhisattva*—the enlightened being who postpones his own nirvana to help others. Unlike Theravadians who prayed only before symbols, such as the Buddha's empty throne or his footprints, Mahayanists also worshipped before depictions of the various Buddhas, other gods and goddesses, and revered bodhisattvas. Over time, Mahayana Buddhism divided into subsects that spread through the Himalayas, including Nyingmapa, Kargyu, Sakya, and Gelug. The Gelug achieved spiritual preeminence in Tibet. Their leader, His Holiness the Dalai Lama, is considered the God

King of Tibet and is currently living in exile in Dharamsala, India.

Pantheon Once you know the symbols that identify the more popular members of the pantheon, they're easy to recognize.

Buddhas **Adibuddha** (Original or Supreme Buddha) is considered infinite or abstract: without beginning or end. Still, he is often depicted in human form, sitting in the lotus (cross-legged) position with his arms crossed. One hand holds a *vajra* (thunderbolt: symbol of the Ultimate Reality); the other hand holds the *ghanta* (bell: symbol of wisdom). His body is usually blue.

The Five Dhyani (Cosmic) Buddhas, which emanated from the Adibuddha, represent the top tier of the Mahayana pantheon and embody the five elements of the cosmos (earth, water, fire, air, ether). They are always shown in a meditation pose. **Vairocana** (Buddha of Resplendent Light or the Buddha Supreme and Eternal) is also known as Buddha in the Center. Both hands appear in front of his chest in an image of a preacher who is "Turning the Wheel of Truth." His color is white, his symbol is the wheel, his element is ether, his vehicle is the lion. **Amitabha** (Buddha of Boundless Light) is also known as Buddha of the West. Both hands usually rest on his lap. His color is red, his symbol is the lotus, his element is water, his vehicle is the peacock. **Aksobhya** (Undisturbed Buddha) is also known as Buddha of the East. The fingers of his right hand usually touch the earth. His color is blue, his symbol is the thunderbolt, his element is air, his vehicle is the elephant. **Ratansambhava** (Jewel Being or Buddha of Precious Birth) is also known as Buddha of the South. His right hand is held low, palm open. His color is yellow, his symbol is the jewel, his element is fire, his vehicle is the horse. **Amoghasiddhi** (Buddha of Infallible Power) is also known as the Buddha of the North. He holds his right hand up in a gesture of fearlessness, which also offers a blessing of confidence. His color is green, his symbol is the double thunderbolt, his element is earth, his vehicle is Garuda (half-man and half-bird).

Sakyamuni (Historic Buddha) has a third eye symbolizing wisdom and usually sits on a lotus throne. His body is gold, his earlobes are long, a protubuerance atop his head is a symbol of his enlightenment, he wears monastic garb. His hands gesture one of three ways: His right hand may touch the earth signifying his realization of spiritual discovery; both hands may be in his lap, palms turned upward as in meditation; or both hands may be near his chest, symbolic of the delivery of his sermon, "The Wheel of Truth."

Bodhisattvas **Maitreya** (Future Buddha) usually appears with one hand held to his chest in the gesture of a preacher delivering "The Wheel of Truth," while the other hand holds a jug of water. His color is yellow, and he usually sits with his feet resting on a flowering lotus.

Avalokitesvara (Buddha of Compassion) has up to 11 heads and 1,000 arms and signifies compassion and wisdom. When he is portrayed with four heads, he is seated in the lotus position; when he appears with his 11 heads, he is standing. One hand holds a *mala* (rosary beads) and another carries a lotus. All Dalai Lamas are considered his incarnation.

Manjushri (Buddha of Transcendent Wisdom) appears with a sword held high in one hand, symbolizing his power to cut through ignorance. His other hand carries a book on a lotus, symbolic of wisdom.

Vajrapani (Buddha of Rain or Power) is blue, appears either seated or standing, and wears a serpent around his neck. In his most ferocious aspect, he carries a thunderbolt; in other depictions, he also holds a lotus.

Amitayus (Buddha of Eternal Life) is bright red, appears seated in meditation in the lotus position, and carries a vase of ambrosia, symbolic of long life.

The Buddha Saktis **Green Tara** (Green Savioress) is the patron goddess of Tibet
(Female Goddesses) and Avalokitesvara's consort. She sits on a lotus throne and holds a lotus in each hand.

White Tara (White Savioress) is also Avalokitesvara'a consort. She usually sits in the lotus position, with her right hand outstretched in a gesture of charity, her left hand holding a lotus in full bloom.

Nagarjuna and **Nagarjuna,** the founder of the Mahayana School of Bud-
Padmasambhava dhism, usually wears a crown with seven snakes, monastic garb, and looks like the Buddha with long earlobes. His hands are normally held palm to palm to his breast.

Padmasambhava (Guru Rimpoche or Lotus Born) appears in royal robes, including the red cap of the Nyingma sect, and sits on an open lotus. His right hand carries the thunderbolt; his left hand holds a *patra* (begging bowl), and tucked in his arm is his *khatvanga* (magic tantric stick), which cuts through evil and ignorance.

Important "Om Mani Padme Hum" is a *mantra* (invocation), which
Symbols means "hail to the jewel in the lotus," reminding the devotee of the Four Noble Truths. The lotus, usually shown as the throne of the enlightened, grows out of mud to reveal its purity and beauty above water. Reciting the mantra helps the devotee rise above imperfection and end the cycle of rebirths.

Mani **Walls** (low stone walls), inscribed with "Om Mani Padme Hum," guard Buddhist villages in the spiritual sense and protect them and nearby crops by diverting the runoff from heavy rains. When a Buddhist passes a mani wall, he repeats the mantra and keeps the wall to his right.

Stupas ("receptacles of offerings") are tall hemispheres made of stone and clay, built near monasteries or villages. Eight early stupas are said to contain the divided ashes of the Buddha. Subsequent stupas hold the remains of sacred *lamas* (monks) or commemorate an event in the Buddha's life. If you see five steps built into the central mound, they stand for the elements that form the cosmos (earth, water, fire, air, either) or the Five Cosmic Buddhas (*see* above). The 13 rings that often lead to a depiction of the moon and sun represent the Path to Enlightenment, frequently symbolized by an uppermost small circle.

Prayer Wheels are prayer-inscribed cylinders that contain paper or cloth strips—each one inscribed with "Om Mani Padme Hum." When the prayer wheel is rotated—always clockwise in respect for the Buddha—it sends the mantra to heaven.

The Wheel of Life, which the Buddha traced for his disciples, appears in most monasteries and represents a visual microcosm of Buddhism. The central image is a large circle or wheel divided into six sections, with a small interior circle and a larger circle around the rim. Often the wheel is held by Shindje, the Lord of Death, whose presence is a reminder of mortality. The interior circle shows the symbols of the root of suffering: a cock (lust), a pig (ignorance), and a snake (lack of compassion). The six sections inside the large circle describe the stations of life that come with rebirth. The bottom half portrays the three lowest forms: animals, ghosts, and the tormented in purgatory. The upper half reveals the inhabitants of the three worthiest realms: the deities, the *ashuras* (fallen deities) who long to rejoin the deities, and the mortals who hope for ascension. The band around this circle depicts allegories of human faults or conditions that man must overcome. A blind woman represents ignorance, the monkey is consciousness, and a woman in labor represents birth, to name a few.

Thang-kas (religious scrolls) or ***Paubhas,*** as they're called in Nepal, appear in monasteries or private shrines. These detailed paintings on cloth show deities, the *mandala* (*see* below), or the Wheel of Life, and are an aid to meditation. The entire painting is often enclosed in a silk brocade border, called its door.

Mandalas, created in sand paintings or thang-kas, are a geometric rendering of the dwelling of the god who resides within a circle that is set inside a square with four entrances, one on each side. During meditation, Buddhists gaze at the mandala to help acquire union with the divine.

The Eight Auspicious Signs The **Jewelled Parasol** protects the mind from evil influences. The **Golden Fish** represents man's rescue from the ocean of misery and is a symbol of spiritual happiness and wealth. The **Conch Shell** proclaims the glory of those who have achieved Enlightenment. (Before the Historic Buddha preached his first sermon, he blew on a conch shell.) The **Holy Vase** represents spiritual wealth and eternal bliss. The **Sacred Lotus** reaffirms the pledge to attain purity and salvation. The **Knot of Eternity,** which has no beginning or end, stands for the Four Noble Truths and eternity. The **Banner of Victory,** which is used in rituals and processions, proclaims the victory of the Four Noble Truths over evil. The **Eight-Spoked Wheel of Truth** symbolizes the Eightfold Path that leads to nirvana.

Hinduism

Hinduism, with its megafamily of gods and goddesses, extends back at least three millenia. Like Buddhists, Hindus believe in reincarnation. Hindus also share the Buddhist goal: liberation from the endless cycle of rebirth and the attainment of nirvana. Hinduism also espouses a similar relationship between dharma (truth) and *karma* (action). If one fulfills one's assigned duty and moral obligation to society, one will be rewarded in the next life.

Sacrifice is an essential part of dharma. An offering to a god blesses the worshiper in return. Sacrifice also calls for the relinquishment of one's individuality, which the Hindu believes frees the *atman* (universal consciousness) and allows the realization of nirvana. This theory explains an important ritual attached to cremation: The head of the deceased is ignited first to free the atman for the journey that will, it is hoped, end in heaven.

Devout Hindus also practice *yoga*, which they consider an indispensable expression of faith. Yoga (which literally means "union") is a series of complex mental and physical exercises that rid the practitioner of all thought to experience a sense of detachment from the realities of the physical world.

Strictures underlying dharma and karma also help to explain the tolerance of the caste system that divided all Hindus into four segregated rankings: *Brahmans* (priests), *Ksatriyas* (nobles and warriors), *Vaisya* (tradesmen), and *Shudras* (menial laborers). *Panchamas* (the filth), more commonly known as "Untouchables," fell outside the system. A member of one of the castes who accidently touched a Panchama was considered polluted until he went through purification rites.

To most westerners, the caste system seems like fuel for revolution. But within Hindu society, even those who sat on the lowest rung accepted their fate, seeing it as a direct result of their karma. If they followed the laws of truth and action, properly fulfilling their assigned duties, they could hope for a better next life. Centuries passed before the Untouchables found a way back from exclusion. The catalyst was Mahatma Gandhi. Through his efforts, the caste system was abolished in 1947—abolished by law, that is. Practically speaking, it still regulates much of Hindu behavior.

Hindu Temple As in Buddhism, the Hindu temple is filled with symbols of belief. Before the structure is built, a priest traces a mandala, which represents the cosmos and determines the placement of all rooms and icons. The center of the temple, called the inner sanctum, represents the egg or womb from which all life originates. This is where the sacred deity resides. The *vimana* (spire) is directly over the inner sanctum. It draws the attention of the devout to the heavenly realm and its connection with the sacred deity.

Many festivals take place in the temple's *mandapa* (a front porch that may be an elaborate pillared pavilion or a simple overhang). Devotees congregate in the mandapa until the deity is revealed. Water is the agent of purification. Ideally, a temple is constructed by a river or lake, but if no natural water source is available, a large tank is built, with steps around it. Before the devout Hindu worships, he takes a ritual dip to rid himself of impurities. Daily worship—usually performed at sunrise, noon, sunset, and midnight—is imbued with sacred traditions. Ancient rituals combine into an elaborate pagentry, with a touching gentleness toward the god's idol.

Hindu Pantheon The Hindu pantheon is dominated by three gods—Brahma, Shiva, and Vishnu—along with their numerous avatars (incarnations). **Brahma,** the Creator of the World and the Progenitor of All Living Things, has four heads and four arms, each one holding sway over a quarter of the universe. The four heads also signify the four Vedas, the most sacred Hindu holy books, which put forth the concept of rebirth. Brahma is the god of wisdom; the rosary that he counts in one hand represents time and his lotus seat represents the earth. Brahma's vehicle is the swan, symbol of the freedom that comes with knowledge. His consort is Sarasvati, the goddess of learning. Unlike Shiva and Vishnu, Brahma has no avatars.

Shiva is the God of Destruction—destruction that gives rise to creation, just as the seedling tears apart the seed. This is why Shiva is also called the God of Creation and Sexual Power and is often worshiped in the form of a lingam (phallic symbol). Images of Shiva have distinctive elements, like the third eye in the middle of his forehead, the tiger skins wrapped around his loins, and the serpents coiled around his body. Shiva often carries a weapon, a trident, or a bowl fashioned from a human skull. **Cosmic Shiva,** a common manifestion of Shiva, shows him as a dancer with four hands poised and surrounded by a ring, which represents the Earth. Since one foot holds down **Apasmara,** the demon of ignorance, his dance ensures perpetual creation. His mount, **Nandi,** the sacred bull, usually guards the entrance to a Shiva temple. Priests who pray to Shiva have three horizontal stripes painted on the forehead. Vishnu priests have three vertical stripes.

Shiva's consort is the most powerful Hindu goddess. With each avatar she assumes, her name and image change. When she is benevolent **Parvati,** wife of Shiva, she's beautiful and sexy. As **Durga,** the goddess of battle, she holds weapons of retribution in each of 10 hands. As **Kali,** the terrible black goddess who conquered time, she wears a necklace of skulls and dangles her red tongue. Devotees must appease her with sacrifices, formerly humans. Now she accepts considerably less.

Ganesha, Shiva and Parvati's son, is the popular god of wealth and good fortune. He has the head of an elephant because, one legend claims, Shiva, unaware he was a father, returned from a trip just after Parvati told Ganesha to guard the house while she slept. When Shiva approached, Ganesha blocked the entrance. Shiva lopped off his head. When he discovered Ganesha was his son, he ordered his servants into the forest to take the head of the first creature they saw—an elephant.

The preserver of the universe, **Vishnu,** has nine known avatars; a 10th is prophesied. Each successive avatar reflects a step up the evolutionary cycle, beginning with the fish and moving up to the ninth, Buddha, accepted by the all-embracing Hindus as a figure within their own pantheon. Vishnu's most popular incarnations are Rama and Krishna, the sixth and seventh, respectively, who are the two gods embodying humanity.

Vishnu appears with four arms that signify the four cardinal directions and his command over the realms they encompass. In one hand, he carries the lotus, the symbol of the universe. The conch shell held in a second hand represents the evolutionary nature of all existence. A wheel in the third hand refers to the rotation of the Earth, with each spoke honoring a specific season of the year. In his fourth hand, Vishnu often holds a weapon to protect him from demons. A common image of Vishnu has him lying on a bed of coils formed by his serpent **Ananta,** who symbolizes time. Creation will begin when Vishnu wakes up. Vishnu has two consorts: **Bhudevi,** the goddess of earth, and **Lakshmi,** the goddess of wealth and prosperity, who rose from the foam of the ocean like Venus. Lakshmi assumes a different name with each of Vishnu's avatars. When he's Rama, she's **Sita;** when he's Krishna, she's **Radha.**

Rama, the hero of the Hindu epic, *Ramayana,* slayed the 10-headed demon **Ravana,** who had kidnapped Sita. This episode, including her rescue by **Hanuman,** the monkey god and Rama's faithful servant, is celebrated at Dussehra, one of India's most festive holidays. **Krishna,** a central figure in another great Hindu epic, *Mahabharata,* is a playful boy god. He plays the flute, has a weakness for teasing young girls, and is colored blue. An embodiment of a human love that has the power to destroy all pain, Krishna represents the ideal man and lover.

Islam

"There is no God but Allah, and Mohammed is His Prophet." This, the *shahadah* (religious creed) and the most important pillar of the Islamic faith, originated with the merchant Mohammed (his name means "highly praised") who was born about AD 570 in the Arabian town of Mecca. A series of revelations from Allah, passed on through the Angel Gabriel, instructed Mohammed to preach against the paganism practiced by the Meccans. Initially, Mohammed saw himself as a social reformer who advocated virtuous life in a city where virtue had vanished. The Meccans, however, saw him as a menace and a threat and forced him to flee to Yathrib (present-day Medina).

This move in AD 622, which Moslems now call *hijra*, marks the beginning of the Islamic era—an era in which Mohammed established the concept of Islam, which means "submission," as a way of life that dictated the proper behavior of the individual. By the time Mohammed died in AD 632, an expanse stretching from the Punjab in India to the Pyrenees in Europe and from Samarkand (in the USSR) to the Sahara had converted to Islam.

The next ruler, called *caliph* (successor of the Prophet), was Abu Bakr, Mohammed's father-in-law. However, some Moslems favored, Ali, the Prophet's nephew, husband of his daughter Fatima and the first convert to Islam. After Ali finally succeeded to the caliphate in AD 656, civil war broke out. Ali moved his capital to Mesopotamia, where he was murdered by Moslem dissidents.

Ali's death signaled the beginning of a period of religious dissension between the traditionalists, Sunnis who followed the orthodox teaching and example of the Prophet, and Ali's supporters, who claimed Ali's right to the caliphate based on his descent from the Prophet. In time, Ali's supporters formed a sect known as the Shias or Shiites (the party of Ali).

Originally political in nature, the differences between the Sunnis and Shiites took on theological overtones. Though the Sunnis retained the doctrine of leadership by consensus; after Syrians massacred Hussain, Ali's grandson, at Karbala in Iraq, the Shiites strengthened their resolve that only Mohammed's rightful heirs should rule. They modified the shahadah: "There is no god but Allah; Mohammed is the Prophet of God and Ali is the Saint of God."

Islam demands submission to God—a God who is invisible yet omnipresent. To represent him in any form is a sin, which explains the absence of icons in mosques and tombs. Every bit of decoration, often fashioned out of myriad tiny gems, is limited to inscriptions of the holy scripture, the *Quran*, and the names of Mohammed and his important followers.

Moslems believe Allah (God) existed throughout time, but men had strayed from his true teaching until Mohammed set them straight. Islam has concepts similar to those of Judaism or Christianity: guardian angels, the Day of Judgment, the general resurrection, heaven and hell, and the eternal life of the soul.

The duties of the Moslem form the five pillars of the faith. These are the recitation of the shahadah; *salat* (daily prayer); *zakat* (almsgiving); *siyam* (fasting); and *haj* (pilgrimage). The believer must pray to Allah five times daily, with each occasion preceded by a ritual washing of hands, feet, neck, and head. Every aspect of salat, during which one always faces Mecca, is predetermined by the *Quran:* the genuflections, prostrations, the actual prayers recited. Whenever possible, men pray at a mosque under a prayer leader; this is obligatory on Fridays. Women may also attend public worship but are segregated from the men.

The ninth month of the Moslem calendar, *Ramadan,* when Mohammed received his revelations, is a month of obligatory fasting from sunrise to sunset for all but the weak, pregnant women, and very small children. During this period of abstinence, smoking, and sexual intercourse are also prohibited.

During his life, a Moslem is supposed to make the haj to the Great Mosque in Mecca to participate in 10 days of special rites held during the 12th month of the lunar calendar. The returning pilgrim is entitled to the honorific "haji" before his name and a turban carved on his tombstone.

The permanent struggle for the triumph of the word of God on earth, the *jihad,* is used to justify wars. However, most Moslems see it in a broader context of a code of ethical conduct that encourages generosity, fairness, honesty, and respect and forbids adultery, gambling, usury, and the consumption of pork and alcohol.

Mosque, or *majid,* means "a place of prostration." It is generally square in shape; is constructed from stone, clay, or brick; and has an open courtyard surrounded with *madrasas* (cloisters) for students who are studying the *Quran.* After the *muezzin* (crier) sings the call for prayer from the minaret, the faithful line up in rows behind the *imam* (one who has studied the *Quran*). The imam stands in the sacred part of the majid facing the *mihrab* (a niche in a wall that indicates the direction of Mecca). When the imam prays, the mihrab—an ingenious amplifier—bounces his voice back to the devotees. Only prayers are heard and prostrations are made; ceremonies connected with birth, marriage, and death occur elsewhere. You won't hear any music or singing either. For the Moslem, the human voice in prayer creates the sweetest sound to Allah.

Sikhism

Guru Nanak, the founder of Sikhism, was born into a Hindu family in 1469 when the Lodi sultanate, a Moslem dynasty from Afghanistan, ruled over his north Indian homeland. From an early age, he railed against the caste system, the corruption of Hindu priests, their superstitious beliefs, their unwieldy family of gods. His anger led to his new theology, which believed in one god, and his title of *guru* (gu: one who drives away darkness and preaches enlightenment: ru).

Nanak's view of Sikhism, recorded in the *Adi Granth* (Sikh Holy Book), subscribed to the Islamic belief that the goal of religion was the union with God, who dwelled within the soul. Through meditation and dharma (Hindu concepts), he believed the devotee could rid himself of impurities, free himself from the endless cycle of rebirth, and attain eternal bliss. For Hindus at the bottom of society, Sikhism offered equality and tolerance. They gladly converted.

3 Bhutan

Introduction

Until the mid-1900s, the tiny kingdom of Bhutan had its back turned to the world. The fabled Land of the Thunder Dragon—a country of Buddhists and *dzongs* (fortresses), yaks and blue sheep, alpine valleys and lofty white peaks—was unknown to foreigners. Then political events forced a change. In 1959 its northern trading partner, Tibet, was consumed by China. In 1975 Sikkim, an independent kingdom to the east, became part of India. Bhutan was now surrounded by two giant powers. It had a friendly alliance with India, but its position with China was less clear. To protect itself, it joined the United Nations in 1971, thus becoming part of the world community of nations. Three years later, the king decided that obtaining foreign currency was a priority and he opened Bhutan's borders.

Unfortunately, foreigners brought Bhutan new problems— visitors touched and unwittingly defiled holy objects, ignored signs prohibiting photographing of religious treasures, and worst of all, bribed *lamas* (monks) to steal sacred scrolls and other precious items for them.

In 1987 the king announced that most monasteries, sacred institutions, and sanctified mountains (all but three peaks) were off-limits to foreigners. Visitors would henceforth travel in groups on fixed itineraries with government guides. Foreigners also had to pay a steep per diem; the cheapest trip, an off-season trek, costs $110 per day.

Is a trip to Bhutan worth the expense? If you visit during the peak season, April and October, the unexpected can happen with annoying frequency. You may end up in a tent instead of your prepaid room and travel around in a junk heap instead of the jeep that is necessary for remote destinations. And when problems arise, the government is ill-equipped to resolve them and loathe to part with the per diem you've paid. You may have the impression that the government wants your money but not you. Perhaps a sign on a door at the dzong in Bumthang sums it up best: "Welcome, no admittance."

This unflattering assessment is meant as a warning. For all trips, use a recommended travel agency (*see* below or in Before You Go in Chapter 1). Be sure your trip includes an employee of the company, who can serve as a tour leader. The tour leader is the key to your understanding Bhutan and acts as an expeditor who can often provide the key to your room or the key to a decent vehicle. Since Bhutan has shut down its overseas tourist bureaus, it's extremely difficult for even the best travel agent to be up on new pitfalls—landslides or latest government edicts. Protect yourself with a trip-cancellation policy (*see* Before You Go in Chapter 1). Finally, if you plan to sign up for a cultural tour, make sure it includes *tsechus* (festivals), which give you a chance to witness the Buddhist rituals in Bhutan.

Trekking is the best and least expensive way to see Bhutan, which is just twice the size of New Hampshire. Routes now open to foreigners take you through spectacular terrain to delightful destinations. You also meet few trekkers.

Bhutan is beautiful. Across its northern border stand the shimmering peaks of the Grand Himalayas, including two revered mountains—Chomolhari, the abode of the Goddess Chomol-

Bhutan *(Numbers on map correspond to numbers in text)*

TIBET (CHINA)

TIBET (CHINA)

INDIA

50 miles
75 km

Sakteng

Radi

Mera

Tashigang

Kurtey

Lhuntsi

10

Mongar

9

Bumthang Valley

7

Ura

8

Kurje

Jakar Dzong

Bumthang

Tongsa

6

Tempelso

Gangker Punsum

Nikkachu

PELE LA BLACK MOUNTAIN RANGE

Manas R.

Manas Game Sanctuary

N

TSENDA KANG

Jejotcangthukang

Thaanza

Gonglokarchung

Po Chu R.

Pela La Pass

Wangdiphodrang Dzong

Lunana

Punakha Dzong

4

5

Laya

Tashithang

Mo Chu

Barshong Chu

Thimphu

3

Chebisa

Gasa

Yali La Pass

Taktsang Monastery

2

Paro

1

Ha

Lingshi

Lemihang

Mt. Jichu Drake

Mt. Chomolhari

Samchi

Phuntsholing

INDIA

hari, and Gangker Punsum, the White Glacier of the Spiritual Brothers—both home to *bharal* (blue sheep) and the rare snow leopard. Only four passes, which once carried traders between the Tibetan plateau and Bhutan, cut through this range. Glaciers tumble down slopes, creating mountaintop lakes and rivers that rush through narrow gorges and wind through wide, sloping valleys.

In Bhutan's central belt, intersected by the Pele La Black Mountain Range, valleys in the west are inhabited by the Nyalops, who are of Tibetan origin, and forested with pine, oak, rhododendron, and fruit trees. Fields are used as pastureland or cultivated with rice, wheat, and maize. Eastern valleys are populated by the Sharchops, descendants of the original inhabitants of Bhutan. Here, a heavy rainfall creates a dense tropical landscape. Cultivated plots are less frequent; life is much harder.

In the south, the home of Nepalese immigrants since the 19th century, the climate is subtropical. A torrential monsoon and sultry heat create an ideal environment for bamboo and banana groves, forests where orchids cling to crooks in trees. This is the site of the Manas Game Sanctuary—a preserve for elephants, tigers, rhinoceros, the rare golden langur (a monkey), and numerous species of bird.

History Historians speculate that until the mid-8th century, Bhutan was under the influence of Indian culture and controlled by rulers from the Cooch dynasty, who also reigned over what is now Assam. When Bhutan pulled free, Padmasambhava, an Indian mystic who was later called Guru Rimpoche, was in Tibet, where he had established the first school of Tibetan Buddhism. Twice Guru Padmasambhava visited Bhutan, spreading his form of Tibetan Buddhism, now known as Nyingmapa, or Old Sect.

Over the years, a rival Tibetan Buddhist faction—the Kahdam (later called Gelug) split into two branches—the Kagyu and the Sakya. The Kagyu, with its austere strictures, gave rise to the Drukpa Kagyus (Thunder Dragons) and the Lhapa Kagyus.

In 1616 the Gelugs seized control of Tibet's Ralung Monastery, the religious center of the Drukpa Kagyus, forcing the lamas and their powerful leader, Ngawang Namgyal, to seek refuge in Bhutan. Over the next 35 years, he unified Bhutan and built massive dzongs and monasteries. An astute military leader, Ngawang Namgyal repulsed invading troops from Tibet, assumed the title of *Shabdung Rimpoche* (Supreme Religious Power), and proclaimed himself the temporal and spiritual ruler of Bhutan. Much of the administrative framework he set up remains intact.

With the end of Ngawang Namgyal's rule in 1651, disparate factions fought for the title of Shabdung Rimpoche. They also battled with Tibet to the north and Cooch Bihar in northeast India. In 1772 struggles in Cooch Bihar pitted the Bhutanese unsuccessfully against Britain's East India Company.

Though the 1865 Treaty of Sinchula ushered in an era of cooperation between the British and Bhutan, internal fighting led to a new civil war in 1869. In 1884 the British recognized Ugyen Wangchuck as the supreme power. In 1907 he became the first hereditary monarch of Bhutan and three years later signed a new treaty with the British in which the Bhutanese agreed to British "guidance" in external affairs, and the British agreed to a hands-off policy inside the kingdom.

With Ugyen Wangchuck's death in 1926, his son Jigme Wangchuck ascended the throne. Jigme Wangchuck instituted numerous reforms—founding schools, repairing monasteries —and concluded a treaty with India after it gained its independence in 1947. His son, Jigme Dorji Wangchuck, who became king in 1952, set up institutions to preserve the language and culture and created the first national museum in Paro. Jigme Dorji Wangchuck abolished serfdom, built roads, instituted long-range economic planning, created a comprehensive educational system, started the postal system, and brought in trained doctors. He established the National Assembly— called Tshogdu—becoming a constitutional monarch who must obtain a popular vote of confidence every three years.

After his death in 1972, his son Jigme Singye Wangchuck assumed the crown. The young king established Bhutan's first factories and telephone facilities, over 100 schools, and numerous hospitals. Though Bhutan still has an estimated per capita income of about $80, overwhelming misery is hard to find, thanks to the government's social programs. The king is committed to maintaining Bhutan's cultural identity. All new buildings, including private homes, must be made with traditional techniques. No nails go into their construction—a marvel of ingenuity considering their complexity and beauty.

The king is much adored. In 1988 he had a formal royal wedding to four sisters whom he had married years earlier during private religious ceremonies. Already the king was father to eight children. A week before the wedding, he named his eight-year-old son, Jigme Gesar Namgyal Wangchuck, the crown prince of Bhutan.

No world leaders or international guests outside Bhutan were invited to the subdued affair. The young king, explained the foreign minister, "is a very simple man. He dislikes public shows, dislikes any kind of ostentation." He does like to play basketball.

The Drukpa Kagyus   After the Buddha, Guru Padmasambhava is the most important spiritual figure in Bhutan. He's considered the second Buddha, and it's a rare shrine that doesn't honor one of his eight manifestations. In his first visit to Bhutan, Padmasambhava appeared as Guru Pema Jungne (Lotus Born); in his second visit, he was Guru Dorje Trolo (Adamantine Ferocity). In this his eighth manifestation, he personifies a process of enlightenment in which the individual realizes that nothing exists by itself. By acquiring this understanding, one overcomes greed, ill will, and ignorance—as represented by the cock, snake, and pig, respectively.

Dorje Trolo's image, which you will notice in religious iconography everywhere, is a reminder of the path that must be taken to break the cycle of mundane existence. His right hand holds the *dorje* (thunderbolt), the symbol of the truth behind the Buddha's teachings. His left hand holds his sacred dagger representing his own miraculous power. Dorje Trolo sits on the back of a pregnant tiger, his consort Tashi Khenden, with her impregnation representing the latent wisdom that exists in all creatures. His fierce appearance accentuates his position as the protector of his consort, who also represents the people of Bhutan. The flames that rise up around them remind the Buddhist of Dorje Trolo's divine energy.

The Drukpa Kagyu sect establishes the Bhutanese code of ethics—based on the teachings of the Buddha and Padmasambhava, which emphasize respect for all life and belief in the importance of subjugating all forms of evil. The sect's rituals are practiced in all Bhutan. The symbols of Drukpa Kagyu Buddhism are the dominant theme in the national flag, the royal crest, and the national anthem.

Before You Go

Government Tourist Offices

The **Permanent Mission of the Kingdom of Bhutan to the United Nations** in New York (*see* Visas, below) has only limited information. Your best bet is to bypass the government and contact the recommended travel agency listed below or tour companies listed in Before You Go to the Himalayas, Chapter 1.

Tour Groups

The following private company offers tours exclusively to Bhutan: **Bhutan Travel** (120 E. 56th St., Suite 1430, New York, NY 10022, tel. 212/838–6382 or 800/950–9908). This company offers the latest excursions and outdoor adventures. Given the limitations placed on the number of annual visitors and mandatory approval for each tour group, you should make all arrangements months in advance.

When to Go

Weather and price will probably determine the timing of most vacations (*see* What It Will Cost, below). Southern Bhutan is best from October to April when daytime maximum temperatures are in the 70s F (about 24° C). From April to the end of August, the maximum daytime temperature climbs into the 90s F (about 35° C), and from June to September, the monsoon brings torrential rains and high humidity.

From November to April in the central belt, including Paro and Thimphu, expect sunny skies and maximum daytime temperatures around 50° F (10° C) and nighttime temperatures around 32° F (13° C). From April to June and September to November, maximum daytime temperatures reach the 60s F (18° C), and nighttime temperatures are in about the 30s F (13° C). In summer, expect maximum daytime temperatures to reach the upper 70s F (about 24° C) and light periods of rain. At press time, travelers can visit eastern Bhutan only from November to March; then the weather is similar to that of Paro and Thimphu.

Moving north to the high mountains, the best time to visit is spring through early autumn. Maximum daytime temperatures climb from the 50s to the 60s F (about 12°–19° C); at night, the temperature can drop to the 40s F (about 7° C). Winters are below freezing.

You can also plan a vacation around an exceptional festival, such as the Paro Tsechu or Thimphu Tsechu, still open to visitors.

Festivals and Seasonal Events

Tsechus in Bhutan enact ancient myths that pit good against evil. A tsechu's dances—Bhutanese morality plays—are bound by tradition, taught by lamas, and usually performed by lamas. Most festivals begin with the appearance of clowns who work the crowds into a festive mood. Then a lama appears with a whip. As he walks across the courtyard, he strikes at objects and people—acts of purification that sanctify the arena for the head lama who signals the start of the festival. If you attend a festival, refer to the following brief descriptions of typical dances.

Shacham (Dance of the Four Stags). Dancers wear knee-length skirts and masks with deer horns; movements are slow and stately. This dance reenacts Guru Padmasambhava's triumph over the demonic King of the Wind who was creating havoc in the world. After his triumph, Padmasambhava leapt on the stag, the mount of the demon. Performing this dance ensures future happiness and peace.

Shana (Black Hat Dance). Dancers wear a large hat, felt boots, brocade robes, but no masks. This dance, accompanied by drums and the sound of the dancers' pounding feet, tells the story of a Tibetan king who once lived in Bhutan and murdered an important lama. A Bhutanese monk killed the king with an arrow concealed in his robe and thus destroyed the power of evil.

Tungam (Dance of the Terrifying Deities). Dancers wear brocade robes, boots, and horrific masks. Tungam reenacts the destruction of evil spirits and the salvation of the world. Dancers representing the power of good encircle evil demons, who are then "killed" by the head performer. Their death liberates them from the evil that controlled them and elevates them to a higher realm.

Pacham (Dance of the Heroes). Dancers wear knee-length yellow skirts and golden crowns, but no masks; they each carry a small bell and drum. This dance, depicting the heavenly abode of Guru Padmasambhava and celebrating the abolition of ignorance, starts with swirls and leaps that create a celestial rainbow of color. Demigods wearing skull masks and beating drums appear from the corners of the courtyard and sanctify the arena for the arrival of Padmasambhava, his face hidden behind the mask of the Buddha. After he's led to his throne, the dancers resume their spinning and reach out for his blessings.

Since the precise date of each tsechu is tied to the lunar calendar, check with your travel agent before you depart.

Jan.: Tongsa Tsechu is a three-day festival in central Bhutan.
Feb.: Losar marks the beginning of the Bhutanese New Year with archery contests and feasts.
Mar.: Shemgang Tsechu in central Bhutan runs for three days.
Paro Tsechu is a five-day festival.
Oct.: Thimphu Tsechu lasts four days.
Nov.: Wangdi Tsechu, near Thimphu, lasts three days.
Dec.: Mongar Tsechu in central Bhutan lasts three days.

Tashigang Tsechu in eastern Bhutan lasts three days. On the **National Day of Bhutan** (Dec. 17), everything's closed to commemorate the establishment of the hereditary monarchy.

What to Pack

Follow the advice in Before You Go to the Himalayas, Chapter 1. If you're planning to trek or go by vehicle to central or eastern Bhutan, bring a sleeping bag. Also bring plenty of film (not available locally) and a flashlight (interiors of the few monuments open to foreigners are poorly lit).

Taking Money Abroad

Bhutan has no restrictions on the amount of foreign currency and traveler's checks you can bring in, but bring checks in small denominations and cash them only when necessary. On departure, Bhutan reconverts only 30% of the total amount cashed.

Changing Money You can change money at **hotels in Thimphu or Paro,** at the **Paro Airport,** or in Thimphu at the **Bhutan Tourism Corporation,** the **Handicrafts Emporium,** or the **Bank of Bhutan.**

Currency

The Bhutanese unit of currency is the ngultrum (nu), equal in value to the Indian rupee, which travelers are not supposed to use in Bhutan. Bhutanese paper money comes in ngultrum 1, 2, 4, 10, 50, and 100 denominations; coins called chetrum, rarely used, come in 1, 2, 5, 10, 25, 50, and 100 denominations, with 100 chetrum equaling one nu. The rate of exchange is approximately U.S. \$1 = 16 nu; £1 = 25 nu.

What It Will Cost

As of 1989, the following per diem rates (per person) are in effect:

April, October: *hotel*, \$250; *lodge*, \$230; *camp/tent*, \$180; *trek*, \$130.

March, May, July, August, September, November: *hotel*, \$200; *lodge*, \$190; *camp/tent*, \$150; *trek*, \$120.

December–March, June: *hotel*, \$150; *lodge*, \$140; *camp/tent*, \$130; *trek*, \$110.

Children up to 3 years of age pay 10% of the per diem; from age 3 to 5, 25%; from 5 to 7, 35%; from 7 to 12, 50%. Individual tourists who enter Bhutan as part of a government-sponsored scheduled-departure tour are charged an extra \$20 per night. Travelers who don't get their prepaid rooms are put up in tents and rebated accordingly.

Visas

To get a visa, you need a valid passport, and you must sign up for one of two types of tours, private or government sponsored. With your visa form, enclose two photographs, and a photocopy of your passport that shows the number, your birthdate and nationality, and the passport's date of issue and expiration; also note your occupation. Send this information to **Bhutan Tourism**

Corporation (Manager, Central Booking, Royal Government of Bhutan, Box 159, Thimphu, Bhutan). You receive your visa when you arrive in Paro.

If you join a tour with a private travel agency, the agency will give you the visa form and do the paperwork for you. If you join a government-sponsored scheduled-departure tour, get a visa form from the **Permanent Mission of the Kingdom of Bhutan to the United Nations** (2 United Nations Plaza, New York, NY, 10017, tel. 212/826–1919). The mission has scanty information about government-sponsored tours, so write at least two months in advance to the Bhutan Tourism Corporation. Currently Bhutan doesn't sponsor government tours in April and October. Bhutan has no embassies or consulates in the United States, Canada, or Britain.

Customs and Duties

On Arrival   Baggage limit on Druk Air, the national airline, is 20 kilograms (44 pounds). You can bring in personal effects; on arrival you must declare all valuables. You can bring in a still or movie camera, but must obtain approval from the Bhutan Tourism Corporation to bring in a video camera. On arrival, you pay $20 in cash or traveler's checks for your visa.

On Departure   Foreigners pay Nu 50 Foreign Departure Tax. You may not export antiques, plants, or animal products.

Staying Healthy

See Staying Healthy in Before You Go to the Himalayas, Chapter 1. No inoculations are required.

Arriving and Departing

By Plane

To reach **Paro International Airport** (currently the only way to enter Bhutan), private tour groups fly in from Kathmandu, Bangkok, Delhi, Calcutta, or Dhaka. Individuals who want to join a fixed-departure government tour must fly in from Delhi, Bangkok, Kathmandu, or Calcutta. The current five-day tour that departs Calcutta Friday and returns Tuesday may be dropped. A weekly four-day tour originates in Kathmandu; two five-day tours originate in Delhi. From Bangkok, you can join a week-long trip. (For information on how to reach Calcutta or Delhi, *see* Before You Go to North India, Chapter 5; for Kathmandu, *see* Before You Go to Nepal, Chapter 4.)

Airline   **Druk Air,** the only airline with access to Bhutan, has flights out of Delhi, Kathmandu, and Bangkok that carry 80 passengers. Since the planes that fly in from Dhaka and Calcutta are 12- and 14-seaters, problems can arise. If a member of the royal family or a dignitary needs an aircraft, your tour group could be bumped and put on a later flight.

Flying Time   The flight from Dhaka, Calcutta, or Kathmandu is about an hour; from Delhi, about three hours; from Bangkok, four hours.

Staying in Bhutan

Behavioral Dos and Don'ts

Don't try to talk your way into off-limit areas; don't climb anywhere that's considered sacred. Don't smoke around a dzong and do remove your hat. Lower an umbrella near the royal palace, inside a monastery compound, or in the presence of a lama. During festivals, don't step onto the dance area to take photos or interfere with the dancers. The Bhutanese are extremely sensitive about each tsechu: They're religious events, no matter how festive they appear. Don't interrupt a Buddhist who's praying. Ask before you take a photograph of any sacred object.

In Bhutan, individuals often wear a long silk scarf. A white scarf, called *khata*, is offered as a gift of respect to high lamas. The king and Je Khempo (head abbot) wear saffron; ministers and deputy ministers wear orange; delegates to the national assembly wear blue; high civil and religious officials and judges wear red; assistant district administrators and village leaders wear red with white stripes. If you get to visit with a lama, it's a nice gesture to bring him a khata, available in shops in Paro and Thimphu.

Getting Around

By Minibus, Car, or Jeep If you're not trekking, you'll travel in Japanese-made minibuses, cars, or jeeps. Though the government's fleet is modern and well maintained, in the peak season, the tourist department often hires unreliable additional cars. The road through central Bhutan to the east is subject to enormous landslides that can shut it down for months. Travelers heading for the east are advised to lobby the tour group operator for jeeps or they may not get there. At press time, the route into Bhutan from Assam was shut down, eliminating the other access into the east and the only road to the Manas Game Sanctuary.

By Helicopter Bhutan hopes to have helicopters by 1991. Check with your travel agency.

Outdoor Adventures

Adventure travel in Bhutan is just beginning. At press time, many options were under development; check with the Bhutan Tourism Corporation or your travel agent for the latest details. Highly recommended adventures are indicated by a star ★. (*See* destination sections, below, for detailed descriptions.)

Climbing and Mountaineering: Permits for some peaks are granted to selected climbers. Contact the Bhutan Tourism Corporation (*see* Visas, above).

Fishing: Once the logistics for travel to Manas Game Sanctuary are worked out, you can fish for trout and *mahseer* (Himalayan river fish) from November to March. Bring your own equipment.

Horseback and Yak Riding: Bhutan plans to offer horse and yak treks. Check with the Bhutan Tourism Corporation (*see* Visas, above). Short horse rides are already available in Paro.

Hot Springs: The trek from Paro or Thimphu to Lunana includes a chance to relax in the Gasa hot springs near Laya.

Rafting: One-day runs are under development between Punaka and Wangdiphodrang northeast of Thimphu.

★ **Trekking.** All treks must be sponsored by a tour operator and approved in advance by the government.

Mt. Chomolhari: From Paro, you can trek for a week to the base of Mt. Cholomari and on to Thimphu, or go north to Laya and swing down to Tashithang near Punakha (28 days total). You visit some of the highest settlements in Bhutan (the home of yak herders) and walk through landscapes of towering glaciers and mountains.

Lunana: From Tashithang near Thimphu, you walk northwest to Lunana, a strikingly beautiful high-altitude area of glaciers, glacier lakes, and mountains. This is one of the finest treks in the entire Himalayas, and one of the most rigorous. You must be physically fit. *East Bhutan:* Take a cultural trek into newly opened eastern Bhutan and visit villages where the weaving of highly detailed silks, wools, and cottons is the traditional occupation. *Winter Treks:* You can take winter treks around Paro, Punakha (near Thimphu), and central Bhutan.

Wildlife Safaris: The government is currently arranging visits (Nov.–Mar.) to the Manas Game Sanctuary in southeastern Bhutan along the border of Assam. This tropical preserve has rhinoceroses, tigers, elephants, leopards, bears, buffalo, wild boar, pythons, many species of deer, the golden langur (a monkey native to Bhutan and Assam), and numerous species of tropical bird. Visitors will be accommodated in a small tourist lodge built in the middle of the forest. To reach the park, you will either trek or enter via the road from Assam. At press time, no further details were available. Contact Bhutan Tourism Corporation (*see* Visas, above) or Bhutan Travel (*see* Tour Groups, above).

Telephones

In Paro and Thimphu, you can make local calls. When you book international phone calls from your hotel, expect to wait an hour for the connection. Payment must be made in local currency; if you're in a hotel, it will also accept traveler's checks. For remote destinations, the wireless is often the only means of communication.

Telegrams and Telex

You can send telegrams and telex messages from Thimphu.

Mail

Receiving Mail An **American Express** office has opened in Thimphu, but it was not equipped to receive mail at press time. Check with your local American Express office before you leave.

Postal Rates The cost of an airmail letter (weighing 10 grams) to Britain, Europe, Canada, or the United States is Nu 5. Postcards are Nu 3.

Tipping

Tipping is prohibited in Bhutan; however, you can give a gift to your drivers or government guides. They will appreciate American- or British-made argyle knee socks, which they wear with their national dress.

Opening and Closing Times

Government offices, banks, and post offices are closed on Sunday and official holidays. Hours for individual establishments are listed.

Shopping

The purchase of antiques is strictly prohibited. There are many other alternatives for souvenirs and gifts. Bhutan creates some of the most elaborate and beautiful stamps in the world—three-dimensional stamps, stamps the size of a postcard. They're available in Thimphu. Bhutan's handwoven, naturally dyed textiles (wool, heavy cotton, and a local silk) are renowned among collectors and irresistibly priced—available by the meter or fashioned into the national dress: *kira* for the women or *kho* for the men—long handsome robes fastened with a *kera* (sash) around the waist. Other good buys are carved masks, woven baskets, wooden butter-tea cups, handmade paper, and new *thang-kas* (religious scrolls).

Dining

Meals offered to tour groups are generally limited to a fixed menu—usually Continental cuisine—and served buffet style. Dishes tend to be repetitive, with a heavy emphasis on noodles, chicken, pork, and vegetables. Expect fruit or fruit salad for dessert. Bhutanese food, hard to find, is delicious. Check the listings in the Thimphu section, below. There are no "dry" days in Bhutan. You can have a daily nightcap when liquor is available.

Mealtimes Expect to eat with your group at an agreed-upon time.

Precautions *See* Staying Healthy in Before You Go to the Himalayas, Chapter 1.

Ratings Since group travel dictates where you eat in most of Bhutan and the cost is built into the per diem, prices are given only for a couple of inexpensive restaurants (under $5) in Thimphu, where you can opt for your own culinary excursion (*see* Thimphu section, below). Prices are per person, excluding drinks, service, and taxes.

Lodging

The government decides where you stay in Bhutan. Most hotels, however, are attractive, conforming to traditional Bhutanese architecture. In Thimphu and Paro, interiors often continue the motif but have Western-style bathrooms. In central and eastern Bhutan, expect simple but adequate tourist guest houses, with attached or shared bathrooms (usually hot water by bucket). Since the number of rooms is limited, you may end up in a tent. Bring a sleeping bag. Finally, though heating is supplied, rooms can be chilly. Pack accordingly. For trekkers, tents and all other equipment, except sleeping bags and day packs, are supplied.

Credit Cards

The American Express card is of limited value in Bhutan.

Paro

Numbers in the margin correspond with points of interest on the Bhutan map.

❶ The law requiring all new buildings to be made in the traditional style gives an ancient appearance to the tiny village of **Paro** constructed in the 70s. Whitewashed facades are trimmed in carved dark wood and painted with Buddhist symbols. Prayer flags rustle from poles along the road, on narrow suspension bridges, and on rooftops. *Chortens* (shrines containing relics) stand at frequent intervals. Lamas walk along fingering their prayer beads or twirling small prayer wheels. Paro's valley is one of the prettiest in the kingdom.

Arriving and Departing by Plane

Currently the only access to Paro is by plane.

Airport and Airline **Druk Airlines** is the only airline that lands at the **International Airport,** 8 kilometers (5 miles) from the center of Paro. A government transport meets your flight and takes you to the one hotel.

Getting Around

The government will take you around in its vehicles on the two tours described below.

Addresses and Numbers

For all tourist information, banking needs, and emergencies, turn to your tour group leader or to your government-run hotel. There are no American, Canadian, or British embassies in Bhutan.

Exploring Paro Village

On this half-day tour, you visit the rebuilt **Paro Dzong.** Constructed in the mid-1600s by Bhutan's great unifier, Ngawang Namgyal, it was destroyed by fire in 1907. Only one thang-ka was saved. Paro Dzong is the district headquarters and home of numerous lamas. The salvaged Thongdel thang-ka is unfurled for a few hours during the Paro Tsechu. The Bhutanese pray before its image of Guru Padmasambhava, believing that will bring them nirvana. Standing on a ridge above the dzong is the former watch tower, **Ta Dzong,** built around 1775, and now the **National Museum.**

The renovated **Dungtse Lhakhang** (monastery), originally built in the 15th century, is shaped like a mandala. According to legend, the mountain behind the monastery was once a mammoth turtle that emitted a foul odor that caused a plague. Thangtong

Gyalpo, who built bridges with massive iron chains, constructed the monastery over the turtle's mouth and put an end to its mischief. The chorten out front contains a large prayer wheel and an image of Gyalpo, with an iron chain in one hand.

Exploring Paro Valley

This day-long tour includes a pony (be sure to reserve in advance) ride or three-hour hike up a mountain opposite the
❷ **Taktsang** (Tiger's Nest) **Monastery,** which clings to the edge of a cliff, 900 meters (2,952 feet) above the valley. You pass chortens with prayer wheels, pass through pine forests, and emerge onto a bluff bristling with prayer flags. You are a short distance from a tea house with an excellent view of Taktsang. At the tea house, you can buy some interesting handicrafts (no credit cards or traveler's checks). Built in 1648 around a cave where Guru Rimpoche and later his follower, Dubthok Singye, meditated, Taktsang's name comes from Guru Rimpoche's novel form of transport. He supposedly flew here on the back of a tiger, and the faithful say that a chorten inside the monastery contains the relics of the sacred creature. Here, continues the legend, the Guru conquered evil demons. Smaller temples, including one from which lamas hurl *vajras* (thunderbolts) at malevolent forces, surround the main shrine. Jutting from a rock above the precarious Taktsang is the **Sang-tog Peri** (Temple of Heaven) **Monastery**—a 300-year-old spiritual retreat.

You also visit **Kyichu Lhakhang,** built in the 8th century and one of Bhutan's most sacred shrines. Inside the compound (ask before you enter it), on the right as you face the complex, is the original monastery. Its golden roof was added in 1830, and in the 1900s the present queen mother built a shrine dedicated to Guru Rimpoche.

Drukgyel (Victorious Druk) **Dzong,** built in 1647 on a spur above Paro Chu (river), commemorates Shabdung Ngawang Namgyal's victory over the Tibetans and his unification of Bhutan. A fire started by a butter lamp destroyed most of the fortress in 1954, leaving just portions of its pressed-mud walls and roofs. Still, Drukgyel provides a good introduction to the basic design of all Bhutanese dzongs. You see two clearly differentiated sections—one for civil administration, the other for lamas. From the top of the spur, you get a good look at the valley and, if visibility is good, a view of Mt. Chomolhari.

Shopping

Lam Dorji (General Store, Shop No. 1) has a good selection of khos, older Bhutanese shawls and hangings, masks, and curios. It's open daily 8–8 and does not accept credit cards or traveler's checks.

Outdoor Adventures

Highly recommended adventures are indicated by a star ★.

★ **Trekking (up to a week):** *Chomolhari Base Camp.* From Paro, a beautiful week-long trek heads up the Paro Valley through Bhutanese villages and alpine meadows to the Chomolhari Base Camp, at 4,039 meters (13,940 feet), and on to Thimphu. You climb through pine forests—home to bear and wild goat—

above the tree line to the base camp, with gorgeous views of Mt. Chomolhari, altitude 7,499 meters (23,977 feet) and Mt. Jichu Drake, altitude 6,901 meters (22,635 feet). You cross Nyele La, and Yali La passes, where gorgeous vistas sweep before you and prayers from flapping prayer flags swirl up to heaven. From here, you walk through rhododendron forests and pass the ruins of the Barshong Dzong and the Cheri Gompa, where lamas practice silent meditation. At Cheri, a vehicle takes you to Thimphu.

★ **Trekking (over a week):** *Northwest Bhutan:* Bhutan Travel Corporation offers a 16-day version of the Chomolhari Base Camp trek. The number of departures is limited. From Chomolhari, you head across the Nyele La Pass, then descend to the village of Lingshi, with its hilltop dzong overlooking a valley crisscrossed with rivers. You traverse flower-covered alpine hills, then climb to Chebisa village, with its many plunging waterfalls. From here, you cross the Gobu La Pass, where the wind rages and your porters (often yaks) pant along with you. The descent is through slopes covered with rhododendron, a multicolored blaze in the spring. Then you head across two more high-altitude passes: Jare La and Shinje La, which lead to a river that must be crossed by horse. At the village of Lemithang, you see Mt. Kancheta (Great Tiger of the Snows), 7,000 meters (22,960 feet)—a shimmer of pink at dawn. The terrain changes again as you walk through rain forests to the second-highest settlement in Bhutan, Laya, altitude 3,850 meters (12,628 feet)— home to yak herders, who raise barley and potatoes on high fields. Here the women keep their hair long (unusual in Bhutan) and wear high-peaked hats that are decorated with coral and turquoise. Homes are constructed of wood, painted with animal iconography. Ghost catchers, wood constructions set on a stone base and surrounded by prayer flags, stand guard in clearings. From Laya, you trek past peaks and glaciers, enter a forest with orchids growing in the trees. Your path leads to the village of Gasa, with its hot springs and dzong. From here, its an easy walk to Tashithang, where vehicles take you to Punakha, then back to Thimphu. InnerAsia Expeditions (*see* Tour Groups in Before You Go to the Himalayas, Chapter 1) offers another version of this same trek.

Dining and Lodging

Olathang Hotel. On a bluff, this government hotel has you stay in the main building or in a private cottage with two double rooms to a unit. Attractive rooms are clean, with attached Western-style bathrooms. The bar is cozy. *Facilities: international phone lines, gift shop, restaurant, bar.*

The Arts

The **National Museum** has an extensive collection of precious ancient thang-kas and sculptures made of butter. Don't miss the shrine on the top floor—an enormous ceramic carving of the Tree of Life, which honors the four sects of Buddhism (remove your shoes before entering this room). There are good wildlife displays, collections of old books, costumes, masks, textiles, Bhutan's stamps, jewelry, weapons, and even the original old jail where the unfortunate were impaled on the walls and rotted to death. *Admission free. Be certain your guide* *gives you at least a full hour to see the 5 floors. No photography allowed. Open Tues.–Sun. 9–4.*

Thimphu

❸ Once a small rural settlement, **Thimphu,** with 20,000 people, is Bhutan's largest city and its capital since 1955—one of the most serene capitals in the world. Architecturally, it's pure Bhutanese. You awake to the sound of chanting. Lamas are everywhere. Shops open early and are a treat for browsers. Streets and sidewalks are fastidiously clean. People are friendly but no longer curious about the presence of foreigners. It's a good place to amble around, if your tour permits.

Arriving and Departing

Thimphu is about 64 kilometers (40 miles) from Paro. The drive in government vehicles takes about two hours.

Getting Around

If you stay in a centrally located hotel, Thimphu is a walker's town. For general sightseeing, the government will take you in vehicles on the tour described below.

Addresses and Numbers

Tourist Information
Visit the **Bhutan Tourism Corporation,** open Monday–Saturday, 9–5.

Emergencies
There are no American, Canadian, or British embassies or consulates in Bhutan. For all emergencies, turn to your government guide or hotel.

Travel Agencies
American Express Travel Service and Banking Facilities (Norzim Lam, tel. 2592) is open Monday–Saturday 9–5. **Druk Air** (LR Market Line, No. 1, Shop 17) is open Monday–Saturday 9–5.

Banks
The **Bank of Bhutan** (Norzim Lam) is open weekdays 9–1 and 2–5. You can also change money at the **Bhutan Tourism Corporation,** open Saturday 3–5, Sunday and government holidays 9–11 and 3–5.

Post Office
The **Post Office** is on a side street near the bank; it's open during the summer, weekdays 8–12:30 and 1:30–5, Saturday 8–1; during the rest of the year, it's open weekdays 8:30–12:30 and 1:30–4:30, Saturday 8:30–1.

Exploring Thimphu

Foreigners can visit the interior of the memorial chorten to the late king Jigme Dorji Wangchuck, constructed in 1974. Each floor has paintings of deities in all their aspects; from the top, you get a good view of Thimphu. The capital's most beautiful structure is **Tashichhodzong** (Fortress of the Glorious Religion), the administrative and religious center of Bhutan, which was originally constructed in 1641 by Ngawang Namgyal. After Jigme Dorji Wangchuck designated Thimphu the capital in 1955, he authorized the complete renovation of Tashichhodzong following the traditional building code—no nails and no architectural plans. The building, off-limits when the monks are in summer residence, has more than 100 rooms, including the throne room of the king and Bhutan's largest monastery, presided over by the Je Khempo, whose residence is in the center of the fort. If you do get inside, you'll find it filled with paintings and sculptures, in particular, a two-story statue of the Buddha that stands behind the altar in the National Assembly Hall.

The **Simtokha Dzong,** just outside Thimphu, is off-limits to foreigners, but you'll notice it if you drive to Punakha or Wangdiphodrang (*see* Excursions, below). This is Bhutan's oldest fortress and seat of religious study, built by Ngawang Namgyal in 1627. Today, it's the home of the Rigney School for monastic studies.

Time Out   Head for the **Swiss Bakery** on a small hill on the left of the main intersection as you head up Norzim Lam from Hotel Druk. You'll find pretty good pastries, tasty breads, hamburgers, hot dogs, and ham sandwiches. *Open Fri.–Wed. 7–6:30. Inexpensive (under $5).*

Shopping

For handsome traditional khos and kiras in wool or silk, scarves, and shawls, visit the following shops, which are open 8 AM–9 PM: **Dorji Gyeltshen Shop** (Line No. 2, Shop No. 35, Norzim Lam), and **Sengay Budha** (Line No. 2, Tshong Khang Shop No. 33, Norzim Lam). These shops have fair, fixed prices and don't accept credit cards or traveler's checks. The government **Handicrafts Emporium** (Norzim Lam, near the American Express office) is the only place authorized to sell older items. You can also buy handicrafts, new thang-kas, fabrics, jewelry, scarves, shawls, wool sweaters, table linens, and sculptures. It's open Monday–Saturday 9–5 and accepts traveler's checks. The **Book Store** of the National Library (Norzim Lam), open weekdays 9–5, sells interesting postcards, a few English-language books on Buddhism, and brass and painted statues of Buddhist deities at very fair prices. It accepts nu only. The **Philatelic Office** behind the Post Office, open Monday–Saturday 9–1 and 2–5, sells stamps for nu only. Bhutan has elevated this necessity into a work of art, treasured by collectors.

Outdoor Adventures

Highly recommended adventures are indicated by a star ★.

★ **Trekking (up to a week):** *Paro:* From Thimphu, you can trek to Paro (*see* Outdoor Adventures in the Paro section, above). *Winter Treks:* The government is planning short winter treks around Thimphu. Contact the Bhutan Tourism Corporation or Bhutan Travel (*see* Before You Go to Bhutan, above).

★ **Trekking (over a week):** *Lunana:* This new, extremely rugged 21-day trek, considered Bhutan's most beautiful, starts in Tashithang (near Thimphu) and heads north along the Mo Chu River through the forested Punakha Valley to the Gasa hot springs, then over the Bale La Pass, at 3,745 meters (12,172 feet). You walk along cliffs, cross the raging Mo Chu River, and head to Laya, a secluded mountain village of farmers and yak herders. From Laya, a narrow trail climbs through woods, up cliffs to the Rodufu River, altitude 4,198 meters (13,645 feet), over the Tsimo La Pass, 4,845 meters (15,748 feet), and the Karakachu La Pass, 5,148 meters (16,733 feet), with great views of snow-covered ranges. A difficult descent leads into the Lunana region, where you follow a river bordered by flowering meadows, climb up the Tsenda Kang ridge, and see the two great mountains, Gonglokarchung and Jejotcangthukang; from here, head through forests, pass an emerald-green lake, and cross the Keshe La Pass, at 4,824 meters (15,680 feet), which leads to Chozo Valley, with charming old villages and an ancient dzong. Finally, you reach the high-altitude Thaanza Valley, the prettiest region in Bhutan, near the border of Tibet and surrounded by peaks. You visit chortens and see farming settlements threaded by a glacial river. From Thaanza, you start your return, passing waterfalls, climbing ridges, and traversing three steep high-altitude passes with great views. You see rare Himalayan birds and flowers and pass the Tempetso Lake; then the terrain turns barren, dotted with moraines and cut by a thrashing river. You reenter dark forests, pass sacred lakes, head through tropical groves with moss hanging from trees and rhododendron growing wild, then reach Nikkachu hamlet and the end of the trek, where a vehicle takes you to Tongsa (Sept.–Oct.). This trek is offered by Bhutan Travel, Inc. (*see* Before You Go to Bhutan, above) and InnerAsia Expeditions (*see* Before You Go to the Himalayas, Chapter 1). You must be physically fit.

Dining

Gahsel Restaurant. In this informal Bhutanese coffee shop, enjoy *shay phalay* (fried dumplings) and the very spicy *erma dashi* (chilis and vegetables). You can also get good *momo* (Tibetan fried dumplings) and Indian and Chinese food. *Shop No. 32, Norzim Lam. No credit cards. Open 9–9. Inexpensive (under $5).*

Lodging

The hotels available to foreigners offer attractive rooms, attached bathrooms with tubs, and identical facilities: room service, bar, restaurant, limited storage for trekkers, and a foreign exchange counter. The government-run Mothithang Hotel, where you're most apt to stay, is a long walk from the center of Thimphu. Taxis may be available. Other hotels are right in the city. The government will decide where you stay.

Excursion from Thimphu to Punakha and Wangdiphodrang

❹ The **Punakha Dzong** is the winter home of the Je Khempo, the religious head of Bhutan. The drive to **Punakha** passes through forests and by waterfalls, chortens, and prayer flags and then heads up to the Dochu La Pass, altitude 3,201 meters (10,500 feet). Here, on a clear day, you can see Mt. Kanchenjunga in neighboring Sikkim and Mt. Everest in Nepal and Tibet.

Just before you arrive in the village of Lobesa, you'll see a hillside monastery dedicated to a Tibetan mystic known as the Divine Madman. In the 13th century, when he was destroying demons in Bhutan, he shot an arrow and said a monastery would appear where it landed. The **Chimi Lhakhang** fulfilled his prophesy. To destroy the demons, the Divine Madman relied on more than his bow and arrow. He used his penis, which was supposedly as long as his body. Those who honor him put a phallic symbol on each side of the house to ward off evil spirits and visit this monastery to worship a statue of him with his famous organ. To devotees, the penis is father heaven, who inseminated mother earth to create mankind—male energy joining with female wisdom to create the cosmic whole.

After Lobesa is Punakha with its famous fortress, the **Punakha Dzong,** built in 1637 on a spit of land at the junction of Pho Chu (male) and Mo Chu (female) rivers on the far side of a narrow suspension bridge. Four fires during the 18th and 19th centuries ravaged this dzong. In 1897 an earthquake caused more damage. Now, the encroaching rivers pose a problem, creeping up to the structure.

The dzong was built by Ngawang Namgyal, whose body lies in perpetual state in the Machin Lhakhang, one of the numerous temples. Only the king and the most important lamas can enter to pay homage.

Once you cross the bridge and enter the exterior grounds, steep steps, which could be pulled up when the dzong was under attack, lead to the entrance pavilion. Two gigantic prayer wheels stand in front of each side wall and frescoes depicting Buddhism's Four Guardian Dieties protect the doorway and the interior structures. When the lamas are in residence, foreigners can go only as far as the first courtyard.

❺ Due south of Punakha is the Wangdiphodrang Valley, the gateway to central Bhutan, set at the confluence of the Mo Chu and Tang Chu rivers. Above the village is the massive **Wangdiphodrang Dzong,** which was constructed in 1645. A legend claims that the dzong was built after a lama saw a little boy named Wangdi playing with pebbles. The boy told the lama that he was constructing a *phodrang* (pebble fortress). The lama took the event as an omen, and the dzong was built and named in the child's honor. Foreigners are allowed inside only during the annual tsechu and then only as far as the first courtyard to witness the dancing and the unfurling of a large thangka depicting Padmasambhava. From Wangdiphodrang, you can also see Mt. Gangker Punsum (White Glacier of the Spiritual Brothers). *For travelers heading back to Thimphu, this is an all-day excursion. Admission fees for all attractions are part of your tour package. The attractions will be open when you arrive.*

Dining and Lodging **Wangdiphodrang Rest House.** Travelers heading to central Bhutan will stay in this simple lodge or in tents pitched on the lawn. Some of the sparsely furnished, clean rooms have attached bathrooms; others share and have an Asian-style toilet. Hot water is available by bucket. Meals are fixed-schedule, fixed-menu buffet. *6 rooms with bath or shared bath. Facilities: limited bar, catering (fixed-schedule fixed-menu buffet).*

Central and Eastern Bhutan

The Bumthang Valley is the cultural and historic heart of the kingdom. Here, old traditions prevail, and the modern age is light years away. As you drive in, you will see few other cars. People walk, often leading small caravans of ponies, and everyone wears the national dress—a sashed robe—and a round bamboo hat that is unique to the area. As you head east through the Pele La Black Mountain Range, forests extend for miles. Hills are topped by massive dzongs and clustered prayer flags.

The paved road comes to an end at the village of **Tashigang,** the major outpost in the east, noted for handwoven textiles produced in outlying villages. Vivid silks, wools, and cottons are worked into ancient designs passed down from generation to generation.

Arriving and Departing/Getting Around

All transportation is by road in vehicles supplied by the government.

Addresses and Numbers

Travelers are advised to bring adequate nu. Turn to your tour guide or government guide for all emergencies.

When to Go

Foreigners can visit eastern Bhutan only from November to March. Central Bhutan may be visited year-round.

Central Bhutan

6 The road east from Wangdiphodrang to your first stop, **Tongsa,** 129 kilometers (80 miles) away, climbs past waterfalls and forests to the Pele La Pass, 3,300 meters (10,824 feet) high, and then into the mountains. Monkeys scuttle along the road or sit in the sun. Sheer cliffs close in on the right; sweeping valleys extend to distant mountains.

The occasional small village set on a slope is a huddle of dwellings built behind low stone walls that protect against landslides and avalanches. Constructed of pressed mud and timber, homes are usually two stories, with the ground floor for livestock and storage and the upper floor for the family living quarters. Here, too, you find the family shrine—entered through a low portal that obliges you to bow your head to the small deity on the altar.

From the Pele La Pass, the road winds down to a valley and the **Chendibji Chorten,** built in the 12th century in the style of Nepalese stupas, with all-knowing eyes peering out in each cardinal direction and a carved band of Buddhas wrapped around its midsection. An enormous *mani* wall nearby protects the village with its inscribed prayers and images of the Buddha.

On a bluff, about 18 kilometers (11 miles) from Tongsa, sits the famous **Tongsa Dzong,** constructed by Ngawang Namgyal in

1648. It is the largest fortification in Bhutan and has over 20 temples. It is also the ancestral home of Bhutan's kings.

Above the dzong stands the watchtower, which foreigners can enter. Steps lead to two tiny shrines with old frescoes depicting earlier kings and the Buddhist goddess, the Green Tara. The altar enshrines an 11-headed Avalokitesvara (Buddha of Compassion) and more images of former kings.

❼ Bumthang Valley, about 68 kilometers (42 miles) from Tongsa, is the site of the **Jakar Dzong,** which sits on the crest of a hill. It is called Castle of the White Bird because when the lamas were choosing an auspicious location for a fortress, an enormous bird rose up and settled on the spur of this hill and gave them their site. The original dzong was built in the 17th century, then rebuilt after a fire and earthquake in the 1800s. The dzong, off limits to foreigners, is encircled by a mile-long wall with a central tower that juts up 45 kilometers (150 feet).

Legends surrounding Guru Padmasambhava figure in two other important local monuments: Jampa Lhakhang and Kurje Monastery. The first, **Jampa Lhakhang,** was built in AD 638 and renovated in the 8th century by Bumthang's ruler after Guru Padmasambhava cured him from a serious ailment, then converted him to the Buddhist faith. Subsequent governors have kept it in excellent repair, adding a gold-leafed roof over the central tower in the late 1800s.

Though it's supposedly off-limits to foreigners, during a recent autumn festival, visitors were allowed to attend the ceremonies held outside the monastery and were permitted into the courtyard. Here three steps leading from the prayer hall to the central altar are slowly sinking. The first step is already at ground level. The faithful say that when the other steps disappear, the Future Buddha will arrive.

Guru Padmasambhava also visited the 8th-century, **Kurje Monastery,** also off-limits to foreigners. Here, the Guru meditated seven days. When he left, there were impressions in rock of his back and his sacred water vessel. The father of the present king is entombed within the shrine.

Dining and Lodging **Tongsa Tourist Lodge.** This lodge, with a cozy common room built around a central fireplace, offers simple rooms with attached bathrooms (hot water by bucket) or modest cottages with similar bathrooms. *6 rooms with bath and about 6 cottages with bath. Facilities: catering (fixed-schedule fixed-menu buffet).*

Jakar Tourist Lodge and Campground. Travelers should insist on staying in the cottages. The tents are inadequate against the wind that rages in the valley. The sparsely furnished, clean cottages have attached bathrooms, Western-style toilet and hot water by bucket. *16 rooms with bath; 12 tents with shared bath. Facilities: catering (fixed-schedule fixed-menu buffet).*

Eastern Bhutan

From the little village of Bumthang, it is 189 kilometers (117 miles) to the village of Mongar, the first night halt. The road winds through the mountains and past tiny hamlets, where men tend fields of rice, maize, millet, and buckwheat or graze yak herds. Women weave, using ancient techniques passed on

from mother to daughter. An hour from Bumthang, you stop at
8 the village of **Ura.**

Ura is an important weaving center. Inside nearly every home
you see textiles in progress—naturally dyed wool, heavy cotton, or intricately patterned *endi* silk spun from cocoons bred
on castor oil plants—set up on wood backstrap looms. In Ura,
you can also visit the new **Ura Dzong.** Inside the temple, detailed frescoes depict the teachings of Padmasambhava.

From Ura, you travel by terraced hills planted with mustard,
millet, and rice, through forests, into stark mountains, and
over the highest pass on the east–west road—Thromseng La,
altitude 3,650 meters (11,972 feet). As you approach Mongar,
you see flowers and Scotch pine, bamboo, and palm groves.

9 **Mongar,** about 60 kilometers (37 miles) from Ura, is the second-
largest settlement in the east and the site of **Mongar Dzong,** one
of Bhutan's newest, built in 1952 on a small hill and visible from
your overnight stopping place. One of the few dzongs open to
visitors, it has images of the Guardian Deities of the North
(with a mongoose) and West (with a chorten) to protect the entrance. Frescoes depicting manifestations of Padmasambhava
cover the exterior of the main temple, which is dedicated to the
Buddhist teacher Dorje Chang.

10 From Mongar, you head north to the remote village of **Lhuntsi.**
During the 70-kilometer (43-mile) journey, you pass prayer
flags and small settlements that add a glimmer of civilization to
dark forests, see a vast expanse of rolling mountains, and
glimpse distant snowy peaks. At Lhuntsi, the first view of its
ancient **Lhuntsi Dzong,** set on a mountain and usually floating
in a halo of clouds, is serene—heavenly. Foreigners aren't
allowed inside. You do spend your night, however, in a government guest house in its shadow.

From Lhuntsi, a day's journey takes you southeast to
Tashigang, formerly an important stop on a trade route to Tibet and now the largest settlement in the east. On a ridge
overlooking the town and Manas River stands the formidable
1667 **Tashigang Dzong,** from which a series of regional kings
ruled the entire eastern region until the unification of the country in the 20th century.

About 44 kilometers (27 miles) from Tashigang is the **Chorten
Kora,** Bhutan's largest stupa, built on a plateau in the foothills.
The chorten, which contains holy relics, has all-knowing eyes
on its spire and conforms to the design of Nepalese stupas,
resting on a square base with wide steps leading to a circular
dome with a gold-leafed umbrella.

Outdoor The most highly recommended adventures are indicated by a
Adventures star ★.

★ **Hiking:** *Kurtey:* The tour to the east with Bhutan Travel Corporation includes a day hike from Lhuntsi to the mountain
village of Kurtey, the most famous weaving center in Bhutan.
You cross one of Bhutan's ancient bamboo bridges, which hangs
across the Kuru Chu river, then follow a steep path to Kurtey,
where the women create textiles for the wealthiest families of
Bhutan and single pieces of cloth can cost as much as $1,000.
You either spend the night in the village or head back to
Lhuntsi.

★ **Trekking (up to a week):** *Mera and Sakteng:* Bhutan Travel Corporation also offers a physically demanding week-long trek to the Mera and Sakteng valleys, home to nomadic yak herders. You go by jeep along the Drangmi Chu River, past precipitous cliffs, through villages with chortens and lush mustard fields, to the village of Phumi, where you start the trek. A steep climb takes you through forests and alpine meadows to rocky cliffs and a ridge dotted with prayer flags. From here, you descend to the Sakteng village, where men wear robes of animal skins, trousers, and knee-high boots. Daggers are tucked into their belts. A turquoise earring hangs from one ear. The women wear long homespun dresses and a dark red cloak. Everyone wears a round black hat of coarse yak hair, with pointed pigtails attached to the brim to keep rain off the face. The trip on to Mera depends on the snow. Sometimes the Nag Chung La Pass, at 4,573 meters (15,000 feet), is closed—especially from November to March, the only time you can visit the east. Mera's valley is similar, home to the same people. Even if you fail to get there, this trek takes you to stunningly beautiful locations. The government is currently constructing tourist community houses—each a large room with a fire pit and toilet facility.

Dining and Lodging The guest houses in the east have lovely locations and conform to the Bhutanese architecture; except for one, they're extremely modest, with fewer than six rooms. Adjoining campsites accommodate the overflow. Some rooms have private bathrooms; others share. The bathrooms have either Western or Asian-style toilet and usually hot water by bucket. Catering includes a fixed-schedule fixed-menu buffet.

4 Nepal

Introduction

Nepal is the world's only declared Hindu nation, but its beliefs are actually a fusion of Hinduism, Buddhism, and remnants of animism. The amalgamation extends to the temples, festivals, and daily rituals celebrated by the faithful. Consider the most revered Hindu goddess in Nepal, the Royal Kumari (Living Goddess), who resides in a palace in Kathmandu and who is honored as the incarnation of the goddess Kali, the wrathful consort of Shiva. Born a Buddhist, once this young child is placed on the throne, she becomes a Hindu goddess, occupying a position of importance in Nepal second to that of the king.

As in India, Vishnu and Shiva in all their manifestations are the most popular Hindu gods. The king is considered a descendent of Vishnu; Shiva is the guardian of Nepal. Though the non-Hindu may be put off by animal sacrifice, it's an important practice in Nepal, and male edible animals are the exclusive offering. An understanding of the ritual of sacrifice places it in a proper context.

As defined by the Vedas, sacred Hindu texts, sacrifice is a symbolic act that allows the devotee to become one with God by means of the surrender of his ego and various negative traits. The death of a water buffalo represents the suppression of anger; a goat, lust; a sheep, stupidity; a duck, apathy; a chicken, fear. An egg is offered as a symbol of all five animals and of the creative process in its purest form.

Hindus believe an animal's death releases its spirit and allows for its rebirth at a higher plane. When an animal is presented to the temple priest, it's head, usually smeared with vermillion or henna (red is auspicious, a symbol of life), is first sprinkled with water, which makes it shake as if agreeing to its death. Should an animal fail to consent, it's not killed.

Hindus and Buddhists (the latter represent 6% of the population) also share each other's gods: Avalokitesvara (Buddha of Compassion) is worshiped as a manifestation of Shiva by Hindus; Ganesh, the elephant-headed god, and Sarasvati, Brahma's consort, are Hindu dieties that often appears in Buddhist sanctuaries. Buddhism and Hinduism—tolerance and harmony. Nepal, which calls itself an "International Zone of Peace," is exactly that. Its peoples get along very well.

Nepal's 18 million people represent numerous races and tribes, each living in different regions, wearing unique traditional dress (although they're slowly shedding them for Western garb), and speaking their own languages or dialects. Gorkhas, who include a variety of tribes—the Gurung, Magar, Rai, Limbu, and Sunwar—are either Buddhist or Hindu and reside primarily within the Annapurna district of central Nepal, where they usually farm or herd livestock.

Moving north into the remote mountains, the people are usually Buddhist and speak Tibetan dialects. Around Mt. Everest, you encounter the Sherpas—intrepid mountaineers and often the indispensable lifeline for a successful climbing or trekking expedition. In the towering peaks to the west of Mt. Everest and due north of Annapurna reside the Lo-pa (the people of the ancient kingdom of Mustang), yak traders whose high-perched homeland remains off-limits to foreigners. Not far from the Lo-

Nepal (*Numbers on map correspond to numbers in text*)

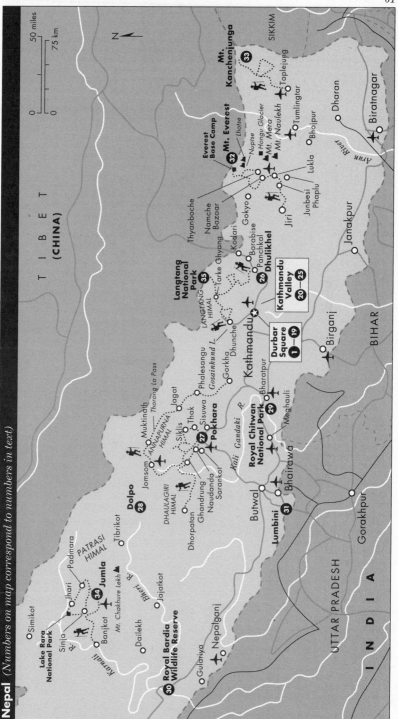

pa are the Thakali, successful traders and farmers. Inhabiting an even higher altitude near Mt. Dhaulagiri are the people of Dolpa, who cultivate barley.

The Newar, predominantly Hindu and claiming as ancestors the original inhabitants of Nepal, constitute the most important ethnic group in the Kathmandu Valley. On the valley fringe, you come across Buddhists called the Tamang, Tibetan for "Horse Trader," who once dealt in horses but now cultivate land. In the tropical southern belt, called the Terai, are Hindu tribes, including the Tharu, who migrated north from the Tharu Desert in India's Rajasthan.

Nepal's topography is also diverse. The fertile plains of the Terai produce rice, wheat, and jute. The rare tiger still roams. Heat rages and rain pours in the summer, turning the wide belt lush green. Dense elephant grass, which covers much of the protected sanctuary lands, grows so high it conceals the tallest tusker.

Throughout Nepal, over a 100 peaks soar over 6,098 meters (20,000 feet), many of them separated by plunging gorges, broken by windswept passes sliced by magnificent rivers. In the extreme north are the giants Everest (Sagarmatha to the Nepalese), 8,877 meters (29,108 feet); Kanchenjunga, 8,598 meters (28,208 feet); Lhotse, 8,511 meters (27,923 feet); and "little" Annapurna I, 8,091 meters (26,545 feet).

Central Nepal has undulating hills and valleys, threaded by rivers that wind through the mountains to the Ganga in the Indian plains. Gentle slopes are covered with terraced fields. Villages and cities show off the indigenous talent that makes this small country a cornucopia of artistic delights.

Legends provide the only clue to the origin of Kathmandu Valley and the early history of the kingdom of Nepal. Hindus tell a story of Krishna, the popular incarnation of Vishnu, throwing a thunderbolt to break open a lake, known as Nagavosa—the abode of serpents (*naga* means snake)—and now called Chorbar Gorge. When the water receded, Krishna's cowherds built a city that became the home of a dynasty.

Buddhists speak of Manjushri (Buddha of Transcendent Wisdom), who traveled into Nepal from China. He saw an enormous jewel-covered lotus, which emitted a powerful flame in the middle of this same lake. Divine revelation told him this was a manifestation of the Adibuddha (Supreme Buddha), called Swayambhu in Nepal. Manjushri decided his followers should settle here. He took his sword and slit open a mountain, which drained the lake and created the valley. One part of the lotus became Swayambhunath, the other Pashupatinath, and the third became Boudanath—three important temples. A story, yes; but modern geologists do believe a lake once filled this valley.

Leaving mythology for recorded history, the earliest known inhabitants were Ahirs, or shepherd kings, most likely Tibeto-Burman migrants from north India, who occupied Kathmandu Valley as early as the 8th century BC. The second wave of inhabitants were the Middle-Eastern Kirats, with a succession of kings who ruled for centuries. Before the 6th century BC, the Shakyas, a Rajput clan from north India, settled in the Terai, where they founded the city of Kapilvastu, renowned for its beauty and sophisticated culture. Here in Lumbini, Prince Siddhartha Gautama, who became the Historic Buddha, was born in 563 BC.

History steps onto firmer ground with the next dynasty, the Licchavis, who most likely migrated from India and took control around AD 300. The Licchavis, who introduced the caste system to Nepal, also ushered in an age of prosperity. Art and architecture flourished. Palaces and temples, in the new and innovative pagoda-style design, cropped up in the valley. Though few buildings of this era survived, an excellent stone carving dating back to the 5th century exists at the Changu Narayan temple on a hilltop west of Kathmandu.

The 13th century saw the rise of the Malla dynasty, whose members were considered descendants of Vishnu. Great patrons of the arts, the Mallas constructed most of the beautiful temples and palaces of Kathmandu Valley. King Yaksha Malla, who ruled until 1482, extended the Malla domain into parts of Tibet and India, but he forgot to watch over his own backyard.

Family fighting left the dynasty vulnerable. In 1768 a Gorkha army, under the rule of Prithvi Narayan Shah, stormed across Nepal. Wary of the British, who had a firm hold on India, Prithvi Narayan Shah and his grandson, Bahadur Shah, conquered nearby rival kingdoms to create a buffer against the British threat, thus unifying Nepal.

In 1846 palace intrigues again erupted into a bloody massacre, which put an end to the Shah dynasty and marked the beginning of the Age of the Ranas. Acting as prime ministers, the Ranas ushered in a period of fragile peace, not to mention secrecy, since they closed Nepal's borders to outsiders. After World War II, fighting between the Ranas, helped along by pressure for meaningful reforms from a newly independent India, set in motion their downfall. In 1950 the titular king, Tribhuvan, took refuge in India. The Nepalese revolted against the Rana government. In 1951 King Tribhuvan returned to Nepal and recaptured the throne, putting an end to more than a century of Rana rule. In 1975 his grandson became King Birendra Bir Bikram Shah Dev.

Before You Go

Government Tourist Offices

No government tourist office exists outside Nepal. The Nepalese embassies and consulates have some free brochures on Nepal (*see* Passports and Visas, below).

Tour Groups

General-Interest Tours To arrange for a car or jeep with driver or a general tour, contact the following reliable agencies:

Adventure Travel Nepal, a division of Tiger Tops (Box 3989, Durbar Marg, Kathmandu, tel. 223328).
Marco Polo Travels (Box 2769, White House, Kamal Pokhari, Kathmandu, tel. 413632).
Natraj Tours and Travels (Box 495, Ghantaghar, Durbar Marg, Kathmandu, tel. 222014).
Yeti Travels (Box 76, Durbar Marg, Kathmandu, tel. 221234).

Special-Interest Tours The following companies offer great outdoor adventures. Their guides are excellent; service is tops. All of them sponsor treks in the Annapurna, Everest, and Khumbu regions; some travel into the remote northeast and northwest. You can join a fixed-departure trip or let the companies custom design a vacation. Make arrangements before you depart (*see also* Special-Interest Tours in Before You Go to the Himalayas, Chapter 1).

Amadablam Trekking (Box 3035, Lazimpat, Kathmandu, tel. 410219) offers numerous treks, including good trips to Mt. Dhaulagiri, Arun Valley, and around Jumla and Rara Lake. It also sponsors rafting runs, wildlife safaris in Royal Chitwan National Park, mountain climbing, and long-distance mountain biking.

Himalayan Horizons (Box 35, Pokhara [Airport], tel. 253) is the only trekking company that focuses exclusively on Pokhara Valley, including Annapurna and Dhaulagiri. It sponsors year-round nature treks, fishing treks, nature and culture treks for children, and treks for the disabled.

Himalayan Journeys (Box 989, Kanti Path, Kathmandu, tel. 226138) is one of the best companies in Nepal. It does all the standard treks, including the long walk to Tibet, and is planning treks into eastern Nepal around Mt. Kanchenjunga and to Dolpo in the northwest. If Mustang opens to foreigners, the company is ready to go.

Himalayan Mountain Bikes (Box 2769, Kamal Pokhari, Kathmandu, tel. 413632 or 418733) offers three bike trips around Kathmandu Valley; trips connected with trekking in Pokhara Valley and Annapurna, Langtang National Park, and Everest; and Terai trips with jungle safaris and rafting or kayaking.

Himalayan River Exploration and Mountain Travel Nepal, part of Tiger Tops International (Box 170, Durbar Marg, Kathmandu, tel. 414508 or 2627 Lombard St., San Francisco, CA 94123, tel. 415/346–3402) is the pioneer in Nepal rafting, trekking, mountaineering, and wildlife safaris. It sponsors all the standard treks, many theme-oriented or family treks, plus the "walk" to Lhasa and other new treks in Tibet. It arranges white-water runs and safaris in its classy resorts at Royal Chitwan National Park and Karnali. It also offers a combination of biking, trekking, and rafting around Kathmandu Valley.

Pokhara Pony Trek (Box 35, Pokhara, tel. 253) is the only horseback-riding outfit in Nepal. Its trips are exclusively in Pokhara Valley and range from a half-day excursion to a 50-day extensive valley tour.

Rapid Adventures Nepal (Box 3863, Thamel, Kathmandu, tel. 412480) offers excellent no-frills rafting excursions (great food and equipment—but no classy extras).

Treks and Expeditions Services (Box 3057, Corner House, Kamal Pokhari, Kathmandu, tel. 412231) offers all the standard treks and mountaineering, plus crafts, cultural, or participatory religious walks and tours around Kathmandu and Annapurna. It also offers high-quality "teahouse" treks (all you need is a backpack) that patronize inns that respect the environment.

The Nepal Mountaineering School, run by the Nepal Mountaineering Association (Ram Shah Path, Kathmandu, tel. 411525), has two excellent courses in mountaineering. Apply months in advance.

When to Go

Nepal's peak season is September to December. Make all travel arrangements well in advance. Mountain views are excellent; temperatures are cool and comfortable. This season also coincides with some of the best festivals, Durga Puja and Indra Jatra. It's also high season for trekking. Unless you go to a remote area, you see many hikers.

For trekkers and outdoor enthusiasts, December and January mean cold nights, some cloud cover, but comfortable daytime temperatures. Trekking can be hazardous; heavy snowfalls can leave you snowbound. February heralds the start of spring—a good chance to see animals, birds, and the mountains, with visibility improving until the onset of the June monsoon. In Kathmandu Valley, Pokhara, and the Terai, expect heavy cloud cover, rain, and steamy heat until October. Trekkers should be aware that the monsoon also brings leeches, but you can trek in higher altitudes where the monsoon doesn't penetrate. The best rafting season is September to June. The best time to visit Royal Chitwan National Park and Royal Bardia Wildlife Reserve is from October to June.

Festivals and Seasonal Events

The lunar calendar determines most dates. Check with Nepal's embassy or consulate or your travel agent before you depart.

Dec. or Jan.: During the week-long Buddhist festival **Seto Macchendranath (Matyendranath) Snan,** devotees remove the sacred idol from its temple in Kathmandu.
Jan.: Prithvi Jayanti honors King Prithvi Narayan Shah, the founder of modern Nepal, with parades.
Feb. 18: A big parade in Kathmandu on **Tribhuvan Jayanti** (National Democracy Day) honors the late King Tribhuvan.
Feb.: During **Shivaratri,** an important Hindu festival celebrating Shiva, pilgrims from India and Nepal attend a massive fair at Pashupatinath Temple near Kathmandu.
Feb. or Mar.: During the week-long **Losar** (Tibetan New Year), monks chant and perform ritual dances—a big event at Boudanath in Kathmandu.
Feb. or Mar.: Holi, an exuberant eight-day Hindu festival, ushers in spring and celebrates the victory of Narsingha (Vishnu) over the demon Hiranyakashipu, an important event depicted on statues throughout Nepal. Children throw red colored water at anything that moves. Wear old clothes.
Apr.: Ghode Chatra is celebrated with a horse race held at the Thundikhel Parade Ground.
Apr.: A four-day festive Hindu and Buddhist celebration, **Seto Macchendranath Rath Jatra,** honors the White Macchendranath (Shiva to the Hindu, Avalokitesvara to the Buddhist), who is drawn in a gigantic chariot through the streets of Kathmandu to Hanuman Square.
Apr.: One of Nepal's best festivals, **Red Macchendranath Jatra** is Patan's week-long chariot pageant honoring this god.
May: Buddhists celebrate **Buddha Jayanti** or **Baishakh Purnima,** which pays tribute to the Buddha's birthday, his enlightenment, and his death. Valuable old *thang-kas* (religious scrolls) are unfurled during ceremonies.
Aug.: A carnival atmosphere surrounds **Gai Jatra,** which honors

the sacred cow and recently deceased family members. Cows and teenagers in cow masks parade through the streets.

Aug. or Sept.: The night before **Krishna Jayanti** (Krishna's birthday), devotees celebrate at Hindu temples honoring Krishna, especially in Patan.

Aug. or Sept.: During **Teej,** Hindu women honor Parvati and Shiva and their own husbands with a fast and a ritual dip in the Bagmati River at Pashupatinath Temple near Kathmandu.

Sept.: An eight-day festival dedicated to Indra, the Hindu God of Rain, **Indra Jatra** honors his victory over the demon Vrita, who had cursed Nepal with a terrible drought. The festival begins with the sacrifice of a goat in Bhaktapur, then moves to Kathmandu where devotees carry the Royal Kumari through the old city in her gold chariot. The huge mask of Bhairav (wrathful aspect of Shiva) is brought out for its annual viewing, and every night masked dancers perform in Hanuman Square.

Oct.: Nepal's most important festival, **Durga Puja,** or **Dassan,** celebrates the victory of Durga, Shiva's consort, over the buffalo demon Mahishasur. Nawa Ratri, the first nine days, honor Durga in her nine manifestations. Devotees take ritual dips. On Kalratri, the eighth night, thousands of animals are sacrificed.

Nov.: A five-day festival, **Tihar** or **Diwali** (Festival of Lights) pays tribute to Yama, god of death. On the third day, candles illuminate the windows of every house in honor of Lakshmi, goddess of wealth and prosperity.

Nov.: During **Mani Rimdu,** a Buddhist festival, lamas perform masked dances at monasteries near Mt. Everest.

Dec. 15: Mahendra Jayanti (Constitution Day) celebrates the beginning of the Nepalese democracy.

Dec. 28: Shri Panch Ko Janma Divas honors the birthday of the present king.

Taking Money Abroad

You can bring any amount of hard currency, including traveler's checks, into Nepal, but you must fill out a Currency Declaration Form when you arrive. There is an illegal black market in foreign currency exchange. Convert your currency at Foreign Exchange Counters authorized by the Nepal Rastra Bank (State Bank of Nepal). A passport is required. Exchange currency in small amounts as needed because on departure, Nepal will reconvert only 10% of the total amount cashed, and only on presentation of an exchange receipt. Non-Indians who enter from India can't exchange Indian rupees for Nepalese currency.

The units of Nepalese currency are the rupee and paisa (100 paisas = 1 rupee). Paper money appears in rupees 1, 2, 5, 10, 50, 100, 500, and 1000 denominations; coins are in 5, 10, 25, 50, and 100 denominations. At press time the rate of exchange was U.S. $1 = Rs. 23; £1 = Rs. 37. Carry lots of small denominations. Few taxi, rickshaw, and scooter drivers have change.

What It Will Cost

Nepal is still a bargain. You can buy a cup of tea for under 30¢ or have a meal for $1. Except for Kathmandu and the wildlife sanctuaries, where fancy accommodations mean fancy prices, lodging is never more than $50 per double and usually inexpensive, under $25 for a double. To protect their profit margin against the frequent devaluation of the rupee, tour operators demand payment for the rental of a car or jeep with driver in U.S. dollars, credit cards, or traveler's checks. For this reason, we provide the dollar cost for car or jeep rental throughout the Nepal listings. A car costs about $60 per day (Rs. 1,380), a jeep about $85 (Rs. 1,955). Also plan on a halt charge of about $6 (Rs. 150) per night. Often a flight to your destination is cheaper.

Visas

Travelers need a tourist visa from the Nepalese consulate or embassy in their home country. You can obtain a 30-day tourist visa that's good for Kathmandu Valley, Pokhara, and other areas linked by highways. To get the visa, you need two passport photos and a valid passport. Cost is $10. If you apply in person, the visa is ready in three working days. If you apply by mail, allow for a month. You can also wait and get a 15-day visa at any valid international entry point, but expect a long line if you do so at the Kathmandu Airport. You can extend this visa at the Central Immigration Office in Kathmandu or at any Police Office in Nepal. You can also extend your 30-day visa at the Kathmandu office. To extend it a second and (maximum) third month, you must fill out a visa application form, present your passport, a passport-size photo, and a foreign exchange receipt proving you've exchanged $5 for each day of the extension. The extended visa fee is $15–$20 per month.

Americans **Permanent Mission of the Kingdom of Nepal to the United Nations** or **Royal Nepalese Consulate** (820 Second Ave., Suite 202, New York, NY 10017, tel. 212/370–4188); **Royal Nepalese Embassy** (2131 Leroy Pl. NW, Washington, DC 20008, tel. 202/667–4550).

Canadians **Royal Nepalese Consulate** (310 Dupont St., Toronto, Ont., tel. 416/968–7252).

Britons **Royal Nepalese Embassy** (12A Kensington Palace Gardens, London, W8 4QU, tel. 01/229–1594).

Customs and Duties

On Arrival Foreigners must fill out a disembarkation card and declare all baggage. Visitors can bring in personal effects, 200 cigarettes or 20 cigars, one bottle of distilled liquor or two bottles of beer, a pair of binoculars, a camera with 15 rolls of film, movie camera, video camera, portable radio, tape recorder, pocket calculator, portable typewriter, tent, sleeping bag, and rucksack.

On Departure Foreigners must fill out an embarkation card and pay Rs. 200 airport tax. Don't export antiques (over 100 years old), animal skins, loose precious stones, drugs, or weapons. Get a certificate or stamp from the Department of Archaeology (National Archives Bldg., Ram Shah Path, Kathmandu) for any reasonably old item and be prepared to show it on departure.

Time Zone

Nepal is 15 minutes ahead of Indian standard time and five hours and 45 minutes ahead of Greenwich mean time.

Staying Healthy

See Staying Healthy in Before You Go to the Himalayas, Chapter 1. An international certificate of vaccination against yellow fever is required if you're arriving from certain specified countries in Africa and Central and South America.

Renting Car with Driver

The cost of a car is determined by your destination. Figure about $26 for three hours or a 60-kilometer round-trip. Hire a tourist taxi or car with driver only from a recommended agency (*see* Tour Groups, above).

Arriving and Departing

By Plane

Airport and Airlines
Only **Royal Nepal Airline (RNAC)** and **Lufthansa** fly in to **Tribhuvan International Airport** from Europe (Frankfurt). Other flights originate in Asia: **Thai Airways** from Bangkok; **Singapore Airlines** from Singapore; **PIA** from Karachi; **Biman Bangladesh Airlines** from Dhaka; **Air India** and **Indian Airlines** from Calcutta and Delhi; **CAAC** (China) from Lhasa (Apr.–Nov.); **Dragon Air** from Hong Kong; **Druk Air** from Paro; **RNAC** from Bangkok, Delhi, Calcutta, Colombo, Dhaka, Dubai via Karachi, Hong Kong, Rangoon, Singapore. Reconfirm your ticket 72 hours before flight time. Arrive at the airport at least two hours before flight time. Planes are frequently overbooked. Tribhuvan Airport can be a nightmare.

Flying Time
Plan on about a 10-hour flight from Frankfurt.

By Hired Car with Driver or Taxi

A road trip to Kathmandu from Delhi or Lhasa means a long journey. At press time, trade disputes had closed the major routes into Kathmandu from Delhi, but this problem will most likely be temporary. Getting through customs at the Nepal/India border is time consuming. If this is the way you decide to travel, hire a car from a tour operator listed in the Delhi section of Chapter 5. At press time, the road from Lhasa was blocked by an extensive landslide, which required a half-day walk on either side of the disaster.

Staying in Nepal

Behavioral Dos and Don'ts

In Nepal, shoes are considered unclean. Remove them before you enter a Nepali house or temple. Follow the guidelines for visiting temples described in Staying in the Himalayas, Chapter 1. Also, it's discourteous to point your finger at a person or statue, to stand with your feet pointed at people or religious objects, or to sit in a position that forces others to step over you. In Kathmandu, beware of pickpockets. Watch your handbag, backpack, and camera, especially in crowded places.

Getting Around

Roads are subject to landslides and washouts in much of Nepal. If you want to trek or mountaineer in remote northern areas, plan to fly to the nearest airport or airstrip. If you plan to visit Pokhara Valley or the Royal Chitwan National Park and Lumbini, you can fly or go by road, even during the monsoon when landslides occur, but it can be slow going. You can also go to Chitwan by raft. For the Royal Bardia Wildlife Reserve in the western Terai, you should fly to Nepalganj, then do a five-hour trip by car. After a trek from Jumla in the northwest, you can raft to Bardia.

By Plane **RNAC,** your only choice, flies between Kathmandu and numerous popular destinations (*see* Arriving and Departing in Kathmandu, below). Fares are reasonable; you must book early, especially in the peak season. Reconfirm each ticket at least 72 hours before departure and arrive at the airport 90 minutes in advance.

Special Fares **RNAC** offers a 25% discount to students with an International Student Identity Card (*see* Student and Youth Travel in Before You Go to the Himalayas, Chapter 1). Some fares are lower during the monsoon. Check with your travel agent before you depart.

By Hired Car or Jeep with Driver From Kathmandu, you can go by road to the border of Tibet in the north, due west to Pokhara, and southwest to Lumbini and Royal Chitwan National Park. The recommended general-interest tour operators (*see* above), who can arrange for a hired car or jeep with driver, also offer standard packages to these destinations, with the cost determined by the length of stay. Make arrangements before you depart.

By Train No trains exist in Nepal.

On Foot You need a trekking permit to trek in Nepal. Go to the Central Immigration Office in Kathmandu or Pokhara and follow the same procedure as for a visa extension (*see* Visas, above). A trekking permit is also required for visits to Nepal's interior (any place not linked by major roads). If you plan to trek into two different areas, you need separate permits. The charge for individual trekkers is Rs. 90 per week for the first month, Rs. 112.50 per additional week. The trekking permit also substitutes for a visa extension. If you use a recommended tour operator, the staff will obtain the permit for you. Trekkers must also pay Rs. 200 tax for trekking in the Annapurna Sanctuary in addition to a Rs. 250 park entrance fee. Trekkers must also pay a Rs. 250 entrance fee to Sagarmatha National Park (the Everest region) and to the National Park in Langtang.

Telephones

Telephone lines connect most major destinations in Nepal. In Kathmandu, you can make international calls at the **Central Telegraph Office** (24 hours daily). If you phone from your hotel, expect a service charge. Except at Western-style hotels that accept credit cards, phone calls must be paid for in local currency. Local calls cost about Rs. 2.

Operators and Information To book an international call, dial 180. For local telephone numbers, dial 197. There's no guarantee the operator will speak English, but if the person does, speak slowly.

Telegrams and Telex You can send telegrams from some popular destinations, but the most expeditious office is Kathmandu's **Central Telegraph Office,** open daily 24 hours.

Mail

Airmail letters weighing 10 grams to Canada and the United States cost Rs. 8; to England and Europe, Rs. 7. All aerograms and postcards cost Rs. 5.

Tipping

The concept of tipping has arrived in Nepal. Follow the guidelines in Chapter 5.

Opening and Closing Times

Nepal has numerous festivals during which government offices and banks shut down. Watch the calendar. Most commercial shops (not necessarily including bazaars) and government offices are closed Saturday, the national day off, and government holidays. Hours are noted for each business establishment.

Shopping

Look for lovely thang-kas, statues, brasswork, masks, wood carvings, jewelry, beautiful wool sweaters, gloves, hats, and carpets. Antiques aren't allowed out of Nepal. With rare exceptions, bargain.

Dining

The standard fare is Nepali (not quite as spicy as Indian cuisine) and Tibetan (with lots of noodle and dumpling dishes). Kathmandu's restaurants offer a wide range of international cuisines and ambiences. Local and imported liquors are available. Expect an early dinner, even in Kathmandu. Many restaurants shut down by 10 PM.

Ratings Highly recommended restaurants are indicated by a star ★.

Category	Cost*
Very Expensive	over $15
Expensive	$10–$15
Moderate	$5–$10
Inexpensive	under $5

per person, excluding drinks, service, and taxes

Lodging

Though Kathmandu, Pokhara, and Royal Chitwan National Park offer a range of options, from expensive Western-style hotels to budget lodges, expect few choices in other areas. In most

Western-style hotels, rupees are accepted only on presentation of a foreign exchange receipt; otherwise, foreign nationals must pay their hotel bills with foreign currency, traveler's checks, or credit cards.

Ratings   Highly recommended lodgings are indicated by a star ★.

Category	Cost*
Very Expensive	over $100
Expensive	$60–$100
Moderate	$25–$60
Inexpensive	under $25

Prices are for a standard double room, including taxes and excluding service charges.

Credit Cards

Western-style hotels, travel agencies, and many shops accept American Express, Diners Club, MasterCard, and Visa credit cards.

Kathmandu

Introduction

In Kathmandu, ringed by the Himalayas, motorcycles roar down the streets. Nepali teens stroll along in jeans and T-shirts. Stalls display posters of Brooke Shields and Michael Jackson next to pictures of the Buddha and Shiva. But despite these signs of the West, Kathmandu's ancient temples, old palaces, and 15th-century homes still dominate the look of this city—a walker's paradise, with countless treasures to explore.

Kathmandu's buildings are more than beautiful—they are manifestions of Nepal's religious beliefs. To understand the essential principles tied to this faith is to increase your pleasure in this rich destination.

On many temples in Old Kathmandu, you see images of the male and female sexually united. This is an artistic rendering of the tantric concept that salvation comes from the union of the male and female forces. Shakti, the consort of Shiva, is an example of the female force. She has numerous manifestations. Like Shiva, she can be benign (as Parvati) or destructive (as Devi, Durga, and Kali). Kali represents the most terrifying form— black, half-naked, wearing a garland of human skulls; her red tongue hangs from her mouth.

Often you see Kali standing on a motionless Shiva. This image represents the universe, where everything is relative—static and dynamic. Shiva without Kali is incomplete, energyless.

Tantrics believe that through meditation; through a series of mysterious rituals; and, above all, through the mystical power of sexual union, you can realize nirvana. In this regard, they compare human existence to the lotus. The root comes from mud; the flower represents perfect beauty. You can't achieve nirvana without emerging from the dark.

A six-sided star on a temple represents the union of the female and male forces. The female triangle points down; the male triangle points up. Their union represents nirvana and the cosmos. The points on the male triangle also stand for Brahma, Vishnu, and Shiva—the Hindu trinity. The points on the female triangle symbolize the consorts Sarasvati, Lakshmi, and Parvati.

Kathmandu's temples' pagoda style originated around 300 BC. The two roofs represent the female triangle moving up to merge with the male. The stanchion in the center of each triangle points the way to enlightenment and stands above the temple's inner sanctum, which enshrines the sacred idol. The Nepalese flag has two triangles. The one on top with the crescent moon represents the female energy; the lower triangle with the sun is the male.

The erotic art on many Hindu temples also depicts the tantric division of the human body into seven *chakras* (centers of energy). One must master the sexual urge at the site of the lowest chakra before one obtains enlightenment. Erotic art is always outside a shrine. Each female image stands for a vowel; each male represents a consonant. If you line up the figures on a temple, they spell out a prayer to the deity in the inner sanctum. Inside the shrine, you usually find a carving of a lotus.

The swastika, a symbol associated so irrevocably with Nazism, confuses the Westerner who sees it on carvings, bronze statues, and thang-kas. "Swastika" is Sanskrit for "well-being" or "doing good for all." Its four arms stand for pure love, compassion, happiness, and indifference—the qualities that lead both Buddhists and Hindus to salvation.

Perhaps these four attributes explain how Kathmandu allowed itself to become a hippy paradise. In the 1960s, when the young flocked to India to find themselves, many were sidetracked when they heard that hashish and marijuana grew wild in Nepal. Years passed before the Nepalese realized these foreigners brought problems, but not the much-needed foreign currency. In 1973 Radio Nepal announced that shirtless foreigners with long beards, mustaches, and flip-flops couldn't get visas. Within a week, all the hippies were "reincarnated." There wasn't a beard in Kathmandu unless it was attached to a wandering *sadhu* (Hindu holy man). In 1975 the government banned trafficking in hashish and marijuana. The owners of land where the wild plants grew had to cut it before it reached three feet. That helped, but now there's a new imported problem: Twelve thousand Nepali children are addicted to heroin.

Arriving and Departing

By Plane
Airport and Airlines
From the domestic terminal near **Tribhuvan International Airport, RNAC** (Kanti Path, tel. 220757 or 214491) flies to Pokhara (two flights daily); Nepalganj—Royal Bardia Wildlife Reserve (over 10 weekly flights); Bhairawa—approach to Lumbini (daily flight); Maghauli—Royal Chitwan National Park (daily); Tumlingtar—gateway to Arun River (five weekly flights); Jumla (two weekly winter flights); Jomsom, north of Annapurna (one weekly winter flight); Lukla, near Everest and Khumbu (three daily winter flights, year-round flights under discussion); Taplejung—gateway to Kanchenjunga (two weekly winter flights). RNAC also arranges numerous charters,

including one to Langtang, due north of Kathmandu. Book all flights early. Reconfirm at least 72 hours before departure and arrive at the airport 90 minutes in advance.

Between Airport and City The airport is 8 kilometers (5 miles) from Kathmandu. A few hotels provide courtesy airport service (*see* Lodging, below).

An airport bus (tel. 521064 or 522144) shuttles among the airport, Sheraton Hotel, Blue Star Hotel, Yellow Pagoda Hotel, Hotel Woodland, New Road Gate, Thamel, Durbar Marg, and Singha Durbar. It runs daily 8 AM–10 PM and costs Rs. 15.

A taxi to Kathmandu should cost Rs. 40; negotiate.

By Hired Car or Jeep with Driver The cost is determined by your destination and length of stay. Hire a car or jeep with driver only from a recommended tour operator and make all peak-season arrangements before you depart.

By Taxi A taxi costs about Rs. 1,050 per day.

Getting Around

By Taxi Taxis, with black-and-white licence plates, are inconvenient in Old Kathmandu. At night, expect to pay twice the normal fare. Call 224374 for night taxis. For longer excursions, insist the driver use the meter or fix the fare beforehand. Offer half what he suggests; then increase your offer.

By Tempo A better option for the old city, *tempo* (auto rickshaw) rides should be cheaper than taxi rides.

By Bicycle Rickshaw A wonderful way to travel through the old city, especially at night, it should be cheaper than a tempo.

By Bicycle Other than walking, bicycling is the nicest way to get around Kathmandu and the surrounding valley. Be prepared for crowds in the old city and for hard pedaling on hills beyond the city limits. Many recommended hotels rent bicycles (*see* Lodging, below). Shops in Thamel and on Freak Street also supply bikes. Figure Rs. 10 per day.

Addresses and Numbers

Tourist Information The **Tourist Information Center** has a counter at the International Airport and an office on New Road, near Basantpur and Old Kathmandu, that is open Sunday–Thursday 9–5 and Friday 9–4. Ask for a free copy of the *Nepal Traveler*, which has useful information and maps.

Emergencies The **American Embassy** (Pani Pokhari, tel. 411179 or 412718) is open weekdays 8–12:30 and 1:30–5. There is no Canadian embassy or consulate. The **British Embassy** (Lainchaur, tel. 411789 or 414588) is open weekdays 9–1 and 3–6. Call the embassy in case of medical emergencies or ask your hotel to recommend a clinic or private physician. As a last resort, head to the emergency room of Bir Hospital near the Thundikhel Parade Ground.

Travel Agencies Most of the indigenous adventure outfits (*see* Before You Go to Nepal, above) and a few overseas outfits (*see* Before You Go to The Himalayas, Chapter 1) have offices in Kathmandu. To hire a guide or car with driver or to arrange excursions, use the following travel agencies. They are open Sunday–Friday 10–5. **Adventure Travel Nepal** (Durbar Marg, tel. 223328), **Marco Polo**

Travels (White House, Kamal Pokhari, tel. 413632), **Natraj Tours and Travels** (Ghantaghar, Durbar Marg, tel. 222014), and **Yeti Travels** (Durbar Marg, tel. 221234).

Bookstores Good bookstores with English-language publications are on Freak Street, in Thamel, and on Rani Pokharai near Durbar Marg. **Tiwari's Pilgrim's Book House** (near Kathmandu Guest House, Thamel), open daily 8 AM–10 PM, has excellent books on the Himalayas. **Tibet Book Store** (Keshar Mahal, Tridevi Marg, Thamel), open Sunday–Friday 9–9, specializes in Buddhism.

Banks **American Express** and **Thomas Cook** are at Yeti Travels (Hotel Mayalu, Jamal Tole, Durbar Marg, tel. 13596). These offices are useful only to report a loss or theft (*see* hours, above); they don't cash checks. **Nepal Bank** is at the intersection of New Road and of Dharma Path. **Rastriya Banijya Bank** is near the Police Headquarters on Tangal Bahal. Banks are open November–mid-February, Sunday–Thursday 10–4, Friday 10–2; mid-February–November, Sunday–Thursday 10–3, Friday 10–2. Outside Kathmandu and Pokhara, carry sufficient rupees. Credit cards and traveler's checks don't work in small villages.

Post Office The **General Post Office** is at Sundhara (near Bhimsen Tower on lower Kanti Path) and is open in winter, Sunday–Friday 10–4; summer, Sunday–Friday 10–5; closed Saturday and government holidays.

Guided Tours

The travel agencies listed above conduct half-day tours by car, minibus, or bus to Bhaktapur (Bhadgaon), Pashupatinath, and Boudanath or to Kathmandu City, Patan (Lalitpur), and Swayambunath; morning tours to Dakshin Kali; and overnight trips to Dhulikhel for a good view of the sunrise or sunset over the Himalayas. During the peak season, book your tour as soon as you arrive.

Private Guides These same operators can supply excellent guides.

Highlights for First-time Visitors

Don't miss Old Kathmandu, Patan, Bhaktapur, and Swayambunath or a sightseeing flight on the Nepalese side of Mt. Everest.

Exploring Old Kathmandu

Numbers in the margin correspond with points of interest on the Durbar Square map.

Walk you must—preferably without a guide. Before you visit the famous monuments that crowd Durbar Square, spend a few hours wandering through the maze of narrow lanes *(gallis)* in **Old Kathmandu.** The typical Newari house was built as early as 1400. Notice the door sills studded with bits of metal; each year a new piece is added to ward off evil spirits.

Step through low portals that lead into *chowks* (courtyards), and most likely you'll discover a small Hindu shrine or Buddhist *chaitya* (small stupa). Houses abutting the courtyard are connected. Public courtyards *(chowks)* are often owned by an extended family. Since one chowk often leads to another, see how long you can avoid stepping back into a main street.

Now head to **Durbar Square** and start your historical and cultural tour of Old Kathmandu, once called Kantipur, "City of Bliss." Many historians believe Kathmandu acquired its pres-

❶ ent name from the three-story **Kashthamandap,** a wood temple at the southwest corner of the square. Built in 1596, it was restored in 1934 after an earthquake. Legend says it was built from the wood of one tree as ransom for a kidnapped god—a remarkable claim, given its 21-meter (68-foot) width and 20-meter (60-foot) height. This and all other attractions mentioned here are best visited sunrise–sunset. Inquire at the Tourist Information Center for times of special events or religious services. Admission is free, but donations are gladly accepted.

In the morning, Hindus come to the Kashthamandap and leave

❷ offerings at the nearby pagoda-style **Maru Ganesh** shrine. *Maru* means nonexistent and may refer to the unusual lack of a spire on the gilded roof. Ganesh is an important Hindu god in Nepal, and his vehicle is the tiny, cunning rat.

The son of Shiva and Parvati, Ganesh has a brother, Kumari, the god of war. One day Shiva held a contest to see which son could circle the universe first. Kumari, tasting victory, flew off. Sad, fat Ganesh discussed his predicament with his rat, who told him to circle his parents and tell them they were the universe. Shiva was so impressed, he blessed Ganesh with the title "God of Auspicious Beginnings." The faithful start each day with an offering to Ganesh, and each king of Nepal comes to this temple to make a gift before he's crowned.

❸ Behind this temple stands the white stucco **Kumari Chowk,** the profusely decorated palace of the Kumari (Living Goddess), built in 1757. The young girl who lives here is not allowed to smile; her feet never touch ground. She leaves her palace only when she's honored in a festival, and then she travels in a gold chariot.

Candidates for the post of the Royal Kumari must be about five years old and a member of the Buddhist Sakya sect. Royal Kumari's horoscope must be compatible with that of the king. Her body must be flawless and conform to 32 requirements, including no body odors, perfect white teeth with no gaps, a small tongue, and the voice of a sparrow. The would-be Kumari must also witness, without flinching, the midnight sacrifice of 108 goats and 108 buffalo (108 is a sacred number for Hindus) and she must spend the night in the temple with the carcasses. Only then is she named the Kumari—a title she keeps until she reaches puberty or cuts herself—if she sheds any blood, her reign is over.

❹ Across the square from Kumari Chowk stands the **Gaddi Baithak,** a neo-Grecian building constructed in 1908. Today the government uses the building, which contains the king's throne, for state functions. Opposite the Gaddi Baithak is the

❺ three-tier **Maju Deval,** a Shiva temple built in 1690. The supporting beams have cornices with animal heads, and the roof struts are covered with erotic carvings.

Statues of Shiva and Parvati peer down from an upper window

❻ in the two-story 1790 **Shiva Parvati Temple.** It's a rare domestic-style temple, resembling a house. Most other temples have

Basantapur Tower, **9**

Degu Taleju
Temple, **13**

Gaddi Baithak, **4**

Hanuman Dhoka
Square, **7**

Indrapur, **17**

Jaganath Temple, **14**

Kalo Bhairav bas
relief, **16**

Kashthamandap, **1**

Krishna Mandir, **15**

Kumari Chowk, **3**

Maju Deval, **5**

Makan Tole, **19**

Maru Ganesh, **2**

Pancha Mukhi
Hanuman Temple, **10**

Pratap Malla
Statue, **12**

Royal Palace, **8**

Seto Bhairav, **11**

Shiva-Parvati
Temple, **6**

Taleju Temple, **18**

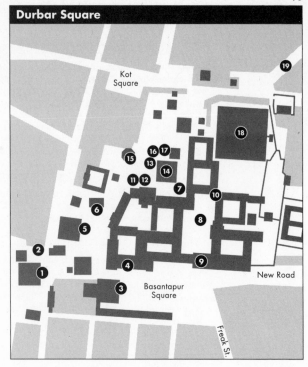

a pagoda design, which was eventually copied in China and Japan.

7 Behind the Shiva Parvati Temple is **Hanuman Dhoka Square,** the cultural and religious center of Old Kathmandu. Hanuman Dhoka means "Gate of Hanuman," the monkey god of Ramayana fame, an obedient servant who performed herculean tasks on behalf of the other gods. The Malla dynasty's kings put Hanuman's image on their battle flags and in 1672 placed his **8** statue outside the **Royal Palace.** Since its installation, Hanuman's statue, dressed in a red cloak, has been the object of devotion, with gobs of mustard oil and red powder dabbed on its surface by the faithful.

Before entering the Royal Palace, notice the two guardian lions near Hanuman. Shiva (the male force) sits on one side and Shakti (the female force) sits on the other. Just inside the Royal Palace, you come to a statue of Narsingha (an avatar of Vishnu) killing the demon Hiranyakashipu, who tortured his son for worshiping this Hindu god. Vishnu turned himself into Narsingha, half-man and half-lion; stretched the demon across his lap; and tore open its stomach with his claws. This image appears throughout the valley.

The palace, much of it off-limits, wraps around several courtyards, with the Golden Door leading into **Nasal Chowk,** where coronations take place. A gilded fish on a pole at the northern end is an avatar of Vishnu and can swim through the world's waters. It is an auspicious sign that represents peace, prosperity, and transcendental wisdom. On the eastern side of this courtyard is a small whitewashed shrine that contains a statue of Nasaleshwar (Dancing Shiva), which gives the square its name.

❾ From the nine-story **Basantapur Tower,** added to the complex in the 17th century, you get a good view of Kathmandu, includ-
❿ ing the unusual round-roofed pagoda, **Pancha Mukhi Hanuman Temple,** dedicated to the monkey god, at the opposite end of the courtyard.

When you leave the palace, notice the huge golden mask on a
⓫ wall hidden behind a carved wood screen. This is **Seto (White) Bhairav,** a wrathful aspect of Shiva, placed here by a rana in 1769 to protect his kingdom from evil and ignorance. During the Indra Jatra festival, the screen is opened. A big pot of *chang* (rice beer) is placed behind the mask's mouth, and the faithful suck the chang through a long bamboo straw—a gift from Seto Bhairav.

⓬ Atop a pillar near the Seto Bhairav is a bronze **statue of King Pratap Malla,** sitting on a lotus-shape pedestal and surrounded by his four sons. Erected in 1670, all the images kneel piously
⓭ facing the **Degu Taleju Temple,** once the Malla's private shrine, the tallest shrine in Hanuman Dhoka, with gilded roofs rising above the square. Its sacred idol, Taleju, is a manifestation of Parvati and was the guardian deity of the dynasty.

On a plinth near the pillar is the many-tiered, 17th-century
⓮ **Jaganath Temple,** dedicated to Jaganath (Krishna) and Guheshwari (Parvati), with erotic carvings on its wood struts.
⓯ Nearby is **Krishna Mandir** (Krishna Temple), an octagonal temple built in the 1600s, with a typical Nepalese first floor and a white plaster north Indian–style second floor.

⓰ On the north wall of the square is the revered 17th-century **bas relief of Kalo (black) Bhairav,** a dreaded aspect of Shiva, with fangs and a necklace of human skulls, trampling his father-in-law, who had insulted him. This image reminds devotees of the inevitability of justice. Legend claims that it once served as a lie detector: Anyone who stood before it and spoke dishonestly
⓱ bled to death. Nearby is the 17th-century temple **Indrapur,** with an open balcony on the second tier. Though dedicated to Indra (the god of rain, who saved Nepal from a destructive drought), the inner sanctum contains a Shiva lingam.

⓲ The famous 16th-century **Taleju Temple,** guarded by a pair of stone lions, is east of Indrapur, and is also dedicated to the guardian goddess. The four-story temple has a gold pinnacle and a gold umbrella atop its gilded roofs. Large bronze faces of the goddess Taleju gaze from upper-floor windows. Except for during the ninth day of the autumn Durga Puja festival, the interior is off-limits to everyone except the royal family and a few priests.

⓳ Walk along **Makhan Tole,** a street heading diagonally northeast of Hanuman Dhoka Square, to the first of three small squares, **Indra Chowk.** Four stone dragons on a second-story balcony guard the tile-covered **Akash Bhairav Temple,** dedicated to a wrathful aspect of Shiva—another example of a domestic-style temple. Non-Hindus can go inside but are not allowed into the inner sanctum, which contains a silver head of Yalambar, a king whom legend claims Krishna beheaded during the Great Battle described in the Hindu epic Mahabharata. The head of the fallen king, whose eyes look up to the sky (the meaning of "Akash") was enshrined here and soon assumed the status of a god, called Akash Bhairav.

In the second square, **Khel Tole,** and set behind a massive gate guarded by two dragons and a small Buddha on a pillar, is one of Nepal's holiest and most ornate temples, **Seto Macchendranath Temple.** Inside are bronze statues of the goddess Tara holding a lotus and a Classical Greek–style statue of a woman. The temple has metal banners hanging from the pinnacle of the gilded roof. Called *dhvajas*, these banners, which decorate many temples, provide a pathway to heaven. Behind the gilded doorway is the inner sanctum with a simple cotton doll-like image of the White Macchendranath. Buddhists revere this idol as Avalokitesvara; Hindus, as a manifestion of Shiva.

Numerous small temples crowd **Asan Tole,** the third and busiest of the squares. The most interesting is the three-story **Annapurna Temple,** dedicated to this benign aspect of Durga. Hindus say this goddess lived in the Indian plains and longed to see the mountain named in her honor. A priest offered to take her to Kathmandu. She turned herself into a *kalash* (sacred vessel), and he placed her here by a tree. Parts of the tree and kalash are enshrined in the inner sanctum.

On **Bangemudha Square,** due west of Asan Tole, try to find **Vaisha Dev** (Toothache Tree) with hundreds of coins nailed into its boulder-shape trunk, which protrudes from the side wall of a corner shop. Bits of metal hammered in by sufferers hoping for relief nearly obliterate the tree and its golden statue of the deity.

Walk south (back toward Hanuman Square) on the narrow road that faces Vaisha Dev to the intersection of Nara Devi Tole. Turn right and walk about a minute to **Yitum Bahal,** a courtyard on the left. One of the oldest courtyards in Kathmandu, the 14th-century Yitum Bahal has a *peepal* tree (fig tree) that has grown around a chaitya. To the right is a 16th-century portal with a handsome carving of the Buddha on the *torana* (carved crest).

Inside a nearby courtyard is **Hum Bahal,** with a Buddhist shrine surrounded by a former monastery *(bahal)*. To your left is an unusual chaitya with four standing bodhisattvas. On the right, examine the carved metal plates with images of Guru Mapa, a demon who ate disobedient children. One depicts his mask; another shows him enjoying a meal. The monastery is now a school, and from the children's behavior, it seems that Guru Mapa remains a powerful disciplinarian.

Time Out	For apple pie, brownies, or cappuccino, stop at **Helena's** (Thamel), open daily 8 AM–10 PM, or **Pizzeria La Cimbali** (Thahity Kwabahal, Thamel), open daily 9 AM–10 PM. For ice cream, go to **Nirula's** (Durbar Marg), open daily 10 AM–10:30 PM.

Shopping

The **Kashmiri Bead Bazaar,** open daily 9–6, is behind Indra Chowk. It's run by Kashmiri Moslems who sell fine glass beads from Belgium, Czechoslovakia, and Japan. Sit on a platform

and pick out strands, which the shopkeeper will quickly make
into a necklace. One of the best bead shops is No. 388. Bargain;
they don't accept credit cards. For good thang-kas, visit
Mannie's Art (Sakya Arcade, Durbar Marg, tel. 223931), open
Sunday–Friday 9:30–7:30. No bargaining here; he accepts
American Express, MasterCard, and Visa credit cards.

For old artwork and curios, visit these shops on Durbar Marg
and bargain: **Karma Lama Ritual Art Gallery** (tel. 223410),
open Sunday–Friday 10–6, no credit cards; **Oriental Handicraft Curio Centre** (Basantpur), open Sunday–Friday 10–7,
accepts American Express cards; **Treasure Art Concern** (Annapurna Arcade, Shop No. 5), open Sunday–Friday 11–7:30,
accepts American Express. In Thamel, don't miss **Yeshi
Phuntsok's Zambala** (12/902 Thamel), open Sunday–Friday
9–1 and 3–8, accepts American Express. This shop sells excellent Tibetan and Bhutanese handicrafts and gorgeous textiles,
especially the traditional raw silk scarves, shawls, blankets,
and vests.

For stylish clothing made from handblocked cotton, stop at
Durga Design (Thamel), open Saturday–Thursday 10–7, no
credit cards. **Roof of the World—D. D. Tibetan Boutique** (Kanti
Path, tel. 220349) is open Sunday–Friday 9:30–7, accepts
American Express cards and sells classy handknit sweaters
and contemporary dresses (Western- and Tibetan-style). You
also find good woolen handknits in other shops in Thamel and
on Freak Street.

Finally, the following shops sell handknits and handicrafts,
with all proceeds helping destitute women or Tibetan refugees:
Women's Skill Development Project in Lazimpat near the
French Embassy, open Sunday–Friday 8–8, and in Pulchowk,
Lalitpur, open Sunday–Friday 10–5. **Mahaguthi Shop** (Durbar
Marg, near the Annapurna Coffee Shop), open daily 10–6:30;
Tibetan Refugee Center (Tibetan Camp, Jawalakhel, tel.
522414), open Sunday–Friday 8:30–noon and 1–5. All these co-
operatives sell at fixed prices and don't take credit cards.

Outdoor Adventures

Highly recommended adventures are indicated by a star ★ .

★ **Bicycling:** Bikes are available for hire (*see* Getting Around,
above). In March and April, Himalayan Mountain Bikes (tel.
413632 or 414192) offers good scheduled-departure and
custom-designed trips around Kathmandu Valley.

Fishing: Fish along the Sunkosi (Oct.–Mar.). Bring your own
equipment. No licence is required.

Golfing: Play at the Royal Golf Course (tel. 412836) near the
airport or head to the Gokarna Safari Golf Club inside the
Gokarna Royal Forest, 10 kilometers (6 miles) northeast of
Kathmandu (tel. 211063). Clubs are available at both.

★ **Hiking:** Pick a destination, bring a canteen and packed lunch,
then have a taxi drop you at the starting point of these day-long
walks.

★ *Mt. Pulchoki:* It's 2,762 meters (9,062 feet) high and about 16
kilometers (10 miles) southeast of Kathmandu. Visit mountaintop shrines, then follow the trail down the mountain through
rhododendron forests to the nearby Godavar Botanical

Gardens—a lovely place to picnic. Catch a taxi back to Kathmandu.

★ *Changu Narayan:* Take a taxi to Bhaktapur. Walk about 6 kilometers (3 miles) due north from Bhaktapur's Durbar Square to Changu Narayan, a historic temple set on a hill (*see* Excursions, below).

Physical Fitness and Yoga: The modern, clean Kathmandu Physical Fitness Center (across from the Ambassador Hotel, tel. 412473) offers inexpensive yoga and aerobic dance classes, massages, and weight training and has saunas and Jacuzzis.

★ **Rafting:** Though rafting is possible year-round on the Sunkosi (east of Kathmandu) and the crowded Trisuli (west of Kathmandu), the September to November period offers the best white water. Short trips (under four days) can be arranged on arrival. Longer trips should be arranged in advance. Use an agency listed under Special-Interest Tours in Before You Go to Nepal, above, or in Before You Go to the Himalayas, Chapter 1.

★ *Sunkosi:* The 10-day journey to Chattra on the Sunkosi is considered one of the best runs in the world. You start at Dolalghat on the road to Tibet. Almost immediately you encounter rapids, which take you by fishing villages, through gorges with bats clinging to cliffs and monkeys scampering through the trees.

Trisuli: Trips on the Trisuli are less rigorous and can last from three to seven days. A typical run starts at Benighat, west of Kathmandu, where two days of fairly mild rapids take you to the Trisuli gorge and challenging white water.

★ **Sightseeing Flight:** A morning hour-long flight (Oct.–May) gives you the mountaineer's glimpse of Everest and other peaks 6,000–8,000 meters (19,680–26,240 feet) high. Book before you depart through a recommended tour operator.

Trekking (up to a week): Many special-interest tour operators offer a good three-day trek around the Kathmandu Valley, ideal in the spring when flowers are in bloom. You walk through villages, terraced fields, and forests and see cultural monuments.

Dining

Kathmandu's private restaurants offer many cuisines: Korean, German, Indian, Nepalese, Japanese, Tibetan, and fast-food American. All those listed below are excellent. Though some restaurants import beef from Calcutta, normally, you're munching on "buff" (as in buffalo). Dress is casual unless stated. Prices are per person, including taxes and excluding service and drinks.

Indian and Nepalese **Naachghar.** A formal restaurant set in a neo-Grecian palace, it has Italian-marble floors, pink walls with ornate plaster moldings, Belgian chandeliers, and a painted ceiling. Nepalese classical music and Indian *ghazels* (romantic ballads) are performed evenings, except Sunday, and accompany traditional specialties, including *banel tareko* (fried wild boar), *charako achhar* (shredded marinated chicken), *hansko sekua* (grilled marinated duck), and *dhukur tareko* (grilled marinated dove). *Yak & Yeti Hotel, Durbar Marg, tel. 413999. Dinner reservations advised. AE, MC, V. Open 12:30–2:30, 7–10:30. Expensive ($10–$15).*

Ghar-E-Kabob. Above a coffee shop, Ghar-E-Kabob has a Moghul decor with miniatures on the walls and ghazels performed nightly, except Thursday. The accent is on the food, which many claim is the best north Indian and Nepalese in Kathmandu. *Hotel de L'Annapurna, Durbar Marg, tel. 221711. Dinner reservations advised. AE, DC, MC, V. Open noon–3, 7–11. Moderate ($5–$11).*

Greenlands Vegetarian Restaurant. Don't be put off by the coffee shop look, the food is great—north and south Indian vegetarian, with especially good *dosa* (vegetable-filled crepe) and *thalis* (small portions of various dishes). *Woodland's Hotel, Durbar Marg, tel. 220123. Open 8 AM–10 PM. Inexpensive (under $5).*

Nepalese and Tibetan

Sunkosi. Very popular, it's cozy, with brick walls and wood trim, and has excellent Nepali and Tibetan dishes. Try *charako sekwa* (grilled chicken), *kalejo sandeko* (mildly spicy liver), or the *golbheda bari* (lamb meatballs). The chef also serves an excellent Tibetan *gyakok* for two (pork, prawns, fish, bean curd, egg, meatballs, and vegetables in a brass pot). Don't miss the famous dessert—*sikarni* (spicy whipped yogurt). *Durbar Marg, tel. 215299 or 220299. Dinner reservations advised. AE. Open 11–10. Moderate ($5–$10).*

Chinese and Tibetan

Arniko Room. Done up in understated Chinese decor, Arniko has excellent spring rolls, fried prawns, and diced and fried spicy bean curd. *Hotel de L'Annapurna, Durbar Marg, tel. 221711. Dinner reservations advised. AE, DC, MC, V. Open noon–3, 7–11. Moderate ($5–$10).*

Golden Gate Restaurant. In this upstairs restaurant with flamboyant Chinese decor, enjoy nonspicy Beijing and Cantonese and spicy Szechuan specialties. *Durbar Marg (opposite Indonesian Bank), tel. 223705. Dinner reservations advised. AE, DC. Open 12:30–2:30, 6:30–10:30. Moderate ($5–$10).*

Ras Rang. Eat in its cozy Newari interior with a large brass fireplace or outside on the lawn. Choose from good Hakka, Cantonese, and Szechuan specialties. *Across from Hotel Ambassador, tel. 414432. Dinner reservations advised. AE. Open 12:30–3, 5–10:30. Inexpensive (under $5).*

Japanese

Fuji Restaurant. Set back from the road, this restaurant, in an old brick palace, is approached via a wood footbridge over a pond. Eat inside at a table, on cushions, on the veranda, in the garden, or at the counter. *Kanti Path (across from the American Embassy), tel. 225272. Dinner reservations advised. No credit cards. Open 10–10. Inexpensive–Moderate (under $10).*

Continental

Coppers. Under construction at press time, this fancy restaurant will feature imported Western specialties—eggs Benedict, steak-and-kidney pie, and pâtés—and have a separate deli providing Western-style sandwiches to go. *Kaisermahal, Thamel (no phone yet). Credit card policy to be announced. Open 7 AM–10:30 PM. Moderate ($5–$10).*

Kokonor. Decorated in traditional Newari style, Kokonor serves the best fish dishes in Kathmandu and good mixed grills. Indian and Nepalese classical music is performed Thursday–Tuesday. *Hotel Shangrila, Lazimpat, tel. 412999. Dinner reservations advised. AE, MC, V. Open noon–2:30, 7–10. Moderate ($5–$10).*

Rumdoodle. This famous hangout, with the best bar in town and good food, has a casual "mountaineering" motif. Tents hang from the ceiling. Walls have "Yeti" footprints auto-

graphed by the Himalayan greats—Sir Edmund Hillary and
Reinhold Messner. Expect a crowd in season. *Thamel, near
Kathmandu Guest House, no phone. AE, V. Open 8–10, 1–3,
5–10; closed Tues. Inexpensive–Moderate (under $10).*

Lodging

In the high season, reserve well in advance. Highly recommended lodgings are indicated by a star ★. Prices are for a
standard double room, including taxes and excluding service
charges.

**Very Expensive
(over $100)**

Hotel de L'Annapurna. This old three-story hotel has a lovely
lobby and excellent service. The rooms are spacious, but have
no inspired decorative touches. The best rooms front the garden and pool. *Durbar Marg, tel. 221711. Reservations abroad:
Utell International in New York, tel. 800/448–8355, or in London, tel. 01/995–8211. 159 rooms with bath. Facilities: air-
conditioning, room service, 4 restaurants, bar, health club,
pool, tennis and billiards, shopping arcade, foreign-exchange
and travel counter, car-rental service. AE, DC, MC, V.*

Soaltee Oberoi. On a ridge 15 minutes from Durbar Square, this
Western-style hotel is decorated in attractive Newari style
with lots of brick and wood trim. Rooms in the Himalayan Wing
are large and lavish; rooms in the older Garden Wing are quiet-
er but less spacious. *Tahachal, tel. 211211. Reservations
abroad: in New York, tel. 212/223–3110 or 800/223–6800; in
Canada, tel. 514/286–4056, 416/281–3491, or 800/341–8585; in
London, tel. 01/583–3050. 300 rooms with bath. Facilities: air-
conditioning, 4 restaurants, bar, room service, baby-sitters,
pool, tennis court, health club, foreign-exchange and travel
counter, car rental, shopping arcade, casino, courtesy bus to
airport and Kathmandu. AE, DC, MC, V.*

★ **Yak & Yeti.** This 18th-century palace, with an additional new
wing, is quiet and elegant. The best rooms face the garden and
pool. *Durbar Marg, tel. 413999. Reservations abroad: Utell International in New York, tel. 212/245–7130, or in London, tel.
01/995–8211. 120 rooms with bath. Facilities: air-conditioning,
room service, 3 restaurants, bar, pool, tennis court, health
club, baby-sitters, shopping arcade, foreign-exchange and
travel counter. AE, MC, V.*

**Expensive
($60–$100)**

Hotel Himalaya. On a hill 10 minutes from Durbar Square,
Himalaya is modern and streamlined, with a marble interior
that highlights an enclosed Japanese rock garden and sleek,
understated decor in the rooms. *Reservations: Box 2141, Sahid
Sukra Marg, Lalitpur (Patan), tel. 523900. 94 rooms with bath.
Facilities: air-conditioning, room service, 2 restaurants, bar,
free center-city shuttle service, foreign-exchange and travel
counter, shopping arcade, pool, tennis court. AE, MC, V.*

★ **Hotel Shangrila.** A handsome Newari hotel in the diplomatic
enclave, the decor has lots of brick, stucco, and wood trim. The
rooms are cheery. The best rooms overlook the garden. *Reservations: Box 655, Lazimpat, Kathmandu, tel. 412999. 57
rooms with bath. Facilities: room service, air-conditioning, 3
restaurants, bar, free airport and center-city shuttle service,
foreign-exchange and travel counter, shopping arcade. AE,
MC, V.*

★ **Hotel Shanker.** The 19th-century former palace and birthplace
of the present queen is opulent, with numerous attractive sitting rooms—some evoke Versailles, others are traditional

Nepalese with brick and wood trim. A few bedrooms have painted ceilings and other rococo touches. The garden and enormous front lawn are ideal for relaxing. The downside: In peak season, service can be indifferent; don't be afraid to complain. *Near the Royal Palace on Lalimpat, Reservations: Box 350, Kathmandu, tel. 410151. 94 rooms with bath. Facilities: room service, air-conditioning, 3 restaurants, bar, travel and foreign-exchange counter, shopping arcade, pool. AE, DC, MC, V.*

Moderate ($25–$60)

★ **Dwarika's Kathmandu Village Hotel.** The only hotel in Nepal to have received the coveted Pacific Area Travel Association Heritage Award for cultural conservation efforts, this hotel is in a shady compound with brick terraces; each room has carved antique windows and traditional furnishings. One drawback: The heating is not great. *Reservations: Box 659, Battisputali, Kathmandu, tel. 414770. 12 rooms with bath. Facilities: dining room, library, bar, foreign-exchange and travel counter. Traveler's checks. No credit cards.*

★ **Summit Hotel.** About 3 kilometers (2 miles) from Durbar Square, this popular two-story hotel is quiet and charming with lovely gardens and lawns and excellent views of the mountains and valley. The cheery rooms have traditional touches—the best ones are upstairs overlooking the lawn and pool. The management is excellent. *Reservations: Box 1406, Kupondole Heights, Kathmandu, tel. 521894. 37 rooms with bath. Facilities: room service, air-conditioning, pool, restaurant, bike rentals, bar, foreign-exchange and travel counter. AE, V.*

Inexpensive (under $25)

Hotel Ambassador. Currently under renovation, this old hotel is in a quiet location near Thamel. The rooms have minimal decor but are clean. *Reservations: Box 2769, Lazimpat, Kathmandu, tel. 410432. 34 rooms with bath. Facilities: air-conditioning, room service, 2 restaurants, bar, foreign-exchange and travel counter, gift shop, bike rentals. AE.*

★ **Kathmandu Guest Hotel and Maya Apartments.** This popular 25-year-old Kathmandu institution caters to the traveler on a budget. The best rooms in the newer Maya Apartments are upstairs with a veranda that overlooks a spacious lawn and garden. Lower-price rooms in the older wing are simpler, without air-conditioning or room service. Reserve well in advance. No smoking is allowed. *Reservations: Thamel, Kathmandu, tel. 413632. 104 rooms with bath. Facilities: air-conditioning and room service for some rooms, kitchen facilities, restaurant, rooftop garden, foreign-exchange and travel counter, car rental service. AE.*

The Arts

Theater

The New Himalchuli Cultural Group performs traditional Nepalese dances daily in its auditorium in the Hotel Shanker compound. *Tel. 410151 for reservations. Admission: Rs. 80. Open Oct.–Mar., 6:30–7:30; Apr.–Sept., 7–8.*

The Everest Cultural Society performs classical and folk dances daily at Hotel de L'Annapurna. *Tel. 220676 for reservations. Admission: Rs. 80. Open 7–8.*

Nightlife

Bars The best bars are at **Rumdoodle** (happy hour with complimentary snacks, 5:30–7; closed Tuesday), at **Hotel Shanker,** and **Yak & Yeti** (classy and contemporary). Most bars close around 11 PM.

Casino **Casino Nepal.** Foreigners flying into Kathmandu get Rs. 100 worth of free coupons upon presentation of a passport and used airline ticket. (The offer expires seven days from arrival.) The entrance makes it look like a dive, but downstairs is pure Las Vegas. *Next door to Soaltee Oberoi Hotel. Open 24 hours.*

Excursion from Kathmandu to Swayambunath

Numbers in the margin correspond with points of interest on the Kathmandu Valley map.

❷⓿ On a hill east of Old Kathmandu stands **Swayambunath,** literally "Place of the Self-born," or as called affectionately by the Nepalese, the Monkey Temple, after the swarms of critters who scavenge for food left by devotees. To reach the top, walk up the 365 steps (benches are located at frequent intervals) on the east side of the hill. You can also drive up the road from the southwest.

After walking through a colorful arch, you head up the steps past statues of the Dhyani Buddhas (Five Cosmic Buddhas) and their animal vehicles, small chaityas, the footprints of Manjushri, Tibetan refugees, pilgrims, and those monkeys. Watch your belongings, these animals are fast.

At the top, crowds of pilgrims circle the 2,000-year-old Swayambunath and its monastery, which belongs to the Nyingma (Old Sect). The large white hemisphere is made of brick and earth; it's called *garbha* (womb) and represents the cosmos. No sacred relic is contained inside. On top, the gilded copper spire consists of 13 concentric circles—the steps to enlightenment, which is symbolized by the intricate metal umbrella above. Below the all-knowing eyes that look out in each cardinal direction is a simple figure that reminds the devout that the Buddha is the only way to salvation.

Start your tour of the complex at the large 17th-century *vajra* (thunderbolt) that belonged to the Hindu god Indra and symbolizes boundless power. It is placed on a plinth decorated with the 12 animals of the Tibetan calendar. The small shrine in front of the vajra contains the first of the five Dhyani Buddhas whose temples encircle the large stupa: Aksobhya (Undisturbed Buddha and Buddha of the East), with his right fingers touching the earth. His vehicle, the elephant, is carved in the base.

From here, walk clockwise around Swayambunath. Vairocana (Buddha of Resplendent Light and the Buddha Supreme and Eternal) holds his hands up like a teacher. His consort, Mamki, is in the shrine to his right. Ratansambhava (Buddha of Precious Birth and Buddha of the South) has his palm open, and a horse, his vehicle, is carved into his pedestal. Pandara, his consort, is in the shrine just before the meditating Amitabha (Buddha of Boundless Light and Buddha of the West). Tara, his consort, is enshrined next to Amoghasiddhi (Buddha of Infalli-

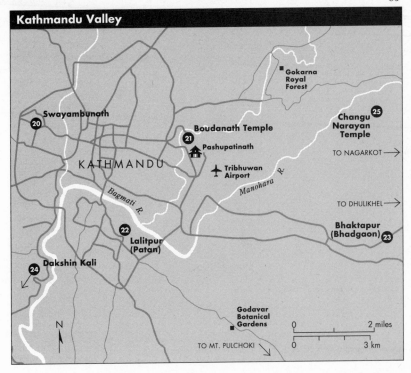

Kathmandu Valley

Gokarna Royal Forest

Swayambunath 20

Boudanath Temple 21

Pashupatinath

KATHMANDU

Tribhuwan Airport

Changu Narayan Temple 25

TO NAGARKOT →

Bagmati R.

Manohara R.

TO DHULIKHEL →

Lalitpur (Patan) 22

Bhaktapur (Bhadgaon) 23

Dakshin Kali

24

Godavar Botanical Gardens

N

0   2 miles

0   3 km

TO MT. PULCHOKI ↘

---

ble Power and Buddha of the North) who holds his right hand
up and has the winged Garuda, his vehicle, set in his base.
Lochana, his consort, brings you back to vajra.

At Swayambunath, you see symbols of the five elements—air,
water, fire, ether, earth—that make up the cosmos. Behind
Amoghasiddhi is the Nagapur Temple honoring water. Behind
Mamki is the Vasupur Temple, which symbolizes the earth. In
the left corner near the Pandara Shrine, the Vayupur Temple
represents the air. From here, leave the main courtyard and
walk west of the Buddhist library to Agnipur, a temple honoring fire. On its right, a path leads to Shantipur, the ether
temple near an enormous statue of Sakyamuni.

This same courtyard has an ornate 19th-century Hindu temple,
Hariti Devi, dedicated to the goddess Hariti, responsible for
both averting smallpox and ensuring fertility. Worshiped by
Hindus and Buddhists, the temple has gilded roofs and a wall of
prayer wheels. Its arch is covered with snakes, protecting the
enshrined deity, who is surrounded by children. Beams are
carved with animal heads. On Saturday, the temple is crowded
with those who come to ask special favors.

Finally, near the Hariti Devi, see the pillared pavilion with
chiseled images of the Green and White Tara and a peacock,
Amitabha's vehicle, facing the shrine that honors this Dhyani
Buddha. In this same area, you find the National Museum. It
has good collections of antique stone and bronze statues, wood
carvings, thang-kas, weapons, and beautifully illustrated old
books, as well as natural science displays. *3 km (2 mi) from the*

*old city. Walk, rent a bike, or take an auto rickshaw or taxi.
Plan 4 hrs if you walk. Museum admission: Rs. 4; Rs. 8 with
camera. Open Wed.–Mon. 10–4. Temple open sunrise–sunset.
You can attend a service in the early morning or later after-
noon; check for time with the Kathmandu Tourist Information
Center.*

Excursion from Kathmandu to Pashupatinath and Boudanath

Dedicated to Shiva, Pashupatinath (Temple of Living Beings) is
the oldest and most sacred Hindu temple in Nepal. It is set on
the banks of the sacred Bagmati River, a tributary of the
Ganga. The original temple was supposedly constructed in the
1400s; much of the present complex was built in 1696.
Pashupatinath is an important cremation site, since the ashes
sprinkled on the water flow down to the Ganga.

During Shivaratri (Feb. or Mar.), pilgrims from all over India
and Nepal flock here; throughout the year, devotees come here
for ritual baths or bring cows, goats, and dogs to the shrine.
The animals are not sacrificed, but honored with a *tika* (red dot
on the forehead), which gives them the right to live undisturbed
within the complex, as befits the temple's name.

Although the main temple is open only to Hindus, you can get a
good look from the far side of the narrow river. Cross the
bridge; as you climb the path, take the first set of stairs on the
left. At the end of the terrace, notice the head of Shiva (its nose
is missing) carved on an 5th- or 6th-century lingam.

From this terrace, you can see the walls and the intricate met-
alwork of the silver doors surrounding the lower level of two-
tier Pashupatinath, which is crowned with gilded roofs. Within
the building is a huge Shiva lingam, and outside stands an
equally large gilded bull, Nandi, Shiva's mount. Continue up
the path, accompanied by as many monkeys as wandering sadhus, and look at the numerous old shrines and small stone
lingams.

Returning to the far side of the river, head left along the bank
to the cremation site; be discreet about photos. At the end of
the walkway, look at the 7th-century head of the Buddha. Its
presence supports the theory that this temple was also a Buddhist shrine—built on a sacred spot where one of the legendary
lotus flowers came to rest.

㉑ Now drive northeast to **Boudanath Temple.** Dating back to AD
600, Boudanath is the second largest stupa in Asia and the most
important Tibetan Buddhist center outside Tibet. Once again,
all-knowing eyes of the Buddha peer from the top of the white
brick-and-earth hemisphere, dedicated to Boudanath (Buddha
of Wisdom), with an unknown relic—some believe it's a tooth of
the Buddha—interred during construction.

As with most Buddhist structures, the stupa's base is shaped
like a mandala, symbolizing the universe and serving as an aid
to meditation. The five elements appear in its design and are
symbolized in the colors of the prayer flags: the base—earth,
yellow flag; the dome—water, blue flag; the central tower—
fire, red flag; crescent—light, pale blue flag; flame on top—
ether, white flag. Thirteen rings wrap around the dome from

base to pinnacle, symbolizing the steps to enlightenment or "Bodhi," hence the stupa's name. Prayer wheels encircle its base.

On your left as you walk clockwise, a huge prayer wheel encloses a shrine covered with 1,000 Buddhas. Beyond this structure is a new monastery, with an enormous gold-painted Buddha seated in meditation. *Pashupatinath is 5 km (3 mi) and Boudanath is 8 km (5 mi) northeast of Kathmandu. Take a taxi to each site and plan 3 hours for this excursion. Visit both sunrise–sunset.*

Excursion from Kathmandu to Lalitpur (Patan)

Tibetan traders once called Patan "Ye Rang" (Eternity Itself). It is the oldest of the three ancient city-kingdoms in Kathmandu Valley that were ruled by the Mallas, who created most of the old structures. Patan is 5 kilometers (3 miles) south of Kathmandu, and you should plan four hours for this excursion. Rent a car with a guide for about $20 or take a taxi for Rs. 40.

㉒ **Patan** is still populated by Newars, two-thirds of them Buddhist—talented artisans who continue to turn out traditional fine arts. As in Kathmandu and Bhaktapur, a fusion prevails between Hinduism and Buddhism. Also as in those cities, it has a Durbar Square and a maze of winding lanes.

As you walk down the main street of Patan toward Durbar Square, you see the first of the old structures built during the Malla dynasty, a small white-domed **Shiva temple** guarded by Nandi. The next building of note is the octagonal-shape 1637 **Krishna Mandir** of black stone, topped with a gold dome. Guarded by lions, symbols of power, its facade is carved with battle scenes from the Ramayana and Mahabharata. Its design is influenced by the Indian shikhara-style temple, with graceful finials adorning the peaked roofs. Inside the shrine stands a black stone image of Krishna with his two consorts, Radha and Rukmani. The second story has sculptures of the nine incarnations of Vishnu. The third story has an image of Shiva.

On a pillar in front of the Krishna Mandir is a large bronze statue of Vishnu's vehicle, **Garuda,** half man and half eagle, erected in 1647 to mark the completion of the temple. Garuda sits on a lotus pedestal and is one of Nepal's finest sculptures.

Across from the pillar is the **Royal Palace,** three buildings set around courtyards. Before you enter the first courtyard, notice three statues on the right front wall: Ganesh, Narsingha ripping open the demon Hiranyakashipu, and Hanuman wearing his familiar red coat and with his hand raised.

The entrance to **Sundari Chowk** (Magnificent Courtyard), constructed in the 1620s, is between Narsingha and Ganesh. The ground-floor rooms surrounding the courtyard were formerly stables, storehouses, and the barracks of the guards. The upper floors were the living quarters of the royal family. In the courtyard, you see the **Taleju Temple,** which contains an image of the patron diety of the king—Taleju Bhavani.

The **Tusa Hiti** (Royal Bath) is an exquisite Newari creation, with a gold waterspout depicting Narayan (Vishnu) and his consort, Lakshmi, astride Garuda. It's a sacrilege to put your feet on the naga encircling the tank or to step into the basin. A stone Garuda faces this royal bath.

Access to the **Mul Chowk** (Main Courtyard), completed in 1660 by Shrinivasa Malla, is to the left of the exterior of the palace. Its two temples are dedicated to the goddess Taleju. On the right of one temple door, Yamuna (Goddess of the sacred Yamuna River) stands on a tortoise, her vehicle. To the left, the goddess Ganga is poised on top of a *makara* (hybrid crocodile-elephant), her vehicle.

At press time, **Mani Keshab Narayan Chowk,** the third courtyard, completed around 1734, was closed for renovation. The entranceway, Golden Gate, is another Patan treasure, with three carved windows and a dazzling torana covered with images of Shiva and Parvati directly above the gate. In the center window is an image of Vishnu.

Near a gigantic bell in Durbar Square is the 18th-century **Hari Shankar Temple,** which you can identify by its three roofs and two stone elephants. It's dedicated to Shiva and Vishnu.

The nearby freestanding pillar has a statue of the late 17th-century King Yoga Narenda, who sits on his throne with his two wives nearby. Over his head is a large cobra with a bird perched on its head. According to legend, this king was kidnapped by the king of Bhaktapur and later killed. But while Narenda was still alive, he sent word to his people that he would continue to live until the bird on the statue flew away, the two elephants guarding the Hari Shankar Temple walked off to drink from a nearby tap, and a statue of a man with a gun fired it once. To this day, people leave Narenda plates of food and prepare his *hookah* (water pipe).

The **Char Narayan Temple,** dedicated to Vishnu and built possibly as early as 1566, has two stone lions—Ajaya and Vijaya—on the front steps heading to the first plinth where two more lions guard the passage up to the second platform leading to the inner sanctum, which contains a lingam supported by four images of Narayan. Erotic carvings on the roof struts apparently depict 84 different positions for sexual intercourse.

Dedicated to Bhim, one of the Pandava brothers of Mahabharata fame, the **Bhimsen Temple,** with a gold roof and a gold *dhvaja* (banner), sits at the end of Durbar Square. Guarded by lions, it is constructed in typical Newari style—three stories with numerous roofs, all resting on an elevated plinth. The animals that stand on the lower roof are more symbols of power. Elaborately carved balconies have images of Shiva, Parvati, and Ganesh.

Patan's most handsome structure is **Hiranya Varna Mahavihar** (Golden Temple), a three-story golden pagoda dedicated to Avalokitesvara and built in the 13th century with periodic later additions. To get to this temple, turn left on the road next to the Bhimsen Temple. At the next wide lane, turn right. When you come to a passageway guarded by lions, turn left, and head toward a gate with an image of Buddha.

You must remove your shoes before you step into the courtyard to examine the small shrine with ornate silver doors and a gilded roof. Inside, you can see numerous statues and chaityas. This is an active monastery with lamas living in the surrounding rooms. Their main prayer hall is up a flight of stairs to the right as you enter (circle around the structure clockwise to enter). Here they pray before an altar filled with statues and surrounded by frescoes and thang-kas.

From the Golden Temple, head down to the river and see the **Khumbeshwar Temple.** The bottom two tiers of this five-story, pagoda-style Shiva temple topped in gold date back to the 14th century, making it one of the oldest in the country. The top three tiers were added in the 17th century. The setting is pastoral, with goats, chickens, and ducks wandering around, women washing clothes, and children bathing in pools. The temple is covered with carvings associated with Shiva.

Inside the courtyard is a gold Nandi on a brick pedestal. Two lions guard the inner sanctum with its multiheaded image of Shiva dressed in orange and covered in sandalwood paste. Around the complex are other shrines with statues of Vishnu, Surya (the Sun God), Ganesh, and the goddess Baglamukhi (Goddess of Poisons), who protects devotees from black magic. The nearby grassy courtyard is a grazing ground for Nandi.

When you head back to Durbar Square from this temple, instead of retracing your steps, go left and walk along the side of the temple. At the next lane, turn right to a lane that leads past more stupas and temples. When you reach Durbar Square, head to **Mahabouddha** (Temple of 1,000 Buddhas). Walk to the far end of the Royal Palace, turn left, and pass through the brass and copper market. A road to the right leads to this well-known temple, concealed behind a painted archway that leads to a courtyard. The tall pyramid-shape, Indian-influenced temple, built of red brick and terra-cotta, crowds the tiny space.

Originally constructed in 1585 as a replica of the temple of Bodh Gaya, where the Historic Buddha attained his enlightenment, the structure was extensively damaged by the earthquake of 1934 and rebuilt—a replica of a replica. Each brick has a tiny image of the Buddha in his meditation pose or of important scenes in his life. All the oil lamps are dedicated to Maya Devi (Sakyamuni's mother).

When you head back to Durbar Square, turn left and see the **Temple of Rato (Red) Macchendranath,** or Matsyendranath (a manifestation of Shiva). Constructed in 1408, it's worshiped by both Hindus and Buddhists. The dark red wood image of Macchendranath, whom many call the guardian deity of Patan, is taken out of the temple and paraded through the city on a huge chariot during the festival of Red Macchendranath Matsyendranath Jatra.

Nearby is the **Minanath Temple,** with an image of Avalokitesvara, whom Buddhists consider a brother of Matsyendranath. The small bronze image of Minanath, which is adorned with clothes, is taken out during the annual procession in his honor.

Excursion from Kathmandu to Bhaktapur (Bhadgaon)

This excursion to Bhaktapur, 13 kilometers (8 miles) east of Kathmandu, will take about four hours. Rent a car with a guide for about $20 or take a taxi for Rs. 50.

㉓ Raja Ananda Malla supposedly created **Bhaktapur** around AD 889, designing his kingdom in the shape of Shiva's conch shell; other sources claim it was Shiva's drum. Today the original shape is impossible to detect. Still, Bhaktapur's beauty and ancient character remain intact, to a large extent because of extensive renovation by the West German government, which is actively involved in the restoration of Nepal's ancient monuments.

A large gate flanked by statues of Bhairav and Hanuman leads to Durbar Square. To your left, behind two ornate stone lions, are 17th-century statues of Bhairav and the goddess Ugrachandi, a manifestation of Durga. Surrounded by female attendants, the goddess is shown killing the buffalo-headed demon, Mahishasur. Legend claims that the king who ordered the construction of these statues was so delighted by the craftsmanship that he had the sculptor's hands chopped off so they couldn't be duplicated.

To your right, as you face Durga, you see another pair of stone lions that guard the entrance to the **Bhatapur Art Gallery,** formerly the Royal Palace, which extends nearly the length of Durbar Square. Its collection of paintings, statuary, and thang-kas spans the 13th to 19th centuries. Most pieces depict Hindu and Buddhist tantric dieties. Statues of Hanuman Bhairav (a hybrid deity with four hands who stands on a demon) and Narsingha Narayan (a manifestation of Vishnu) stand behind the lions on either side of the door. *Admission: Rs. 3. Open Wed.–Mon. 10–5.*

The main entrance to the Royal Palace is through Nepal's most famous **Golden Gate** (actually copper and gold), which has in the center an image of the goddess Taleju, with three heads and numerous arms. It was constructed in 1745 by King Ranjit Malla, who put the now-famous image of wrestlers along the bottom edge. Facing the gate is a bronze statue of King Bhupatindra Malla, seated with his hands together in a gesture of devotion to the goddess. To his right is the royal residence, the famous Durbar Hall, or Palace of 55 Windows, which was constructed in 1427. Renovated in the 17th century, each balcony has carved windows that are increasingly more ornate at each ascending level. The wood carvings are considered the best in Nepal.

Walk through the Golden Gate to the entrance of **Taleju Chowk.** Inside the courtyard (closed to non-Hindus) is the **Taleju Temple.** Look for a wood pole in the open area. During Dassan Festivities, the army sacrifices 108 water buffalo—each one killed with one strike of the knife. The blood is given to the goddess; the meat is distributed to government employees.

Return to Durbar Square and look for two large bells. The smaller of the two is the **Bell of the Barking Dogs.** Its ring triggers croons from canines. Hemmed in by the bells is the **Vatsala Temple,** dedicated to Shiva and constructed in 1737. Behind the Vatsala Temple is the oldest temple in Bhaktapur, the two-story **Pashupatinath Temple,** which some historians claim was constructed in 1492, others say 1682. It is a replica of the famous Pashupatinath Temple in Kathmandu.

Head down a short street behind the Pashupatinath to **Taumadhi Tole** (Taumadhi Square), dominated by the tallest temple in Nepal—the **Nyatapola**—built in 1708 and one of the finest examples of Nepal's pagoda-style temples. Five platforms lead up to the temple with its five-tier roof. On each platform stands a set of guardians, with each pair supposedly 10 times stronger than the pair below. At the bottom are the pair of famous wrestlers, Jaya and Pata, who were 10 times stronger than ordinary men. The deity enshrined inside, the tantri goddess Siddhi Lakshmi, is the strongest of all. Since the temple was never officially inaugurated, its doors have never been opened.

The large **Bhairavanath Temple,** dedicated to Bhairav, is also on Taumadhi Tole. It's worshiped by Hindus and Buddhists. Constructed in stages from 1617 to 1718, it is often the scene of sacrifices. Don't be surprised if you see animal heads and inflated intestines hanging from its beams.

Head north from Taumadhi Tole back to the edge of Durbar Square; then turn right and see the **Dattatreya Square,** which contains buildings with intricately carved windows. The Peacock Windows, carved in 1492, which grace the **Pujari Math** Hindu monastery are considered among the finest examples of Newari wood carving. Pujari Math stands beside the three-story **Dattatreya Temple.** A legend asserts that the wood for this temple came from the trunk of a single tree in 1458. This date makes it one of the oldest temples in the valley. Statues standing out front are the famous Bhaktapur wrestlers. On the opposite side from Pujari Math is the **Brass and Bronze Museum,** which houses a collection of Nepalese brass and bronze work dating from the 18th century. *Admission: Rs. 3. Open Wed.–Mon. 10–5.*

Excursion from Kathmandu to Dakshin Kali

A trip to Dakshin Kali is best taken by hired car with driver; the cost is about $25 and you should plan two hours for the trip. The best times to visit the temple are Tuesday or Saturday morning. **Dakshin Kali,** 22 kilometers (14 miles) south of Kathmandu, is dedicated to Kali, the black goddess of destruction, and was built 300 years ago by a Malla king whose people were dying from a cholera epidemic. In a dream, Kali told him to build a temple for her in Dakshin, south of his kingdom, and then to sacrifice 108 buffalo. The king obeyed Kali's command, and the epidemic ended.

A sacrifice at Dakshin Kali is a highly charged event. Follow the lane from the hillside parking area past stalls selling Nepali fast food, including *khuwa* (sweet milk-and-cheese curd served on a large leaf); vendors offering handicrafts and garlands; and, no doubt, at least one praying Shivite sadhu in an orange dhoti, his face smeared with ash. Go under an arch and take steps leading down to a bridge that crosses over a stream. From here, you see two groups of pilgrims—men and women—lining up for the temple, plus numerous others bathing, picnicking, and washing their animals by the stream.

The temple is designed as a female tantric triangle, point aimed at the ground. Lion figures, vehicles of the goddess, guard the temple. A Bhairav idol stands under the canopy. On the side wall is a Ganesh idol. On the left side of the main temple entrance is the idol Dakshin Kali, with eight arms, lifting her body onto Shiva, who lies motionless.

The priest, nearly hidden, sits inside the inner sanctum and sprinkles holy water on each animal as it's presented to him. The temple butcher grabs the squawking animal, usually a chicken or rooster, walks over to the image of Kali and Shiva on the side wall, and lops off the head. Blood drenches the statue red. He hands the headless creature to its owner and dabs a speck of its blood onto his own forehead, sanctifying himself. In front of the temple, in the midst of the ruckus and surging crowds, holy men sitting under a covered pavilion read aloud from holy scriptures.

Excursion from Kathmandu to Changu Narayan

Changu Narayan is 13 kilometers (8 miles) west of Kathmandu. The excursion will take three hours if you travel by taxi. You can also do a delightful day walk to Changu Narayan from Bhaktapur (*see* Outdoor Adventures, above).

This excursion requires a 20-minute walk up a steep hill to great vistas and the site of **Changu Narayan,** a Hindu temple complex set in a courtyard and dedicated to Narayan (Vishnu). Many call it the most beautiful group of temples in Kathmandu Valley.

Historians believe the original temple was constructed in the 3rd or 4th century and restored in 1708 after a fire. Changu Narayan also celebrates Garuda, "Changu" in Nepali. Once when Garuda was fighting with a snake-god who prevented his son from worshiping Vishnu, Vishnu intervened to restore peace. To prove his friendship, the snake wrapped himself around Garuda's neck. Vishnu jumped aboard, and the three of them flew off to this hill, where a statue of the trio remains.

In the courtyard, elephants flank the entrance to the two-story temple. Oil lamps and bells hang from the lower tiled roof. Birds are perched on each corner. Roof struts are carved with colorfully painted deities, animals, and erotic images. The finely wrought portal has a gilded overhead torana depicting Vishnu with his consorts. His symbols—conch shell, lotus, disc, and mace—appear repeatedly. A 5th- or 6th-century statue of Garuda kneels out front.

Nearby is the sole surviving monument from the reign of the Licchavis—a stone pillar with an inscription that dates to the 4th century. To the left of the temple stands the black statue commemorating the legendary flight—an image duplicated on Nepal's Rs. 10 note. Finally, notice the sculpture of Vishnu in all his incarnations—one of the finest examples of 6th-century art in the subcontinent.

Excursion from Kathmandu to Dhulikhel

Numbers in the margin correspond with points of interest on the Nepal map.

For the best view of the northeastern Himalayas, including 12 peaks over 6,098 meters (20,000 feet), head east to **Dhulikhel** in the foothills of Panchkhal Valley, 34 kilometers (21 miles) east of Kathmandu. Hire a car with driver. The cost for a half-day trip is about $25. You drive along the Chinese Highway that leads to Tibet, passing by Bhaktapur and through the village of Banepa, a former city-kingdom.

Once you climb a low pass, you enter the valley and the village of Dhulikhel, with a main square surrounded by temples. You can stay at the **Dhulikhel Mountain Resort.** Thatched cottages (two doubles in each) have mountain views or overlook lovely gardens and lawns. There's no electricity—only candlelight—a romantic touch. *Reservations: Box 3203, Durbar Marg, Kathmandu, tel. 220031. 26 rooms with bath (shower). Facilities: good multicuisine restaurant, bar, cultural programs on request; arrangements for trekking, camping, rafting, hikes. AE. Expensive ($60–$100), including full board.*

Pokhara

㉗ Until the mid-1900s **Pokhara** bustled only in the winter, when Tibetans from the north arrived with their mule trains to barter salt and raw yak wool for grain. In 1959, after the Chinese seized Tibet, their route was closed. But by then, new arrivals had discovered the valley.

Though the advent of tourism sped up the arrival of electricity, an airport, new roads, and improved social services, it also increased the cost of necessities for local villagers. The creation of teahouses on popular trekking routes also made trekking too easy by eliminating the need for camping gear and food portage. Trails are now overburdened.

Visitors who want to trek near Pokhara should heed the advice of conservationists and avoid Annapurna, especially during the peak season. Consider a new destination: At press time, the **㉘** government had removed the restrictions on trekking in **Dolpo,** northwest of Pokhara. An ancient kingdom and the site of the sacred Crystal Mountain, it is a land of deep river gorges and jagged, barren peaks and the home of Buddhists who ride ponies and herd yak and sheep. To visit this area, contact a travel agency listed in Before You Go to Nepal, above, or Before You Go to the Himalayas, Chapter 1.

Addresses and Numbers

Tourist Information Nepal's **Tourist Office** (across from the airport, tel. 28) is open Sunday–Friday 10–5. Also visit **Check List Service** (at the airport, tel. 253), open Sunday–Friday 10–5.

Emergencies The nearest embassies are in Kathmandu. Turn to your hotel for the name of a reliable doctor. As a last resort, Pokhara has two hospitals: Gandaki Zonal Hospital (Ramghat, tel. 67) and Shining Hospital (northern edge of Pokhara, tel. 111). In Jomsom (*see* the Around Annapurna trek, below), the government has a small clinic.

Travel Agencies For outdoor adventures contact **Himalayan Horizons** and **Pokhara Pony Treks** (near the airport). For excursions by car, make arrangements through the recommended hotels.

Bookstores Small shops near Phewa Lake sell new and secondhand English-language books.

Banks **Rastriya Banijva Bank Exchange Counter** at Ratnapuri is open daily 7–7.

Post Office Post offices are at **Pardi** and near the **Mahendra Bridge** and are open Sunday–Friday 10–5.

Arriving and Departing

By Plane
Airports and Airline
From Kathmandu, **RNAC** (in Pokhara, tel. 40) makes two daily flights to Pokhara (year-round) and one weekly winter flight to Jomsom (north of Annapurna and gateway to Dolpo). Reserve your ticket in advance. Reconfirm 72 hours before departure; arrive at the airport 90 minutes in advance. Airport tax for each departure is Rs. 25.

Between Airport and City
The airport is on the southern edge of Pokhara. A taxi to most hotels is about Rs. 45. Hotel New Crystal offers a free shuttle service.

From the Jomsom airstrip, you will walk to the beginning of your trek.

By Hired Car with Driver
The cost of a two-night excursion by car with driver from Kathmandu to Pokhara costs about $175 round-trip. For longer trips, expect to pay an additional $60 per day. Hire a car only from a recommended travel agency in Kathmandu (*see* above) or from your hotel in Pokhara (*see* below).

By Taxi
A taxi costs about Rs. 1,050 per day.

Getting Around

By Taxi
Taxis are unmetered. Ask your hotel for reasonable fares.

By Bicycle
Bicycles cost Rs. 20 per day. Flat stretches and quiet streets make pedaling easy. Biking into the hilly valley is more rigorous (*see* Outdoor Adventures, below).

By Pony
See Outdoor Adventures, below.

Outdoor Adventures

Highly recommended adventures are indicated by a star ★.

★ **Biking:** Himalayan Mountain Bikes (Box 2769, Kamal Pokhari, Kathmandu, tel. 413632 or 418733) offers mountain bike trips combined with trekking around Pokhara Valley and Annapurna. Arrange before you depart.

Boating: Paddle around Phewa Lake.

Fishing: Fish for trout along Mardi Khola River, east of Pokhara. No license required; bring equipment.

★ Hikes: *Sarankot:* Head to the hilltop Bhindyabasani Temple in Pokhara and follow the trail through rural villages to Sarankot, the ruins of an 18th-century fort, with beautiful mountain views. Plan for about eight hours round-trip; bring a picnic lunch.

★ *Begnas and Rupa lakes:* Drive to the village of Sisuwa, 15 kilometers (9 miles) east of Pokhara and hike through Nepali hamlets to the village of Panchbhaiya, with views of the Himalayas and the two beautiful lakes in a tropical valley. Plan six hours and bring a picnic lunch.

Hot Springs: From November to May, trek about a week (*see* Trekking, below) or take a two-day pony ride to the base of Macchapuchhre and enjoy hot springs at Diprang Bridge.

★ **Horseback Riding:** Contact Pokhara Pony Trek (Box 35, Pokhara, tel. 253) to arrange for numerous tours by horse with guide around Pokhara Valley. You can also sign up for year-round scheduled-departure tours that last from a half day to six days. For excursions over three days, make all arrangements before you depart.

Swimming: Swim only in tame meandering rivers and at Begnas and Rupa lakes.

★ **Trekking (up to a week):** *Royal Trek:* This four-day trip, designed by Tiger Tops International for Britain's Prince Charles, goes around the lush rim of Pokhara valley and concentrates on quaint hilltop villages, with great views of Himalayan giants. At the end of the trek, you descend to Rupa Lake and then return to Pokhara.

President's Trek: This four-day trek, created for Jimmy Carter by the same outfit, starts south of Pokhara. You climb lush slopes to the village of Bhumdi, head through forests to a mountain ridge, and then go to Panchase Lekh (Black Mountain)—a sacred Hindu destination that offers the best views in Pokhara. You descend to the Harpan Khola River (good swimming), then return to Pokhara. Both treks occur November–May.

★ *Siklis:* This six-day Tiger Mountains trek is demanding, with lots of up-and-down climbing, but you meet few trekkers and get fabulous views of all the great peaks. You pass through farming land and tiny settlements to a mountain ridge above the village of Kalikathan. Descend to a lush valley and the Madi Khola River, then climb through a scrub forest to the village of Thak. The next two days you climb to an altitude of 2,250 meters (7,380 feet), passing through rhododendron forests to Siklis village, populated by the Buddhist Gurung. You descend through forests and mountain pastures to Pokhara.

★ *Macchapuchhre:* This seven-day trek also involves rugged climbing. You head north of Pokhara through rhododendron forests to high pastures, altitude 3,660 meters (12,000 feet), until you reach the base of Macchapuchhre, at 6,997 meters (22,950 feet). The return route leads to hot springs at Diprang Bridge, then through the rugged Seti Khola River's gorge back to Pokhara. These last treks are made November–May.

Trekking (over a week): *Around Annapurna:* To trek in the Annapurna Sanctuary, you must pay a Rs. 200 entrance fee at the Pokhara Airport or through your tour operator. This rigorous 24- to 26-day trip (Mar.–Nov.) takes you around the massif. Most trekking companies start the hike at the old city of **Gorkha,** the site of the 18th-century palace of King Prithvi Narayan Shah, who was responsible for the unification of Nepal. From here, you walk through the Marsyangdi Valley, threaded by a river and terraced with rice fields and mango groves. The trail winds up slopes to hilltop Buddhist Gurung villages. Following the Khudi Khola River's canyon, you climb to old villages that are Tibetan in appearance. At times the trail is gouged out of rock; then suddenly you veer into a forest that opens into a mountain-top meadow before you descend into the Manangbhot Valley, hemmed in at the south by numerous mountains, including the Annapurnas. To the west lies the glacier-fed Tilicho Lake. From here, it's an arduous climb to the Thorong La Pass, at 5,396 meters (17,700 feet), where you may see the *bharal* (blue sheep) scampering along distant cliffs. From the pass, you see the entire Annapurna Range and the Dolpo district to the west, before descending to Muktinath.

This 2,000-year-old sacred grove is revered by Buddhists and Hindus who flock here in August to the small Jawala Mai Temple, dedicated to Vishnu and enshrining a mysterious water that burns with a blue flame caused by natural gas seepage. On a rock north of the shrine, Buddhists claim that footprints imbedded into the surface belong to Guru Padmasambhava who introduced Buddhism to Tibet. From here, it's on to the Kali Gondaki Gorge, home of the Thakalis who used to control the salt trade route between Nepal and Tibet. You enter forests and bamboo groves and pass rice paddies as the trek comes to an end.

Annapurna Sanctuary Trek: This moderately difficult 14- to 16-day trek (Mar.–Nov.) avoids high altitudes but keeps you surrounded by mountains. Our recommended companies try hard to avoid the over-used teahouse route; they start the trip south of Pokhara, then head to the Panchase Lekh (*see* President's Trek, above) before joining the main route that heads through rhododendron forests to Pon Hill, with its majestic views of Macchapuchhre, Annapurna, Dhaulagiri, and the Kali Gondaki Valley. You cross the Deorali Pass, at 2,522 meters (8,275 feet), which leads to the Kyumnu Khola River (good swimming) and the last village before you enter the sacred sanctuary—home of the Hindu goddesses Annapurna and Gangapurna. You climb to the Hinko Cave, then on to the Macchapuchhre Base Camp and deeper into the Annapurna Sanctuary. You descend through rhododendron and bamboo forests to the Madi Khola Valley and Ghandrung, a wealthy Gurung village. After Ghandrung, it's a steep descent to the Madi Khola River, then a steep climb up to the village of Landrung before you head down through meadows and back to Pokhara.

★ *Dhorpatan:* This moderate 23-day trek (Mar.–Nov.) is an excellent alternative to "Around Annapurna." You get views of all the great mountains and walk along a beautiful ridge leading into Dhorpatan. The trek begins at Sarankot, above Pokhara, where you follow the ridge northwest to the village of Naudanda. Sharing the trail with mule trains, you head through Gurung villages, then descend into a pine forest and follow the Modi Khola River. A moderate up-and-down trail leads into the Kali Gondaki and Mayangi Khola valleys, with lovely river campsites. Again, the trail climbs sharply, taking you past hamlets still unaccustomed to foreigners to the Jaja La Ridge, at 3,414 meters (11,200 feet). You descend into the Dhorpatan Valley—alpine beautiful with shepherd's huts huddled around its rim and the Dhauligiri Range in front of you. This is the year-round home of Tibetan refugees, the summer home of Nepali shepherds. From Dhorpatan, you proceed to the mountains and glaciers that drain into the Gusung Khola. You climb another pass, 4,573 meters (15,000 feet) high, where you may see bharal and pheasants. To return to Pokhara, the trek follows the concluding days of the Annapurna Sanctuary trek.

★ *Macchapucchre Sanctuary:* This 14-day trek (Mar.–Nov.) is also a good alternative. From Sarankot, you climb through beautiful grazing country, retracing the end of the Annapurna Sanctuary trek until the middle of the second day. Then you leave the main trail and make a steep climb before you descend into the Mardi Khola Valley and wade across the Mardi River.

To get to Odane Hill requires a difficult climb to a ridge and forests of rhododendron and, finally, great views of Annapurna and Macchapucchre and a glimpse of Dhaulagiri. The next day is rough. You travel a narrow trail along a gorge to the sanctuary, at 4,054 meters (13,300 feet)—an open plateau, with astonishing views of the south side of the Annapurna Range. You relax and recoup for two days, then climb to 4,634 meters (15,200 feet) to see the Macchapucchre Glaciers. From here, you start your descent; you pass scattered hamlets, then reach Diprang Bridge, where you can jump into hot springs before heading on to Puran Chaur, just outside Pokhara.

★ *Lamjung Himal:* This difficult 14-day trek (year-round) starts after a day-long arduous drive to Phalesangu village. You trek along the Marsyangdi River, picking up a trail that goes through farms and villages before you start the climb up slopes and through forests to the Buddhist Gurung village of Ghanpokhara. You hike along a ridge through rhododendron and bamboo forests filled with birds. The next day, when you climb up to the Telbrong Danga Ridge, is tough, with great views that stay with you until you cross the Namun Pass, at 3,506 meters (11,500 feet). You descend through forests, past waterfalls, then climb to the Rambrong Danda Ridge, with excellent views of the Annapurna Range. From here, you climb to Thulo Lake, at 4,024 meters (13,200 feet), then descend a mountain-goat trail to Jagat, the first village you see after nine days of trekking. You walk through the Madi Valley, with great views of Dhauligiri, before you reach the Gurung village of Syang. Two days later you reach Pokhara.

Dining

All restaurants are casual and multicuisine, unless noted. From October to March, make dinner reservations. Highly recommended restaurants are indicated by a star ★. Prices are per person, including taxes and excluding drinks and service.

Fishtail Restaurant. It's cozy, with a fireplace in the middle of the circular room. The bar is nearby. Though waiters push the fixed menu, you can eat à la carte. *Fishtail Lodge, tel. 20071. AE, DC, MC, V. Open 7–9:30, noon–2, 7–9:30. Moderate ($5–$10).*

★ **New Crystal Restaurant.** On the second floor of the hotel, this handsome restaurant serves a good mixed grill, chicken butter masala (chicken in a spicy tomato sauce), and mixed vegetable curry. *Nagdhunga, tel. 227932. AE, DC, MC, V. Open 7–9:30, noon–2:30, 7–9:30. Moderate ($5–$10).*

★ **Solo.** Solo is unpretentious, with a few antique Buddhist urns and thang-kas and good views of the mountains. Try the tasty soups and curries. *Dragon Hotel, Pardi, tel. 20391. No credit cards. Open 7–10, noon–3, 6–10. Moderate ($5–$10).*

★ **Himalchuli Restaurant.** A spacious *khar ko jhupadi* (thatched hut), Himalchuli is very informal. The menu is hearty multinational fare, including pizza and Mexican cuisine. *Pardi Damside, Phewa Lake, tel. 20189. AE, V. Open Sept.–June daily, 5:30 AM–11 PM; June–Sept., daily 7 AM–10 PM.*

Lodging

Highly recommended lodgings are indicated by a star ★. Prices are for a standard double room or cottage, including taxes and excluding service charges.

★ **Pokhara Mountain Lodge.** At press time, Tiger Tops was starting construction of a Gurung-style village on a ridge east of Pokhara. The lodge will offer the amenities of other excellent Tiger Tops facilities (*see* Before You Go to Nepal, above, for the address). Projected opening is the end of 1990. *Very expensive (over $100).*

Dragon Hotel. In a quiet neighborhood away from the lake and center of town, modest Dragon Hotel is impeccable; the service is excellent and the rooms are simple. There are great views of the mountains from the roof terrace. *Box 15, Pardi, Lakeside, Pokhara, tel. 20391. 22 rooms with bath. Facilities: room service, restaurant, bar, cultural performances in season, air-conditioning, fans, car rental, foreign exchange and travel counter. No credit cards. Moderate ($25–$60).*

Fishtail Lodge. Space-age-style Fishtail Lodge is secluded in landscaped gardens on Phewa Lake island. The rooms are in modular units; the best ones have mountain views. *Box 10, Pokhara, tel. 20071, or reserve through Hotel de L'Annapurna or Utell International (see Hotel de L'Annapurna in Kathmandu, above). 50 rooms with bath (shower). Facilities: air-conditioning, fans, restaurant, bar, cultural programs in season, travel and foreign exchange counter. AE, DC, MC, V. Moderate ($25–$60).*

★ **Pokhara View Point.** On a mountain spur about 15 minutes from the airport, this complex under construction (projected opening 1990), will offer privacy and views, plus a chance to stay in an impeccable clay-and-wood Gorkha-style cottage. *Reserve through Dragon Hotel (see above). About 4 cottages with bath. Facilities: to be announced. No credit cards. Moderate $25–$60.*

★ **Gurka Lodge.** Hidden on an interior lane, you have to search for this charming lodge in a lush garden. You'll likely be greeted by a water buffalo outside the gate. Clean, sparsely furnished rooms are in idyllic thatched cottages. *Lakeside, Pokhara, no phone. 3 rooms with bath. Facilities: restaurant. No credit cards. Inexpensive (under $25).*

Nightlife

Bars The best bar is at **Fishtail Lodge,** with its island setting. It's open daily 11–11.

Theater Four hotels sponsor nightly cultural programs (Oct.–Mar.): **Dragon Hotel** (tel. 20391 for details), **Fishtail Lodge** (6:30–7:30, Rs. 45 for nonguests), **New Hotel Crystal** (7–8 in the bar; Rs. 25), and **Hotel Mount Annapurna** (near the airport, tel. 20027 for details).

The Terai

Introduction

A trip south to the Terai takes you from the mountains to the heat of the Indo-Gangetic plains and groves of bamboo and banana trees jutting above rice paddies. The slow-paced Terai is home to the Tharu, former nomads who migrated from the Thar desert in India during the 12th century to escape conversion to the Moslem religion. First the women came, accompanied by male servants who served as helpmates and later became the women's lovers. Today women still rule the roost. Even the man designated the village chieftain must bow to their power. When his wife serves him his meal, she kicks it to him across the mud floor.

Their dark complexions make the Tharu easy to recognize. Many of the men wear a loincloth—ancient garb that contrasts with the modern black umbrellas that shield their exposed bodies from the sun. The women usually wear white saris and heavy silver ornaments on the ankles, wrists, and necks; gold adorns the ears and nose. Women also tattoo their legs. In the past, these markings kept away Moslems, offended by the practice. Now it's primarily an artistic embellishment. Many Tharu also wear around the neck or wrist a white thread—symbol of purity—and a black thread—to ward off evil spirits.

In the Terai, you can visit the **Royal Chitwan National Park,** southwest of Kathmandu, and the **Royal Bardia Wildlife Reserve** in the extreme west of Nepal. The town of **Lumbini** is midway between the two parks, a destination with minimal lodging but important cultural significance—the birthplace of Sakyamuni, the Historic Buddha. To the extreme northeast is the Arun River, an excellent rafting alternative to Trisuli and Seti Khola. Travelers who head to Chitwan in December should try to see the annual five-day elephant polo match held at Tiger Tops. For details, write to the World Elephant Polo Association (Box 242, Kathmandu) or contact Tiger Tops (*see* Travel Agencies under Important Addresses and Numbers, below).

Addresses and Numbers

Tourist Information — Three **Tourist Information Centers** are in the Terai, none at convenient locations: **Birgunj** (tel. 2083); **Janakpur** (no phone); **Bhairawa** (on the way to Lumbini, tel. 304).

Emergencies — The nearest embassies are in Kathmandu. Small government hospitals are at **Bharatpur** (near Chitwan), **Nepalganj** (near Lumbini and the approach to Bardia), and **Biratnagar** (near the Arun River). If you're staying at Chitwan or Bardia, turn to your lodge for assistance.

Travel Agencies — **Lodges** in Chitwan and Bardia can make all travel arrangements. **Tiger Tops** runs a summer package to Tharu Village in Chitwan that includes an excellent day excursion to Lumbini, (*see* Tiger Tops in Dining and Lodging, Chitwan, below).

Banks — There are banks in Nepalganj and other towns. They are out of the way if you are going to a game park. Bring sufficient rupees.

Arriving and Departing

By Plane
Airports and Airline

From Kathmandu, **RNAC** flies daily to Maghauli (Chitwan) and Bhairawa (approach to Lumbini). RNAC makes over 10 weekly flights to Nepalganj (Bardia), and five weekly flights to Tumlingtar (gateway to Arun River). On trips to Bardia, once you arrive at Nepalganj, you can get to Tiger Tops by jeep or raft (*see* Outdoor Adventures, below).

By Hired Car with Driver

For trips to Chitwan, the recommended lodges have numerous packages that offer transportation by car or raft. (*See* Outdoor Adventures, below.) The recommended tour operators in Kathmandu arrange an overnight excursion to Lumbini for about $160. In high season, make all arrangements before you depart. All recommended lodges at Chitwan offer packages that cover the cost of surface transportation.

Outdoor Adventures

Highly recommended adventures are indicated by a star ★.

★ **Biking:** Himalayan Mountain Bikes (Box 2769, Kamal Pokhari, Kathmandu, tel. 413632 or 418733) offers bike trips in the Terai, with a jungle safari. Amadablam Trekking (Box 3035, Lazimpat, Kathmandu, tel. 410219) is planning to arrange similar trips. Write for details.

Fishing: Fish for *mahseer* (Himalayan river fish) along the Karnali river. Equipment available through Tiger Tops.

★ **Rafting:** *Chitwan:* To raft to Chitwan, lodges offer a one- to three-day trip (Sept.–May; Tiger Tops also rafts in the summer). From the Kaligondaki River, south of Kathmandu, you leave the forested hills and enter the Terai plains and the Seti Khola River. You pass Hindu shrines and villages, then float into the park to see wild animals.

Bardia: To raft from Nepalganj to Bardia (a three-day trip), you start at the Bheri River, with its rapids that lead to a narrow gorge, broken by an occasional valley with small villages. On the final day, you reach the confluence of the Bheri and Karnali rivers and then enter a final narrow canyon that opens into the Terai and the wildlife reserve.

Arun River: This river in the east has just opened for rafting, with runs rated from moderate to difficult and trips averaging about five days. The tropical terrain is lush and remote (Oct.–June).

For all trips, make arrangements in advance. In Chitwan or Bardia, you can arrange your trip through a lodge in the sanctuaries, or if you prefer to tent, some outdoor-adventure outfits now offer rafting trips with their own private campsites (*see* Before You Go to Nepal, above, or Before You Go to the Himalayas, Chapter 1).

Swimming: Swim at the game parks, but watch out for the freshwater crocodiles.

Royal Chitwan National Park

Bordering the Rapti River, the Royal Chitwan National Park was once the private playground and hunting preserve of

Nepal's rana prime ministers. In 1962 King Mahendra turned the area into a wildlife sanctuary. Only 22 tigers and 100 rhinoceros had survived the hunter's gun. Eleven years later, Chitwan was declared a national park. Today, it's closely guarded by armed forces who keep out poachers. Even the Tharu are restricted to one annual two-week harvesting of the elephant grass they use for thatching.

By 1987, 100 tigers and over 400 rhinoceros were spotted in the park. The sanctuary is also home to leopards and other jungle cats, elephants, buffalo, sloth bear, *gaur* (wild oxen), wild boar, langur and rhesus monkeys, freshwater dolphins, freshwater crocodiles, pythons, and king cobras, plus over 350 species of birds, including giant hornbills, peacocks, and eagles. Chitwan has been called the best sanctuary in Asia, and its excellent accommodations, beautiful vistas, and the splendid wildlife justify the claim.

The best way to explore the park is from a four-wheel-drive vehicle, on the back of an elephant, in a dugout canoe cruising quietly down the Rapti River, or from the cover of a *machan* (watchtower) built deep in the forest. Unlike Africa, where animals roam in herds, most of the protected species in Chitwan rarely move in large groups. The elusive tiger is a nocturnal hunter. Your best chance of a sighting is early morning or early evening, when numerous lodges arrange excursions. Also remember to wear neutral-color clothes.

Dining and Lodging To get the most of the park, you should stay a minimum of three days and two nights. Rates include full board (with a fixed multicuisine menu), elephant safaris, nature walks, birdwatching, canoeing, and jeep rides. All lodges have bars, but drinks are extra. Exceptions or additions are noted with each option. Highly recommended lodges are indicated by a star ★. Prices are per person in a standard double room, tent, or cottage, including taxes and excluding service charges. Most prices are very expensive (over $100 per person per night).

★ **Chitwan Jungle Lodge.** Nine kilometers (about 6 miles) inside the park and 4 kilometers (3 miles) from the river, this lodge offers a popular two-night package by road from Kathmandu or Pokhara for about $225 per person. You can also raft a day for an additional $50 per person. Stay in thatched clay huts with attractive furnishings. Swim in the nearby river. At night, you eat in a roundhouse and can attend lectures by naturalists or watch cultural programs. *Reservations: Box 1281, Durbar Marg, Kathmandu, tel. 410918. 22 rooms with bath (shower). AE. Closed June–Aug.*

Gaida Wildlife Camp. Also in the park, Gaida offers cottages and tents. Each thatched cottage, built on stilts, has two double rooms and verandas overlooking the Dungla River. The nearby lodge serves good food; the bar is well stocked. At night, you can attend cultural programs and wildlife lectures. Safari-style tents (cheaper) are located farther in the jungle. Gaida offers a three-day package ($250 per person) or a fourday package that includes one day of rafting (about $325 per person). *Reservations: Box 2056, Durbar Marg, Kathmandu, tel. 220940. 20 rooms with bath; 10 tents with nearby bath. AE, DC.*

Machan Wildlife Resort. You can stay in a shady grove in a mudand-timber cottage near an attractive lodge and small swimming pool or go deeper into the park and stay in a safari-style tent (cheaper) and eat your meals around a campfire. Machan offers the three-day package by road (about $225 per person), with an extra day of rafting (about $275). *Reservations: Box 3140, Durbar Marg, Kathmandu, tel. 222823. 15 rooms with bath, 10 tents with nearby bath. AE. Summer discount.*

★ **Tiger Tops.** Set deep within the park, Tiger Tops is the class act in Chitwan. You can stay in attractive rooms in the Jungle Lodge. (The best views are on the upper floor.) Or stay in an island-based fancy safari-style tent, with separate showers and bathrooms. Or stay in a typical mud hut in Tharu Village, just outside the park, and see Tharu cultural programs, observe the Tharu lifestyle, and enjoy a new swimming pool. You can also design a package that includes all three. Tiger Tops offers two special packages: a three-day deluxe rafting trip down to Chitwan (Oct.–May, $890 per person) and a five-day excursion with two days of rafting, two days at Tharu, and a trip to Lumbini (May–Sept., $770 per person). It also offers a three-day package from Kathmandu (by car or plane) and will make pickups from Pokhara. Reserve well in advance. *Reservations: Box 242, Durbar Marg, Kathmandu, tel. 222706 or through the Tiger Tops offices abroad (see Tour Groups in Before You Go to the Himalayas, Chapter 1). 20 rooms with bath in the lodge, 10 tents with nearby bath, 12 rooms with bath at Tharu. Cost for lodge: $250 per night; tented camp: $180; Tharu Village: $110. Camp and lodge are closed mid-June–mid-Sept. AE.*

Hotel Elephant Camp. At the edge of the park by the Rapti River, this modest resort has great service and a pleasant ambience. Individual thatched cottages are nicely decorated. The National Park Museum and its park elephants are nearby. You're also close to Tharu villages. Elephant Camp offers two three-day packages: by road from Kathmandu ($300) or with a day of rafting (slightly more expensive). *Box 78, Durbar Marg, Kathmandu, tel. 213976. About 12 cottages with bath (showers). No credit cards. Summer discount.*

Excursion from Chitwan to Lumbini Lumbini is 136 kilometers (83 miles) from Chitwan. You can arrange an excursion with Tiger Tops and do the trip in a day. You can also fly into Bhairawa or make a two-day car excursion to Lumbini from Kathmandu (use a recommended travel agent).

At this isolated spot near the Indian border, Lord Buddha was born around 563 BC. In 1895 a German archaeologist discovered an inscribed pillar honoring Lumbini as the birthplace of Sakyamuni, left behind by north India's Emperor Ashoka in 250 BC. The discovery triggered other archaeological excavations, currently assisted by the United Nations. Since then, Lumbini has become one of the holiest destinations for Buddhists.

Today Ashoka's pillar marks the formal Royal Garden at Lumbini as the birthplace of Siddhartha Gautama, the prince who later became Sakyamuni, the Enlightened One. Behind the pillar is the Maya Temple, a 3rd-century brick shrine, which honors the Buddha's mother, Maya Devi. Inside, fine stone carvings portray the birth of the Buddha. In the nearby brick *ghat* (temple tank), Maya Devi bathed before giving birth. Not far from these remains, foreign Buddhist sects have built *gompas* (monasteries) and shrines, including the Dharma Swami Maharaj Buddhavihar, a Tibetan monastery with a golden statue of the Buddha. In Bhairawa, two simple Western-style hotels offer reasonable but clean rooms with attached bathrooms and decent restaurants: Hotel Himalaya Inn and Lumbini Garden

Guest House. Both are inexpensive (under $25) and do not accept credit cards.

Royal Bardia Wildlife Reserve

In the western Terai, the Royal Bardia Wildlife Reserve is a vast stretch of *sal* (hardwood) forest. The Karnali River threads through it, bordered by Tharu villages. You can see black buck and swamp deer, wild boar, otters, monkeys, and many species of birds. The lucky will see wild elephants, wild boar, the solitary tiger, freshwater crocodiles, and freshwater dolphins.

Dining and Lodging Rates include full board, park activities, and taxes, but not alcoholic drinks or service charges. Prices are per person in a standard double room or tent and are very expensive (over $100).

Tiger Tops Karnali Lodge and Tented Camp. The lodge is on a grassy plain outside the jungle. The rooms have an attractive ethnic-style decor, and the attached bathrooms are modern. Tucked in the forest and overlooking the Karnali River, the tented camp (cheaper) has secluded safari-style tents. In both facilities, you can go on nature walks, take a jeep, ride an elephant, embark on a river cruise, visit Tharu villages, and go fishing. *Reservations: Box 242, Durbar Marg, Kathmandu, tel. 222706 or through the Tiger Tops offices abroad (see Tour Groups in Before You Go to the Himalayas, Chapter 1). 10 rooms with bath, 14 tents with nearby bath. AE.*

Everest and Northeast Nepal

㉝ Mt. Everest: Look at it from one angle and jagged pinnacles jut up like daggers and glaciers mirror the heavens; look at it from another direction and black rock contrasts with icy slopes and snow massifs. Wild animals roam craggy cliffs.

Sightings of Everest's most famous inhabitant, the Yeti, which means "wild man of the mountain" not "abominable snowman," date back to the 14th century when Asian travelers reported seeing enormous, hairy, foul-smelling creatures that attacked men, kidnapped women, and drank yak blood. Eric Shipton, the famous 20th-century mountaineer, took a photograph of his foot next to a gigantic snowprint with an extended big toe. Scientific expeditions have attempted to track the elusive Yeti, a far more difficult quest than climbing the 8,877-meter (29,108-foot) peak that is the creature's supposed home.

According to devout Buddhists, the successful ascent made by Sir Edmund Hillary and Tenzing Norgay was not the first. A shaman priest challenged Guru Padmasambhava (the 8th-century Indian mystic who brought Buddhism to Tibet) to a race to Everest's summit. The guru waited for the first rays of the sun, which carried him and his chair of wisdom to the top. The priest never appeared, lost en route astride his magical drums, now heard in the periodic claps of thunder that crash around the mountain—his drums calling out for their master. As for Padmasambhava, he left behind his chair as a symbol of power and casually ambled down the mountain.

When Hillary and Norgay made their ascent, they paid their respects to this giant, called Sagarmatha (Mother Goddess of the Universe) by the Nepalese and Chomolungma (Mother Goddess of the Winds) by the Tibetans. Norgay, a Buddhist, buried a small parcel of sweets as an offering. Hillary added a crucifix.

Today's climbers and trekkers have left behind less touching souvenirs. In 1987 Sir Edmund announced, "Everest is a junkpile." Fully 75% of the forest cover at the base of the mountain is gone. Many local Sherpas, who used to revere the trees, now prefer the money they make selling bundled firewood to trekkers. By the year 2,000, if the current rate of deforestation persists, visitors to Sagarmatha will see not the mountain's massive forest mantle, but barren slopes.

A trip to Everest means accommodations only in trekker's huts, dormitories, or the lodges used by private trekking outfits—unless the classy and very expensive (over $100) Everest View Hotel near Namche Bazaar is reopened (check with your travel agent). When you choose your trek, the agency will determine where you will stay and will supply all basic food and tents and, most likely, sleeping bags. Kathmandu and Namche are the best places to buy extra supplies. Other villages have minimal provisions. Trekkers heading into the Everest area, declared the Sagarmatha National Park in 1976, pay a Rs. 250 entrance fee at the Visitors Center in Namche. Numerous trekkers now crowd the route to Everest from Lukla during the fall, so plan this trip for between December and March. Many trekking outfits also offer a trip to Sherpa villages and monasteries; the same advice applies.

33 Or, consider a new option. At press time, the Nepalese government made available remote, unspoiled **Mt. Kanchenjunga,** the third-highest peak in the world. To visit this area to the east of Everest, you must trek with an authorized trekking agent (*see* the outdoor adventure outfits listed in Before You Go to Nepal, above, and in Before You Go to the Himalayas, Chapter 1).

Addresses and Numbers

Tourist Information There are no sources of information in the Everest area. Get information in Kathmandu.

Emergencies The nearest embassies are in Kathmandu. The hospital Sir Edmund Hillary founded, primarily for villagers, is at **Kunde.** The **Himalayan Rescue Association** has a clinic at Pheriche (open Oct. to May), and the government runs small hospitals at **Jiri** and **Phaplu.**

Banks Bring sufficient rupees from Kathmandu. There are few banks in this area.

Arriving and Departing

By Plane
Airport and Airline From Kathmandu, **RNAC** makes three daily winter flights to Lukla (near Everest and Khumbu) and two weekly winter flights to Taplejung (gateway to Kanchenjunga). Book all flights early. Reconfirm at least 72 hours before departure and arrive at the airport 90 minutes in advance. Foreigners must pay Rs. 25 airport tax.

Outdoor Adventures

Highly recommended adventures are indicated by a star ★.

Biking: Contact Himalayan Mountain Bikes (Box 2769, Kamal Pokhari, Kathmandu, tel. 413632 or 418733 for details about mountain bike trips combined with trekking around Everest.

Climbing and Mountaineering: Expeditions to Everest are booked until 1991. If you're determined to climb a peak in this area, contact the recommended special-interest tour operators who offer scheduled-departure expeditions, usually to Island Peak, altitude 5,600 meters (18,368 feet), southeast of Everest (*see* Before You Go to Nepal, above, or Before You Go to the Himalayas, Chapter 1).

Trekking: For all treks in the Everest area, you must be physically fit and prepared for high altitudes, especially if you fly into Lukla. Recommended trekking season is October to May.

★ **Trekking (up to a week):** *Around Namche:* The shortest trek you can take in the Everest area is about seven days and starts from Lukla. You head through terraced hillsides to Namche Bazaar, at 6,987 meters (11,270 feet), a thriving Sherpa market village, then pass through the riverside Phunki village, with its water-powered prayer wheel, and head up to the Thyangboche Monastery, an important Buddhist center, under renovation, in Khumbu. From its setting, surrounded by pine and backed by the sacred Ama Dablam peak, altitude 6,858 meters (22,494 feet), the views of Everest, Lhotse, and Nuptse are worth every photo. During November and December, the lamas, members of the Nyingmapa (Old Sect), perform the colorful Mani Rimdu masked dance that depicts Guru Padmasambhava's triumph over the Bon religion, which predated Buddhism. From here, head on to the 300-year-old Pangboche Monastery, the oldest in Khumbu. Circle back through Khumjung village, at 3,780 meters (12,400 feet), which has a monastery with relics that include a sacred yeti scalp, then pass through rhododendron forests that lead to Namche.

★ **Trekking (over a week):** *Sherpa Villages:* Popular in the autumn, this moderately difficult 10- to 24-day trek goes through a series of villages around Khumbu Valley. The accent is on culture and monasteries, yet the views are spectacular. Longer versions take you on a wider circle, which allows for more variety of terrain, yet the altitude never exceeds 4,115 meters (13,500 feet). This trek is less crowded after the autumn peak season.

★ *"Walk in"* from Jiri to the Everest base. This is the best trek—20 to 30 days, depending on side trips. You start in the Hindu-Buddhist world of Nepal's hill people. From their lush verdant terrain of rhododendron forests and bamboo groves, you cross the Kharubas Pass, at 2,713 meters (8,900 feet), and descend to a region dominated by Buddhism. Villages have gompas, mani walls (to protect the village), and prayer flags. At Junbesi, you can visit Nepal's largest monastery, Thubten Chholing, the present seat of the Tulshi Rimpoche, who was one of two abbots who presided over the Rongbuk Gompa in Tibet until he fled the Chinese invasion. Cross the Tragsindo La Pass, at 3,072 meters (10,076 feet), and then Khari La Pass, at about 3,900 meters (12,792 feet), which leads to Lukla and Namche and offers good views of Everest and surrounding peaks. Now it's on to the Everest Base Camp. The mountains are rough and dark, with upper slopes caked with glaciers and snow. You climb steep ridges, with the Buddhist mantra "Om Mani Padme Hum" ("Hail to the jewel in the lotus") carved into the surfaces. You traverse the Changri Glacier, strewn with rubble and frozen daggers of ice, then head higher into yak grazing lands. Local people, accustomed to the altitude, pass by with ease as you trudge along. Kala Pattar, or "Black Rock," 5,545 meters (18,188 feet), provides a close-up view of the famous peak—the moment to remember. The entire South Face, the West Ridge, and the pass leading into Tibet loom defiantly before you. From here you circle back to Lukla.

Lukla to Everest Base Camp: Besides the "walk-in," many companies also offer a 20-day trek from Lukla to the base.

Lukla to Gokyo Peak and Everest Base Camp: This 20-day trek follows a trail along the Dudh Kosi River to its source near the Gokyo Lakes. From here, you climb up Gokyo Peak, 5,483 meters (17,984 feet), and have wonderful views of nearby giants, Cho Oyu, Everest, Lhotse, and Makalu. After crossing the Chyugima La Pass, at 5,422 meters (17,783 feet), you head into the Everest Base Camp and on to Kala Pattar.

All these treks are popular in the autumn; however, the low-altitude regions of the "walk-in" up to Lukla don't see as much traffic.

Jumla and Northwest Nepal

Because it's in an area long closed to foreigners, not many have ㉞ heard of **Jumla** or Nepal's largest body of water, Lake Rara, tucked in the northwest. This lake, at an elevation of 2,980 meters (9,777 feet), is the showpiece of Lake Rara National Park, considered by many the prettiest park in Nepal. The lake is idyllic, encircled by pine slopes, with white peaks in the distance.

The distant Himalayas form a ridge—a natural barrier that guards what was the summer capital of the Mallas, who ruled Nepal in the 14th century. The land is reminiscent of the American West, with wide rough valleys dotted with scrub and occasional huddled settlements of houses with flat stone roofs. This area, compared to the rest of Nepal, is sparsely populated. Its people are unaccustomed to foreigners. There are no tourist hotels or restaurants, few phones, and few roads. You will be camping exclusively. Once trekkers start coming in large numbers, though, this situation will change.

Addresses and Numbers

Tourist Information Get all your information in Kathmandu; there are no services here.

Emergencies The nearest embassies are in Kathmandu. The government has a small hospital at **Jumla** and a dispensary in **Gumgarhi** at Rara Lake.

Banks   Bring sufficient rupees from Kathmandu. There are no convenient places to change money in this area.

Arriving and Departing

By Plane   RNAC makes two weekly flights to the Jumla airstrip from
Airport and Airline   Kathmandu and four weekly flights from Nepalganj. Book all flights early. Reconfirm at least 72 hours before departure; arrive at the airport 90 minutes in advance. Foreigners must pay Rs. 25 airport tax.

Outdoor Adventures

This is such a new destination that adventures are just being developed. Highly recommended adventures are indicated by a star ★.

★   **Hot Springs:** Tatopani, three hours west of Jumla, has good hot springs.

Trekking: Though you can get some provisions in Jumla, you should bring in supplies from Kathmandu or Nepalganj.

Trekking (over a week): *Lake Rara National Park:* This fairly easy eight-day trek with two overnights at the lake takes you to the park and back to Jumla. You follow the Chaudbise Khola River, pass through pine forests, and head up to the Ghurchi Lagna Pass, at 3,545 meters (11,627 feet), with good views of the snow-covered Patrasi range. You cross footbridges, one suspended 2,743 meters (8,997 feet) above the water. You traverse steep slopes until you reach the hilltop hamlet of Jhari, at 2,500 meters (8,200 feet), where you see the lake spread out in the valley below. On the return trip to Jumla, the highlight is the climb to the top of Ghorosain, altitude 5,351 meters (17,548 feet), with good views of much of Nepal's northwest. From here, you head to the village of Sinja, where you can visit a temple on a hill and the ruins of Lamathada, the old capital of the Mallas. The last two days are for the descent into Jumla.

★   **Trekking and Rafting:** *Trek to Karnali River* and *Run to Bardia Wildlife Reserve:* This 20-day trip (6 days of trekking, 12 days of rafting, 2 days in the Royal Bardia Reserve in the Terai) begins in Jumla. You follow the Tila River west past mud houses surrounded by rice paddies. At Tatopani, three hours west of Jumla, you can enjoy hot springs. You walk through rhododendron forests, follow a ridge over a pass, altitude 1,212 meters (4,000 feet), and descend to Banjkot village at the confluence of the Tila and Karnali rivers. From here, you run the rapids to Bardia, camping on beaches, swimming in the water, and visiting temples and villages not far from the bank. The landscape turns tropical, with cultivated paddies, terraced slopes, and occasional Tharu villages and their thatched clay homes. (For a description of your destination, Bardia, *see* the Terai section, above). This trip is best from mid-November to mid-December or mid-February to June.

Langtang Valley and Helambu

㉟ Glaciers, high-altitude lakes, imposing mountains, and proximity to Kathmandu and the Tibetan plateau make **Langtang** and these valleys a popular trekking alternative to Everest or Annapurna, especially for the visitor who is short on time. In this area, 75 kilometers (47 miles) north of Kathmandu, you're surrounded by gigantic peaks, including Langtang Lirung, altitude 7,246 meters, (23,771 feet), the highest in this area. Huge glaciers sprawl down mountain slopes, spread across high valley floors, and empty into the sacred Gosainkund Lake. As in neighboring Everest, the people who inhabit Langtang are Sherpas. Their handsome villages and gompas add a peaceful touch to the formidable landscape.

In 1976, to save the beauty of Langtang Valley and Gosainkund, Nepal turned the area into its second-largest national park, a protected area for the endangered musk deer, Himalayan *thar* (wild goat), pandas, and the elusive snow leopard.

Trekkers who plan to visit this area should bring all necessary supplies and provisions. The entrance fee to the national park is Rs. 250.

Addresses and Numbers

Tourist Information There is no tourist information office in this area. Get whatever information you need in Kathmandu.

Emergencies The nearest embassies are in Kathmandu. At press time, no hospitals or clinics existed.

Banks Bring sufficient rupees from Kathmandu. There are no convenient places to change money in this area.

Arriving and Departing

The only flights into Langtang are by prearranged **RNAC** charters. Most people trek in from the village of Dhunche, a five-hour drive north of Kathmandu, or walk in from Panchkhal, a village on the road from Kathmandu to Tibet.

Outdoor Adventures

Highly recommended adventures are indicated by a star ★.

★ **Trekking (over a week):** *Helambu Trek.* This moderately difficult 9- to 13-day trek starts from Panchkhal, 52 kilometers (32 miles) north of Kathmandu. You follow the Indravati Khola River and ascend to Taramarang village, then up to Tarke Ghyang, at 2,560 meters (8,397 feet), the biggest Sherpa village in Helambu, tucked under towering mountains. At its monastery, lamas perform masked dances on the March full moon. From Tarke Ghyang, trekkers have two choices. One option is a 13-day trek over the Ganja La Pass, 5,122 meters (16,767 feet), and through villages to a view of the Langtang glaciers tumbling down from Langtang Lirung. The second 9-day route affords great panoramas of the Jugal Himal and its tallest peak, altitude 6,989 meters (22,930 feet). You proceed to

Shermathang village and monastery, encircled by alpine hills, then head back to Taramarang.

Lantang, Gosainkund, and Helambu: This 25-day trek starts from Dhunche, north of Kathmandu. You follow the Trisuli River north (an old caravan route to Tibet), then head east through a dense forest and into a gorge that opens into the alpine Langtang Valley. This trek includes most of the villages visited on the shorter treks described above, and takes you to Gosainkund Lake, altitude 4,380 meters (14,366 feet), encircled by craggy peaks. You walk through evergreen forests and alpine meadows, by cascading waterfalls, and up barren slopes. All treks can be done year-round, but the Ganja La Pass is open only from May to October.

5 North India

Introduction

The Himalayas span the entire northern stretch of India—an astonishing arc nearly 3,200 kilometers (1,984 miles) long—and within this mass of peaks and valleys are some of the country's most lovely states. In the northwest is the state of Jammu and Kashmir and its Ladakh district. No other state offers such scenic diversity. Jammu and Kashmir has green, alpine vales, flower-strewn meadows, rushing rivers and streams feeding numerous lakes, and glacier-topped mountains. In Kashmir, the Moghul emperors left beautiful gardens and mosques. Ladakh and its little-known Zanskar Valley transport you to the high-altitude world of dramatic landscapes, rugged passes, and ancient Buddhist *gompas* (monasteries).

The mountains and valleys of the small state of Himachal Pradesh, east of Jammu and Kashmir, include a smaller mountaintop Buddhist kingdom called Lahaul. Himachal has two well-known destinations: Manali, tucked beneath the mountains on the edge of Kulu Valley, and Shimla, a popular British getaway during the Raj, now the capital of the state. For the tourist who wants to explore the quiet side of India, this is the state to visit. Here, the people aren't so accustomed to tourists; the beautiful haunts are less traveled.

Heading east, you'll find northern Uttar Pradesh, also known as Uttarakhand, a place that represents the essence of Hinduism, which holds sway in this part of the Himalayas. Here, too, you find the source of the Yamuna and the Ganga, India's holiest rivers. Uttarakhand is the abode of the Hindu gods; four revered shrines—Badrinath, Yamunotri, Gangotri, Kedarnath—are each set atop a remote peak. To visit this state is to feel Hinduism permeate the land: You're in the heart of its ancient mythology.

Sikkim, north of West Bengal and east of Uttar Pradesh, is in India's Eastern Himalayas. Once a separate kingdom, Sikkim became an Indian state in 1975. The five peaks of Kanchenjunga, the third-highest mountain in the world, loom over this tiny state and its friendly people. Buddhism, though no longer the religion of the majority, still dominates the landscape. Buddhist prayer flags, prayer wheels, and monasteries are sprinkled throughout the green valleys and mountains.

In northern West Bengal, the terraced slopes of the tea-growing Darjeeling district, the "Queen of the British Hill Stations" (summer getaways), spread across a jagged ridge in the shadow of Mt. Kanchenjunga. Both Buddhism and Hinduism flourish here.

To the east sits Assam, a state sliced by the wide Brahmaputra River. Paddy fields threaded by canals surround clusters of thatched bamboo homes where villagers still honor traditional customs. Assam claims 12 of the best wildlife sanctuaries in north India.

Tucked in the Himalayan foothills below Assam is exotic Meghalaya. In its Garo Hills, elephants frequent the road, bamboo watchtowers dot the landscape, and bare-breasted women work the fields. Once Christian missionaries did serious damage to the area's unique local cultures; foreigners were evicted and kept out until recently.

History When the Aryans from eastern Europe and central Asia migrated into the Indus Valley around 1,750 BC, they found a sophisticated local civilization. During the Aryans' 1,000-year tenure, they developed the Hindu religion, the Sanskrit language, the caste system and a well-ordered trading and agrarian society.

Outsiders continued to affect the history of India. Alexander the Great marched through the northwest around 325 BC. Today, many tribes trace their ancestry back to his armies. Chandragupta, a young Indian prince, took advantage of the confusion left by Alexander's retreat and established the Mauryan empire. Ashoka, Chandragupta's grandson, whose reign began in 274 BC, established Buddhism in the subcontinent.

During the next centuries, kingdoms rose and fell. In the 11th century, the Afghan Sultan Mahmud of Ghazni, known as the "Idol Breaker," conquered north India. He ransacked the temples of the Hindu "infidels" and made slaves of his captives—creating a bitterness between Hindus and Moslems that would have a lasting impact.

In 1556 Akbar, an important Moghul emperor, began his reign over northern India, where he created the first of the beautiful summer retreats in Kashmir. Though the two dominant religions, Islam and Hinduism, remained distinct, beginning with Akbar's reign, their peoples commingled and intermarriages occurred. The last of the Great Moghuls, Aurangzeb, who ruled from 1658 to 1707, exhibited extreme intolerance once again, destroying Hindu temples and building Moslem mosques from the rubble.

By 1818 the British East India Company had emerged as a political force that controlled almost the entire subcontinent through a divide-and-conquer process that pitted Hindu against Moslem.

The British might have unified India, but unlike other invaders, they stayed aloof, creating their exclusive hill stations and establishing their own caste system in which the *sahib* (white man) was superior. A call for independence came from two distinct factions—the Hindu-dominated Indian National Congress, established in 1885, and the Moslem League, created in 1906. The movement for freedom could not be stopped, nor could the British halt the increasing friction between the two religions.

When civil war threatened in 1947, England appointed the Earl of Mountbatten as the new Viceroy of India to supervise the transition of power. He argued for an undivided India, but Moslem fear of disenfranchisement was too well entrenched. They rallied behind Muhammad Ali Jinnah, the president of the Moslem League, and demanded their Islamic nation of Pakistan. In the end, Mountbatten and Jawaharlal Nehru, head of the Congress Party, capitulated.

Mountbatten authorized a land survey to determine the new boundaries and offered all the Hindu rajas and Moslem nawabs who held title to private states the right of choice: Pakistan or India. At the time of partitioning, as many as a million persons —Moslems moving from India to Pakistan and Hindus moving from Pakistan to India—were killed in a religious holocaust.

Only Mahatma Gandhi had held fast to the dream of one nation. He renounced partitioning and shunned the Independence Day celebrations that were held on August 15, 1947. When an assassin's bullet cut him down on January 30, 1948, he died filled with the pain of his sundered homeland.

The impossible chore of breaking up the subcontinent had fallen to Sir Cyril Radcliffe, who worked feverishly in the one month allotted to him, carving up the northwest and northeast of India into the new nation of East and West Pakistan. Meanwhile, the Maharajah of Kashmir, a Hindu, struggled over the question of allegiance. Pathan tribes from new Pakistan forced the issue, invading Kashmir. In a panic, the maharajah cast his lot with India, which sent troops.

Unfortunately, the maharajah's decision failed to reflect the will of his people, most of whom were Moslems. Kashmir—Nehru's homeland—became a source of conflict that still stands in the way of friendship between the two young nations.

Before You Go

Government Tourist Offices

In the U.S. 30 Rockefeller Plaza, Room 15, N. Mezzanine, New York, NY 10020, tel. 212/586–4901; 230 N. Michigan Ave., Chicago, IL 60601, tel. 312/236–6899; 3550 Wilshire Blvd., Suite 204, Los Angeles, CA 90014, tel. 213/380–8855.

In Canada 60 Bloor St. W, Suite 1003, Toronto, Ontario M4W 3B8, tel. 416/962–3787.

In the U.K. 7 Cork St., London, W1X 2AB, tel. 01/437–3677.

Tour Groups

The following indigenous companies, some with international offices, organize high-quality, full-service trips.

General-Interest Tours **Journeyworld International** (410 E. 51st St., New York, NY 10022, tel. 212/752–8308 or 800/635–3900).
Sita World Travel (Indrama, Suite 1708, 501 5th Ave., New York, NY 10017, tel. 212/972–5500; in the U.K.: Chesham House, 136 Regent St., London W1R 5FA, tel. 01/437–6900).
Tours of Distinction (141 E. 44th St., New York, NY 10017, tel. 212/661–4680 or 800/888–8634).
Travel Corporation (TCI, Suite 6E, 20 E. 53rd St., New York, NY 10022, tel. 212/371–8080; in CA: Suite 1509, 3200 Wilshire Blvd., Los Angeles, CA 90010, tel. 213/389–2113; in the U.K.: Suite 235, High Holborn House, 52/54 High Holborn, London WC1V 6RL, tel. 01/242–9930).
Trade Wings (Suite 805, 25 W. 43rd St., New York, NY 10036, tel. 212/354–8328).

Special-Interest Tours **Arventures Adventure Holidays** (Post Bag 7, Dehradun, Uttar Pradesh, India; tel. in India, 29172). Primarily a trekking, mountaineering, and rafting outfit, this full-service company creates every conceivable fixed or customizable outdoor experience: treks by elephant, bike, horse, jeep; wildlife-park safaris; and water trips by *shikara* (Kashmiri gondola). It creates "theme" treks that focus on nature, photography, village life, or religion.

Himalayan River Runners (188-A Jor Bagh, New Delhi, tel. in India, 615736). This is the best rafting company in India, sponsoring the latest runs in the Indian Himalayas with excellent personal attention and equipment. Fixed departures and customized trips are available.

Package Deals for Independent Travelers

Contact the **Government of India Tourist Office** for information on "special packages" that can take you to, from, and around India at bargain rates. **Air India, Indian Airlines,** and **Vayudoot** also offer special packages for those making numerous flights.

When to Go

If the good time you expect hinges on the weather, pay attention to the following factors.

Northwest India In and around Himachal Pradesh's Shimla, early fall and spring bring moderate crowds. Winter turns Shimla romantic white. The Shivaratri Festival, a Hindu celebration, makes the small city of Mandi a February plus. Expect crowds in Manali from June to August. Kulu will be packed during the October Dussehra festival—but with villagers who add a cultural dimension to this event. Skiers should head to Manali from December to April. With the exception of Lahaul, Himachal Pradesh experiences a monsoon—periodic showers—during July and August.

In Kashmir, winter means good skiing and cold-weather adventures. Some houseboats are open and supply heaters. By May the snow melts; the state bursts into bloom. Crowds descend on Srinagar from mid-June until August. In the fall, autumn flowers and the chenar trees add a new splash of color. You can fly to Leh in Ladakh all year, but bad road conditions restrict travel if you arrive in winter. You can plan your trip around the Hemis Festival (usually in June) at the Hemis Gompa in Ladakh—one of the best Buddhist events in Asia. The Amar Nath Yatra (pilgrimage) in July or August is a three- to-five day round-trip walk to a Hindu shrine with thousands of pilgrims—a religious experience you won't forget.

Unless you're a skier or want a white holiday, the best times to visit Uttar Pradesh are from mid-May to July and mid-September to mid-November. The Char Dhams (Hindu shrines) in Garhwal are accessible May to late October (opening and closing dates subject to the weather). The Valley of Flowers is in bloom in July and August, the time of the monsoon. The three important cities—Mussoorie, Haridwar, and Rishikesh—are year-round destinations. Corbett National Park is open from mid-November to mid-June, with the best viewing time from March to June.

Jammu, northern Uttar Pradesh's Corbett National Park, Mussoorie, and Haridwar can experience a heavy monsoon from mid-June to September. In Ladakh and Lahaul in Himachal Pradesh, the passes are usually clear of snow from mid-June to October.

Northeast India The best time to visit Assam is September to June. You can also plan a vacation around the Rongali Festival in April or Durga Puja in October. The best time to visit Meghalaya is October to

April. Try to plan your vacation around Ka Pamblang Nongkrem or Wangala—terrific tribal festivals held in November. The most popular seasons in northern West Bengal are from April to mid-June and mid-September to November. The winter is cold, but you'll find no crowds in snowy white Darjeeling. The most popular times to visit Sikkim are from mid-February to June and October to mid-December. From December until February, though temperatures drop, Sikkim is lovely, and this is the time of the Losar festival.

The monsoon brings torrential rain from May to October in Assam and Meghalaya, and moderate rain from June to September in Northern West Bengal and Sikkim.

Festivals and Seasonal Events

India's a land of festivals—practically a celebration each day; what follows is a list of highlights. The lunar calendar often determines the exact date. Check with the **Government of India Tourist Office** or your travel agent before you go.

Jan. 26: Republic Day celebrates India's adoption of its Constitution—a festive day all over the country; big parade in Delhi.
Feb.: Losar, the Buddhist New Year, is a festive occasion with colorful dances at monasteries; especially big in Sikkim.
Feb.: Maha Shivaratri, in honor of the Hindu god Shiva, is a big celebration at all Shiva temples—especially interesting in Guwahati in Assam and in Mandi and Baijnath in Himachal Pradesh.
Feb. or Mar.: Holi is a festival of spring, celebrated with gusto. On the first night, Hindu devotees light a bonfire in which a demoness goes up in flames as people dance. On the second day, kids throw colored water on each other and you. Dress in dispensible clothes.
Feb. or Mar: The Haridwar Kumbh Mela in Uttar Pradesh is the largest fair in India and honors the city's special religious sanctity. The next scheduled Kumbh Mela is 1998. Ardh (Half) Kumbh Mela is in 1992.
Mid-Apr.: Rongali, an exuberant week-long festival, celebrates the advent of spring and the Assamese New Year with energetic dancing and singing in traditional costumes.
Apr. or May: During the remarkable festival of **Trimundiya,** held in a temple in Joshimath in Uttar Pradesh, a man who is considered the reincarnation of a religious spirit eats 50 pounds of rice and a sacrificed goat in honor of the Hindu goddess Durga.
May: Buddha Jayanti celebrates the birthday of Sakyamuni with rituals and chantings at monasteries; it's especially big in Sikkim.
May: Eid-ul-Fitr signals the end of Ramadan—a month-long period of daytime fasting by Moslems to commemorate the descent of the Quran from heaven. Alms are given to the poor, prayers are offered and, there is much feasting and rejoicing—big in Kashmir.
June: The Hemis Festival in Ladakh honors the birthday of Guru Padmasambhava with masked *lamas* (monks) and musicians performing ritual *chaams* (dances).
July or Aug.: The three- to five-day Hindu pilgrimage to Amar Nath cave in Kashmir celebrates the moment when Shiva re-

vealed the mystery of salvation to his consort Parvati—a festive religious experience.

July or Aug.: The pilgrimage to Lake Manimahesh near Chamba in Himachal Pradesh is a memorable holy trek, with thousands of Hindus going to purify themselves in frigid waters.

Aug. 15: Independence Day celebrates India's independence from Britain in 1947.

Aug.: Bakrid or **Eid-ul-Zuhu** celebrates the sacrifice of Harrat Ibrahim (who willingly killed his son at the behest of God) with animal sacrifices. This solemn festival concludes with a feast and joyous celebration; big in Kashmir.

Aug. or Sept.: In Sikkim, **Pang Lhabsol** offers thanks to Mt. Kanchenjunga, Sikkim's guardian deity. Stately dances are performed in monasteries by costumed lamas.

Sept.: Muharram is the Shiite Moslem time of mourning, with all-night chanting and self-flagellation that commemorates the martyrdom of Mohammed's grandson, Hussain; big in Kashmir.

Sept. or Oct.: Dussehra or Durga Puja is a nine-day festival in honor of the Hindu goddesses Durga, Lakshmi, and Saraswati celebrating the victory of the hero Rama over the demon Ravana. It's especially thrilling in Calcutta, in Kulu Valley in Himachal Pradesh, and at the Kamakhya Temple in Assam.

Oct. Sikkim sponsors a month-long **Autumn Festival** in Gangtok highlighting Sikkim's culture.

Oct. or Nov.: Diwali/Deepavali, the most important Hindu festival in India, starts the New Year and celebrates the day the hero Rama ended a 14-year exile.

Nov.: The Shillong Tourist Festival in Meghalaya coincides with **Ka Pamblang Nongkrem,** a five-day knock-out Khasi ceremony with days of colorful tribal dances.

Nov. or Dec.: Wangala, the Hundred Drums Festival, is a four-day tribal celebration in Meghalaya. The Garos, dressed in traditional costumes, dance for days to traditional musical accompaniment.

Currency

The units of Indian currency are the rupee and paisa (100 paisas equal one rupee). Paper money comes in the following denominations of rupees: 1, 2, 5, 10, 20, 50, and 100. Don't accept ripped or torn bills. Coins are in denominations of 5, 10, 20, 25, and 50 paisas, 1 rupee, 2 rupees, and 5 rupees. The rate of exchange is approximately U.S. $1 = Rs. 16; £1 = Rs. 25.

Cash, bank notes, and traveler's checks up to the equivalent of U.S.$1,000 don't have to be declared at the time of entry. Visitors in possession of more than that amount are required to fill out a Currency Declaration Form on arrival. This form allows you to exchange back your unused currency (provided you've held onto your encashment slips) at the end of your stay and lets you leave the country with your unchanged money. You receive an encashment slip every time you cash money or checks. If you want to pay a hotel bill in rupees, you must have this slip.

What It Will Cost

India is a bargain destination and a shopper's dream. Only posh hotels will cost more than a $100 for a double; these hotels are primarily in big cities like Calcutta and Delhi. In the mountains, the most expensive accommodations run $50–$75 per double, often with meals included. Meals are also economical, especially if you eat outside your hotel. Unless you order a feast, you'll find it hard to spend more than $10 per person for a hearty meal.

Transportation by a car with driver is also affordable. Figure about Rs. 4–5 per kilometer, with an added Rs. 100 halt charge per night on the road.

Rates for car with driver, taxis, and auto rickshaws vary from state to state; indeed, this is true of the cost of all your expenditures, including taxes. Check each separate destination section for the details.

Visitors should also plan on paying an airport departure tax when they leave India. If you're heading for Bhutan, Nepal, Pakistan, and other neighboring countries, the tax is Rs. 150; for all other international destinations, the tax is Rs. 300.

Visas

Citizens of all countries must have a valid tourist visa obtained from **Indian Consulates or High Commissions** (*see* list, below). To get a visa, you need a valid passport and a passport photo. The visa cost for Americans and Canadians is $15, for Britons, $40.50. The visa is good for four months, with a four-month extension possible. You must arrive in India within six months of the date your visa is issued. Individuals who need to extend their visas should visit the **Foreigners' Regional Registration Office** in New Delhi or Calcutta or any of the **Offices of the Superintendent of Police** in the various district headquarters. If you appear in person at an Indian Consulate or High Commission, your initial visa is usually granted within 48 hours. If you apply through the mail, allow a month and include a self-addressed envelope.

Americans U.S. citizens can apply to the following offices of the **Consulate General of India:** 3 E. 64th St., New York, NY, 10021, tel. 212/879–7800; 150 N. Michigan Ave., Chicago, IL 60601, tel. 312/781–6280; 540 Arguello Blvd., San Francisco, CA 94118, tel. 415/668–0662. You can also apply to the **Embassy of India,** 2107 Massachusetts Ave., Washington DC 20008, tel. 202/939–7000.

Canadians Canadians can apply to the **Indian High Commission** at 10 Springfield Rd., Ottawa, Ont. K1M 1O9, tel. 613/744–3751, or **Consulates General** at 2 Bloor St., Suite 500, West Cumberland, Toronto, Ontario M4W 3E2, tel. 416/960–0751; or 325 Howe St., Vancouver, British Columbia V6C 1Z7, tel. 604/662–8811.

Britons British citizens can apply to the **Indian High Commission,** India house, Aldwych, London WC2B 4NA, tel. 01/836–8484.

Restricted Area Permit

A Restricted Area Permit is obligatory for Assam, Meghalaya, and Sikkim. You also need the permit to travel by train or car to northern West Bengal. If you fly into Bagdogra Airport to visit Darjeeling or Kalimpong in West Bengal, the permit is not necessary. At press time, you could visit Meghalaya only as part of a group traveling with a government-recognized tour operator.

Obtain a copy of the Restricted Area Permit from the consulate, but don't go through it to get permission, which many travel agents or even the Government of India Tourist Office will suggest. Apply directly to the **Ministry of Home Affairs,** Government of India (Lok Nayak Bhavan, Khan Market, New Delhi, India). The consulate is more likely to say "no" than to go through the paperwork to make your trip happen.

When you fill out the permit, you must be specific about your trip plans and provide a precise list of destinations. If you list the northeastern states collectively or even list them individually, you'll run into trouble. For acceptable destinations, see the permit guidelines in each destination chapter. Also note the time restrictions and figure them into your itinerary. Once you fill out the permit, make two copies; for Sikkim, make three. Send the original to the Ministry of Home Affairs and keep the copy for your records. Send the other copy to Sikkim Tourism in Delhi (New Sikkim House, 14 Panchsheel Marg, Chanakyapuri, Delhi). It will expedite the process.

Allow a minimum of three months for clearance. When you get your permit, make three copies and keep them with you when you travel. Travelers have recounted terrible stories in which they've either lost their one copy due to carelessness or because it was inexplicably taken from them by the police at a checkpoint—which meant they couldn't proceed on their trip. The permit must be shown repeatedly at various checkpoints and to every hotel manager when you check in (or you won't be given a room).

Travelers can also visit this part of India as part of a tour group. (*See* Travel Agents in Before You Go to the Himalayas in Chapter 1 or in the individual destination sections.)

Customs and Duties

On Arrival The foreign tourist who enters India for a period up to six months has a choice of two channels for Customs clearance. The Green Channel is for passengers who don't have dutiable articles or unaccompanied baggage. The Red Channel is for passengers with dutiable articles, unaccompanied baggage, or high-value articles that must be entered on a Tourist Baggage Re-Export Form (TBRE). If you leave behind an item declared on the TBRE, you will have to pay duty on the missing item.

You can bring in the following duty-free articles: personal effects (clothes and jewelry), a baby carriage or stroller, a camera with five rolls of film, binoculars, a portable musical instrument, a radio or portable tape recorder, a tent and camping equipment, sports equipment (fishing rod, canoe, bicycle, pair of skis, two tennis racquets), 200 cigarettes or 50 cigars, .95 liters of liquor, and gifts not exceeding a value of Rs. 500 (about $30). You may not bring in dangerous drugs, gold coins, gold and silver bullion, silver coins not in use, or live plants.

On Departure Gold jewelry purchases can't exceed Rs. 2,000. For jewelry set with precious stones, the limit is Rs. 10,000. You can't take out art objects more than 100 years old or animal and snake skins.

Time Zone

Indian standard time is 5½ hours ahead of Greenwich mean time and 9½ hours ahead of the U.S. eastern standard time.

Staying Healthy

See Staying Healthy in Before You Go to the Himalayas, Chapter 1. For entry into India, no vaccination certificate or inoculation is required.

Car Rentals

Self-drive cars are not available for hire in India.

Rail Passes

Many areas of the Himalayas don't have tracks; only buy the Indrail Pass if you plan to stay in India a while or intend to travel in areas other than the Himalayas. To obtain the pass, go to the **Railway Central Reservation Office** in Calcutta or New Delhi. The cost for the Indrail Pass for first class (with air-conditioning) is $190 for 7 days, $230 for 15 days, $280 for 21 days, $350 for 30 days.

Arriving and Departing

If you intend to visit the western Himalayas, fly into **Delhi.** For the eastern Himalayas, you can fly from Delhi to **Bagdogra** at the foot of the mountains in northern West Bengal. You can also fly to **Calcutta** and head north to various airports in the northeastern states. (*See* Arriving and Departing in the Delhi or Calcutta sections, below).

Staying in North India

Getting Around

By Plane   For domestic flights on **Indian Airlines** or **Vayudoot,** get your tickets when you purchase your international ticket to the subcontinent. In the summer, tickets are hard to get once you've arrived. Reconfirm your ticket in person or through your hotel at least 72 hours before departure and arrive at the airport an hour in advance.

Bad weather can delay or cancel scheduled flights into remote regions. Structure your trip with time for unexpected delays. Never schedule back-to-back flights. If your trip schedule is tight, fly into a major destination in the Himalayas—Shimla or Kulu in Himachal Pradesh, Srinagar in Kashmir, Dehradun in Uttar Pradesh, to name a few possibilities—then proceed in a hired car or jeep with driver.

Currently Indian Airlines flies between the following destinations: from Delhi to Bagdogra (gateway to northern West Bengal and Sikkim), Calcutta, Chandigarh (to Himachal Pradesh); Guwahati (Assam and Meghalaya), Jammu, Srinagar (Kashmir), and Leh (Ladakh); from Calcutta to Bagdogra, Delhi, Guwahati, and Kathmandu.

Vayudoot is expanding fast. Ask your travel agent about new destinations. Currently the airline flies between the following destinations: from Calcutta to Guwahati (Assam) and Shillong (Meghalaya); from Chandigarh (Punjab) to Delhi, Kulu, and Shimla (Himachal Pradesh); from Delhi to Chandigarh, Dehradun, and Pantnagar (Uttar Pradesh), and Kulu and Shimla (Himachal Pradesh); and from Kulu to Shimla (Himachal Pradesh). Usually, from October to June, Vayudoot runs a four-hour Himalayan Airtrek Flight from Delhi to Dehradun, then up around the mountains and back again to Delhi.

Special Fares
General Discounts

Discover India. Indian Airlines offers unlimited travel for 21 days within India for $375. Payment must be made in foreign currency.

Tour India. 14 days on Indian Airlines for $300. Same payment restriction.

India Wonderfares-North. This Indian Airlines package for $200 is good for unlimited travel for seven days and covers Chandigarh, Delhi, Jammu, Srinagar, and Leh (plus other non-Himalayan destinations in the north).

India Wonderfares East. Again, $200, same restrictions, this tour covers flights to Calcutta, Bagdogra, Guwahati (and other eastern destinations).

Winter Discount to Srinagar. From November to April, Indian Airlines offers a 30% discount on round-trips to Srinagar for groups of four or more persons staying 3–14 nights.

Student Discounts

Students aged 12–26 with a valid student ID card qualify for a 25% concession (payable in foreign currency) on Indian Airlines flights.

Youth Discounts

A child under age 2 who sits on your lap pays 10% of the adult fare. Children aged 2–12 pay 50%.

By Helicopter

You can fly by helicopter from Bagdogra in West Bengal to Sikkim or around Meghalaya and into Assam. Consult each destination section for details.

By Car or Jeep with Driver

Some destinations are only accessible by jeep, car, or foot. Hire a tourist taxi or car or jeep with driver only from a government-approved and licensed operator. For reliable companies, consult the listings in each destination section. You can also hire a car from your travel agent or the **India Tourism Development Corporation** (ITDC, Kanishka Shopping Plaza, Ashok Rd., New Delhi). Write well in advance.

By Train

Few tracks run through the Himalayas. If you go first class, the cost of the ticket comes close to the price of airfare. If you travel overnight, you must reserve a sleeping berth or you could be put off the train.

There are two train rides travelers with time should consider: the narrow-gauge chugger, built by the British, that winds through the mountains from Kalka to Shimla, Himachal Pradesh (*see* Arriving and Departing by Train in the Himachal Pradesh section, below, for details). The other famous narrow-gauge train running from Siliguri to Darjeeling is recently in service again. (*See* Arriving and Departing by Train in the northern West Bengal section, below.)

Telephones

In remote areas, there are few phones, and the connections may be temperamental; but armed with patience, you can make your call—international, domestic, or local. The easiest, most expensive way to place a call is from your **hotel.** You can also call from a **main post office** or from **telegraph offices** that provide public phones.

Local Calls A local pay-phone call in India costs a rupee. Lines often cross; dial the number slowly or push the buttons carefully, then drop in the money once the connection is made—or just ask a resident of India to make the call for you.

International Calls The cost is generally equal to what you would pay in your home country. Travelers can place a more expensive lightning or urgent call that gives them priority booking. Except at Western-style hotels that accept credit cards, expect to pay for phone calls in local currency.

Operators and Information In India, if you need telephone assistance, dial 199; for directory inquiries, dial 197. Hopefully, the operator will speak English; if so, speak slowly. There's no guarantee you'll get the number you need.

Telegrams and Telex Head to the **local post office** or **telegraph office** (if you're in a reasonably large city), fill out the proper form (it's in English), and your message will be on its way.

Mail

Receiving Mail The easiest way to receive mail in India is through a local office of **American Express.** Mail is held for 30 days before it's returned to the sender. It can also be forwarded for a nominal fee. To get your mail, show your American Express card or American Express travelers checks, plus one piece of identification, preferably a passport. It's a free service to American Express traveler's check or card holders.

Postal Rates The cost of an airmail letter (weighing 10 grams) to England, Europe, Canada, and the United States is Rs. 6.50. Aerograms cost Rs. 5; airmail postcards are Rs. 4.50.

Tipping

Indian restaurants don't necessarily impose a service charge, but those in most major hotels do include a service charge of 10%. Hotel employees all expect to be tipped. Bellboys and bell captains should be paid Rs. 2 per bag. For room service, tip Rs. 2. If you're staying in a private home, tip the domestic workers Rs. 5 per day. Taxi drivers don't expect tips unless they go to a great deal of trouble. Railroad porters should be paid Rs. 2 per bag. Set the rate before you let them take your bags.

Opening and Closing Times

India has numerous government holidays when the commercial world shuts down. Hours also vary throughout India. Check listings of individual establishments for hours.

Shopping

Wonderful handicrafts are available all over India. Check each destination section for best buys. Except for fixed-price stores, shoppers are expected to bargain (*see* Shopping in Staying in the Himalayas, Chapter 1). Don't be too eager to buy. Be prepared to walk out; even do it. Usually the merchant will call you back. It's part of the process.

Dining

The cuisines of India vary from region to region, and just as there's more to India than the Taj Mahal, there's more to Indian food than "curry," which in fact is a British misnomer—a corruption of "kari," the local name of an aromatic spice used in south Indian gravies. There's also more to Indian cuisine than hot. In big cities and popular tourist destinations, you can pore over a menu that features Continental, Chinese, Japanese, and even Thai cuisine. Regional specialties are described in destination sections.

Consuming alcohol is a tricky business in India. Dry days are observed in some states. In some states, only beer is available. Some states only allow liquor in hotels. (*See* each destination section for details.)

Mealtimes In Delhi and Calcutta, mealtimes are similar to ours, and restaurants normally stay open until 11 PM or midnight. In remote areas, expect an earlier dinner unless you're staying in a Western-style hotel.

Precautions *See* Staying Healthy in Chapter 1.

Ratings Highly recommended restaurants are indicated by a star ★.

Category	Cost *
Very Expensive	over $15
Expensive	$10–$15
Moderate	$5–$10
Inexpensive	under $5

per person, excluding drinks, service, and taxes

Lodging

In India, you find a range of accommodations. In some mountain destinations, you won't have much choice, but in popular tourist centers, expect options to suit all budgets.

Western-style Hotels Western-style hotels are the most expensive option and offer little local ambience. Popular chains have foreign reservation offices, as well as reservation offices within India. The **Ashok Group** has hotels in Delhi, Calcutta, Jammu, Shillong (Meghalaya), and Guwahati (Assam); a hotel under construction in Gulmarg (Kashmir); and traveler's lodges in Kulu and Manali in Himachal Pradesh. To make a reservation from the United States, call **Golden Tulip World-Wide Hotels** (tel. 212/247–7950 or 800/344–1212) or call the **Air India** office in your home country. The **Taj Group** has a hotel in Delhi and one under construction in Calcutta. To make a reservation from the United States, call 212/972–6830 or 800/458–8825; in the United Kingdom, call 01/834–6635. **Oberoi** has hotels in Delhi, Calcutta, Shimla (Himachal Pradesh), and Srinagar (Kashmir) and a hotel under renovation in Darjeeling (West Bengal). To make a reservation in the United States, call 212/682–7655 or 800/223–1474/5; in the United Kingdom, call 01/541–1199. **Welcomgroup Chain** has hotels in Delhi and Calcutta and houseboats in Srinagar. To make a reservation in the United States, call **Sheraton Central Hotels,** 212/581–1000; worldwide, 800/325–3535. **Hyatt** has a hotel in Delhi. To make a reservation, call (worldwide) 800/233–1234.

Indian-style Hotels An Indian-style hotel is less fancy and less costly and often comes with a bathroom that has the traditional Indian-style toilet; the Western-style toilet, however, is beginning to show up with some frequency. Most likely, you'll find a shower, not a tub. But don't think primitive; the bathroom will be clean—just different. Though many of these hotels offer an ample share of amenities, very few accept credit cards. Some will take traveler's checks; all take rupees.

Inns and Lodges If only more inns and lodges existed in India! The traveler with an old-fashioned notion of class and charm must stay in any of the recommended places. Some are rustic properties tucked away in the mountains; others are in hill stations and are elegant down to the sterling silver tea service that appears with breakfast and afternoon tea. Pampering is part of the experience. The cost is a bargain, and usually meals are included. Don't expect to use your credit cards or even your traveler's checks. Make your reservation well in advance.

Houseboats These are exclusive to Kashmir and another opportunity that shouldn't slip by. (*See* Lodging in the section on Srinagar, below.) Reserve before you arrive. The best houseboats are popular in the summer season.

Camping Camping is possible in most of the Indian Himalayas. Some areas have camping sites set up with roomy safari-style tents available at a nominal cost, or you can rent equipment from private companies or the state tourist department.

Ratings Highly recommended lodgings are indicated by a star ★.

Category	Cost*
Very Expensive	over $100
Expensive	$60–$100
Moderate	$25–$60
Inexpensive	under $25

All prices are for a standard double room or a cottage, including taxes and excluding service charges.

Editor's Note

Because of the enormous distances covered by North India, we have divided the span into two sections. Section 1: Northwest India and Delhi is the gateway to Himachal Pradesh; Jammu and Kashmir, including Ladakh; and Northern Uttar Pradesh:

Uttarakhand. Section 2: Northeast India and Calcutta is the departure point for Assam, Meghalaya, Northern West Bengal, and Sikkim. Delhi and Calcutta have the major airports providing access to these regions.

Section 1
Northwest India & Delhi

In the mid-1600s, when Bombay and Madras were trading posts and Calcutta a simple village, Delhi flourished as the 450-year-old capital of a string of empires. Each ruler, in turn, appended his own capital (all eight still exist), with the two crowning achievements the palaces and mosques created by the Moghul Emperor Shah Jahan in the mid-1600s and government buildings built by the British in the early 1900s, which today serve as the capital buildings of independent India.

Arriving and Departing by Plane

There are no nonstop flights from the United States to the **Indira Gandhi International Airport** in Delhi. Most flights touch down in Europe or Great Britain. Since these routes are heavily traveled, the passenger has many airlines and fares from which to choose. Fares change with stunning rapidity, so consult your travel agent and check fare-structuring information in Arriving and Departing, Chapter 1.

From North America   Be sure to distinguish between (1) direct flights—no changes but one or more stops and (2) connecting flights—two or more planes, two or more stops.

Airlines   **Air India** (in the U.S., tel. 800/223–7776; in Montreal, 800/268–9582; in Vancouver, 800/663–3433; in Toronto, 416/865–1033) and **Pan American** (tel. 800/221–1111) offer direct flights with a short stop in London or Frankfurt.

The following airlines offer connecting flights: **KLM** (tel. 212/759–3600), **Air France** (tel. 800/237–2747), **British Airways** (tel. 800/247–9297), **Lufthansa** (tel. 718/895–1277), **Pakistan Airlines** (in New York, tel. 212/370–9157; in Chicago, 312/263–3082; in Los Angeles, 213/559–6409; in Montreal, 514/626–5250; in Toronto, tel. 416/591–5490), **Gulf Air** (tel. 800/772–4642), **Kuwait Airways** (tel. 212/308–5454), **Thai Airways** (tel. 800/426–5204), **Royal Jordanian** (tel. 800/223–0470), **Singapore Airlines** (tel. 800/742–3333), **Air New Zealand** (tel. 800/262–1234). To fly on to Calcutta usually involves an overnight stay and a next-day departure on **Indian Airlines.**

Flying Time   From New York to Delhi is about 16 hours, not including stops.

From the U.K.   **Air India** (tel. 01/491–7979), **British Airways** (tel. 01/759–5511), *Airlines*   **Pan American** (tel. 01/409–0688), and **Thai Airways** (tel. 01/499–9113) have direct flights to Delhi. **Lufthansa, Royal Jordanian, Gulf Air, Air France, KLM,** and **Emirates Airways** offer connecting flights.

Flying Time   From London to Delhi is about nine hours, not including stops.

Between Airports and City   Numerous hotels provide airport pickup service. The traveler can also take the airport bus (Rs. 10 from the national airport, Rs. 15 from the international airport), which runs frequently to major hotels and the center of town. Taxis are also available. Use the Prepaid Taxi Counter; your destination determines the exact rate (about Rs. 70 to the center of Delhi). Don't give the driver your payment slip until you arrive. If he demands more rupees, complain to the hotel doorman.

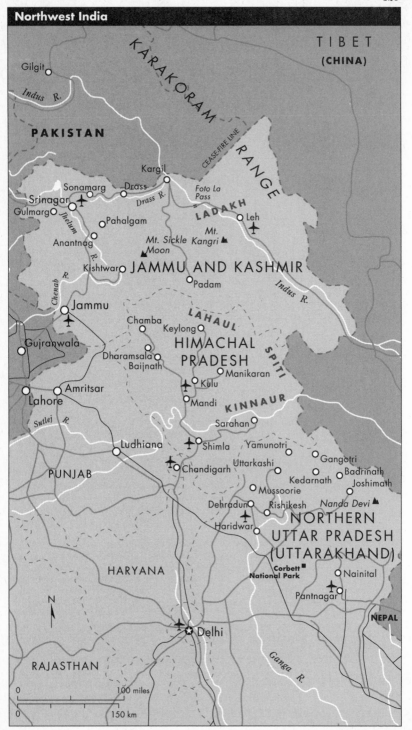

Arriving and Departing for the Himalayas

By Plane
Airports and Airlines
International flights use the **Indira Gandhi International Airport.** Domestic flights use the nearby **National Airport** (Air Bus terminal or Boeing and Vayudoot terminal). Both airports are about 15 kilometers (10 miles) from the center of Delhi.

Indian Airlines makes international flights to the following Himalayan destinations: Kathmandu in Nepal (daily); Lahore in Pakistan (twice weekly). Indian Airlines makes the following domestic flights: Bagdogra in northern West Bengal, the gateway to Sikkim (daily); Calcutta (three daily flights); Chandigarh for Himachal Pradesh (daily); Guwahati in Assam, the gateway for Meghalaya (twice daily); Jammu (daily); Srinagar (three daily flights); Leh in Ladakh (twice weekly). **Druk Air** flies into Paro in Bhutan (weekly).

Vayudoot flies to Dehradun (twice daily) and Pantnagar (twice weekly)—both in Uttar Pradesh; Kulu (twice daily) and Shimla (daily)—both in Himachal Pradesh. From Delhi, Vayudoot also makes the Himalayan Air Trek twice daily, October to June (subject to the monsoon).

By Hired Car with Driver
Hire a car from a recommended travel agency (*see* Travel Agencies, below). Except for a jaunt to Corbett National Park—250 kilometers (155 miles) away—most Himalayan destinations are more quickly and cheaply reached by plane.

By Train
The **Delhi Railway Station** is 7 kilometers (4 miles) north of Connaught Place and the **New Delhi Railway Station** is directly north of Connaught Place. Most trains leave from the New Delhi Railway Station, but check before you set out. For tickets and information, contact the **Northern Railway's Tourist Guide** (Delhi Railway Station, tel. 3313535), open daily 10–5. Before you board any train, you must have a ticket and, if you will be traveling at night, a reservation for a sleeper *and* a berth.

Getting Around Delhi

By Taxi
Taxis are Rs. 3.30 for the first kilometer, Rs. 2.40 for additional kilometers.

By Auto Rickshaw
Auto rickshaws charge Rs. 2.50 for the first 1.6 kilometers and Rs. 1.20 per additional kilometer.

By Bicycle Rickshaw
In Old Delhi, try a bicycle rickshaw—cheaper than the auto rickshaw. Ask a local merchant for the appropriate fare.

Addresses and Numbers

Tourist Information
Most tourist offices are open Monday–Saturday 10–5, except where noted. The **Government of India Tourist Office** (tel. 3320005) is at 88 Jan Path. The **Domestic** and **International Airports** and the **Delhi Railway Station** have counters open 24 hours a day. The following Himalayan states have tourist offices in Dehli: **Assam** (B-1, Baba Kharak Singh Marg, tel. 325897), **Himachal Pradesh** (Chanderlok Building, 36 Jan Path, tel. 3325320), **Jammu and Kashmir (and Ladakh)** (Kanishka Shopping Plaza, 19 Ashok Rd., tel. 3325373), **Meghalaya** (9 Aurangzeb Rd., tel. 3014417), **Sikkim** (New Sikkim House, 14 Panchsheel Marg, Chanakyapuri, tel. 3015346), **Uttar Pradesh**

(Chanderlok Building, 36 Jan Path, tel. 3322251), **West Bengal** (A-2, State Emporia, Baba Kharak Singh Marg, tel. 353840).

Emergencies **Police** (tel. 100). For health emergencies: **ambulance** (tel. 102) and **All-India Institute of Medical Sciences (hospital)** (Ansari Nagar, Aurobindo Marg). Better yet: Most hotels have excellent house physicians who have access to top-flight private clinics, or call the appropriate embassy.

Embassies **American** (Shanti Path, tel. 690351), **Canadian** (7/8 Shanti Path, tel. 619461), **British** (Shanti Path, tel. 690371).

Bookstores **Book Worm** (B-29 Connaught Pl.), **New Book Depot** (B-18 Connaught Pl.), **Oxford Book and Stationery Co.** (N-Block, Connaught Pl.), and **Piccadilly Book Stall** (Shop 64, Shankar Market, off Connaught Pl.) sell English-language publications. Bookstores are open Monday–Saturday 10–6.

Foreign Banks Hours are weekdays 10–2, Saturday 10–noon. **American Express** (Wenger Building, A-Block, Connaught Pl., tel. 344119), **Thomas Cook** (Hotel Imperial, Jan Path, tel. 312468), **Bank of America** (Hansalaya Bldg., Barakhamba Rd., tel. 3310296), **Citibank** (Jeevan Deep Bldg., Parliament St., tel. 311116), **Grindlays Bank** (H-Block, Connaught Pl., tel. 321335).

Indian Banks **Reserve Bank of India** (6 Parliament St.) and **State Bank of India** (SBI New Bldg., Parliament St.). The **Central Bank of India** (Hotel Ashok, Chanakyapuri, tel. 600121) is open 24 hours.

Post Offices Post offices are open Monday–Saturday 10–4:30. A good **central branch** is near American Express on Connaught Place. At the **Eastern Court Post Office** on Jan Path, you can send a telegram or telex or make a domestic or international phone call.

Travel Agencies Agencies are open Monday–Saturday 10–5. **India Tourism Development Corporation** or ITDC (L-Block, Connaught Pl., tel. 320005) has counters at the Ashok and Lodhi hotels. Other agencies include **American Express** (A-Block, Connaught Pl., tel. 344119), **Thomas Cook** (Hotel Imperial, Jan Path, tel. 312468), **Mercury Travels** (Jeevan Tara Bldg., Parliament St., tel. 321403), **Sita World Travel** (F-12, Connaught Pl, tel. 3311122), **Travel Corporation** (TCI, Hotel Metro, N-49, Connaught Pl., tel. 3315181).

Exploring Old Delhi

Put on walking shoes, grab a rickshaw, and lose yourself in Old Delhi, north of Connaught Place (the hub of Delhi). Once you pass through Delhi Gate, you see the silhouette of the massive **Lal Qila** (Red Fort), Shah Jahan's statement of Moghul power. Today, you have to reckon with crowds and an ongoing renovation, but try to imagine the imperial elephants swaying by with their *mahouts* (elephant drivers), the royal army of eunuchs, and the court ladies hidden in their palanquins.

Continue along the **Chhatta Chowk** (Vaulted Arcade), once the shopping district for ladies of the royal harem and now a bazaar selling significantly inferior goods. The arcade leads to the two-story **Naubat Khana** (Drum House), where ceremonial music was played five times daily. A spacious lawn, once the boundary at which all but the nobility had to stop, leads to the great **Diwan-i-Am** (Hall of Public Audiences).

The hall, raised on a platform and open on three sides, evokes a time of past glory. Here, the emperor sat on a throne inlaid with countless precious stones and set under a pearl-fringed canopy in a marble alcove in the center of the back wall. Watched by the throngs in the courtyard below, the emperor heard the pleas of his subjects. The rest of the hall was reserved for maharajahs and foreign envoys, all standing with lowered eyes, prohibited from looking at the emperor.

Behind the Diwan-i-Am stands a row of palaces that overlook the Yamuna River. To the extreme south is **Mumtaz Mahal,** now the **Red Fort Museum of Archaeology,** with relics from the Moghul period and numerous paintings and drawings. Next is **Rang Mahal** (Painted Palace), once richly decorated with a silver ceiling that was dismantled to pay the bills when the treasury ran low.

The third palace is **Khas Mahal** (Living Quarters). On a marble screen, you see carved the Scale of Justice—two swords and a scale that symbolize punishment and justice. From the attached octagonal tower, **Muthamman Burj,** the emperor would appear before his subjects each morning or would watch elephant fights.

The next palace is the famous **Diwan-i-Khas** (Hall of Private Audience), the most exclusive pavilion. A couplet written in gold above an archway sums up Shah Jahan's sentiments about his city: "If there be a paradise on earth—It is this! It is this! It is this!" Here, Shah Jahan, sitting on his solid-gold, jewel-inlaid Peacock Throne, consulted with his ministers. Nadir Shah, the Persian invader who sacked Delhi in 1739, hauled the throne back home.

Finally, you reach **Royal Hammams,** exquisite Moghul baths with a state-of-the-art steam bath and inlaid marble floors, every square inch a reminder of the self-indulgence these rulers exhibited as a matter of course.

From here, a short path leads to **Moti Masjid** (Pearl Mosque), designed by Shah Jahan's son, Aurangzeb, for his personal use and that of his harem. The prayer hall is inlaid with *musalla* (prayer rugs) outlined in black marble. Though the white marble of the mosque implies purity, some claim the excessively ornate style reflects the decadence that set in before the end of Shah Jahan's reign. *Admission: Rs. 0.50, free Fri.; Lal Qila is open sunrise–sunset; museum closed Fri. A sound and light show is held nightly 7:30–8:30; tickets (Rs. 4 and Rs. 8) available at the fort.*

The domed minarets of the red sandstone and white marble **Jama Masjid,** India's largest mosque, completed in 1658 by Shah Jahan, loom majestically over the Lal Qila. Broad steps lead to double-story gateways and a mammoth courtyard where thousands gather to pray. Each dome, portico, and minaret of this mosque is subordinated to the design of the whole, producing an overall impression of harmony. Just standing in the courtyard, tranquility sweeps around you. Inside the prayer hall, the pulpit is carved from a single marble slab. *The best time to visit is Fri., the holy day; check with your hotel or tourist department for the exact hour and to be certain you'll be able to go inside. For Rs. 1, you can climb up a minaret (a woman must be escorted by a "responsible" male).*

The northern gate of Jama Masjid leads into **Chandni Chawk,** the former imperial avenue, where Shah Jahan would ride at the head of his lavish cavalcade. Today, bullock carts, taxis, private cars, dogs, auto rickshaws, bicycle rickshaws, horse-drawn carts, and pedestrians pack the avenue. If you suffer from claustrophobia, you're in trouble. If not, you're in for an adventure.

Within Chandni Chowk, intense aromas fill the air: the pungent odor of oriental spices and the smell of garbage. As in the days of the Moghuls, astrologers set up on the pavement, shoemakers squat to repair sandals and other leather articles, medicine booths conceal doctors attending patients, oversize false teeth grin out of windows of local dentists, sidewalk photographers with aged box cameras happily take your picture for a small fee.

The heart of Old Delhi is nothing if not the glory and the guile, grandeur and grime, of the fascinating and slowly changing East. The twisting and turning streets beg you to meander, to lose yourself, though you're never really lost. Indeed, have some fun and turn this gigantic maze into a treasure hunt. Look for **Dariba Kalan** (Silver Street) and bargain for jewelry, turn down **Kinari Wali Gulli** (Street of Trimmings) aglitter with bridal accessories and saris, have a snack on **Paratha Walan** (Street of Bread Sellers). Lucky wanderers will stumble onto a picturesque lane of painted row houses and find peace and quiet in the exquisite **Jain Sweitamna Temple** situated at the far end. Here's a clue: the lane's off Kinari Wali Gulli. The entrance to the temple is via the brass doors on the left.

Directly across from the Lal Qila is one final attraction worth a 15-minute visit: the **Charity Birds Hospital** where vegetarian birds (and rabbits) are treated inside and nonvegetarian birds and other needy animals are treated in the courtyard. Look for the flocks of birds flying over the roof. *Allow 2 hrs for a casual stroll. Most shops in Chandni Chowk open Mon.–Sat. Admission to the temple free. It is best visited 5–8 PM.*

Time Out   **Kake da Hotel** (Think Restaurant) serves the best butter chicken in town. Bring towelettes or wear old clothes. Expect a crowd and a steal of a meal in ethnic surroundings. *74 Outer Circle, Connaught Pl. (between L and M Blocks). No credit cards. Open Mon.–Sat. 11 AM until the chicken is gone.*

Dining

Dry days are strictly observed in hotel restaurants—no alcohol is available on the first and seventh day of the month and national holidays. Unless noted, restaurants accept American Express, Diners Club, MasterCard, and Visa credit cards, require reservations, and allow casual dress. All restaurants listed are excellent. Prices are per person, excluding drinks, service, and taxes.

Indian   **Bukhara.** This handsome copper-and-wood-decorated restaurant emphasizes superb northwest-frontier specialties: leg of lamb, *tandooris,* and *kebabs. Maurya Sheraton, Diplomatic Enclave, tel. 3010101. Open 12:30–2:30 and 8–midnight. Expensive ($10–$15).*

Frontier Room. This rustic-style restaurant gets high marks for great northwest-frontier cuisine served in a subdued setting. Roving minstrels entertain at night. Try the kebabs. *Ashok Hotel, Chanakyapuri, tel. 600121. Open 1–2:45 and 8–11:45. Expensive ($10–$15).*

Mayur. This Indian restaurant is romantic: You eat under a painted blue sky with live performances of Indian *ghazels* (romantic ballads) at night. Choose from a wide range of dishes. *Maurya Sheraton. Open 12:30–2:30 and 8–midnight. Expensive ($10–$15).*

Chinese **House of Ming.** With just a few Chinese decorative touches on the walls, this elegant restaurant serves wonderful Cantonese and Szechwan food. *Taj Mahal Hotel, 1 Mansingh Rd., tel. 3016162. Open 12:30–3 and 7:30–midnight. Expensive ($10–$15).*

Tea House of the August Moon. Eat in a tea house complete with a pond filled with goldfish, a bridge, a bamboo grove, and dragons on the wall that emit smoke at night. You enjoy very good Cantonese, Szechuan, and *dim sum* (snacks). *Taj Palace Inter-Continental, Sardar Patel Marg, Diplomatic Enclave, tel. 3010404. Open 12:30–2:45 and 7:30–11:45. Expensive ($10–$15).*

Continental **Cafe Promenade.** The best nightly buffet in Delhi serves Continental and Indian cuisines, with imported cheeses and cold cuts, a well-stocked salad bar, and tasty desserts. Sometimes you have to contend with a rock band. *Hyatt Regency, Bhikaiji Cama Place, Ring Rd., tel. 609911. Open noon–3 and 7:30–11:30. Moderate–Expensive ($5–$15).*

Machan. Any time of day or night, you can have good Continental and Thai cuisine at Machan, done up in light and airy tropical colors with reminders of wildlife. "Machan" means wildlife lookout tower. After 3 PM, it serves great pizza. *Taj Mahal Hotel, 1 Mansingh Rd., tel. 3016162. Reservations not necessary. Moderate ($5–$15).*

Lodging

Unless noted, all hotels accept American Express, Diners Club, MasterCard, and Visa credit cards and have these facilities: shops, swimming pool, cable TV, restaurants, travel agencies, secretarial services, and international communication setups. Bedrooms have low-key modern decor; all have well-appointed bathrooms. Prices are for a standard double room, including taxes and excluding service charges.

Very Expensive **Oberoi.** A marble high rise with black marble floors and bou-
(over $100) quets of flowers in the lobby, this is Delhi's classiest hotel. Best rooms overlook the pool. *Dr. Zakir Hussain Marg, tel. 363030. 20 km (12 mi) from the airport; 8 km (5 mi) from Connaught Pl. 288 rooms.*

Taj Mahal Hotel. This white marble hotel is fancy glitz. You might catch sight of a lavish wedding; you can visit the resident astrologer. *1 Mansingh Rd., tel. 3016162. 18 km (11 mi) from the airport; 5 km (3 mi) from Connaught Pl. 300 rooms.*

Expensive **Ashok Hotel.** Its palatial red-and-white sandstone exterior be-
($60–$100) fits India's first national hotel, still run by the government and popular with visiting VIPs. The rooms aren't exquisite, but they're spacious. *Chanakyapuri, tel. 600121. 10 km. (6 mi) from the airport; 6 km (4 mi) from Connaught. 576 rooms. Facilities: 24-hr bank.*

Claridges Hotel. This is an old British staple—tidy, nearly stodgy. The primary aim is to please the guests. *12 Aurangzeb Rd., tel. 3010211. 12 km (7 mi) from the airport; 4 km (2 mi) from Connaught Pl. 140 rooms.*

Hyatt Regency. Super posh, this hotel even has a microwaterfall in the lobby. Make sure your room doesn't face the parking lot or the shanty town out back. *Bhikaiji Cama Pl., Ring Rd., tel. 609911. 8 km (5 mi) from the airport; 8 km (5 mi) from Connaught Pl. 535 rooms.*

Moderate–Expensive ($25–$100)

Hotel Imperial. This British Raj hotel and Delhi landmark is ragged around the edges, but its location in the heart of Delhi makes it very popular. Good ambience for the nonflashy traveler. *Jan Path, tel. 3325332. 23 km (14 mi) from the airport. 175 rooms.*

Taj Palace Inter-Continental. If Taj Mahal Hotel is booked up, try its other hotel, which also has less glitz. *2 Sardar Patel Marg, Diplomatic Enclave, tel. 3010404. 12 km (7 mi) from the airport; 8 km (5 mi) from Connaught Pl. 504 rooms.*

Welcomgroup Maurya Sheraton. Another posh marble monolith, its good restaurants make this a popular choice. *Diplomatic Enclave, tel. 3010101. 6 km (3.8 mi) from the airport; 7 km (4.4 mi) from Connaught Pl. 500 rooms.*

The following three guest houses in Sunder Nagar, about 16 kilometers (10 miles) from the airport and 5 kilometers (3 miles) from Connaught Place, are quiet havens with attractive lawns and clean, air-conditioned rooms, usually without television. All rooms have Western-style bathrooms. Lacking dining rooms, the guest houses offer room service. With prices at the low end of the Moderate category, they're great bargains. They accept rupees only.

Jukaso Inn. *50 Sunder Nagar, tel. 690308. 55 rooms.*
Kailish Inn. *10 Sunder Nagar, tel. 617401. 10 rooms.*
Maharani Guest House. *3 Sunder Nagar, tel. 693128. 25 rooms.*

Himachal Pradesh

Introduction

Place five mountain ranges across Himachal Pradesh like fingers on an open hand: the Siwalik, Dhauladhar, Pir Panjal, Great Himalayas, and Zanskar; ring the fingers with cool twining rivers; set the rings with sparkling lakes. Himachal Pradesh, surrounded by India's Jammu and Kashmir and Uttar Pradesh, as well as Tibet, has fertile valleys and barren snowy peaks where the monsoon never penetrates. Every road in this state (the size of Indiana) continually climbs and descends. Except for the few cities, such as the capital, Shimla, the pace is slow and pastoral. This is a state of villages, where you find numerous adventures and cultural diversity.

In Kulu Valley, the black-garbed people of Malana prohibit visitors from touching all buildings. An Aryan people who speak an unusual Tibetan dialect, their isolated mountain village is what historians call the world's oldest surviving democracy, lending credence to the claim that they're the descendents of Alexander the Great, who attempted to conquer this area in about 325BC.

In Chamba Valley, you encounter the Hindu-animist Gaddi and
Moslem Gujjar. The Gaddi move with vast herds of sheep, goats,
and cattle, the men wearing a *chola* (white thigh-length woolen
coat) over *sutthan* (tight woolen trousers) and the women wearing a *luanchari* (long colorful dress) and lots of jewelry—for
good luck and as an indication of wealth. Their homes are small
wood or stone dwellings, their possessions limited to what will
fit on the back of a few horses.

The Gujjar travel with large herds of buffalo, making their living by selling fresh milk and *ghee* (butter). The men, who are
usually bearded, wear turbans and long robes. The women
wear typical Moslem female dress: a *kurta* (long blouse) and
churidar (loose trousers), accented by paisley scarves and
chunks of silver jewelry.

Buddhists from Tibet live among Hindus in Dharamsala, the
home of the exiled Dalai Lama. They also live in remote Lahaul
and in Sarahan, near Shimla, where the Hindu Bhimakali Temple is sacred to Buddhists, too.

Staying in Himachal Pradesh

Addresses and   Monday–Saturday, 10–5, contact the **Himachal Pradesh Tour-**
Numbers   **ist Office** (Daizy Bank Estate, Shimla, H.P., tel. 5488) or
Tourist Information   the **Himachal Pradesh Tourism Development Corporation**
(HPTDC), a government undertaking (Ritz Annexe, Shimla,
H.P., tel. 3294). There are also government tourist offices in
the following cities: Chamba, Dharamsala, Kulu, Manali, and
Mandi (*see* individual destination listings, below).

Emergencies   For all emergencies, turn to your hotel or the tourist department or contact your embassy in Delhi: **American** (Shanti Path,
tel. 690351), **Canadian,** (7/8 Shanti Path, tel. 619461), **British**
(Shanti Path, tel. 690371).

Travel Agencies   **Himalayan Adventurers** (May Flower Guest House, Manali,
H.P., tel. 104) is the best adventure outfit. **Himalayan River**
Runners (188-A, Jor Bagh, New Delhi, tel. 615736) offers the
best rafting runs. **HPTDC** offers good inexpensive tours, treks,
and all travel needs, including cars with drivers (*see* Tourist Information, above). The **Mountaineering Institute of Manali and**
Allied Sports Complex, (Manali, H.P., tel. 42) has excellent
courses in climbing, trekking, and skiing (*see* Outdoor Adventures, below).

Arriving and Departing

By Plane   To see Shimla and south Himachal, fly into the **Jubbarhati Air-**
port. For all other destinations, fly into **Bhuntar Airport** near
Kulu. All flights arrive from Delhi's **National Airport** and take
about 1½ hours. Flights are subject to delays or cancellation
due to bad weather.

Airports and   **Vayudoot** flies a small plane daily into **Jubbarhati Airport,** 23 ki-
Airlines   lometers (14 miles) from Shimla, and into **Bhuntar Airport,** 10
kilometers (6 miles) from Kulu and 52 kilometers (32 miles)
from Manali. Call for fares and schedules (tel. 3312587). Book
seats before you depart from home.

Between Airport   From **Jubbarhati Airport** into Shimla, you can go by taxi (45
and City   minutes, Rs. 100) or by bus, the **Airport Coach Service** (one

Himachal Pradesh *(Numbers on map correspond to numbers in text)*

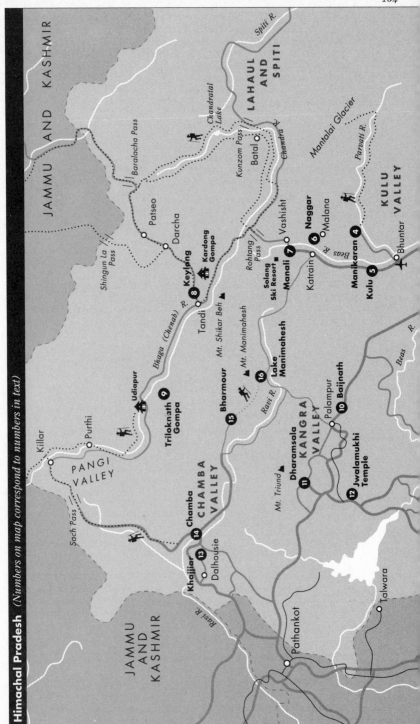

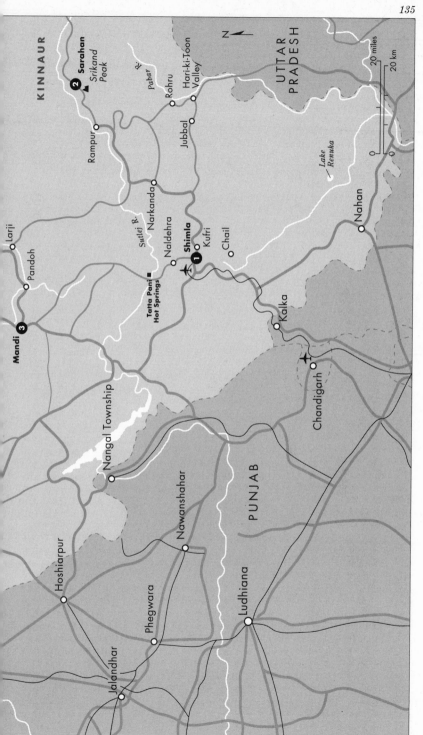

hour, Rs. 20), which often waits for additional flights before making the trip. For pickup locations on the way back to the airport, contact HPTDC (Shimla, tel. 3311).

From **Bhuntar Airport, Himachal Pradesh Road Transport Corporation** (HPRTC) charges Rs. 10 for buses to Kulu (15 minutes) and Manali (90 minutes); you may have to wait. Taxis to Kulu (Rs. 40) or Manali (Rs. 180) are plentiful and fast.

By Hired Car with Driver From Delhi to Shimla, 370 kilometers (229 miles), brace yourself for a seven-hour journey on a dusty highway through the Indian state of Haryana. The trip turns scenic and slows down once you reach Himachal. Hire a car from a recommended Dehli travel agency (*see* Addresses and Numbers in the Delhi section, above).

By Train Take the *Himalayan Queen*, which departs late at night from the **New Delhi Railway Station** for Kalka, 96 kilometers (59 miles) from Shimla. This train connects with the morning departure of the British-built *Toy Train*, which winds for five hours through the mountains to Shimla. You sit on a wood bench, but it's fun. Book your ticket in advance: first (air-conditioned or non-air-conditioned) or second (air-conditioned) class. Reserve a sleeper *and* a berth. Call **Northern Railway's Tourist Guide** between 10 and 5 (New Delhi Railway Station tel. 3313535; in Shimla, tel. 2915).

Highlights for First-time Visitors

Himachal's roads, frequently blocked by herds of animals, require a slow pace. If your visit is under two weeks, concentrate on one or two valleys. To follow the itinerary outlined in this section takes about three weeks traveling by car (without any long stops or outdoor adventures).

Best bets include walks around Naggar and Manikaran in Kulu Valley, with a four-day round-trip trek to Malana or a 10-day round-trip trek to the Mantalai Glacier (May–mid-Oct.); a night at Chapslee Inn in Shimla and an excursion to Buddhist Sarahan, combined with a walk or short trek (May–mid-Oct.); eight days for a summer trip from Chamba to Bharmour, the home of the Gaddi and Gujjar, timed with the pilgrimage to Lake Manimahesh in July or August; the nine-day autumn Dussehra Festival in Kulu; the new 10-day journey by jeep through Lahaul to Ladakh (open July–Oct.); and a five-day rafting trip on the Sutlej plus seven days of exploration (Nov.–mid-Dec. and Feb.–Apr.).

Getting Around

By Plane **Vayudoot** makes a daily flight between Shimla (tel. 3311) and Kulu (tel. 2286). Book early.

By Hired Car with Driver Except for Lahaul, where you must hire a jeep or walk, a car with driver is the best way to travel. You make better time, stop when you want, and take any road that appeals to you. The cost is about Rs. 4 per kilometer with a halt charge of Rs. 50 to 100 per night. Contact the **HPTDC** or our recommended travel agencies.

Guided Tours

At press time, there are no scheduled-departure statewide tours.

Outdoor Adventures

Highly recommended adventures are indicated by a star ★.

★ **Climbing and Mountaineering:** Six-thousand-meter (20,000-foot) mountains test your courage near Manali and in Lahaul; the climbing season is July–October. Arrange in advance with the **Mountaineering Institute of Manali and Allied Sports Complex** (Manali, H.P. tel. 42), which also organizes courses in high-altitude trekking, mountaineering, rock climbing, and skiing and Outward Bound–type courses for children. (*See* Travel Agencies, above or Special-Interest Tours in either Before You Go to the Himalayas, Chapter 1, or in Before You Go to North India above).

★ **Fishing:** You'll find trout in the Pabar River near Rohru, a day-long excursion from Shimla, and in the Beas River near Manali. Try for *mahseer* (Himalayan river fish) on the Beas near Dharamsala. For the required license, contact the tourist department in each district.

Golfing: Golfers can test Naldehra's nine-hole course, India's oldest, near Shimla (May–Nov.). Equipment is available.

★ **Hang gliding:** Soar in Kangra Valley (from Mar.–Apr. and mid-Aug.–Nov.) and take courses through HPTDC (*see* Tourist Information, above). All equipment is provided. Arrange in advance.

★ **Hot Springs:** Relax in enclosed cubicles all year long in Tatta Pani, north of Shimla, in Manikaran near Kulu, and in Vashisht near Manali.

Ice-Skating: Ice skaters can use Shimla's rink (Nov.–Feb.). Skates are available.

★ **Rafting:** *Sutlej River.* Take a 12-day trip (Nov.–mid-Dec. and Feb.–Apr.) that includes six days of rafting on the Sutlej River from Narkanda to the Salapar Bridge northwest of Shimla, and six days of walks. *Beas River.* Take a day run on the Beas in Kulu Valley (mid-May–mid-July and mid-Aug.–mid-Sept.). *Chandra River.* A three-day run is under study on this river in Lahaul (mid-Aug.–mid-Sept.). Arrange in advance. Contact Himalayan River Runners (*see* Travel Agencies, above).

★ **Skiing:** Near Shimla, slopes at *Kufri* and *Narkanda* aren't challenging, but the price is low, including cost of equipment, and the Himalayan views are great (Jan.–Mar.).

★ At *Solang*, near Manali, you ski against a backdrop of glaciers and towering peaks. Instruction and equipment are available (Dec.–Mar.). You can also combine trekking with skiing and extend the season to June. Arrange in advance with Himalayan Adventurers (*see* Travel Agencies, above). For ski courses, contact HPTDC (see Tourist Information, above).

Trekking: For Manali; Shimla; and the Kulu, Chamba, and Kangra valleys, the best time to trek is May–June and September–mid-October. The trekking season in Lahaul

(June–Oct.) is determined by snow. Lahaul treks are strenuous; you're rarely below 3,700 meters (12,000 feet). For all treks, except the pilgrimage in Bharmour, you should have a guide and you should arrange before you depart with Himalayan Adventurers or special-interest tour operators listed in Before You Go to the Himalayas (Chapter 1) or Before You Go to North India. You can rent camping equipment or hire a porter or guide from Himalayan Adventurers, HPTDC, or the Mountaineering Institute (*see* Climbing and Mountaineering in this section, above).

Trekking (up to a week): ★ *Jubbal to Hari-ki-Toon Valley.* From Jubbal, 100 kilometers (62 miles) northeast of Shimla, you can go by foot or pony along the Toms River through forests, fields of wildflowers, and remote hamlets to the Hari-ki-Toon Valley (three–five days). For details, contact Chapslee Inn (Lakkar Bazar, Shimla, H.P., tel. 77319 or 78242).

★ *Naggar to Malana.* From Naggar, 18 kilometers (11 miles) south of Manali, you can take a rugged three–four-day hike up a mountain to the isolated village of Malana. Follow local customs: don't bring or wear any leather in the village—hide your shoes in a bush—walk on the right of any path, and don't touch any person or building.

Lake Manimahesh. Take the six-day Hindu pilgrimage (July or Aug.) from the temple town of Bharmour in Chamba Valley to the Shiva temple at Lake Manimahesh. Follow a meandering stream into the mountains, walk through alpine meadows, and finally ascend a steep path to a rocky ridge. The area is home to the Gaddi and Gujjar. During the pilgrimage, you don't need a guide or advanced planning. Tea and snack stalls are set up along the route; bring your own camping gear and extra provisions. Before or after the pilgrimage, a guide is advised.

★ **Trekking (over a week):** *Pangi Valley.* From Chamba Valley, head north 137 kilometers (85 miles) to the dry, rugged Pangi Valley beyond the Sach Pass, 4,428 meters (14,523 feet) up. The Chenab River (Chandra Bhaga) lashes through a deep narrow gorge. Numerous high-altitude peaks challenge mountaineers. Every village and hamlet has its own temple, the two most important being Mindhal Vasni, about 15 kilometers (9 miles) from Killar, and Purthi, about 30 kilometers (18.6 miles) from Killar. From Killar, you can trek northwest to Kishtwar in Jammu and Kashmir or turn east on the way to Kishtwar and cross the Umasi La Pass into the Zanskar Valley. You can trek southeast to Keylong in Lahaul and on to Manali or trek from Killar through Lahaul to Purthi and a convenient rest house on the banks of the Chandra Bhaga. This entire area is rarely explored and offers numerous routes rated short to long, easy to hard. Plan at least eight days.

Mantali Glacier. This 10-day trek (May–June, Sept.–mid-Oct.) to Kulu Valley starts in the sulphur springs village of Manikaran, then heads up the mountains to Parvati Valley, where hot springs crop up in the forests and meadows. You pass through hamlets and see ancient Hindu temples and a magnificent glacier, 4,462 meters (14,635 feet) high, the source of the Parvati River.

Lahaul. The "circular trek" takes 15 days and gives you the most complete excursion through this area. Start at Batal, about six hours from the Rohtang Pass, and hike to high-altitude Chandratal Lake (Lake of the Moon). You follow and finally crash through a raging river, cross snow bridges, traverse the 8-kilometer (5-mile) Baralacha Pass, surrounded by a sea of snow-covered peaks 5,000–6,000 meters (16,400–19,680 feet) high. You climb up to the Phirtse La Pass, at 5,435 meters (17,826 feet) to see the glacier, then descend into the valley of Shangse with its small *gompa* (monastery). You walk to Fuktal and see its gompa, then head over the Shingu La Pass, 5,096 meters (16,714 feet) up, before ending in Darcha, a day's drive from Manali.

You can do an 11-day version of this trek—the *Chandratal Trek*—by eliminating the Phirtse La Pass and the last valleys. You can also do 10- or 12-day treks from Lahaul that take you to Padam in Zanskar Valley, Ladakh. Each route is rugged; you see few foreigners and discover civilized valleys in this seemingly uncultivated world.

★ **Jeep Safari:** A new road just opened from Manali to Leh (mid-July–mid-Oct.) that takes you through this remote Buddhist realm. Arrangements must be made in advance to cross this sensitive border area. Contact Himalayan Adventurers (see Travel Agencies, above). If you're short on time or stamina, you can also spend six days (mid-July–mid-Oct.) seeing Chandratal Lake and most of Lahaul's best monasteries by jeep. Arrange in advance through Himalayan Adventurers.

Shimla

Numbers in the margin correspond with points of interest on the Himachal Pradesh map.

After wresting Shimla from Nepal in 1819, the British decided that this 2,000-meter- (7,000-foot-) high ridge was the ideal escape from the summer heat of the capital in Delhi. By 1860, **①** they had **Shimla** looking as much like England as possible.

Some of their homes were gingerbread-trimmed bungalows; others were estates with granite manor homes that signaled the change in England's status. The men who spent summer in Shimla were the new *rajas* (kings) of India and controlled the subcontinent.

Opulence set the tone in Shimla. It became the unofficial summer capital—the premier British hill station in India—with the Gaiety Theater, named for the Gaiety in London, putting on the latest Noel Coward plays.

Today, a crowd of new buildings is overwhelming Shimla. Developers are obliterating all traces of the fastidious English gardens and the British air of exclusivity. Shimla—no longer a getaway but rather the state capital of Himachal Pradesh—buzzes year-round. Use Shimla as a base for good nearby excursions or as the start for a tour of the state.

Arriving and Departing For futher information, *see* Arriving and Departing Himachal Pradesh, above.

Getting Around Shimla is a walker's town, with The Mall and some parts of The Ridge prohibited to vehicles. For trips beyond pedestrian thoroughfares, hire a taxi from **Kalaka Taxi Union** (tel. 3985) or **Vishal Taxi Union** (tel. 5123). Bargain using Delhi rates: Rs. 3.30 first kilometer, Rs. 2.40 per additional kilometer. You can travel around pedestrian areas in a rickshaw. Set the fare before you start; it should be less than a taxi.

Addresses and Numbers

Tourist Information Obtain information about tours and hiring a car with driver from the **Tourist Information Office** (The Mall, tel. 3311) or **HPTDC** (Ritz Annexe, tel. 3294 or 5071). They are both open Monday–Saturday 10–5.

For travel assistance, contact **Himalayan Travels** (The Mall, tel. 2411), open Monday–Saturday 10–6.

Banks **Grindlays Bank** and **Bank of India** are on The Mall, open weekdays 10–2, Saturday 10–noon.

Post Office The **General Post & Telegraph Office** is also on The Mall, open Monday–Saturday 10–4:30.

Bookstores Good English books are at **Maria Brothers** (78, The Mall, tel. 5388), open daily 10:30–1 and 5–8 or **Minerva Book House** (46, The Mall) open daily 9–7.

Guided Tours HPTDC (tel. 3294) has daily luxury bus tours to see the countryside near Shimla. You can also go by car.

Exploring See the mountain views from the peaceful grounds of the Elizabethan-style **Indian Institute of Advanced Studies**—the former Viceregal Lodge constructed in 1884–88. (Visitors aren't normally allowed inside.) On the way back, stop at the **Himachal State Museum** and see a good display of Pahari miniatures and other regional schools of painting and sculpture. *The institute is near Summer Hill. Grounds are open sunrise–dusk. The museum is near Chaura Maidan. Admission: Rs. .50. Open Tues.–Sat. 10–1:30 and 2–5. Closed government holidays.*

On The Mall, notice **Christ Church,** the second-oldest church in north India, built in 1857. Finally, walk through the **Middle and Lower Bazaars.** Here, merchants who oversee the crowd of tiny stalls—Tibetans in long woolen garments and the various hill people of Himachal—bring you back to the heart of Asia.

Shopping Handloomed woolen shawls and carved wood products are good buys in fixed-price shops along **The Mall.** The shops are open daily 10–7 and don't accept credit cards. For rare books on the Himalayas or old etchings, visit **Maria Brothers** (78, The Mall, tel. 5388), open daily 10:30–1 and 5–8.

Outdoor Adventures Hike 2 kilometers (about a mile) from The Mall up to Jakhoo Hill, with its temple dedicated to Hanuman, the Hindu monkey god. On a clear day, you get a good view of the Himalayas straight to Ladakh. For a nominal charge, try **skating** at the Skating Rink (below the Rivoli Cinema, tel. 2344), open November–February, daily 10–6. Rent reasonable skates from Capital Boot House on The Mall.

Dining Except for two special dining rooms, Shimla has few good restaurants. Most of the hotels listed in Lodging, below, serve decent Indian (sometimes vegetarian), Continental, and even Chinese cuisine. Dress is casual. Highly recommended restaurants are indicated by a star ★. Prices are per person, excluding drinks, service, and taxes.

★ **Chapslee.** This home-turned-inn is filled with antiques and elegance, and the meals—fixed menu—match the ambience. Expect Indian cuisine at lunch, Continental at dinner. The formal dining room can accommodate about 12 people. *Lakkar*

Bazar, tel. 77319 or 78242. Reservations required. No credit cards. Closed Jan.–Mar. 15. Moderate–Expensive ($5–$15).

★ **Woodville Palace.** Shimla's other culinary treat, this villa has an interior dining room filled with antiques. Expect a fixed menu and a small dining room. *Himachal Bhawan Road, tel. 2722. Reservations required. No credit cards. Moderate–Expensive ($5–$15).*

Oberoi Clarkes. This low-key restaurant with mountain views serves good Continental, Chinese, and Indian food. *The Mall, tel. 6091. Reservations advised. AE, DC, MC, V. Open 8–10, 1–2:30, 8–10. Moderate–Expensive ($5–$15).*

Lodging Shimla offers two special accommodations that evoke the Raj. Highly recommended lodgings are indicated by a star ★. Prices are for a standard double room, including taxes and excluding service charges.

★ **Chapslee.** The height of understatement: Its lawn is modest, exterior far from grand. But step inside this private home of a *kanwar* (prince) and his wife and you're surrounded by sumptuous antiques. Forget about Western amenities; this is Indian high class, with a hot water bottle slipped into your bed at night, afternoon tea, a library with old books. The Pink Suite is gorgeous: three fireplaces, for starters. Gourmet meals are included. Reserve well in advance. *Reservations: Lakkar Bazar, Shimla, H.P., tel. 77319 or 78242. 7 rooms with bath. No credit cards. Closed Jan.–Mar. 15. Expensive ($60–$100).*

Oberoi Clarkes. Despite its 50-year history and chalet-style exterior, it has such an uninspired interior decor, you feel cheated unless you ask for a fireplace and good views. It offers mid-November–April discounts. *The Mall, Shimla, H.P., tel. 6091. 33 rooms with bath. Facilities: TV, restaurant, bar, room service, foreign exchange desk, travel desk, and car-rental service. AE, DC, MC, V. Expensive ($60–$100).*

★ **Woodville Palace Hotel.** This stately villa, owned by a kanwar and converted into a hotel, offers grand living. The rooms have original Victorian and Art Deco decor. Hollywood stars spent (and spend) time here, carousing and playing billiards and croquet. Meals are included. *Reservations: Himachal Bhawan Rd., Shimla, H.P., tel. 2722. Reserve well in advance. 11 rooms with bath. Facilities: gardens, tennis court under construction, billiard room. No credit cards. Expensive ($60–$100).*

Hotel Holiday Home. Run by HPTDC, this clean, recently refurbished Western-style hotel, set on a ridge beneath The Mall, offers good value; luxury rooms are spacious. *Cart Rd., Shimla, H.P., tel. 6031. 65 rooms with bath (shower). Facilities: multicuisine restaurant, bar, room service, TV, car-rental arrangements. No credit cards. Inexpensive–Moderate (under $60).*

Nightlife The old **Gaiety Theatre** (The Mall, tel. 4035) still has occasional productions in the summer. The best bar is at **Oberoi Clarkes.** You can imbibe until 10 PM. If you're staying at Chapslee or Woodville, you'll have a nightcap in style.

Excursions from Shimla

Contact the Tourist Information Office or HPTDC (*see* Important Addresses and Numbers, above) for information on excursions to the mountain-top year-round Kufri resort, to the nine-hole golf course at Naldehra, to the Palace Hotel—once a majarajah's lavish playground—in Chail, to skiing in Narkanda, and to the exquisite scenery of Rohru, the peaceful Lake Renuka, nestled in the mountains.

Contact the kanwar at Chapslee in Shimla (tel. 77319 or 78242) for information on a romantic new destination: the rustic guest house of the Maharajah of Jubbal's golden-spired palace, set in a tiny hamlet beyond a mountain pass.

Excursions from Shimla to Rampur and Sarahan

Foreigners rarely head northeast of Shimla to Rampur, 140 kilometers (87 miles) away, and on to Sarahan, 41 kilometers (24 miles) farther, a beautiful trip through remote villages and over a pass into a Buddhist-Hindu world. **Rampur,** a commercial outpost with tiers of houses rising up from the banks of the Sutlej River, provides a peaceful setting for a Buddhist monastery with a huge prayer wheel. Rampur is also the site of the November **Lavi,** one of Himachal's most jubilant fairs. From Rampur, head to **Sarahan,** which sits above a valley with grand views of the Himalayas. Climb to a hilltop peak called **Srikand** and a stone image of Shiva, known as Srikand Mahadev. Here, worshipers offer a cup of *charas* (hashish) to the god.

Visit the 200-year-old **Bhimakali Temple** set in a courtyard: a multistory wood structure that evokes China with its pagoda-shape roofs and Himachal with its rough wood walls. Note the elaborate turn-of-the-century silver doors made by silversmiths from the region of Kinnaur (off-limits to foreigners). The Hindu part of the temple, rectangular towers at one end of the courtyard, contains an inner sanctum with Hindu and Buddhist bronzes, numerous masks, and an image of Bhimakali, a manifestation of Kali, the Hindu goddess of destruction. Hire a car with driver in Shimla. To spend the night, a must for this trip, arrange for basic accommodations in the new **Tourist Lodge,** run by the HPTDC. *174 km (108 mi) from Shimla. Reservations: HPTDC, Shimla, H.P., tel. 3311. 15 rooms with bath (Indian shower). Facilities: restaurant, lounge. No credit cards. Inexpensive (under $25).*

Mandi

At first glance, **Mandi,** 156 kilometers (97 miles) to the north of Shimla and set in a valley of the Beas River, looks like an old New England mill town, with rickety wood houses packed against the riverbank. Then you see the granite temples, unmistakeably Indian. The town's name is attributed to a Hindu saint, Mandava Rishi, who performed penance along the water.

Mandi is a typical north Indian city, easy to explore in a day. Its people are friendly and hospitable; you see few tourists. Its temples, dedicated to Shiva, are an odd mix. Some, recently constructed, are painted splashy reds and yellows. Other granite temples from the 16th and 17th centuries fill a Moghul mausoleum-shaped exterior with a Hindu interior and its ornately carved pillars and inner sanctum where the deity resides.

Arriving and Departing *See* By Hired Car with Driver in Arriving and Departing Himachal Pradesh, above.

Getting Around   Walk through Mandi's narrow lanes. For excursions, take a taxi. Bargain using Delhi rates: Rs. 3.30 for the first kilometer, Rs. 2.40 per additional kilometer.

Addresses and Numbers   Visit the **Tourist Information Center** (HPTDC Tourist Bungalow, tel. 2575), open Monday–Saturday 10–5. The **State Bank of India,** open weekdays 10–2, Saturday 10–noon, and the **General Post & Telegraph Office,** open Monday–Saturday 10–4:30, are in the center of Mandi.

Exploring   The 16th-century **Panchvaktra Temple** is on the riverbank, not far from the bridge leading to Mandi. Shiva's mount, the bull Nandi, carved from one piece of rock, guards the inner sanctum. It contains not the usual lingam, but rather a five-faced Shiva, who sits in a meditation pose, with his consort, Parvati, on his lap.

Walk 1 kilometer (a half mile) to the heart of Mandi and stroll through the maze of cobblestone lanes lined with tiny shops or stalls and an occasional temple. Sloping roofs overhang second-story balconies. The city is an Italian hill town gone Asian. Try to find **Ravi Nagar,** a spacious courtyard garden; then circle down to the river and the **Bhutnath Shrine.** Here Nandi is outside the temple, facing the inner sanctum. A sculpted archway draws your attention to the interior and the sacred lingam. Whenever there's a drought, the devout bring water from the Beas and pour it over the lingam. They say that by the time it trickles back to the river, it rains. *Allow 4 hrs for this tour. The Bhutnath is near a group of new temples on the river's edge in the heart of Mandi. Open sunrise–sunset.*

Dining   Mandi has only simple restaurants. Dress is casual, reservations are not necessary, and cost is inexpensive (under $5). No credit cards are accepted.

Cafe Shiraz. Run by HPTDC, it has institutional decor and reliable Indian, Chinese, and Continental food. *In a central Mandi square, near Bhutnath Shrine. Open 8 AM–9 PM.*
Tourist Bungalow Restaurant. Also run by HPTDC, expect the same decor and same cuisine, but you'll find a bar. *Just outside Mandi, tel. 2575. Open 7 AM–10 PM.*

Lodging   **Tourist Bungalow.** On a hill just outside the city, this old two-story building has clean, simple rooms. The best rooms are upstairs off the veranda. *Reservations: Manager, Tourist Bungalow, Mandi, H.P., tel. 2575. 7 rooms with bath (Indian shower). Facilities: bar, room service, restaurant, HPTDC office (which can arrange car rental). No credit cards. Inexpensive (under $25).*

Excursion from Mandi to Kulu Valley, Manali, and Lahaul

On to Kulu Valley and Manikaran   Put film in your camera and prepare to move at a slow pace on a 110-kilometer (68-mile) trip east from Mandi to the Kulu Valley via the Kulu Road. At Pandoh, about 15 kilometers (9 miles) out, the road climbs and the Beas River thrashes against cavernous walls of the Mandi-Larji Gorge. At Aut, about 25 kilometers (15 miles) farther, the river cuts north. Precipices tower overhead, boulders hang over the road. You've entered **Kulu Valley** (literally, "Abode of the Gods"), an 80-kilometer (50-mile) stretch through wild mountains tempered by an occasional cultivated slope. Suspension bridges cross the river and connect to hamlets of stone homes: the only clues that somehow this area has been civilized.

At Bhuntar, about 70 kilometers (43 miles) farther, turn east and cross the narrow suspension bridge. Continue on the circuitous road to **Manikaran,** which emerges behind a veil of steam bubbling up from the Parvati River. A complex of granite temples by the river fades in and out of the mist. Wood houses, weathered dark brown with gray slate roofs, crowd together in the mountain hamlet.

Manikaran
Visit the **HPTDC** Office (Hotel Parvati, tel. 35), open Monday–Saturday 10–5. There are no banks or post office.

Getting Around
Manikaran is a walker's destination. You see nothing by car.

Exploring the Sacred Springs
A Hindu legend explains the name Manikaran (Jewel in the Ear). Long ago, when Shiva and Parvati broke a journey here to begin a 1,000-year meditation (short by their standards), Shesh Nag, an underworld demon, stole Parvati's earring. Shiva shook the earth with such ferocity that the demon coughed up the jewel, plus others he had hoarded, creating the numerous holes in the area from which steam now bubbles. To commemorate this miracle, the river was named Parvati and a Shiva Lingam, still visible, was installed by the water's edge. To this day, the devout swear by the medicinal value of each spring.

Any walk in Manikaran passes hot sulfur water sputtering up between stones in cobblestone lanes, in rectangular pits where pots of food cook, in temple baths, out of holes in the earth. Visit the 15th-century **Sri Ramchandra Temple.** Open 24 hours.

Spend time in the **Gurdwara Sri Guru Nanak Dev Ji,** built in 1940 and always crowded with pilgrims taking their ritual dip. Through the thick vapor, you can barely see Sikhs reclining by the tanks and you nearly trip over dogs napping on the mud-caked floor. Upstairs is the communal kitchen, mist-clear, where free food is served to visitors staying in surrounding rooms. On the top floor is the prayer hall with the sacred holy book, Granth Sahib, displayed on the altar. The Gurdwara has a morning and evening service that's open to visitors. Women sit separate from men. Don't point your feet at the holy book or turn your back on it when you leave.

Outdoor Adventures
Hike up the path that leads south out of the tiny hamlet into the mountain. You pass a small tea stall—a great stop—before continuing to the Brahmganga River, which intersects with the Parvati. Search for exquisite wild flowers or tasty fruit or just picnic. Plan three hours for the 4-kilometer (2½-mile) hike. Luxuriate in a **hot sulfur bath:** Become a pilgrim and jump into the gender-segregated temple baths at the busy Gurdwara or recline in a private cubicle on the main floor of Hotel Parvati. *To reserve a Hotel Parvati cubicle, tel. 35. Towel and soap provided. Nominal charge. Open daily 24 hrs.*

Dining and Lodging
There's only one hotel and restaurant. The establishment doesn't accept credit cards and is inexpensive (under $25 per standard double room, including taxes and excluding service charges).

Hotel Parvati. An earthquake in 1988 put some cracks in this clean, simple two-story hotel, but they should be repaired by the time you arrive. Ask for a river view. *Reserve in advance:*

HPTDC, Manikaran, H.P. tel. 35. 12 rooms with bath. Facilities: multicuisine restaurant, room service, terraces, sulfur baths.

On to Manali
Kulu's Dussehra Festival
5

From Manikaran, head to **Kulu,** 46 kilometers (29 miles) away. On the city's outskirts is the Dhalpur Maiden (grass field)—the site of Himachal's famous **Dussehra,** the Hindu festival that celebrates the triumph of good over evil. This is the Super Bowl of India, except the outcome is known. Crowds jam the maidan to watch the pursuit and conquest of the demon Ravana by the hero Rama (an avatar of the god Vishnu). On the first day, hundreds of idols, brought down from hill temples in palanquins, are paraded before Lord Raghunathji, the valley's presiding diety. Nine days later, Dussehra ends with Lord Raghunathji sitting on the edge of the River Beas, watching over a large bonfire and the sacrifice of a bull and various small animals. To spend the night in Kulu, stay in the clean rooms with fans at **Hotel Salvari.** *Reservations: Tourism Development Officer, Kulu, H.P. tel. 2349. 8 rooms with bath. Facilities: restaurant, bar, garden, TV lounge. No credit cards. Inexpensive (under $25).*

Naggar and Malana
6

Two roads lead from Kulu to Manali, 56 kilometers (35 miles) away. Turn right at Katrain, 20 kilometers (12 miles) north of Kulu, and cross the Beas River. Head north and see **Naggar,** the seat of the former rajas of Kulu, now a sleepy village. This is also the start of the trek to mysterious **Malana,** the world's oldest democracy. Perched on a mountainside, Naggar's 400-year-old castle, built of weathered wood and stone and looking like a fort, is now a refurbished government-run hotel, with great views from its veranda. Down below rests the village, surrounded by orchards and fields that spread down to the river.

Walk through narrow lanes to an old stone **Shiva temple.** Stop at a tea stall, meander along footpaths that take you into backyards, and climb to the nearby pagoda-style **Tripura Sundari Temple.** In the **Roerich Museum,** see the 20th-century paintings of Kulu Valley by the Russian artist, Nicholas Roerich. To stay at Naggar's **Hotel Castle,** contact *Tourism Development Officer, Kulu, H.P. tel. 2349. 14 rooms with bath. Facilities: restaurant, outdoor cafeteria. No credit cards. Inexpensive (under $25).*

Manali
7

Manali sits at the foot of mountains, many of them unscaled and unnamed. In the summer, tourists jam the small city, the base for Himachal's greatest adventures: trekking into Kulu Valley and Lahaul. Many travelers come to relax on the veranda of a cozy guest house, such as John Banon's Guest House and the May Flower Guest House, old staples that live up to their reputation for good food and genuine hospitality.

Getting Around

Taxis are available at the **taxi stand** (tel. 23) in the center of town. Bargain and use Delhi rates: Rs. 3.30 for the first kilometer, Rs. 2.40 per additional kilometer.

Addresses and Numbers

Visit the **Tourist Information Office** (Manali center, tel. 25), open April–October, Monday–Saturday 8 AM–midnight; November–March, Monday–Saturday 9–7. For outdoor adventures, contact **Himalayan Adventures** (c/o May Flower Guest House, tel. 104 or 182); the **Mountaineering Institute** (tel. 42); or the **HPTDC** (Tourist Information Office, tel. 25), also a good source of cars and jeeps with drivers. **State Bank of India** and

Punjab National Bank are in the center of town and are open weekdays 10–2, Saturday 10–noon). The **General Post and Telegraph Office** is near Model Town and is open Monday–Saturday 10–4:30.

Guided Tours   **HPTDC** (Tourist Information Office, Manali, H.P. tel. 25.) runs three daily seven-hour tours around Manali (Apr.–mid-Oct.): the sights around Manali and up to Rohtang Pass, the gateway to Lahaul; Manali to Naggar; and Manali to Manikaran. Guides and porters for short treks are available through **HPTDC** or the **director, Mountaineering Institute** (tel. 42).

Exploring   Walk 1 kilometer (a half mile) from the village center to the 600-year-old **Hadimba Devi Temple,** dedicated to a wife in the legendary Pandava family, who figure prominently in the Hindu epic, Mahabharata. Set in a secluded cedar grove, the somber wood structure with a four-tiered pagoda-shape roof, is a typical north Indian Hindu temple. The local king was so enamored of the work of the artist who carved the shrine's exterior and door that he cut off the artisan's hand to prevent him from making a more beautiful temple. Undaunted, the artist used his left hand to create a second masterpiece: the Triloknath Temple at Chamba. The people who lived in Chamba chopped off his head.

In Manali, Tibetan refugees have left a Buddhist mark. See the new **Tibetan Monastery** just behind the bus stop in an area called Model Town and walk through the **Tibetan Bazaar.** Plan four hours for this walk.

Time Out   Near the taxi stand and Punjab Bank are numerous stalls that serve a plate of *paapri* (a mess of pastry, potatoes, and yogurt, covered in a sweet-and-sour sauce). It's delicious.

Outdoor Adventures   Try **fishing** for trout on the Beas River (Apr.–Oct.). Contact HPTDC for a license (tel. 25; Rs. 10 per day). For Rs. 12, enjoy **hot water springs** in a private cubicle at Vashisht, HPTDC Complex, 3 kilometers (2 miles) from Manali. Contact the Tourist Information Office (tel. 25) for a license; the springs are open 7 AM–10 PM. Take a one-day **rafting** trip on the Beas (mid-May–mid-July and mid-Aug.–mid-Sept.) Contact Himalayan Adventurers (tel. 104). The cost is $60 per person. **Ski** at Solang Valley, 13 kilometers (8 miles) away, on good slopes surrounded by glaciers and the Himalayas (mid-Jan.–mid-Mar.). Contact the Tourist Information Office (tel. 25). Equipment is for hire at a third what you pay in the West. In summer, take the three- or four-day **trek** to the secluded village of Malana (*see* Outdoor Adventures in Staying in Himachal Pradesh, above).

Shopping   Best buys are great handknit sweaters, socks, hats, mittens, and gloves; handloomed Kulu shawls; and Kulu jackets. Wander from shop to shop; they're open daily 9–8; shops have fixed prices and don't accept credit cards.

Dining   With one exception, the best meals are served in the recommended lodgings, where the dining rooms are restricted to guests.

Mount View Restaurant. This simple restaurant is crowded with booths; music plays unobtrusively; a photo of the Dalai Lama smiles down from the wall. The Buddhists who run this restaurant provide tasty Tibetan, Chinese, Indian, and Japanese meals. *Across from the Tourist Information Office. No phone. Dress: casual. No credit cards. Inexpensive (under $5*

*per person, excluding drinks, service, and taxes). Open 8 AM–
10 PM.*

Lodging   Manali is bursting with hotels, many poor substitutes for the
trees they replaced. Highly recommended lodgings are indicated by a star ★. Prices are for a standard double room or a
cottage, including taxes and excluding service charges.

Log Huts. Part of the Manali Complex run by HPTDC, these
two-bedroom cottages overlook a river, with the mountains
right outside the door. Write ahead. *Reservations: Area Manager, Tourist Information Office, Manali, H.P. tel. 25. 12 huts
with bath. Facilities: cafeteria, room service, restaurant. No
credit cards. Expensive ($60–$100).*

Span Resorts. These fancy Western-style cottage hideaways,
set on 12 acres by the Beas River, are 15 kilometers (9 miles)
from the heart of Manali. Fish and play croquet, table tennis,
or miniature golf. Meals are included; winter discount is offered. Write ahead. *Reservations: Kulu-Manali Highway,
Katrain, Kulu, H.P., tel. 38. 25 rooms with bath. Facilities:
restaurants, bar, room service, travel counter, doctor on call,
gift shop. AE. Expensive ($60 to $100).*

★ **John Banon's Guest House.** Though this isn't Manali's most
beautiful lodge, there's a garden and orchard, and the owner is
a delight and ensures a pleasant stay. Cozy rooms have fireplaces, upstairs rooms, a veranda. The mountains and town
center are a short walk away. *Meals are included. Write ahead.
Reservations: The Manali Orchards, Manali, H.P., tel. 35. 10
rooms with bath. Facilities: room service, restaurant, travel
and outdoor adventure assistance. No credit cards. Moderate
($25–$60).*

★ **May Flower Guest House.** Up the road from John Banon's is a
charming inn that steals your heart once you step onto the spacious veranda and look back at the orchard. The family-style
dining room sets the tone: everything comfortable and orderly.
Meals are included. Each room has a fireplace. You're treated
with care. Book well in advance. *Reservations: Manali, H.P.,
tel. 104. 6 rooms with bath. Facilities: room service, restaurant, travel and outdoor adventure assistance. No credit cards.
Closed Nov. 15–Feb. Moderate ($25–$60).*

Hotel Pinewood. Near the other nice inns, this lodge is set on a
lovely lawn and offers a winter discount. Ask for an upstairs
room, which opens onto a porch. The rustic rooms have fireplaces. Write ahead. *Reservations: Manali, H.P., tel. 118. 10
rooms with bath. Facilities: restaurant. No credit cards. Inexpensive (under $25).*

On to the Lahaul begins 51 kilometers (32 miles) north of Manali on the
Lahaul District far side of the Rohtang Pass, 3,978 meters (13,050 feet) high. To
travel through its commingling of religion and nature is memo-
rable. The area's one rough road hugs cliff edges with cold
rivers racing in gorges hundreds of feet below. Streams shoot
across the road. Rocky mountains bear in from all directions.
Crossing windswept passes, you feel as if you've arrived at the
top of the world. Glaciers are somber. An occasional lake spar-
kles under a hot sun. Prayer flags or rare green valleys beckon
with their unexpected display of color; so do the red and white
gompas. Lahaul is just now experiencing an influx of tourists,
but, unlike Ladakh, quiet prevails.

The Buddhists of Lahaul, in their dark trousers and long over-
coats are Mongolian and follow a Tibetan form of Tantric

Buddhism, usually the *Gelug* (Yellow Hat Sect), led by the Dalai Lama. The women twist their hair into numerous pigtails, held in place by a silver ornament that hangs to the waist. As with most Buddhist communities, you'll also notice that men and women share all tasks—from raising a family to fieldwork. To see Lahaul, you must be prepared for high altitude. You're usually above 3,658 meters (12,000 feet). To get around, you have two good options: your feet or a jeep—which limits you to areas accesible by road only. Even if you go by jeep, the journey is slow. Roads pass over creaking bridges that you must inch across and wind around narrow passages blasted through rock, bump through debris from landslides, or make strenous climbs up to passes chiseled through hard snow.

Getting Around For the best way to experience Lahaul, see the description of the top trekking routes under Outdoor Adventures in Staying in Himachal Pradesh, above. Arrange well in advance for a jeep through **Himalayan Adventures** (*see* Travel Agencies in Staying in Himachal Pradesh, above) or **HPTDC** (Manali, tel. 25).

Staying in Lahaul All travelers should bring water purification tablets and canteen, lots of energy-producing snacks (available in Manali), provisions, sleeping bag and all camping gear, flashlight with ample batteries, sunglasses that keep out ultraviolet rays, powerful sunblock, and hat with broad brim. Except for small villages and Keylong, where you find simple Tibetan meals, the food—inexpensive (under $5)—will be cooked vegetables, *chappatis* (unleavened fried bread), and rice. All lodging is inexpensive (under $25 for a standard double room, including taxes and excluding service charges) and spartan except for Keylong. Credit cards are not accepted.

Exploring Keylong Lahaul's capital, no larger than a village, is **Keylong,** 117 kilometers (72 miles) from Manali. This is the site of Lahaul's most **8** important monastery, the 12th-century **Kardong Gompa,** whose monks and nuns belong to the Gelug. Follow a narrow path, shaded by willows, that winds about 4 kilometers (2½ miles) up the steep hill to the monastery overlooking Keylong and the Bhaga River. Near the summit, just before a cluster of square clay homes, is an enormous *chorten* (shrine containing sacred relics). The four Kardong chapels are decorated with thang-kas (religious scrolls), murals, and cylindrical prayer wheels, including an enormous one that contains 1,000 strips of paper, each inscribed with the sacred mantra: *Om Mani Padme Hum* (Hail to the Jewel in the Lotus). Inside the most sacred chamber are the holy ashes of Lama Narbhu Rimpoche, who reconstructed the gompa in the early 1900s. Walk slowly at this high altitude. Plan five hours for this hike.

Dining and Lodging Stalls in Keylong serve Tibetan food and are usually open 8–8.

Keylong Tourist Hotel. By 1991, the renovation will be completed at this hotel; it will operate under solar power and have a swimming pool and more rooms. You can also stay in safaristyle tents with cots. *Reservations: Area Manager, Tourist Information Office, Manali, H.P., tel. 25. 3 rooms with bath (Indian shower), numerous tents with shared bath. Facilities: catering service. No credit cards. Closed mid-Oct. to May. Inexpensive (under $25).*

Excursions from Keylong to Guru Ghantal The hilltop gompa, **Guru Ghantal,** is at the confluence of the Chandra and Bhaga rivers, southwest of Keylong. This is Lahaul's oldest monastery, reputedly 800 years old, which

belongs to the Nyingmapa (Old Sect) founded by Padmasambhava, Guru Rimpoche. Next to the Ghantal is an eight-
story castle of wood and stone belonging to the thakur (king) of
Ghantal. Lamas perform *chaams* (ritual dances) during an August fair. Check with the tourist department for the date. *The
walk—11 kilometers (about 7 miles) each way—to the gompa
requires an early morning start, or spend the night in a tent.
Bring all supplies and a flashlight. Gompa open sunrise–
sunset.*

**Excursion from
Keylong to
Udaipur
and Triloknath**

9

Go by jeep or on foot 49 kilometers (30 miles) northwest of
Keylong to **Udaipur** and **Triloknath,** two important pilgrimage
destinations. In Udaipur, Hindus flock to the wood 11th-
century **temple,** dedicated to a manifestation of the goddess
Kali. It has ornate interior carvings. *Open 24 hours.* The
Indian-style stone and brick **Triloknath Gompa,** 3 kilometers
(1½ miles) from Udaipur, sits behind a wall, a modern addition.
Open sunrise to sunset.

Excursion from Mandi to Dharamsala and Kangra Valley

From Lahaul or Manali, head southwest to Mandi for a trip
northwest into **Kangra** and its district capital, **Dharamsala,**
home of the exiled Dalai Lama. Located 147 kilometers (91
miles) from Mandi, the valley's civilization dates back 3,500
years to the age of the Vedas (sacred liturgical texts); it's described in the Mahabharata epic and Puranas (sacred legends),
which makes it one of the oldest hill states in India.

During the 16th- and 17th-century Moghul rule, this was the
place to get a nose job. People from Nepal and India flocked to
the valley to have their proboscises reconstructed after they
had been lopped off, a popular punishment for minor infrac-
tions. Artistry also flourished in more conventional media:
Kangra miniatures, paintings with minute detail and exquisite
color, are considered among the finest in the world.

The road winds through small villages and orchards, past goats
nibbling grass in nearby fields. Water buffalos amble on the
road. You enter pine forests and groves of eucalyptus and sugarcane, with monkeys scampering in the branches. Finally, you
enter a wide valley with the snow-covered peaks of the
Dhauladhar Range in the distance.

Baijnath Temple

10

Your first stop is **Baijnath,** with its important Hindu temple
dedicated to Shiva Vaidyanatha(Lord of Physicians). (Hang-
gliders take note: Billing, east of Baijnath, is the start for
flights.) The **Baijnath Temple,** constructed in the spire-topped
Shikhara style, is considered the oldest north Indian Shiva
temple. Like most stone temples in Himachal, Baijnath is not
massive; it sits on the crest of a low mountain, with stone steps
leading down to the Bindwakund River. You enter the temple
through the *mandapa* (pavilion), supported by four pillars with
handsome carvings, including an unusual composite image of
Vishnu and his consort Lakshmi. The mandapa leads to the inner sanctum and its Shiva lingam, one of 12 natural lingams
(*jyotorlingas*) worshiped in India.

*Dining and Lodging
in Baijnath*

If you want to spend the night, stay in the lovely **Palace Motel,**
an antique-filled former palace (don't think grand) turned into
a hotel. *Write ahead. Reservations: Palace Motel, Taragarh,*

Kangra Valley, H.P., tel. 34. (Baijnath). 12 rooms with bath.
Facilities: restaurant (open 6 AM–11 PM), room service, TV in
lounge. No credit cards. Inexpensive (under $25).

Dharamsala From Palampur, 10 kilometers (about 6 miles) beyond
Baijnath, tea gardens and forests of pine lead to the former
⑪ British Hill Station of **Dharamsala,** surrounded by snow-
capped peaks. Dharamsala is broken into two centers. In **Lower
Dharamsala,** you find the Kotwali Bazar, schools, businesses,
government offices, and a bustle that's distinctly Indian and
Hindu in character. **Upper Dharamsala,** Mcleod Ganj, 10 kilometers (about 6 miles) away, has a quiet aura that's decidedly
Tibetan and Buddhist and is the original location of the hill station. This is where the Dalai Lama lives; Buddhists from all
over the world come here to study with His Holiness.

Getting Around Taxis, unmetered, are at the **bus stand** in Lower Dharamsala.
Use them for excursions in and around Dharamsala (tel. 2243).
Bargain using Delhi rates: Rs. 3.30 for the first kilometer, Rs.
2.40 per additional kilometer. If you stay in Upper Dharamsala, everything worth seeing is within walking distance.

Addresses and Visit the **Tourist Information Assistant** (HPTDC) (Kotwali Ba-
Numbers zar, Lower Dharamsala; tel. 2363), open Monday–Saturday
10–5. The **State Bank of India,** open weekdays 10–2, Saturday
10–noon, and the **General Post and Telegraph Office,** open
Monday–Saturday 10–4:30, are in Lower Dharamsala.

Exploring Upper In Mcleod Ganj, visit the **Tibetan Medical and India Astro Insti-**
Dharamsala **tute,** where students study astrology and a style of holistic
medicine originally expounded by Sakyamuni (the Historic
Buddha). Here, medicines are created at auspicious times under specific conditions, such as in the light of the moon. The
pharmacy produces over 200 medicines, including the Great
Iron Pill for eye ailments, Precious Old Turquoise for liver ailments, and Purified Moon Crystal to prevent wrinkles and
white hair.

Also see the **Namgyal Monastery,** where hundreds of monks
gather inside the new gompa to sit and pray beneath an enormous golden image of the Buddha. *Non-Buddhists enter the
interior of the shrine from a side entrance. Open sunrise–
sunset.*

On Sunday, wander through the **Tibetan flea market,** a short
walk from the heart of Mcleod Ganj. Just ask anyone to point
the way. This outdoor event is also heavily attended by inquisi-
tive monkeys.

Also visit the one stalwart monument that survived the earthquake of 1905—St. John's Church in the Wilderness—set in a
cozy pine grove 2 kilometers (about a mile) from the center of
Mcleod Ganj.

Outdoor Adventures From August to June, fishing enthusiasts can try for mahseer
in the Beas River near Nadaun, 10 kilometers (about 6 miles)
away. Obtain a licence from the District Fisheries Officer in
Dharamsala. From Dharamsala you can take a one-day, 12-ki-
lometer (about 7-mile), **hike** to Triund, 2,865 meters (9,397
feet) up, at the base of snow-clad mountains. Start early.

Shopping In Upper Dharamsala, visit the **Tibetan Handicraft Center,**
open Monday–Saturday 9–5, and numerous small stalls (open

daily) that sell Tibetan curios, new carpets, and thang-kas. None of these shops takes credit cards.

Dining This is a town where restaurants come and go, many of them started by Western Buddhists who later moved on. Dress is casual, and reservations are not necessary. All are inexpensive (under $5) and don't take credit cards.

Highly recommended restaurants are indicated by a star ★. Prices are per person, excluding drinks, service, and taxes.

★ **Toepa.** This is a tiny, laid-back Tibetan "coffee house." You meet Buddhists studying the scriptures and eating tasty Tibetan food. *On the main street of Upper Dharamsala. Open 8 AM–9:30 PM.*

Hotel Dhauladhar Restaurant. Sit outside on the terrace surrounded by views or sit inside the multicuisine restaurant with its institutional decor. *Lower Dharamsala, tel. 2107. Open 8–10 and 1–3: snacks: 5–7 and 8–10.*

Lodging Highly recommended lodgings are indicated by a star ★. Prices in the moderate range are for a standard double room, including taxes and excluding service charges. Dormitories are inexpensive.

★ **Hotel Bhagsu.** Within walking distance of the prime attractions, this simple bungalow is set back on a pleasant lawn in Upper Dharamsala. All rooms are spacious and pleasant. *Write ahead. Reservations: The Manager, Hotel Bhagsu, Dharamsala, H.P., tel. 2290. 15 rooms with bath. Facilities: restaurant. No credit cards. Inexpensive (under $25).*

Hotel Dhauladhar. In Lower Dharamsala, the bungalow portion offers more amenities. The hotel also has two very inexpensive dormitories (Rs. 20 per bed). Though the views from the hotel are fine, it's 10 kilometers (about 6 miles) from everything worth visiting. Write ahead. *Reservations: The Manager, Hotel Dhauladhar, Dharamsala, H.P., tel. 2256. 21 rooms with bath and 2 dormitories with shared bath. Facilities: restaurant, terrace, bar. No credit cards. Inexpensive (under $25).*

Nightlife Inquire at the HPTDC (tel. 2363) about Tibetan music and dance at the **Tibetan Institute of Performing Arts,** 1 kilometer (a half mile) up the hill from the center of Mcleod Ganj. Starting the second Saturday in April, the institute puts on a 10-day festive Tibetan opera.

Excursion from Dharamsala to Jwalamukhi Temple ⑫ According to Hindu legend, when Shiva circled the earth with the dead body of his consort Sati (Parvati) and created turmoil, Lord Vishnu put a stop to his agony by cutting Sati's body into pieces. Sati's tongue fell at the site of the **Jwalamukhi Temple,** southwest of Dharamsala, and flames appeared, over which the raja of Chamba built a temple. Supposedly, the Moghul Emperor Akbar tried and failed to smother the flames. Out of respect, he left behind a solid gold umbrella, which still remains. The flames continue to burn, kept alive by attendent priests. Inside the temple, you find no idol, only the flames shooting up from rock crevasses. The huge brass bell inside the mandapa was a gift of the king of Nepal. To this day, the Jwalamukhi is one of the most important pilgrim centers in north India and the site of an important April festival. Allow five hours to get there by car. *56 km (35 mi) from Dharamsala. Open sunrise to sunset.*

Excursion from Dharamsala to Chamba and Chamba Valley	**Dalhousie,** 124 kilometers (77 miles) from Dharamsala, the gateway to **Chamba Valley** is set on five hills rising from the main ridges of the Dhauladhar. A former British hill station, it has seen far better days. Move on.

Khajjiar
⓭

From Dalhousie, head to **Khajjiar,** 22 kilometers (14 miles) farther, a beautiful saucer-shape meadow with a tiny sacred pond in the center surrounded by pine trees. An idol of the local diety, Khajinag (a serpent), is enshrined in a nearby temple covered with a golden dome. You see more horses than people.

You can spend the night and have a meal in the **Hotel Devdar** on a hill overlooking the meadow. Run by the HPTDC, the old bungalow has minimally furnished doubles with Indian-style bathrooms (hot and cold water available) and a six-bed dormitory with shared bath. Write ahead. *Reservations: The Area Manager, HPTDC, Dalhousie, H.P., tel. 36. 11 rooms with bath; dormitory with shared bath. Facilities: restaurant, heaters available, room service, horseback riding. No credit cards. Closed Dec.–mid-Apr. Inexpensive (under $25).*

Again, a narrow road climbs until you look straight into the Himalayas. On a mountain crest, the road begins its slow descent to Chamba, 53 kilometers (33 miles) from Dalhousie, winding continuously while hugging the edge of the mountains that slope down to the nearby Ravi River. The land is now terraced and cultivated. Dusty footpaths cut across the hills. You

⓮ round a bend, and **Chamba,** the district capital of the Chamba Valley, spreads out on both sides of the Ravi River. You are now 180 kilometers (111 miles) from Dharamsala.

Getting Around Chamba

Unmetered taxis are available. Bargain using Delhi rates: Rs 3.30 for the first kilometer, 2.40 per additional kilometer.

Addresses and Numbers

Visit the **Tourist Information Center** (Hotel Iravati, tel. 94). The **State Bank of India,** open weekdays 10–2, Saturday 10–noon, and the **General Post and Telegraph Office,** open Monday–Saturday 10–4:30, are in the middle of Chamba.

Exploring Chamba

Walk into the center of Chamba and see the **Lakshminarayan Temple complex** with numerous shrines built between the 8th and 10th centuries. The temples dedicated to Vishnu or Shiva are in the typical Himachal Shikara style with two parasol roofs; the other temples, which are dedicated to the goddess Durga or to *nagas* (serpents), are in a less ornate flat-topped indigenous style. *Open 24 hours.*

Down by the river, near the entrance to the Chaugan Maidan (town green), you find the **Hari Rai Temple,** dedicated to Vishnu, which dates back to the 11th century and contains a beautiful bronze statue of Chaturmurti (Vishnu with four arms). *Open 24 hours.*

Also visit the **Bhuri Singh Museum,** right in town, with its excellent collection of miniature paintings from the Kangra and Basoli schools. *Admission: nominal. Open Tues.–Sun. 10–5.*

If you visit Chamba after the harvest, the Chaugan Maidan comes alive during the week-long **Minjar Fair,** which starts on a Sunday at the old Chamba Palace. Hill people wearing golden silk *minjars* (corn tassles) follow a colorful palanquin containing Lord Raghuvira, Chamba's presiding deity, and other palanquins with other temple gods through the city to the holy

Ravi River. The devotees invoke the rain god, Varuna, and immerse their minjars in the water.

Dining and Lodging The only place to eat and stay is the hotel run by the HPTDC.

Hotel Iravati. This multistory hotel has spacious rooms with overhead fans. Some rooms have balconies. *Reservations: Area Manager, HPTDC, Dalhousie, H.P., tel. 36. 12 rooms with bath (shower). Facilities: multicuisine, inexpensive restaurant; room service; tourist office. No credit cards. Inexpensive (under $25).*

Excursion from Chamba to Bharmour
15

From Chamba, head southeast by car on a day trip to **Bharmour:** the base of the Gujjar and the Gaddi, who prod herds of sheep and cattle along well-worn footpaths up steep inclines to small clusters of simple dwellings. Bharmour used to be their summer home. Now families are encouraged to stay year-round and develop cash crops: wheat, walnuts, almonds, maise, and apples.

The road cuts through a mountain valley that first winds along the Ravi, then turns with the swift-moving Buddhal River. Streams splash across the pavement. The river gorge widens, revealing a quick glimpse of a distant peak or a splinter of sky. Suspension bridges carry villagers and their animals across the water. All along the way, you see the intrepid Gaddi.

The small village of Bharmour, 69 kilometers (43 miles) from Chamba, dates back at least to the 7th century and isn't much larger than its central square with 84 temples—many of them small structures with simple lingams.

Pilgrimage to Lake Manimahesh
16

If you're near Bharmour during the six-day Hindu pilgrimage to **Lake Manimahesh** during July or August, go. This pilgrimage is an astonishing adventure (*see* Festivals and Seasonal Events, in Staying in Himachal Pradesh, above). You can also trek from here into the rugged Pangi Valley (*see* Outdoor Adventures in Staying in Himachal Pradesh, above).

Jammu and Kashmir, Including Ladakh

Introduction

No part of the Himalayas has captured the traveler's heart as much as Kashmir, surrounded by India's Himachal Pradesh, Pakistan, and Tibet. The mountains add majesty to Kashmir's vales, lakes, and glacier-fed rivers. Starting with Akbar in the late 1500s, it charmed the Moghul emperors, who came from their winter palaces in the southern plains to their Persian-style Kashmir gardens, architectural gems whose beauty rivaled that of the landscape.

When Jammu and Kashmir's maharajah, who controlled the vale until India's independence, denied the British the right to own land, they devised a charming solution: the houseboat. Soon a flotilla, outfitted with Victoriana, sat smugly in the water.

Given nature's blessings, Kashmir should be nothing but enchanting, but 20th-century tourism has taken its toll. During summer in Srinagar, the state capital, instead of Moslem chants that praise Allah, more often you hear children cry "one rupee, one rupee." You see man-made ugliness more often than wild animals and rip-off prices for dubious merchandise. The road trip from Kashmir to Ladakh has become a Himalayan car rally.

Having said all this, is a visit to Jammu and Kashmir and Ladakh worth the time or expense? Yes, if you plan your trip wisely. (*See* Highlights for First-time Visitors, below.)

Addresses and Numbers

Tourist Information   Contact the **Directorate of Tourism** (Shervani Rd., Tourist Reception Center, Srinagar, J. & K. tel. 72449 or 77303), which is open 24 hours a day. The tourist department has branches in other state destinations. (*See* destination sections for addresses and telephone numbers.)

Emergencies   For all emergencies, turn to your hotel or the tourist department or contact your embassy in Delhi: **American** (Shanti Path, tel. 690351); **Canadian** (7/8 Shanti Path, tel. 619461); **British** (Shanti Path, tel. 690371).

Travel Agencies   For good treks and outdoor adventures, contact **Boktoo and Sons Travel Agency** (Box 95, Srinagar, J. & K., tel. 74547) and **Dragon Tours & Travels** (4 Polo View, Srinagar, J. & K., tel. 77330). To raft the Zanskar River in Zanskar Valley, contact **Himalayan River Runners** (188-A Jor Bagh, New Delhi, tel. 615736). To raft the Lidder and Sindh rivers in Kashmir, contact **Travel Corporation** (India) TCI, Kaul Bldg., Maulana Azad Rd., Srinagar, J. & K., tel. 73525).

Highlights for First-time Visitors

If you're curious about Hinduism and want to trek, go to Jammu, the city of golden-spired temples. An excellent trek, overlooked by foreigners, starts in Kishtwar, a 10-hour drive from Jammu. In Kashmir, stay on a Victorian-style houseboat in Srinigar and go to sleep to the sound of Moslem chanting.

Art lovers must not miss the antiquities of the Buddhist monasteries in Ladakh. Go by jeep on a glorious trip over mountain passes from Kargil in Ladakh into Zanskar Valley, a high-altitude, temple-strewn valley just opening up to tourism. From tiny Padam, the district capital, you can do a rugged 10-day trek over soaring passes or take the most harrowing and scenically beautiful rafting trip on the subcontinent.

Getting Around

Travel by plane is the fastest (unless the flight is canceled) way to get around. With a private car or jeep (best for Ladakh), the trip is more expensive, but you decide what you see and where you go. Taxis are good for long hauls to popular destinations, and you can share the cost with other travelers.

By Plane   **Indian Airlines** flies daily between Jammu and Srinagar (30 minutes) and makes five weekly flights between Leh and Srinagar (45 minutes). Book well in advance.

By Hired Car with Driver To hire a car with driver, use a travel agency listed below in each major city section. Figure about Rs. 4 per kilometer with a halt charge of Rs. 50–Rs. 100 per night.

By Hired Jeep with Driver If you want to visit Zanskar, south of Kargil, you must go by jeep unless you walk or hitch a truck ride. Figure about $400–$500 for a good tour of Ladakh from Srinagar; add $100 for Zanskar. Hire your jeep and driver through a travel agency listed under Leh or Srinagar.

By Taxi Taxi drivers don't like to adhere to fixed rates determined by destination. But before hiring a taxi, get the legal rate from the tourist department, then haggle with the driver. From Jammu to Srinagar, the cost should be around $50; from Srinagar to Leh, $125.

Guided Tours

There are no state-sponsored tours of Jammu and Kashmir. You can take tours around Jammu, Srinagar, or Ladakh that are arranged by the Jammu and Kashmir Tourism Development Corporation (J&KTDC).

Outdoor Adventures

Highly recommended adventures are indicated by a star ★.

Bicycling: The Srinagar Tourist Reception Center rents 10-speed bikes.

★ **Climbing and Mountaineering:** many mountains throughout the region are open to expeditions; the climbing season extends from mid-May to mid-October. To climb a mountain in India demands advance planning and prior permission from the Indian Mountaineering Foundation (Benito Juarez Rd., New Delhi, tel. 671211). It can take two years to get a climb approved. You can also join an organized expedition offered by a special-interest tour group listed in Before You Go to the Himalayas, Chapter 1, or in Before You Go to North India, above.

★ **Fishing:** From March to October, Kashmir has the best trout fishing in the Indian Himalayas. Get a six-day permit and information on locations and equipment from the Department of Fisheries (Srinagar's Tourist Reception Center) or at Yennar near Pahalgam.

★ **Golfing:** Golfers can play at Srinagar, Pahalgam, and Gulmarg (Apr.–Oct.). Equipment is available. If your handicap is under 15, you can enter tournaments. For details, contact the J&K Tourist Department (Tourist Reception Center, Srinagar, tel. 72449).

★ **Horseback Riding:** Contact J&K Tourist Department to arrange rides in Pahalgam, Sonamarg, and Gulmarg. Go by pony for up to a week on the Amar Nath Pilgrimage (*see* Trekking).

Hot Springs: Good hot springs await the trekker who heads from Kishtwar to the tiny village of Totowain in Kashmir. In Anantnag, near Srinagar, you also find springs.

★ **Rafting:** *Lidder and Sindh rivers:* In Kashmir, rafters can take a one-day run on the Lidder or a two-day run on the Sindh (May–June and mid-Aug.–Sept.).

Jammu and Kashmir, including Ladakh

PAKISTAN

Drass

Mt. Harmukh ▲

Bandipur

Wular Lake

Wangath

Sonamarg 🥾 **8**

Sopore

Sindh R.

🏠 **Amar Nath cave**

Nasim Bagh

Shalimar Bagh

Dachigam National Park

Baramula

Mansabal Lake

Mahagunus Pass

Nagin Lake

Dal Lake

3 🛫

Nishat Bagh

7

Pahalgam 🥾

4 Tangmarg

Srinagar

Chasma Shahi

Gulmarg

Pampore

Totowain

Jhelum

Inshan

Liddar R.

Bijbehara

🥾

Anantnag **5**

Lehinvan

Achabal

Daksum

Verinag **6**

Kishtwar

Vaishno Devi **2**

Katra

Uidhampur

🛫 **1** **Jammu**

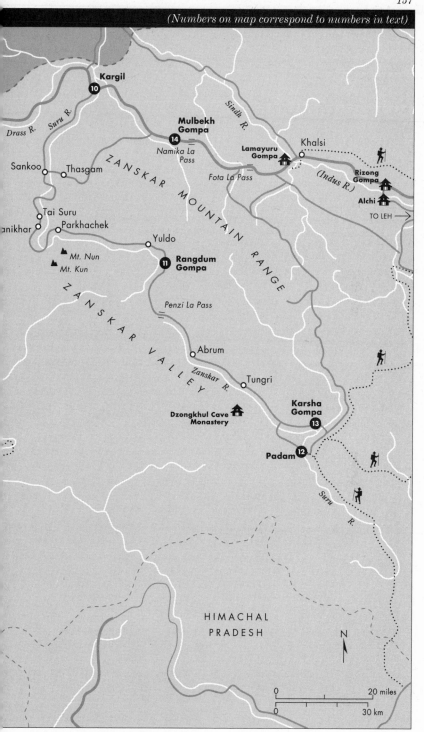

Kargil **10**

Drass R.

Suru R.

Sindh R.

**Mulbekh
Gompa** **14**

*Namika La
Pass*

**Lamayuru
Gompa**

Khalsi

(Indus R.)

**Rizong
Gompa**

Fota La Pass

Sankoo

Thasgam

Alchi

TO LEH →

Tai Suru

nikhar

Parkhachek

ZANSKAR MOUNTAIN RANGE

Yuldo

▲ Mt. Nun

▲ Mt. Kun

11 **Rangdum
Gompa**

Penzi La Pass

Z A N S K A R   V A L L E Y

Abrum

Zanskar R.

Tungri

**Karsha
Gompa**

**Dzongkhul Cave
Monastery**

13

Padam **12**

Suru R.

H I M A C H A L

P R A D E S H

N

0   20 miles

0   30 km

★ *Zanskar River:* Experienced rafters can make the six-day run from Padam to the Indus River (mid-July–mid-Sept.). Arrange in advance. Contact Himalayan River Runners (*see* Travel Agencies, above).

★ **Skiing and Heliskiing:** You can ski (mid-Dec.–mid-Apr.) at Gulmarg near Srinagar, at a third of what you pay in the West. You can rent excellent equipment. Slopes have T-bars and a chair lift; a gondola car is scheduled for completion in 1990. Lessons are available. Heliskiing in remote valleys, a new sport for the accomplished skier, is available through Adventure on Skis (815 North Rd., Rte. 202, Westfield, MA 01085, tel. 800/628–9655 or 413/568–2855).

Shikara Trips: From Srinagar, you can go by *shikara* (gondola) for three to seven days to nearby lakes. A very lazy way to travel, it's not recommended to the active. The scenery is magical; you explore small villages and camp on bucolic little islands. Contact our recommended outdoor adventure outfits; if you're staying on a houseboat, the owner can arrange a trip.

Trekking: Trekking season in Kashmir is April–November; in Ladakh, July–October. No special permits are required. You can rent good camping gear from the tourist departments in Srinagar, Kargil, Kishtwar, Sonamarg, and Pahalgam. For any trek over a week, advance planning is recommended. Contact our recommended outdoor adventure agencies. Highly recommended treks are indicated with a star ★.

Trekking (up to a week): ★*Vaishno Devi*. Make a 13.5-kilometer (8-mile) trek to the venerated cave that honors three Hindu goddesses. The pilgrimage begins at Katra, near Jammu.

★ *Amar Nath Pilgrimage*. This strenuous five-day trek (July or Aug.) starts at Pahalgam, near Srinagar, and ends at the sacred Amar Nath Cave. Bring tenting gear. You follow the Lidder River, pass flower-strewn meadows, cross the Mahagunus Pass, then wait with thousands of chanting devotees to see the revered lingam. Children under age 12 are not allowed—too many people. To go by pony, arrange in advance with Assistant Director Tourism, Pahalgam, J. & K.

★ *Around Leh*. For five to seven days, you can visit Lamayuru, Shey, Hemis, and Thikse monasteries and hike through Ladakh's mountaintop landscape of sand dunes surrounded by snow-covered peaks. Bring camping gear and provisions and hire a guide through the local tourist department or our recommended travel agencies.

Trekking (over a week): ★*Kishtwar to Lehinvan or Srinagar*. From Kishtwar near Jammu, you head through the Margan Pass into the remote Marwa and Warvan valleys, with their gorges, rivers, glaciers, rice paddies, flowering meadows, and orchards. You share the trail with mule trains and shepherds. Relax in hot springs in Totawoin village; get a close look at Himalayan peaks. You can extend this nine-day trek to 25 days and go through Zanskar Valley across windswept passes to Ladakh.

★ *Zanskar to Leh*. From Zanskar Valley, you can do a tough, high-altitude 10-day trek from Padam. You cross a rope bridge; wind through gorges; climb up steep ridges and over high passes; and, if you're lucky, see wild animals. You meet Tibetans, Ladakhis, and yak herders.

Wildlife Parks: *Dachigam National Park*. Near Srinagar, this former exclusive preserve of the maharajah of Kashmir is home to leopards, red deer, *hanguls* (rare Kashmir stag), and the Himalayan brown bear, plus 150 species of birds. For passes into the year-round sanctuary and reservations in simple huts (sleeping bags are advised), contact the Chief Wildlife Warden (Tourist Reception Center, Srinagar, J. & K., tel. 72449 or 77303).

Kishtwar High Altitude Park in Jammu has musk deer, Himalayan black and brown bear, and 50 species of birds. Best viewing season is March–May. No pass is required.

In Ladakh's *Hemis High-Altitude National Park*, you may see rare bharal sheep, great Tibetan sheep, ibex, and snow leopards, plus numerous high-altitude birds, including the Himalayan snow cock. Best viewing season is September–May. For passes or permission to camp, contact the Wildlife Warden, (Tourist Department, Leh, J & K).

Jammu

Numbers in the margin correspond with points of interest on the Jammu and Kashmir map.

① **Jammu,** known as the "City of Temples," has long been a center of Indian arts and culture. For centuries, Pahari painters have created lovely miniatures of Hindu subjects, which show a dexterity of line and matchless blend of color. Before Independence, unlike Kashmir, Jammu was a private domain, where the local maharajah had his winter palace. No European could enter Jammu without his permission.

Arriving and Departing
By Plane

If you plan a summer visit, get your ticket months in advance and reconfirm your flight 72 hours before departure. **Indian Airlines** makes a daily two-hour flight to Jammu from Delhi's **National Airport.** On arrival, foreigners must register at the **Foreigners' Regional Registration Office** in the terminal. The **Jammu Airport** is 6 kilometers (4 miles) from Jammu. Call for **flight information** (in Delhi, tel. 3312587; in Jammu, tel. 42735).

Between Airport and City

No scheduled airport bus operates in Jammu; take a taxi into town (about Rs. 20).

By Hired Car with Driver

It takes a day to get from Delhi to Jammu. Hire a car with driver from one of our recommended travel agencies.

By Train

The afternoon-departing *Shalimar Express* and the late-night *Pune Jammu Jhelum Express* leave daily from the **New Delhi Railway Station.** The trip takes about 15 hours. Reserve a sleeper and a berth. For maximum comfort, book first or second (air-conditioned) class. Call for train information in Delhi (tel. 3313535).

Getting Around

Taxi drivers hate to use their meters. Bargain using Delhi rates: Rs. 3.30 for the first kilometer, Rs. 2.40 per additional kilometer. You can take an auto rickshaw, which is cheaper than a taxi, or, cheapest of all, a *tonga* (horse-drawn cart).

Addresses and Numbers

Visit the **Tourist Reception Center** between 8 AM and 10 PM (Veer Marg, tel. 48172). For travel arrangements or to hire a car with driver, contact **J&KTDC** (Tourist Reception Center, Veer

Marg, tel. 5421), **Razdan Travel Service** (Sohan Singh Market, below Gumal, tel. 49379), or the travel counters at the **Asia Jammu Tawi Hotel** (Nehra Market, tel. 49430) or **Hotel Jammu Ashok** (Jammu Tawi, tel. 43127). For a long-distance taxi, contact the **Special Tourist Taxi Association** (Tourist Reception Center, Veer Marg, tel. 46266). Most offices are open daily 10–6. The **State Bank of India,** at Hari Market and at Raghunath Bazar, is open weekdays 10–2, Saturday 10–noon. The **General Post Office** on Pacca Danga Raja Ram, is open Monday–Saturday 10–4:30.

Guided Tours The **J&KTDC** at the Tourist Reception Center (Veer Marg, tel. 5421) provides a tour to Amar Mahal Palace Museum, Dogra Art Gallery, Ranbireswar Temple, Raghunath Mandir, and Bahur Fort.

Exploring Visit the largest Hindu temple complex in Northern India; the multitower, lavishly gold-leafed, 19th-century **Raghunath Temple** in the heart of the city is dedicated to the Ramayama epic's hero Rama (also the god Vishnu's eighth incarnation). Attend the joyous ritual of a morning or evening *arti* (prayer service). Ask the Tourist Reception Center for times. Nearby **Ranbireswar Temple,** with its 75-meter (246-foot) tower, was built soon after Raghunath and is dedicated to Lord Shiva. Inside are 12 large crystal lingams, plus thousands of smaller lingams attached to stone slabs. *Open sunrise–sunset.*

Bahu Fort, surrounded by gardens, sits on a rocky ridge by the Tawi River. The oldest building in Jammu, it was started over 3,000 years ago and contains a temple dedicated to Kali, the Hindu goddess of destruction. *Open sunrise–sunset.*

The **Amar Mahal Palace Museum** sits above the Tawi—looking like a French chateau. It displays graceful Pahari miniatures and portraits of the former rulers of Jammu and Kashmir. *Admission: Rs. 1. Open winter, Mon.–Sat. 10–noon and 3–5, Sun. 10–noon; summer, Mon.–Sat. 3–7, Sun. 10–noon. Closed state holidays.*

Also see the **Dogra Art Gallery,** with its fine Pahari miniatures. *Gandhi Bhawan, opposite the New Secretariat. Admission free. Open Tues.–Sun. (winter) 11–5; (summer) 7:30–1.*

Dining Hotels in Jammu are your best bet. Dress is casual. Reservations are not necessary. Prices are per person, excluding drinks, service, and taxes. Highly recommended restaurants are indicated by a star ★.

★ **Cosmo Bar and Restaurant.** This unpretentious, air-conditioned restaurant has great local ambience and serves good food—Indian, Mughlai, Chinese, and Continental. *Hotel Cosmopolitan, Veer Marg, tel. 47561. DC, V. Open noon–10. Inexpensive (under $5).*

Lodging Highly recommended lodgings are indicated by a star ★. Prices are for a standard double room, including taxes and excluding service charges.

Hotel Asia Jammu Tawi. A Western-style hotel, about 1½ kilometers (1 mile) from the center of town, it has reasonably attractive air-conditioned rooms, and best, a swimming pool. *Nehru Market, Jammu, J. & K., tel. 49430. 44 rooms with bath. Facilities: pool, health club, room service, restaurant*

*with live music, bar, TV, foreign exchange and travel counter,
shopping arcade, doctor on call. AE, DC. Moderate ($25–$60).*
★ **Hotel Asia Jammu Ashok.** Across from the Amar Mahal Palace,
this government hotel is modern with pleasant rooms. *Jammu
Tawi, J. & K., tel. 43127. 49 rooms with bath. Facilities: pool,
bar, restaurant, coffee shop, shopping arcade, TV, foreign exchange and travel counter, doctor on call. AE, DC, MC, V.
Moderate ($25–$60).*

Excursion from Jammu to Katra

From April until the end of August, make the 13-kilometer (8-
mile) **pilgrimage from Katra**—50 kilometers (31 miles) from
❷ Jammu—to the **cave** that honors the goddess Vaishno Devi. The
gods created her to overcome evil, which she did when she
slayed the demon Bhairon who had chased her to this mountain
retreat. Slosh through water to reach a dimly lit cave—an inner sanctum dedicated to the Hindu goddesses Lakshmi, Kali,
and Sarasvati, whose images are protected under gold and silver canopies. Snacks are available. You need a pass from
officials in Katra to get into the cave. You can spend the night at
the clean, Western-style **Asia Vaishnodevi Katra Hotel,** a short
walk from the bus stand. *Katra, J. & K., tel. 627. Reservations
advised. 37 rooms with bath. Facilities: vegetarian restaurant,
health club with sauna and massage, prayer room, travel
counter, barbershop, room service. DC. Moderate ($25–$60).*

Srinagar

❸ **Srinagar,** the gateway to Kashmir, is nestled in the mountains
about 112 kilometers (70 miles) north of the Banihal Pass.
Crisscrossed by canals and bridges, this city has been compared to Venice and Amsterdam. But Srinagar is definitely
Eastern, decidedly Moslem; it's also guarded by the towering
Himalayas, and these distinctions create a spirituality and a
beauty unique to this city.

Moslems represent about 90% of the population. To the summer
tourist, their life appears idyllic. The soulful chanting of their
daily prayers fills the air. Men, women, and children paddle
around in small punts. Young boys cavort in the water. In villages, a sense of caring goes beyond blood ties—a pivotal
Islamic concept. But for most Kashmiris, when the tourists
leave, their income leaves, too. Winters are harsh. In early
spring, when the snow melts and heavy rains begin, the rivers
and lakes flood, washing away crops and livestock. By June, nature calms down and the tourists return—bringing cash but
pushing up the cost of daily necessities. Step inside a village
home, and you see few material possessions.

In Kashmir, few women observe strict *purdah* (isolation). They
paddle around the lakes and canals with their faces unveiled
and stare curiously at visitors. But they follow strict Islamic
customs. At dinner, men eat first and women eat later with the
children. In mixed company, women are reluctant to speak.
And in Srinagar, when they're walking down a street, they're
completely concealed in a long *burka* (tentlike robe) with eyes
peeking from behind lace, high heels clicking on the pavement.
Men run the shops and stalls. The only female merchants are
Buddhist Tibetans.

Arriving and If you plan a summer visit, get your ticket months in advance
Departing and reconfirm your flight 72 hours before departure. **Indian**
By Plane **Airlines** makes three daily flights from Delhi to Srinagar. For
Srinagar, take the **airbus**, which is a 1¼-hour flight and leaves
from the **Air Bus Terminal.** The other flights leave from the **National Airport** and take a longer three-hour route. On arrival,
foreigners must register at the **Foreigners' Regional Registration Office** in the terminal. The **Srinagar Airport** is 14.5
kilometers (9 miles) from Srinagar. Call for flight **information**
(in Delhi, tel. 3312587; in Srinagar, tel. 73270).

From the Srinagar Airport, take a **taxi** for Rs. 60 to Srinagar or
for Rs. 90 to Nagin Lake, 18 kilometers (11 miles) and the location of the best houseboats. You can also take a **J&K Road
Transport Corporation** (J&KRTC) coach from the airport to the
Tourist Reception Center in Srinagar for Rs. 10 per person.

By Hired Car Due to political problems in the Punjab, a state south of Jammu
with Driver and Kashmir, foreigners skirt its boundaries, which means a
two-day trip from Delhi to Srinagar. Hire a car with driver
from one of our recommended travel agencies.

By Train There are no trains to Srinagar.

Getting Around Best rates on hired car or jeep with driver are through
By Hired Car **J&KSRTC** (Tourist Reception Center, Sherwani Rd., opposite
the main taxi stand, tel. 76107). It also has a list of approved
taxi operators. Taxis always claim broken meters. Get the
rates for your destinations from the Tourist Reception Center,
then bargain hard. Or use Delhi rates: Rs. 3.30 for the first kilometer, Rs. 2.40 per additional kilometer.

By Auto Rickshaw Auto rickshaws are cheaper but also demand bargaining. Aim
for half the opening price.

By Cart The horse-drawn cart is cheapest of all.

By Shikara The most attractive form of transport is the shikara. Rates are
determined by the government and posted at all major *ghats*
(stairways leading from the river), but boatsmen don't observe
them. Figure Rs. 30 per hour.

Addresses and Visit the **Tourist Reception Center** (Shervani Rd., tel. 72449 or
Numbers 77303) to arrange for private cars, jeeps, taxis, government ac-
Tourist Information commodations, rental of trekking and mountaineering
equipment and bikes, and reservations for major houseboats
and hotels. The following offices are in this complex: **Department of Fisheries** (for fishing permits), the **Chief Wildlife
Warden** (for permits to visit Dachigam National Park), **Indian
Airlines** booking and reconfirmation office, **J&KSRTC**, where
you must reserve your seat for all bus trips to the valleys
surrounding Srinagar and to Ladakh.

Travel Agents Two good private adventure outfits are **Boktoo and Sons Travel
Agency** (Dal Gate, tel. 74547) and **Dragon Tours & Travels** (4
Polo View, tel. 77330). For general travel needs, contact **Mercury Travels** (Hotel Oberoi Palace, tel. 78786), **Sita World Travel**
(Maulana Azad Rd., tel. 78891), or **Travel Corporation of India**
(Maulana Azad Rd., tel. 73525). Most offices are open in summer, daily 10–6.

Bookstore For good English books, go to **Kashmir Bookshop** (Sherwani
Rd., tel. 72426, open Monday–Saturday 10–6).

Banks, Post and **Grindlays Bank** and the **State Bank of India** (Sherwani Rd.) are
Telegraph Offices open weekdays 10–2, Saturday 10–noon. The State Bank of India also has a branch, open weekdays 4–7, in the Tourist
Reception Center. The **General Post Office** (Maulana Azad Rd.,
near the **Central Telegraph Office**) is open Monday–Saturday
10–5.

Guided Tours **J&KTDC** (Tourist Reception Center, tel. 72698) runs daily bus
and shikara tours around Srinagar and to the famous valleys.
For helicopter tours, call the J. & K. Tourist Department (tel.
77305).

Exploring the Old If you're staying on a houseboat on Lake Nagin or on the quiet-
City by Shikara er end of Dal Lake, take a shikara to the city; otherwise hire
one at Dal Gate. From Nagin, you glide past hamlets, under
wood bridges, and past tall brick houses with carved balconies
that hang precariously over the water. Finally you come to Dal
Gate, which leads to the old city.

Beyond Dal Gate, nearly every hundred feet a riverside ghat
leads to a thoroughfare, an alley, or even directly into a mammoth house. You maneuver around *dongas* (large flat-bottom
vessels) on which entire families live, lumber-laden barges,
fancy houseboats, ducks, swimming children, and other
shikaras. Once you turn into the Jhellum River, you pass by the
Raghunath Mandir, the largest Hindu temple in Kashmir.

Your first stop is the pagodalike **Shah Hamdan Mosque,** first
constructed in the 14th century. Repeatedly destroyed by fire,
it was rebuilt a final time in 1732 without the use of a single nail
or screw. The walls and ceilings are covered with delicate
painted woodwork brightened by chandeliers. Only Moslems
are allowed inside the complex; take a peek from outside.

Return to your shikara and stop upriver at the limestone **Pather
Masjid,** built in 1620 on the instructions of the Moghul Emperor
Jahangir's wife, Nur Jahan, as a mosque for Shiite Moslems.
Your next and last stop is at a large ghat near a poorly main-
tained 15th-century tomb.

Climb the ghat and stroll through the market, **Lal Chowk.** Robust horses with shaggy coats and jangling bell necklaces pull
canopied tongas filled with Kashmiris, the women hidden from
view. The streets are lined with open stalls where merchants,
smoking *hubbly-bubbly* (water pipes) sit crosslegged on raised
platforms behind displays of apples, pears, nuts, fresh-killed
chickens and skinned goats, and copper and silverplated pots.

This Moslem market leads to the **Jamia Masjid,** the largest
mosque in Kashmir. Reconstructed several times since it was
first built in 1400, its vast interior contains 400 cedar pillars,
each made from a single tree trunk. The mosque is also considered holy to Hindus, whose craftsmen created the fine wood
carvings inside the structure. Its grounds are revered by Buddhists, who call it Tsitsung Tsublak Kang. *Bring a packed
lunch to eat on this day-long tour.*

Time Out In the old market, stop at any crowded stall selling fresh
snacks. If you're staying on Nagin Lake, stop at laid-back
Moma Mia's Hotel and Restaurant. You can sip decent espresso
on the sun deck.

Exploring the Moghul Gardens by Shikara No trip to Srinagar is complete without a tour of the waterside Moghul pleasure gardens where the emperors created their vision of earthly paradise—sustained by water and filled with trees, symbols of creation and knowledge. You also notice that a water channel cuts each level of any of the more prominent gardens into four sections, which represent the Persian notion of a world divided into quadrants.

Begin your shikara tour at **Nasim Bagh** (Garden of the Morning Breeze) on the northwest side of Dal Lake. The oldest garden (created in 1586), Nasim Bagh is a small forest of giant chenars. From here, take a boat across the lake to the **Shalimar Bagh** (Garden of Love).

As you float to the garden, you see stately chenars screening secluded Shalimar, a garden site chosen in the early 1600s by the Emperor Jahangir for his wife, Nur Jahan. Time your arrival at **Nishat Bagh** (Garden of Pleasure) for the late afternoon. As you head ashore, you see a spectacular series of terraces rising from the lake into the Himalayan foothills. Purportedly, when the garden's creator, Nur Jahan's brother, Asaf Khan, refused to offer it as a gift to Jahangir, the emperor blocked the water. The garden withered, upsetting a servant who removed the dam. Jahangir sent for the servant, who confessed his crime. Jahangir's love of nature overcame his anger, and he let the servant live and the garden flourish.

Ascending from level to level, you enter formal gardens of roses, zinnias, dahlias, and cosmos. Look back at the lake from the top terrace. Slanting rays of sun shoot color across the water, bathing the lower levels of the Nishat and the lake in a tangerine glow.

Return to your shikara and pass by Shah Jahan's **Char Chenar,** (Four Plane Trees)—an island garden of three chenars and a small pavilion that seem to float in the water. Illuminated at night, the smallest garden, **Chasma Shahi** (Royal Spring), with its terraces, waterfalls, and fountain, offers a view of Dal Lake and the surrounding mountains. Approach it by rickshaw or taxi. Start this five-hour tour around 2 PM. *Admission: Rs. 1 to some of the gardens. Evening sound-and-light show is presented at Shalimar Bagh, May–Oct.*

Shopping If you stay on a houseboat, floating emporia with merchandise crammed into sacks and metal trunks hover around your boat like sharks. Pay attention to what you buy: Silver is frequently not silver; good-quality papier-mâché items should be well laquered and heavy; carpets touted as silk or wool are often synthetic. Give a minimum deposit to any tailor, and don't give him the rest until you're satisfied with the garments. The houseboat owners listed under Lodging, below, perform two valuable services: They can keep away the shikara touts and they can judge the quality of any item you want to buy.

If you're not up to bargaining, shop in the **Kashmir Government Arts Emporium** (Shervani Rd.) and in the **Government Central Market** (the Boulevard). You will want to bargain at **Suffering Moses** (the Bund), who has good merchandise at high prices. **Ali Sons** (Dal Gate, 1st Boulevard La., tel. 74266) has good old carpets and curios. Bargain here also. These shops take American Express and Visa cards, and are open Monday–Saturday 10–6, closed Sunday. Other shops are open daily 10–6.

Outdoor **Bicycle** around Srinagar on a 10-speed bike rented from the
Adventures Tourist Reception Center. Rent good **golf** equipment and play
at the Kashmir Government Golf Club (Maulana Azad Rd., tel.
76524). Take an early morning, three-hour **hike** to the hilltop
Hindu Shankaracharya Temple. Play **tennis** at the Amar Singh
Club (tel. 76848); racquets are available. **Waterski** at the Water
Sports Institute on Nagin Lake. Go on a three-day **shikara ride**
(with camping) to Mansabal Lake, which is filled with lotus
flowers and birds, or a five-day trip (with camping) to
mountain-ringed Wular Lake, the largest freshwater lake in
India. Contact our recommended outdoor adventure agencies
or, if you stay on a houseboat, ask the owner to make arrangements.

Dining In Srinagar, try Kashmiri food, with its Middle-Eastern fla-
vors and recipes dating back to the Moghuls. Try kebabs (small
pieces of meat broiled on a skewer); *birianis* (fowl or mutton
cooked with rice, butter, and spices); *gustava* (meatball curry
cooked in a yogurt gravy); *rista* (beaten spicy lamb); *rogan josh*
(mutton cooked on the bone in a spiced curry); and if you're
lucky, you'll find a chef who can prepare fried spinach cooked in
mustard oil, tumeric, and an aromatic water in which dried
cockscomb flowers have been soaked. After your meal, have
sweet Kashmiri tea. Most good restaurants are in the better
hotels and are mentioned in Lodging, below. Lunchtime is
12:30–3, dinnertime is 7:30–11. Dress is casual. Reservations
are advised in all hotel restaurants.

If you stay on a houseboat, meals are included. Discuss the
day's menu with your host. The few independent restaurants
that offer memorable ambience or food are listed below. They
don't take credit cards and are inexpensive (under $5). Highly
recommended restaurants are indicated by a star ★. Prices are
per person, excluding drinks, service, and taxes.

Adhoo's. This simple restaurant, which is usually crowded with
customers, has a terrace out back and offers Kashmiri specialties at a very low price. *Residency Rd., tel. 72593. Open 9 AM–
11 PM.*

★ **Lhasa.** If you like Tibetan food, eat in the supercasual Lhasa's
candle-lit garden. *Boulevard La. tel. 71438. Open noon–11.*

Lodging Highly recommended lodgings are indicated by a star ★.
Prices are for a standard double room or cottage or for a double
occupancy on a houseboat, including taxes and excluding service charges.

Houseboats A visit to Srinagar can be a vacation on a legendary houseboat
moored on Dal and Nagin lakes and the Jhellum River. Book in
advance or on arrival through the Accommodations Counter in
the Tourist Reception Center in Srinagar. Before you commit
to a boat not listed below, take a shikara to see it. If you want
peace, choose Nagin or the remote arm of Dal (a 30-minute car
ride from the city). If you stay near Srinagar, expect noise.

If you're on a low budget or privacy is all-important, choose a
small Class A or B boat. If grand is your fantasy, go for Deluxe.
The best new boats have carved wood walls and fragrant cedar
ceilings, formal dining room, a handsome sitting room, bedrooms, a sun deck on the roof, a cozy veranda from which you
can watch the sun rise or set. The listed houseboats are beautiful; the owners treat you with care. They'll pick you up at the
airport and arrange all your excursions. Deluxe boats are at the

low end of the moderate ($25–$60 per double room) range; Class A and B boats are inexpensive (under $25 per double room). All meals are included.

Reshu Boktoo & Sons. These houseboats are nestled on the western side of Nagin Lake. The classiest is the three-bedroom *Golden Lotus.* Nice two-bedroom boats are also available. The owners supervise excellent treks in Kashmir and Ladakh and know the best fishing spots. *Dal Gate, Box 95, Srinagar, J. & K., tel. 74547. Deluxe and Class A boats. All rooms with bath. AE, DC, MC, V.*

Clermont Houseboats. These houseboats are on the remote arm of Dal Lake. The best boats are old and with two bedrooms; you're surrounded by beautiful furnishings and memorabilia. Newer boats with two or three bedrooms are fancy and come with the same classy service. *G. M. Butt & Sons, Clermont Houseboats, Dal Gate, Srinagar, J. & K., tel. 72175. Deluxe. All rooms with bath. AE, DC, MC, V.*

Abdud Rashid Major & Bros. When you step aboard the small one-bedroom *H.P. Peony* and *Young Peony*, you feel like someone's grandmother supervised the decorating. They're a real bargain. *Nagin Lake, Srinagar, J. & K., tel. 74850. Class A. All rooms have baths. No credit cards.*

Hotels Srinagar also has good hotels to fit every budget.

Centaur Lake View Hotel. This gigantic hotel on Dal Lake has modern rooms. *Chesmeshahi, Srinagar, J. & K., tel. 75667. 251 rooms with bath. Facilities: excellent multicuisine restaurants, bar, room service, swimming pool, health club, tennis court, travel and foreign exchange counter. AE, DC, MC, V. Expensive ($60–$100).*

Nedous. The oldest hotel in Srinagar, Nedous has just been purchased by the Welcomgroup chain and is under total renovation—to be completed in late 1990. Inspection was impossible at press time. But set back on a lawn against the river, not far from the heart of the city, this two-story British bungalow with verandas is beautiful from the outside. It could become the hotel of choice. *For information, contact Welcomgroup: in the U.S., tel. 212/581–1000, or worldwide, tel. 800/325–3535. Facilities: all amenities are planned. Expensive ($60–$100). AE, DC, MC, V.*

Oberoi Palace. This was the former home of the maharajah; its beautiful lawns and six-hole golf course overlook Dal Lake. Its spacious rooms need refurbishing. Ask for an upper-floor lakeview room. The hotel is a distance from the road and from Srinagar. *Guptar Rd., Srinagar, J. & K., tel. 75751. 100 rooms with bath. Facilities: TV, room service, excellent multicuisine restaurant, bar, badminton, golf course, shopping arcade, travel and foreign exchange counter. AE, DC, MC, V. Expensive ($60–$100).*

★ **Lake Isle Resort.** Set on a secluded island in Nagin Lake, this 50-year-old two-story bungalow with spacious front lawns and great views is a delight. The rooms are in simple Kashmiri decor. An upstairs library is perfect for reading. Meals are included. *Naseem Bagh, Srinagar, J. & K., tel. 78446, or in the U.S., BGA Corporation, 790 Shirley Dr., Tipp City, OH 45371, tel. 513/667–8071. 11 rooms with bath. Facilities: good multicuisine restaurant, bar, sightseeing arrangements, badminton, boating and fishing, room service. AE, MC, V. Closed mid-Nov.–Apr. Moderate ($25–$60).*

★ **Cheshma Shahi Hutments.** On a hill overlooking Dal Lake, near the Cheshma Shahi Moghul garden, these charming new government-run cottages are economical and popular. Reserve well in advance. *Reservations: J&KTDC, Tourist Reception Center, Srinagar, J. & K., tel. 73688 or 72644. About 12 huts. Facilities: restaurant, bar, room service. No credit cards. Inexpensive (under $25).*

Nightlife   If you want a good nightcap and you're staying on a houseboat, buy your own liquor in Srinagar and sit on your veranda. The best hotel bars are at **Oberoi, Centaur,** and **Lake Isle Resort.** Most bars are open until 11 PM.

Excursion from Srinagar to Gulmarg

4   A bowl-shape vale tucked in mountains, **Gulmarg,** 2,730 meters (8,200 feet) high, was a favorite retreat of the Moghul emperors and the British. It sits 56 kilometers (32 miles) northwest of Srinagar. Today, you can golf, trek, play tennis, and horseback ride in the warm weather. You can ski or sled in winter.

Contact the **Gulmarg Tourist Department** (tel. 39) for all outdoor adventure arrangements. Plan for a two-hour trip by car or taxi from Srinagar. You can also go by **helicopter** (*see* Guided Tours, above). A quick look at the area, including a short walk and lunch, will take a day.

Dining and   The few hotels in Gulmarg are rustic, except for Highlands
Lodging   Park and a new one under construction. Restaurants are in the hotels. Highly recommended lodgings are indicated by a star ★. Prices are for a standard double room or a cottage, including taxes and excluding service charges.

★ **Hotel Highlands Park.** Old hunting trophies hang over the fireplace in this chateau-style hotel's lobby. Pine-paneled rooms are comfortable, with ample heat in the winter. Meals are included. *Gulmarg, J. & K., tel. 30. 39 rooms with bath. Facilities: bar, good multicuisine restaurant, foreign exchange counter, room service, health club. Traveler's checks; no credit cards. Closed Nov.–Dec. 10. Expensive ($60–$100).*

Ashok. The government is currently constructing a new 28-room Western-style high rise. Rooms could not be inspected at press time. *For latest information, call an Ashok representative; in the U.S., tel. 212/247–7950 or 800/344–1212 or Air India offices worldwide. Moderate ($25–$60).*

★ **J&K Tourist Department Huts.** These small, very popular, wood cottages dot the slopes of the valley. They're not fancy, but with a fireplace in each bedroom, they're just right for Gulmarg. Bring your own sleeping bag or rent linen at a nominal cost. Reserve 2 months in advance in the summer. *J&K Tourist Department, Tourist Reception Center, Srinagar, J. & K., tel. 72449; or in Gulmarg, tel. 39. 14 huts with bath. No credit cards. Inexpensive (under $25).*

Excursion from Srinagar to Pahalgam via Anantnag, Verinag, and Achabal

To see Hindu and Moghul monuments, loop south of Srinagar to Pahalgam, 96 kilometers (59 miles) away in the Lidder Valley— the start for many good treks.

⑤ Anantnag, 54 kilometers (33 miles) from Srinagar, is the abode of Ananta, the serpent on which the Hindu god Vishnu often rests. Walk through the **Hindu temple complex** where *sadhus* (holy men) sit, hair matted and faces covered with ash. If you want to enjoy the sulphur springs, men should use the open tank, and women should enter the enclosed cubicle.

From here, head south to **Achabal,** 4 kilometers (2½ miles) away, and visit one of the loveliest of Moghul retreats, the **pleasure garden** of the Empress Nur Jahan, set in a forest with three pavilions on the upper terrace. Water from a natural spring gushes down each level and shoots up from fountains below. A government-run cafeteria offers good snacks and lunch.

⑥ The largest spring in Kashmir is at **Verinag,** 22 kilometers (14 miles) south of Achabal. It spills into pools in another beautiful Moghul **pleasure garden,** called "the glory of Kashmir" by Emperor Jahangir. Many of the original pavilions are gone, but the extensive lawns backed by cedar-covered hills and the remaining architecture are lovely. Have snacks or lunch in the government-run cafeteria.

⑦ Pahalgam resort, 68 kilometers (42 miles) northeast of Verinag, set at the junction of the Lidder and Sheshnag rivers and surrounded by mountains, used to be a sleepy shepherd's village. Now it's immensely popular. Summer brings a rush of campers, fishermen, golfers, and horseback riders. Just 2,195 meters (7,200 feet) above sea level, the scenery is exquisite. If you go by car or taxi and follow the route described in this excursion, this is a day trip. The J. & K. Tourist Department in Srinagar (tel. 77305) offers helicopter flights. For outdoor adventure information, contact the Pahalgam Tourist Department (tel. 24). Ideally, you should spend the night at Pahalgam.

Dining and Lodging The good restaurants in Pahalgam are attached to the hotels. Highly recommended lodgings are indicated by a star ★. Prices are for a standard double room or a cottage, including taxes and excluding service charges.

★ **Pahalgam Hotel.** Set on the main street, this wonderful lodge has been renovated and offers Western-style amenities and attractive, centrally heated rooms. The best rooms have a river view. Meals are included. December–January discounts offered. *Pahalgam, J. & K., tel. 26. 46 rooms with bath. Facilities: room service, TV, very good multicuisine restaurant, heated pool, health club. AE, DC. Expensive ($60–$100).*
Plaza Hotel. This attractive lodge, enclosed by a pleasant garden, is well managed. Not fancy, it's also not expensive; its rooms have a cozy charm. Meals are included. *Pahalgam, J. & K., tel. 39. 30 rooms with bath. Facilities: multicuisine restaurant, bar. No credit cards. Closed mid-Nov.–mid-Mar. Moderate ($25–$60).*
★ **Hotel Woodstock.** This weathered gray lodge is under renovation. Spacious rooms will be carpeted and centrally heated and have a rustic modern decor. The best rooms have a view of the river. November–March discounts offered. *Pahalgam, J. & K., tel. 27. 95 rooms with bath. Facilities: TV, bar, good multicuisine restaurant, room service, doctor on call, car rental, health club, shopping mall. AE, DC. Moderate ($25–$60).*
★ **J. & K. Government Tourist Bungalow and Huts.** These accommodations are a bargain. The stone bungalow is old, with clean,

spacious rooms. The huts are charming: little stone dwellings with ample rooms and verandas. Reserve well in advance. *Reservations: J. & K. Tourist Department, Tourist Reception Center, Srinagar, J. & K., tel. 77305. 7 rooms with bath in the bungalow, 57 huts with bath, and safari-style tents (very cheap) with shared bath. Facilities: restaurant, bar. No credit cards. Inexpensive (under $25).*

Excursion from Srinagar to Sonamarg

Because of its dubious status as the starting point for the "road rally" to Ladakh, **Sonamarg,** at the edge of Kashmir, is chaotic and dusty. It's recommended only as the start for a trek.

Ladakh: Kargil and Leh

Tucked between the Karakoram and the Great Himalayas, the world's two highest ranges, Ladakh is a prime destination for the traveler searching for great adventure combined with a journey into the world of the Mahayana Buddhist. Ladakh's *gompas* (monasteries), old and new, are splendid, with beautiful interior frescoes and statues.

Only about 150,000 people live in these windswept mountains. You see yak and blue sheep, the lucky see the snow leopard, and you see evidence of Ladakh's Buddhism: gompas set on high cliffs, *chortens* (shrines containing sacred relics), and *mani* walls that keep evil spirits from entering a village. Prayer flags snap in the wind.

Read about high-altitude sickness under Staying Healthy in Before You Go to the Himalayas, Chapter 1. Even if you're not trekking, bring high-altitude pills, a powerful sunblock, a wide-brimmed hat, sunglasses that block ultraviolet rays, a good flashlight, water-purification tablets, a quart-size canteen, and snacks. If you intend to go to Zanskar Valley, bring a sleeping bag, camping gear, and other basic food provisions. There is no tourist infrastructure, and there are few shops. All your needs can be purchased or rented in Srinagar.

Arriving and Departing *By Jeep* A jeep is the best way to travel—obligatory for Zanskar. The road is too rough for taxis or cars. When you travel in Zanskar, be prepared for landslides and vehicular breakdowns. Consider them part of the adventure. You can also travel by hired car with driver or by taxi (which you can share). Make arrangements with J&KTDC in Srinagar.

Don't trek without a guide, and for all lengthy outdoor adventures in Ladakh, make arrangements through our recommended agencies before you depart from home. Once you enter the village of **Drass** on the far side of the Zojila Pass, you must stop and register with the police.

By Plane **Indian Airlines** makes two weekly flights to Leh from Delhi and five weekly flights to Leh from Srinagar. Flights to Leh are subject to the weather. When flights are delayed or canceled, you're not booked on the next plane. You could get stuck in Leh. On arrival in Leh, foreigners must register at the **Foreigners' Regional Registration Office** in the terminal. The **Leh Airport** is 8 kilometers (5 miles) from Leh. For **flight information** in Delhi, call 3312587; in Leh, call 76. If your schedule's tight, fly into Srinagar, then visit Ladakh by jeep or car.

Between Airport and City No scheduled airport bus operates in Leh; take a taxi into town (about Rs. 30).

Kargil

⑩ Long ago, **Kargil,** the halfway point to Leh, used to be an important trading stop for caravans from China, Afghanistan, Turkey, and India. Today, Kargil is an obligatory overnight halt on the winding road that passes through the valley of Drass, the second-coldest place in the world after Siberia. In the few villages you pass, mud-and-brick homes are built low for warmth. Yet by day, the sun is fierce: Apricot trees grow here, as do gigantic radishes.

Addresses and Numbers The **Tourist Office** (tel. 29) is off the main street toward the lower government-run Tourist Bungalow and is open Monday–Saturday 9–5; you can also contact the proprietors of the recommended hotels. The **State Bank of India,** open weekdays 10–2, Saturday 10–noon, and the **Post and Telegraph Office,** open Monday–Saturday 10–4:30, are in the center of Kargil.

Dining Except for one restaurant, which is inexpensive (under $5) and does not accept credit cards, the best food is in the hotels listed.

Naktul Chinese Restaurant. This small, friendly eatery serves large portions. *On the road to the lower Tourist Bungalow. Open 7 AM–10PM.*

Lodging Facilities are limited; book in advance. Stay away from budget hotel, where bedbugs are rampant. Highly recommended hotels are indicated by a star ★. Prices are for a standard double room or a cottage, including taxes and excluding service charges.

★ **Hotel Broadway.** This excellently managed hotel off the main street has a simple lobby and clean, sparsely decorated rooms. The best rooms overlook the Suru River. *Suru View, Kargil, J. & K., tel. 13. 26 rooms with bath. Facilities: very good multicuisine restaurant, room service, transport and trekking arrangements, doctor on call. No credit cards. Moderate ($25–$60).*

Hotel Carvan Sarai. Perched above the center of Kargil, this simple, clean hotel, built in tiers, has a Middle Eastern ambience. Upper-floor rooms have a great river view. *Kargil, Ladakh, J. & K., tel. 79. 40 rooms with bath. Facilities: multicuisine restaurant. No credit cards. Moderate ($25–$60).*

★ **Hotel Siachen.** On the banks of the Suru River and off the main street, this excellently managed, popular hotel has a garden in its parking lot and clean, simple rooms with verandas. *Kargil, J. & K., tel. 22. 27 rooms with bath. Facilities: room service, doctor on call, foreign exchange and travel counter, excellent multicuisine restaurant. DC. Moderate ($25–$60).*

Excursion from Kargil to Zanskar

From Kargil, travelers heading to Padam, 247 kilometers (153 miles) away in the Zanskar Valley, should bring a packed lunch, leave by 6 AM, and expect a long day of driving. The road is a work in progress, with nature keeping the upper hand by sending down landslides. The landscape is dramatic, with patches of pastureland and flourishing crops—shocks of color below the dusty-hued Zanskar Range. Men and women, walk by—their backs hunched under loads of firewood. You also see the black-and-white hushen, a high-altitude bird.

As you approach Trispune, 20 kilometers (12 miles) from Kargil, sheep, cattle, and the hybrid *dzou* (a shaggy combination of a cow and a yak) graze. You pass simple mosques with tin-plated domes.

At Sankoo, 40 kilometers (25 miles) from Kargil, the mountains close in. Narrow bridges carry you back and forth across the Suru River. Nun Peak soars into view; within moments, to its left, you see the killer Kun peak, dreaded by mountaineers.

In Tespar, 3 kilometers (2 miles) later, you see barren fields with Islamic burial mounds with two thin oblong slabs indicating the placement of the head and feet. In the next village, Tai Suru, two large imambaras, constructed along typical Turkish lines, tower over the hamlet.

After Panikhar, 70 kilometers (43 miles) from Kargil, the road turns shabby. You bump along. Vistas grow rugged. Narrow bridges cross gorges where fallen boulders hang trapped in crevices, sheets of rock jut out over the road. The few Suru Valley inhabitants wear animal skins over their robes.

In Parkhachek, 89 kilometers (55 miles) from Kargil, the green fields are irrigated by man-made canals that channel melting snow. Forget tractors. Here the sod is tilled by the wood plow. Robust horses, the main means of transport, still buck at the sound of a vehicle.

About 140 kilometers (87 miles) from Kargil, you reach the small village of Yuldo, Buddhist in every respect, with the tall spikes of prayer flags mounted on low roofs and chortens standing in fields. This is the only village between Kargil and Padam with a private hotel (a hotel of last resort). Stop and eat your packed lunch with the hotel's tea. Just beyond Yuldo, you see ⓫ the first gompa: 250-year-old fortress-shaped **Rangdum** sits atop a hill at the base of a mountain.

Soon after, on your left, another monastery stands apart from the village, an oasis for meditation. The mountains turn dark. Peaks gleam like coal. When the road divides into numerous tracks, take the well-traveled set to minimize bumps and dust. There's more of a road as you climb toward the Penzi La Pass.

A sign announces that you've entered Zanskar Valley; then a blue-green lake emerges on your right. Another sign announces the Penzi La Pass, 4,268 meters (14,000 feet) high. The Suru heads off, and a towering glacier feeds water into the Zanskar River. At first the valley is no more than a rocky desert, then bits of green appear along with dzou and the famous Zanskar ponies. The Zanskar River races along in a deep gorge. The vast valley sweeps up to soft-hued mountains.

Americans may now think of the Wild West. But the chortens, the Mongolian features of robed men galloping by, the dzou, and the low flat houses are unmistakeably Himalayan.

You pass through Abrum, with its small roadside monastery, then Tungri with a dirt road leading up to the distant cave monastery, **Dzongkhul**—attributed to the 10th-century Indian teacher Naropa, who spent years here in meditation. His footprints are said to be imbedded in the rock. The monastery also contains his sacred staff, numerous small shrines, and sacred idols.

Padam Finally you reach **Padam,** former capital of the kingdom of
⑫ Zanskar and now valley headquarters, set on the edge of a sweeping circular basin ringed by mountains. Ten kilometers (6 miles) away, you see the tiny, cliff-side village of Karsha. You're surrounded by Buddhist shrines. The only noise comes from chattering birds, the whipping wind, and countless flapping prayer flags.

Padam and its valley are slowly becoming a tourist destination. The people are friendly and getting accustomed to foreign faces and foreign ways. If you're invited into a typical Zanskar house, called *niu lem lem,* don't refuse the invitation or the tea that will be offered along with fresh *chappati* (unleavened fried bread). Houses are built of stone and clay with a flat roof of thick mud-filled branches. Some houses are a single story with a separate dwelling for livestock; others are two story with animals downstairs and the family above. Each room is immaculate, especially the kitchen, which also serves as bedroom and common room. Kitchen utensils and a churn for making butter tea neatly line shelves against a wall. You'll notice cushions and *chaktse* (stools, honored seats for the elders). Traditionally, women sit opposite the men.

Exploring Karsha In Padam, see the splendid **Karsha Gompa,** Zanskar's biggest
Gompa monastery, built in the 11th century by Rinchen Zangpo, the
⑬ founder of the Alchi Monastery on the way to Leh. The gompa sits on a bluff, 10 kilometers (6 miles) from the valley on the far side of the Doda River, which you cross via a creaking rope bridge. Climb through the village.

The Gelug (Yellow Hat Sect) gompa sits in a courtyard with an enormous prayer flag. The Lhabrang (Main Prayer Hall) has frescoes of guardian deities surrounding the entrance. Inside, numerous statues crowd the main altar, including a gold statue of Guru Rimpoche (a copy of the famous statue in the Potala Palace in Tibet). There are also statues of the Sakyamuni (Historic Buddha), Maitreya (Future Buddha), Avalokitesvara (Buddha of Compassion), and a chorten that contains a statue of the founder of the monastery. Five-hundred-year-old frescoes portraying the life story of the Buddha, old *thang-kas* (religious scrolls), and shelves holding the Holy Scriptures cover the walls.

When you leave the prayer hall, take steps to the right that lead to another prayer chamber with a statue of the Buddha and more holy books. Return to the courtyard and climb the steps to the red section of the gompa, called Gonkhang, in which you find a ferocious guardian diety—in this case, Lhamo. The color red is said to ward off evil. Steps in the Gonkhang lead to a tiny door and small chamber where daily prayers are held. All around the space are religious articles, including the statue of Lhamo, her face under cover.

This is a day-long walk to and from Padam (bring your canteen); you can also go by jeep and just walk 4 kilometers (2½ miles), which reduces a visit to a half-day excursion. *Admission: Rs. 10. Open sunrise–sunset.*

Dining and Most places are primitive, so it's far more pleasant to sleep in a
Lodging tent. The one hotel/restaurant is also in high demand.

Padam Tourist Bungalow. If you can get a room in this government bungalow, you'll need a sleeping bag. Linen is clean and
there are blankets, but the simple rooms get cold. The restaurant serves good basic Indian and Continental food. Some
tenting is allowed. Reserve well in advance. *J&K Tourist Officer, Kargil, J. & K., tel. 29. 5 rooms with bath (hot water by
bucket). Facilities: restaurant. No credit cards. Inexpensive
(under $25).*

Trips from Kargil to Leh

On to Mulbekh   Travelers who go to Zanskar from Kargil can trek or raft part
of the way from Padam to Leh (*see* Outdoor Adventures in
Staying in Jammu and Kashmir, above); otherwise the trip by
vehicle to Leh, 230 kilometers (142 miles), resumes from Kargil
and demands an early morning start to see important monasteries along the way.

14 In the village of **Mulbekh,** 39 kilometers (24 miles) from Kargil,
the transition to Buddhism is abrupt. A gompa is perched on a
cliff, and in the center of the village, the Chamba Statue of Buddha is carved into the face of an enormous rock—its legs
concealed behind a small gompa. Walk through the decorated
entrance to the courtyard and the towering Buddha. On your
left is the Chok Chung (Prayer Hall). Set behind the altar is a
statue of Avalokitesvara, with 1,000 eyes and numerous heads.
Frescoes cover the walls. *Open sunrise–sunset.*

Beyond Mulbekh, the road climbs to the highest point between
Srinagar and Leh—Fota La Pass, at 4,147 meters (13,602 feet).

*Numbers in the margin correspond with points of interest on
the Fota La Pass to Stok map.*

Exploring   From the Fota La, you descend toward the village of **Lama-**
Lamayuru Gompa **yuru,** 108 kilometers (67 miles) from Kargil, nestled in a green
15 valley with its famous gompa, which belongs to the Kargyu
(Red Hat Sect), above huddled dwellings. To enter the village,
take the dirt road to the right—a short walk to the village and
gompa, which is behind a courtyard. Stairs to the left of the
gompa lead to an interior courtyard.

The biggest prayer hall is called Chamba Dukhang. The four
statues at the left of the front altar are deities connected to
Buddhism's Nyingmapa (Old Sect), which contended with the
Yellow Hat Sect for control of the monastery from the 11th century until the 15th century, when a reformed offshoot of the
Red Hat Sect, Kargyu, assumed control. The chamber is filled
with religious articles: thang-kas, statues, photos of the Dalai
Lama, and elaborately painted wood boxes containing holy
books. Silk streamers and oval banners hang from beams as offerings to the dieties.

According to legend, the great *Arhat* (Saint) Nimagon visited
this area of Ladakh when it was under water. He prayed to
nagas (water serpents): "May a monastery be founded in this
place." As an offering, he threw some grains of corn into the
water and the lake disappeared. The grains collected together
and a plant, called *yung-drung*, which is another name for
Lamayuru, appeared in the shape of a swastika—an ancient
sanskrit symbol for well-being and an omen that led to the
eventual creation of the monastery by Naropa, who converted
to Buddhism during an 11th-century visit to Ladakh. He medi-

174

Fota La Pass to Stok (Numbers on map correspond to numbers in text)

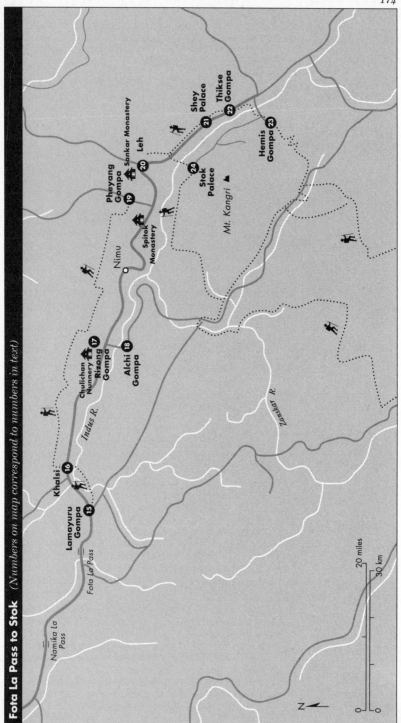

Namika La Pass

Fota La Pass

Lamayuru Gompa **15**

Khalsi **16**

Chulichan Nunnery

Rizong Gompa **17**

Alchi Gompa **18**

Indus R.

Nimu

Pheyang Gompa **19**

Spitok Monastery

Sankar Monastery

Leh **20**

Stok Palace **24**

Mt. Kangri

Zanskar R.

Shey Palace **21**

Thikse Gompa **22**

Hemis Gompa **23**

N

20 miles

30 km

tated inside a cave, marked now with his statue; the cave and the statue are inside the Chamba Dukhang in an opening on the wall to the right of the entrance.

A door at the front of the chamber leads into a small anteroom, the original small prayer hall, called Upching Khang. The statues behind glass at the front altar include a statue of Skyabsje Toldan Rimpoche, the founder of the presiding sect whose reincarnations are its spiritual leader. From the courtyard, steps lead up to a small chamber, with old frescoes, painted clay statues, and small silver chortens studded with coral and turquoise and embellished with gold. *Admission: Rs. 10.*

On to Alchi After you leave Lamayuru, Ladakh's lunar landscape begins— gigantic piles of sand rise up in front of you, backed by tiers of peaks spreading in every direction. The basin below is filled ⑯ with sand. Gigantic chortens lead the way into **Khalsi,** 141 kilometers (87 miles) from Kargil, which straddles the Indus River and is a good place for lunch. Look for the roadside stall with a sign, PUNJABI VEGETARIAN, and two benches out front (open 5:30 AM until the electricity runs out). For less than a dollar, you can have delicious *chana masala* (tomato curry with potato), chappati, rice, and tea.

After Khalsi, the mountains turn red, then white with sand blanketing the lower slopes. Sheets of rock overhang the road. Debris from continual landslides lie in haphazard heaps. About 167 kilometers (104 miles) from Kargil, a dirt track to the left ⑰ leads to a valley and the **Rizong Gompa** and nearby **Chulichan Nunnery,** which require a 5-kilometer (3-mile) walk each way once the road ends. The monks and nuns follow austere traditions. They own only robes and books, live in spartan rooms, and eat only a midday meal of *tsampa* (roasted barley).

Exploring Alchi At 176 kilometers (109 miles) from Kargil, take the road to the **Gompa** right across a bridge and head for the village of **Alchi,** with its ⑱ spectacular gompa, 5 kilometers (3 miles) from the main road. Unlike most gompas, Alchi's sits in the middle of a village— serene and enchanting—with two-story clay homes showing off the best in Ladakhi architecture. You walk past numerous chortens, mani walls, and prayer wheels. Stop and peer into some of the smaller hollow chortens. Inside are small conical mounds made of human ashes and clay.

Alchi Gompa, with its numerous modest-size chambers and courtyards, was founded by the Great Translator Rinchen Zangpo, who visited Ladakh from AD 1020 to 1035. He brought artists from Kashmir and Tibet to create the wood and clay statues, carve the elaborate pillars, and paint the gompa's priceless frescoes. Be certain to see these five chambers.

Lhakhang Soma (Prayer Chamber) has a five-foot white chorten standing in the middle of the room. Its walls are covered with 1,000 images of the Buddha depicting scenes in his life. Sum Tsek (Three Tiers) Temple sits in a courtyard. Exterior trim is carved with elaborate religious iconography; note the image of the Buddha on the archway. Inside the temple is an enormous chorten surrounded by three towering statues: Avalokitesvara is white; Manjushri (Buddha of Transcendent Wisdom) is red; Vajrapani (Buddha of Rain or Power) is blue. At the base of Avalokitesvara is an inscription (use a flashlight) that records the restoration of the temple under the reign of King Tashi Namgyal in the 16th century. The ladder set against the entrance way is not just the approach to the roof but to heaven. Today, visitors are prevented from climbing up because the roof is in danger of collapse; but in the past, if you could make it to the top without touching the wall, you'd go straight to the highest realm at death. If you failed, you could try again in your next life.

The Dukhang (Main Prayer Hall) has a chorten standing in the middle of the courtyard that you can walk under. Exterior walls are painted with the Historic Buddha's life story. In the chamber to the left of the temple is a gilded statue of Avalokitesvara. In the first chamber to the right of the door are three statues, Avalokitesvara between two Bodhisattvas. The chamber to the extreme right contains an enormous statue of Maitreya. Inside the temple are numerous frescoes and mandalas, thang-kas, a prayer drum, and precious silver chortens. But the real treasures lie behind glass in a tiny sanctuary at the front. If you're lucky or persuasive, a lama may unlock the door and let you look at the statues, which represent the top tier of the Mahayana pantheon. A four-headed Vairocana (Buddha of Resplendent Light) is in the center. On the right are Amitabha (Buddha of Boundless Light) with Amoghasiddhi (Buddha of Infallible Power) beneath him; on the left are Aksobhya (Undisturbed Buddha), with Ratan-sambhava (Buddha of Precious Birth) underneath.

Lotsawa Lhakhang contains three statues in front of a fresco that duplicates the carvings: Rinchen Zangpo, the translator and founder of the monastery, is on the left; Sakyamuni sits in the middle; Avalokitesvara is on the right. The surrounding walls are covered with beautiful mandalas and frescoes that include an unusually large number of animals and whimsical gods.

Jampal Lhakhang, also called the Manjushri Temple, has an elaborate stucco statue of Manjushri, in which each side represents the god who lords over each cardinal direction: blue for Aksobhya (Buddha of the East); yellow for Ratansambhava (Buddha of the South); red for Amitabha (Buddha of the West); and green for Amoghasiddhi (Buddha of the North). Alchi has few resident lamas. Getting into these five chambers requires perseverance. *Admission: Rs. 10. Open sunrise–sunset.*

On to Leh From Alchi, mountain vistas turn red, pale green, tan, and gray. As you approach the village of Nimu, 205 kilometers (127 miles) from Kargil, at the confluence of the Zanskar and Indus rivers, a sensitive border area, the presence of the Indian Army intensifies. You see barracks and pass convoys. From Nimu, you follow the Indus and enter the Indus Plain, with occasional villages appearing at the base of the Karakoram Mountains to the left and the Ladakh Range to your right. In the distance on the right, the 447-year-old **Pheyang Monastery** guards its green village. Inside its main chamber are large statues of Vairocana and Sakyamuni, as well as of numerous reincarnations of the Kargyu (Red Hat Sect) head lamas. Its walls are covered with frescoes. *Open sunrise–sunset.*

⑲

Leh

From the village of Spitok, at the base of a hill with its gompa perched on the crest, you see Ladakh's capital, 8 kilometers (5 miles) ahead, built into the base of the snow-covered Karakorams. Back in the 3rd century BC, **Leh**, altitude 3,506 meters (11,500 feet), was an important Buddhist center. Later

⑳

it became a major commercial center on the Silk Route in Central Asia. The 20th century has turned Leh into an important Indian military base and tourist boomtown.

Getting Around   Hire a taxi or jeep from the **taxi stand** near the Tourist Bungalow. Get a list of reasonable fares from the Tourist Department.

Addresses and Numbers   Visit the **J&K Tourist Department** (on the road to the airport, tel. 97) between 8 AM and 8 PM. To reconfirm all flights out of Leh, go to **Indian Airlines** (on the main road, tel. 76), open 10–6. The **State Bank of India,** open weekdays 10–2, Saturday 10–noon, and the **Post Office,** open Monday–Saturday 10–4:30, are in Leh Bazar. **Dragon Tours and Travels,** an excellent outdoor adventure outfit, has an office in Leh (tel. 8) and is open Monday–Saturday 9–6. Also, contact the **Students' Educational and Cultural Movement of Ladakh** (SECMOL), a nonprofit organization that sponsors inexpensive treks around this part of the state (Compound Karzoo, tel. 284, ext. 2).

Guided Tours   SECMOL has excellent guides for tours to monasteries, palaces, and even private homes. Charges are based on your itinerary and are reasonable.

Exploring   The 1594 **Shiite Mosque** in the main bazaar is a good example of Turkish/Iranian architecture. Near the post office at the upper end of the bazaar, narrow lanes veer to the right and wind their way through the old city. You pass old dwellings clustered together on the slope and finally end up at the 16th-century **Leh Khar Palace** and its gompa, the **Temple of the Guardian Deities,** both in ruins, perched on top of the hill. Inside the palace are crumbling, barely visible frescoes. Numerous small shrines in the gompa contain old artifacts, including a six-armed *mahakala* (guardian) and a solid-gold one-ton statue of the Buddha; but the caretaker is a guardian demon himself and is loathe to let anyone inside. Higher up on the same ridge are the towers of an old fortification (now off-limits). *Admission: Rs. 5. Currently the palace and gompa are open summer 7 AM–9:30 PM, but don't be surprised if they're shut down completely. Ask the Tourist Department before you go.*

Shopping   Shops in Leh entice you with fraudulent claims of antiques from the region. When the articles are old, their acquisition was usually unscrupulous. The following fixed-price shops in **Now Shar Bazaar** have lovely merchandise: **Dragon Curios,** open 10–8, no credit cards; **Ladakh Art Palace,** open 9–7, accepts credit cards; and **Lhasa Leh Curios,** open 9–6:30, no credit cards. SECMOL plans to sell local handicrafts. It could be in business when you arrive (Compound Karzoo, tel. 284, ext. 2). The two **Tibetan Refugee Handicraft Centers** sell carpets, paintings, woolen shawls and sweaters, and other handicrafts. All proceeds go to the refugees. One is on the outskirts of Leh and the other is on the road to Thikse Gompa; they are open Monday–Saturday 10–4 and do not accept credit cards.

Outdoor Adventures   Take a short 3-kilometer (2-mile) **hike** north of Leh to the **Sankar Monastery,** on a valley floor and the home to lamas who belong to the Gelug (Yellow Hat Sect) and worship his Holiness, the Dalai Lama. The temple is filled with statues, including Avalokitesvara and Sakyamuni. Walls are covered with frescoes. The monastery is usually open from 6–8 AM to 5–7 PM. Check with the Tourist Department before you go. **Hike** or **camp** in the Hemis High Altitude National Park, where you may see the rare bharal sheep, great Tibetan sheep, ibex, and snow leopards, plus numerous high-altitude birds, including the Himalayan snow cock. For passes or permission to camp, contact the Wildlife Warden, Tourist Department, Leh.

Dining   Except for two restaurants—inexpensive (under $5), no credit cards, no reservations necessary—the best food is in the hotels, which usually include meals in the cost of lodging.

Dreamland Restaurant. This small, informal restaurant is crowded with young Ladakhis chatting with foreigners and eating good Tibetan and Chinese dishes. *Fort Rd. No reservations. No credit cards. Open 8 AM–10 PM. Inexpensive (under $5).*

Potala Hill Top Restaurant. Don't be put off by the dingy stairwell that leads to this informal and popular restaurant with a quasi-Chinese decor and good Chinese and Tibetan specialties. *Lal Chowk. No reservations. No credit cards. Open 9 AM–10 PM. Inexpensive (under $5).*

Lodging   Leh has numerous lovely hotels to fit all budgets. Highly recommended lodgings are indicated by a star ★. Prices are for a standard double room, including taxes and excluding service charges.

Ladakh Sarai. Here, you stay in a *yurt* (tent) in a meadow below the Stok Gompa, 15 kilometers (9 miles) from Leh. Large, lantern-lit circular tents are attractively furnished. Toilets and solar-heated showers are separate. The separate lobby is Ladakhi-style with comfortable low platforms and a little shrine. Meals are normally eaten outside. Meals and sightseeing are included in the cost of the lodging. *Reservations: Mountain Travel India, 1/1 Rani Jhansi Rd., New Delhi, tel. 52204, or through the Mountain Travel office in your home country. Check General-Interest Tours in Before You Go to the Himalayas, Chapter 1. 12 tents with bath. Facilities: multicuisine restaurant, bar. AE, DC, MC, V. Closed Nov.– Mar. Very Expensive (over $100).*

Hotel Kang-lha-chhen. Near the center of old Leh, this simple, clean hotel has a distinctly Ladakhi look to its black-trimmed two-story white stucco exterior. The best rooms are on the upper floor and overlook the interior courtyard and garden. Meals are included in the room cost. *Leh, J. & K., tel. 144. 25 rooms with bath. Facilities: travel agent, doctor on call, room service, good multicuisine restaurant (nonguests must call in advance). AE. Moderate ($25–$60).*

★ **Hotel Lha-Ri-Mo.** A short walk from all markets and nestled behind a garden, this is the loveliest hotel in Leh. The restaurant is especially charming, with intricately hand-painted beams. The rooms are simple but pleasing. *Leh, J. & K., tel. 101. 30 rooms with bath. Facilities: travel agent, doctor on call, excellent multicuisine restaurant (for hotel guests). AE. Closed Nov.–May. Moderate ($25–$60).*

★ **Jorchung Guest House.** The traveler looking for the ultimate in peace and quiet should stay in this private Ladakhi home, made of clay and surrounded by a garden and fruit trees in a residential area that's a 10-minute walk from Leh. The rooms are simple but very clean. Gracious hospitality: bed-and-breakfast Ladakhi-style. Write in advance. *Reservations: Tukcha, Leh, J. & K. No phone. 5 rooms with shared bath (Indian shower). No credit cards. Inexpensive (under $25).*

Nightlife SECMOL stages wonderful Ladakhi dances and songs for tourists in an open-air theater. *Contact SECMOL, Compound Karzoo, tel. 284, ext. 2. Admission: Rs. 60. Shows start at 6 PM.*

Excursion to Spitok Gompa The **Spitok Gompa,** built 500 years ago on top of a hill overlooking the Indus River, was the first Gelug monastery built in Ladakh. The royal seat of the Head Lama of Ladakh, Spitok has tiers of chambers with beautiful thang-kas and relics. In the main prayer hall is a throne reserved for the Dalai Lama and surrounded by statues of Avalokitesvara and Yamantaka, the fiercesome guardian of this sect. A separate chamber farther up the hill also pays tribute to Yamantaka and the six-armed Mahakala, "the Black One." The numerous faces on Yamantaka remain veiled except for one day of festive celebration in January. This chamber also contains an exceptional collection of old masks. Some rooms are off-limits to tourists. *About 8 km (5 mi) west of Leh. Admission: Rs. 10. Open sunrise–sunset.*

Excursion to Shey Palace, Thikse, Hemis, and Stok Head southwest on the main road from Leh. After 7 kilometers (4 miles), the **Summer Palace of the Dalai Lama** comes into view—a lovely golden-roofed two-story home. Farther along, you pass clay mounds in a barren stretch on the left—a Buddhist cremation ground.

Exploring Shey Palace **㉑** The 1670 **Shey Palace,** its reflection mirrored in water, sits on a bluff 11 kilometers (7 miles) from Leh. Belonging to the Namgyal royal family, Shey served as the ancient capital of Ladakh. It's now in danger of collapse; you can only view its exterior, with beautiful wood carvings, especially around the entrance portico. You also see numerous chortens and the palace gompa, which has a 12-meter (30-foot) copper-gilt statue of a meditating Sakyamuni, called Shey Thubha (Lord Buddha).

Exploring Thikse Gompa **㉒** Up ahead is the 12-story 800-year-old **Thikse Gompa**—on a mountain spur and approached by a road on the left. The gompa is 19 kilometers (12 miles) from Leh. The road winds to the monastery with a panoramic view of the Indus Valley. After you climb the steps, you pass under a painted arch into a courtyard. Stairs on the right lead to the temple dedicated to Maitreya, with painted doors and facade. Inside, you see an enormous painted clay statue of Maitreya in the meditation pose, made between 1979 and 1981. Frescoes, adding a riot of color, portray the life of Maitreya, yet to come, whose life experience will be the same as Sakyamuni.

On the opposite end of the courtyard, steps lead to a small terrace painted with frescoes. In the interior chamber, called Szok Khang (Meeting Place for Prayer), lamas pray each morning, surrounded by old frescoes and elaborately carved wood pillars, each topped with a clay statue. Prayer drums are stationed near the left and right walls. Gold-plated statues of the Buddha are placed on the front altar. Within a small chamber behind the front altar are three more gold-plated statues: on the left is Jamyang (a king of Ladakh), in the center is Sakyamuni, on the right is Maitreya.

Outside, the temple steps to the left lead to the Gonthang, the red portion of the gompa. Here, you find the fierce guardian deity, Yamantaka, face under cover with the horns of a dzou rising up on either side. Above the cover is Jamyang, wearing a crown. Thikse has a good festival with chaams—usually held in

September. (At the road that leads to Thikse, stop at the Chamba Restaurant, run by the monastery, and have a good, cheap meal of Tibetan noodles, tea, cold drinks.) *Admission to Thikse: Rs. 10. Open sunrise–late at night.*

Exploring Hemis Gompa
(23)

Hemis Gompa, on the opposite side of the Indus, 32 kilometers (20 miles) from Leh, was built in the 17th century and is the current home of 300 lamas of the Nyingmapa (Old Sect). Its famous courtyard is the site of the Hemis Festival—a three-day celebration that marks the birthday of Guru Padmasambhava with ritual chaams performed by masked lamas who fight demons by gyrating slowly to the loud drone of the long Himalayan trumpet.

Frescoes of guardian deities protect two large temples. More fearsome paintings are in the Dukhang (Main Assembly Hall). A beautiful statue of Sakyamuni stands in the Tshogkhang (Main Temple), surrounded by numerous precious gold and silver chortens and the serene statue of the goddess Tara.

At the far end of the courtyard, a passage leads to the Lhakhang Nying-Pa (Old Temple) with exquisite old frescoes and another statue of Tara. From the Lhakhang, a staircase leads up to a terraced roof with numerous smaller temples, including one with a statue of the founder of the gompa and a beautiful gold-and-silver chorten. *Admission: Rs. 10. Open sunrise–sunset.*

Exploring Stok Palace Museum
(24)

On the way back to Leh from Hemis, keep the Indus River on your right and head to the **Stok Palace Museum,** 17 kilometers (10.5 miles) from Leh. The 1825 palace houses the jewels and ceremonial dress of the kings of Ladakh, as well as beautiful thang-kas, precious stones, and musical instruments. *Admission: Rs. 20. Open 7–6.*

Northern Uttar Pradesh: Uttarakhand

Introduction

This Himalayan region, bordered by India's Himachal Pradesh, Tibet, and Nepal, has figured prominently in every text revered by Hindus—the Vedas, the Puranas, the Ramayana, and the Mahabharata. Here, the Aryans arrived as early as 3000 BC, calling their new home Aryavarta (Land of the Aryans). Here, mythic kings—the Kauravas and Pandavas—fought the Great Battle recorded in the Mahabharata. Here, in Lumbini (now part of Nepal), Siddhartha Gautama, the Historic Buddha, was born in 563 BC.

Uttarakhand is the mythological abode of the Hindu pantheon. Goethe called Uttarakhand the "Holiest of Holies." Every year thousands of pilgrims set out on *yatras* (pilgrimages) to the Garhwal mountains and the sacred Char Dhams (Four Temples)—Yamunotri, Gangotri, Kedarnath, and Badrinath—the homes of the Hindu gods Vishnu and Shiva and the source of the holy Yamuna and Ganga rivers.

Uttarakhand is also a land of adventure. Its Garhwal mountains, with more than 100 peaks towering above 6,000 meters (20,000 feet), draw the climber and trekker. For the rafter searching for serious white water, Uttarakhand's runs, ranked with Asia's best, are swift and long. Race down the Alakananda with rapids that qualify as the "wall" and "roller coaster"— passing villages that rarely see Westerners. Fly down the Bhagirathi through gorges, past silver beaches and old cities.

Winter visitors can ski at Auli, India's newest ski resort. Though the current facilities don't rival what you'd find in the Rockies or the Alps, the Himalayan vistas outclass views any- where. Set in the lower foothills, Corbett National Park, India's first tiger preserve, is a protected area for tigers, ele- phants, hyenas, hog deer, and other animals. The traveler with an eye for opulence can experience the British Raj in sumptu- ous hotels in Mussoorie that serve elegance and civility along with great food.

Since Uttarakhand is so inextricably bound to the source of Hinduism, the suggested itinerary in this chapter is organized around a series of myths you will pursue. You start in the city of Haridwar—Gateway to the Gods—then continue north, keep- ing the sacred dimension in mind.

Addresses and Numbers

Tourist Information   Contact **Garhwal Mandal Vikas Nigam,** or GMVN (Trekking and Tour Executive, Mountaineering Division, Munkireti, Rishikesh, U.P., tel. 373), an Uttar Pradesh government orga- nization and the best source of information on Uttarakhand. *(See* the various destination sections for branch offices.)

For information about **Corbett National Park,** contact the Field Director (Project Tiger, Ramnagar, U.P., tel. 189) or the Chief Wildlife Warden (Lucknow, U.P., tel. 46140). Offices are usual- ly open Monday–Saturday 10–5.

Emergencies   Contact your hotel, the local tourist office, or your embassy in Delhi: **American** (Shanti Path, tel. 690351), **Canadian** (7/8 Shan- ti Path, tel. 619461), **British** (Shanti Path, tel. 690371).

Travel Agencies   **Arventures Adventure Holidays** (Post Bag 7, Dehradun, U.P., tel. 29172) is the best private adventure outfit in Uttar Pradesh. **Himalayan River Runners** (188-A, Jor Bagh, New Delhi, tel. 615736) is the best rafting company. **GMVN** provides inexpensive tours, treks, skiing at Auli, and all travel needs, including cars with drivers (*see* Tourist Information, above).

Arriving and Departing

This section is for travelers going to the cities of Mussoorie and Haridwar. See Arriving and Departing Corbett National Park for information on that destination.

By Plane   Fly into northern Uttar Pradesh from Delhi's **National Airport.** Flights take about one hour.

Airports and Airlines   **Vayudoot,** with 40-seat planes, flies twice daily from Delhi into **Dehradun's Jolly Grant Airport.** From here, it's 41 kilometers (25 miles) to Haridwar or 60 kilometers (37 miles) to Mussoorie, the starting point for destinations in the north. For fares and schedules, call, in Delhi (tel. 3312587). Try to book your ticket before you depart from home.

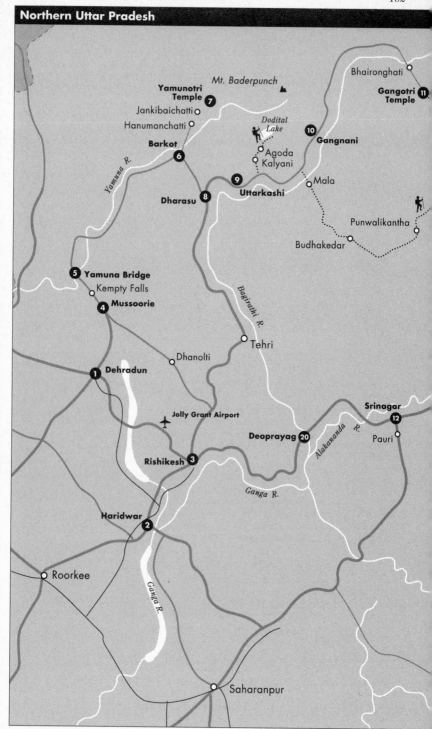

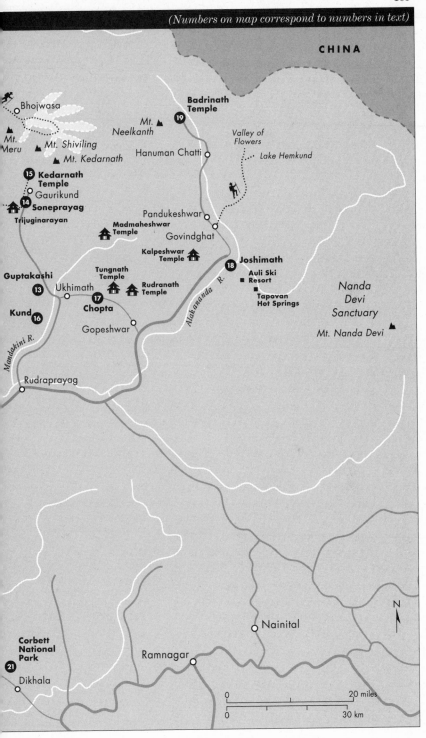

(Numbers on map correspond to numbers in text)

CHINA

Bhojwasa

Mt. Neelkanth

Badrinath Temple **19**

Valley of Flowers

Hanuman Chatti

Lake Hemkund

Mt. Meru

Mt. Shiviling

Mt. Kedarnath

15 Kedarnath Temple

Gaurikund

14 Soneprayag

Trijuginarayan

Pandukeshwar

Govindghat

Madmaheshwar Temple

Kalpeshwar Temple

18 Joshimath

Auli Ski Resort

Tapovan Hot Springs

Nanda Devi Sanctuary

Guptakashi **13**

Ukhimath

Tungnath Temple

Rudranath Temple

Mandakini R.

Alakananda R.

Kund **16**

17 Chopta

Gopeshwar

Mt. Nanda Devi

Rudraprayag

N

Nainital

Ramnagar

Corbett National Park

21

Dikhala

0   20 miles

0   30 km

Between Airport and City   From Jolly Grant Airport, no hotel in Haridwar provides free pickup service; the Hotel Natraj (Dehradun Rd., tel. 1099) in Rishikesh, 26 kilometers (16 miles) from Haridwar, does provide this service. A taxi, always available, will take you to Haridwar for about Rs. 200. To go to Mussoorie, take either a taxi from the airport (Rs. 250) or the airport bus (Rs. 18), which meets each plane, to Dehradun, a distance of 26 kilometers (16 miles), and get off at the taxi stand. From there, a taxi costs Rs. 100 for the remaining three-hour trip.

By Hired Car with Driver   If you fly into Dehradun's airport, save time and money by hiring a car with driver in Haridwar. To drive from Delhi, about 200 kilometers (124 miles) to Haridwar, plan for five hours on decent roads. Hire a car from a travel agency listed in the section on Delhi, above.

By Train   Trains to Haridwar or Dehradun (the departure point for Mussoorie and points farther north) are reasonably clean and comfortable, but they do take time. Two daily trains—the early morning Dehradun Express and the late-night Mussoorie Express—go from the **New Delhi Railway Station** (all information: tel. 3313535) to Haridwar in about seven hours.

If you book an overnight journey, reserve both a sleeper and berth, or you'll be put off the train. Get your ticket well in advance in first (air-conditioned or non air-conditioned) or second (air-conditioned) class.

Highlights for First-time Visitors

Begin a trip through Uttarakhand at the religious city of Haridwar, with its mesmerizing nighttime *Arti* (prayer service) of the Ganga. From Haridwar, head north by hired car with driver—the best way to get around. Your first stop should be Mussoorie, a former British hill station that still evokes the Raj and offers two classy hotels—the Savoy and Carlton's Hotel Plaisance.

Then push north into Garhwal, where you find the best treks. If you're not trekking, then go by car and visit these two of the Char Dhams: Gangotri, the home of *swamis* (Hindu masters) and *sadhus* (wandering Hindu holy men), and Badrinath, the holiest of the four temples. If you're willing to do a two-day round-trip trek from the end of the car-worthy road to the temple, then skip Gangotri and see Kedarnath, considered the most beautiful of the Char Dhams.

A trip to these temples takes you through the mountainous terrain of Garhwal, with its alpine valleys and perennially white-capped peaks. You'll see religious mendicants; Buddhist Bhutias, originally from Bhut in Tibet; the Gujjar, Moslem nomads who herd water buffalo; and the Garhwali villagers. This entire trip, starting and ending at Haridwar or Dehradun, takes 10–14 days, allowing for a couple of side trips, such as a five-hour walk from the village of Chopta to Tungnath, the highest temple in Garhwal, and a dip in the clean temple baths at the Parashar Kund hillside shrine.

Getting Around

By Hired Car with Driver   This is the best way to travel within Uttarakhand; figure about Rs. 4 per kilometer, with a halt charge of Rs. 50–100 per night.

Hire a car from a travel agency listed in the city sections below or from GMVN *(see* Tourist Information, above). Once you head to northern Uttarakhand or Mussoorie, expect roads to be winding and pitted from landslides. Near the Char Dhams in Garhwal, they're at the mercy of the weather. Be flexible: though you wanted to see Kedarnath, you may end up at Gangotri instead.

Guided Tours

Special-Interest Tours Garwhal Mandal Vikas Nigam (Yatra Manager, Yatra Office, GMVN, Munikireti, Rishikesh, U.P., tel. 372) runs scheduled 4- to 12-day tours by coach, minibus, and tourist taxi from Rishikesh and Mussoorie to the Char Dhams and the Valley of Flowers in Garhwal from May until October. From December to June, it sponsors a weekend conducted tour to Corbett from Delhi. Contact the Uttar Pradesh Tourist Department (Chandralok Bldg., 36 Jan Path, New Delhi, tel. 3322251).

Personal Guides Contact GMVN in Rishikesh (tel. 372 or 357) or in Mussoorie (tel. 2863); pay about Rs. 75 per day. You can also hire a guide from one of the private travel agencies listed in the Haridwar and Mussoorie sections. In Corbett, you can get a free park guide (tips should be offered) from the Reception Center at Dhikala.

Outdoor Adventures

Highly recommended adventures are indicated by a star ★.

Bicycling: GMVN can arrange a six- to eight-day trip (including bike) for excursions from November to June near Corbett National Park. Pedal through sal and bamboo forests and see wild animals. Bring binoculars and your fishing rod. Arrange in advance.

★ **Climbing and Mountaineering:** The Nehru Institute of Mountaineering in Uttarkashi offers courses in mountaineering. Experienced climbers can tackle soaring peaks like Nanda Devi from May to June and September to October. Arrange in advance through our recommended travel agencies.

★ **Fishing:** Use your own equipment at Yamuna Bridge near Mussoorie, near Corbett National Park, and at Dodital Lake near Uttarkashi.

Day Walks: A steep four-hour hike from Chopta (on the route from Kedarnath to Badrinath temples) up to the Tungnath Temple, the highest shrine in Garhwal, takes you through a forest and pastures to the summit with its ancient temple and views of some of Uttarakhand's highest peaks, including Nanda Devi. A day walk from Soneprayag follows a river gorge before veering into the mountains to great views and the sacred Trijuginarayan Temple, where the gods Shiva and Parvati were married.

Hot Springs: The best springs are at Parashar Kund (also called Rishikund) Temple near Gangnani, 56 kilometers (35 miles) north of Uttarkashi, and at Tapovan near Joshimath. They're free.

★ **Rafting:** You can raft from one to three days (Oct.–mid-Dec. and Feb.–June) on the Ganga from Deoprayag to Rishikesh;

take a six-day run (Nov.–mid-Dec. and Feb.–Apr.) on the
Alakananda from Rudraprayag to Rishikesh; or run the
Bhagirathi from Tehri to Rishikesh, the greatest challenge
(Nov.–mid-Dec. and Feb.–Apr.). Arrange in advance through
Himalayan River Runners *(see* Travel Agencies, above).

★ **Skiing:** From January to March, skiers can whoosh down slopes
at Auli, 16 kilometers (10 miles) from Joshimath, India's newest
ski resort with a 4-kilometer (2½-mile) ropeway. Costs of skiing, equipment rental (good quality), and lessons are less than
a third of those in the United States. Arrange in advance for
courses through GMVN in Rishikesh *(see* Special-Interest
Tours, above). *Reservations for cottages: GMVN, 74/1 Rajpur
Rd., Dehradun, U.P., tel. 26817. Facilities: catering. No credit
cards. Inexpensive (under $25).*

★ **Trekking (up to a week):** *Dodital Lake.* Atop a forested mountain, it's unspoiled by pollution; you'll meet few visitors on this
steep 21-kilometer (13-mile) climb. Start with an early morning
taxi ride 11 kilometers (about 7 miles) north of Uttarkashi to
the tiny village of Kalyani for a 5-kilometer (3-mile) climb to
Agoda, a Garhwali forest hamlet with a temple. After another
16 kilometers (10 miles), you reach Dodital Lake, fed by natural
springs and set in a pine and rhododendron forest. Allow three
to five days. The region is approachable year-round, but come
prepared for cold (30–40° F) in the winter. Trekkers without
tents can sleep in the small, minimally furnished forest rest
houses (under $5 per room) in Agoda and Dodital. Bring a
sleeping bag and food. Obtain permission from the Divisional
Forest Officer at the Tourist Bureau in Uttarkashi, U.P. (tel.
190).

★ *Gaumukh.* The two-day trek to Gaumukh, the source of the
Ganga, requires an 18-kilometer (11-mile) hike, not arduous,
from the Gangotri Temple. From Gaumukh, you have a perfect
view of Shivling Peak, flanked by Meru and Kedarnath, plus
other Himalayan peaks that top 6,400 meters (21,000 feet). You
also see the looming Gangotri Glacier—a wall of snow that
changes hue with the light and time of year, pilgrims taking ritual baths in the river, and meditating sadhus. Gaumukh is
approachable May–October. Food is available at stalls along
the route, but bring snacks, a canteen, water-purification tablets, a flashlight, and insect repellent. Bring all your camping
needs, or bring your sleeping bag and stay at the rustic Tourist
Rest House at Bhojwasa, 8 kilometers (5 miles) from the glacier. You can stay either in a "deluxe" double with attached
bath or a dormitory with shared bathroom. All bathrooms are
Indian-style with hot water by bucket. *Reservations: Assistant General Manager (Tourism) GMVN, Munikireti,
Rishikesh, U.P., tel. 372 or 357. 4 rooms with bath and dorms
with shared bath. Facilities: catering service. No credit cards.
Inexpensive (under $25).*

Valley of Flowers and Hemkund Lake. This seven-day trek
starts from Govindghat on the road to the Badrinath Temple
and follows a 19-kilometer (12-mile) mule track into the alpine
Valley of Flowers, surrounded by peaks and threaded with
streams. Over 200 species of flowers are in bloom between mid-
July and mid-September. The 6-kilometer (4-mile) climb to
Hemkund Lake and its shrine brings you to a heavenly pilgrimage destination. You need a permit from GMVN *(see* the
preceding trek) to camp in this area, now a national park.

★ **Trekking (over a week):** There are numerous excellent treks in Garhwal; all require a guide and advance planning *(see* Travel Agencies in Important Addresses and Numbers, above; in Special-Interest Tours in Before You Go to the Himalayas, Chapter 1; and in North India, above). Many are year-round, such as the trek from Gangotri to Kedarnath, but expect cold winter nights. Treks into the Nanda Devi Sanctuary are closed at press time due to environmental damage. The Panch Kedar trek is best from April to October.

★ *Gangotri to Kedarnath.* This rough 10-day walk takes you past determined Hindu devotees, up the steep ridges of the ancient pilgrim route from the Gangotri Temple to Kedarnath Temple.

★ *Panch Kedar trek.* You travel for two weeks through pastoral Garhwali villages, meet the Gujjar nomads, and see five important shrines set against a backdrop of white-capped Himalayan peaks.

★ **Wildlife Safaris and Jungle Excursions:** Corbett National Park *(see* section on this destination, below) is India's oldest sanctuary and one of its best. From the back of an elephant, from inside a jeep, or from a *machan* (watch tower), you may see elephants, tigers, leopards, black bear, wild boar, deer, snakes (including the python and king cobra), crocodiles, and birds. Stay in rustic lodging inside the park or at a fancy private camp an hour away. The park is open from November to mid-June.

Haridwar

Numbers in the margin correspond with points of interest on the Northern Uttar Pradesh map.

❶ The plane to Uttarakhand lands near **Dehradun,** the largest Uttar Pradesh city in the lower Himalayan foothills and a congested town. Head to **Haridwar,** 41 kilometers (25 miles) away.

❷

Hari means god; *dwar* means door—a geospiritual description of Haridwar's location: the point where the holy Ganga emerges from the Sivalik Mountains. Haridwar's religious energy rivals that of the holy city of Varanasi, but with an unexpected twist—a trip here means party time. Indians from all over the country celebrate an exuberant nightly prayer service called Arti of the Ganga. Every 12 years, the city is jammed with millions of pilgrims who come to the Kumbh Mela celebration.

Haridwar originated during an intense battle between gods and demons who fought over a *kumbh* (jar) of nectar that promised immortality. Four drops spilled, one on Haridwar's Har-ki-pauri Ghat. Vishnu, the Hindu deity, appeared in disguise and conned the demons into letting him distribute the rest. He gave all the nectar to the gods, who took their treasure to paradise.

Getting Around Taxis are unmetered. Bargain using Delhi rates: Rs. 3.30 for the first kilometer, Rs. 2.40 per additional kilometer. You can also take an auto rickshaw, unmetered and cheaper than a taxi. But the two-seater bicycle rickshaw is the best way to see Haridwar. Hire a rickshaw for a morning or afternoon. Ask your hotel to suggest a fare and fix it with the driver before you start.

Addresses and Numbers For tourist information, visit the **U.P. Tourist Bureau** (Lalta Rao Bridge, Station Rd., tel. 19) or the **Tourist Information Counter** (Railway Station, tel. 817), open Monday–Saturday 10–5. To hire a car with driver, contact **Wings** (tel. 878), **Konark** (tel. 210), **Vikrant** (tel. 930), or **GMVN** at Munikireti in nearby Rishikesh (tel. 372), all open Monday–Saturday 10–5. Cash traveler's checks at the **State Bank of India** (Station Rd., near Chitra Talkies), open weekdays 10–2, Saturday 10–noon. The **General Post & Telegraph Office,** on Upper Road, is open Monday–Saturday 10–4:30.

Exploring Haridwar Start your walk at the **Lalto Rao Bridge.** As you proceed northeast along **Jodhamal Road,** the facades of buildings—some Art Deco and all done up in bright pastels with highlighted trim—make you think of Miami Beach. But this is India, and these are *ashrams* (religious retreats) and *dharmshalas* (guest houses). Inside, along with pilgrims, you find ornate marble gods and goddesses dressed in festive clothes.

In **Moti Bazaar,** one long bustling street, *ayurvedic* (herbal) medicine shops sell *jalzeera* (spice powder for stomachaches); religious shops sell polished stone lingams, framed photos of deities, and sandstone prayer beads. Vendors sell *dias* (little woven leaf boats containing flowers and a thimble-size clay pot with oil and a wick). Buy one (about Rs. 10) to set afloat in the Ganga during Arti.

Walk down to the Ganga and **Har-ki-pauri Ghat,** surrounded by a complex of temples, new except for the 16th-century Shri Ganga Mandir. From the *ghat* (stairway to the water), a short bridge leads to the **Pant Dweep,** a terraced island that is the best vantage point for the service.

Arti begins with the clang of temple bells. Chanting priests carrying large brass lamps filled with oil descend the steps of the ghat and ignite the lamps. Flames shoot up as the priests swing the lamps over the Ganga. Temple bells chime, drowning out the chanting; the air sweetens from *dhoop* (incense). Hundreds of burning dias flicker away down the Ganga.

In 10–15 minutes Arti is over, but you have more to experience. Head back to the bridge via the **walkway along the canal.** Masseurs offer to rub your head, arms, and back; an armless artist draws with his feet; sadhus in deep meditation sit in temporary shrines erected under trees; beggars call out for rupees and food. *Plan at least 3 hours, with 1 hour for Moti Bazaar. Arrive at Har-ki-pauri Ghat 30 minutes before Arti begins—usually at sundown.*

Haridwar's Religious Fun Houses *Pawan* means "holy," *dham,* "house"—but step into Haridwar's **Pawan Dham** and those who subscribe to more sedate religions might think they've entered a religious fun house. Elaborate frescoes made of inlaid and painted glass depict mythological events. Step up close to cubicles with gaily dressed and decorated marble deities and look into the mirrored walls to see infinite reflections of each statue. The crowning pièce de kitsch is a gigantic freestanding, sparkling, glass-inlaid chariot drawn by horses with Krishna (an avatar of Vishnu) and the hero Arjun inside and Hanuman, the monkey god, on top.

Swami Satyamitrananda Giri, who founded the **Bharat Mata Mandir,** also on the same road, says his seven-story building "is

not only art—it is an act of devotion." It's a lot more than that.
Every floor is done up in an India-as-Motherland theme. The
ground floor, Shrine of Bharat Mata (Mother India), gets you
into the mood with her statue and a large map of the country.
On the top floor is the abode of Shiva, Mt. Kailas, complete with
an inner sanctum where Shiva sits in deep meditation. Since
most of the signs are in Hindi, you'll want to buy the English-
language brochure (Rs. 5) when you enter. *Admission free to
all ashrams. They are about 5 km (3 mi) from the center of
Haridwar on the road to Rishikesh. Take a bicycle rickshaw.
Allow 2 hours for this excursion. Open sunrise to sunset.*

Exploring In dusty **Rishikesh,** 24 kilometers (15 miles) north of Haridwar,
Rishikesh visit Maharishi Mahesh Yogi's **Transcendental Meditation Cen-**
❸ **ter** (across the Ganga River at Shankracharya Nagar, tel. 121),
which once hooked the Beatles; Swami Sivananda's **Divine Life
Society** (Shivanand Nagar, tel. 40); the **Yoga Sadhan Ashram**
(Railway Rd.); and **Yoga Niketan** (Munikireti, tel. 227). *Medi-
tate or attend an evening lecture at a nominal cost. Admission
to facilities free otherwise. Generally open sunrise–sunset.*

Dining All food in Haridwar is vegetarian. If you want meat or eggs,
head to Hotel Surprise, outside Haridwar's city limits. Dress is
casual. Highly recommended restaurants are indicated by a
star ★. Prices are per person, excluding drinks, service, and
taxes.

Hotel Surprise. The decor at air-conditioned Gazal is Western,
the food nonvegetarian Continental and Chinese. You can also
dine outside at Barbeque for South Indian and *tandoori* (marinated meat) items or at the Rooftop Restaurant for grilled
specialties, with good views in either place. *Hotel Surprise,
Haridwar-Delhi Rd., Jwala Pur, tel. 1146. Gazal open 8–11,
noon–3, 7–midnight; Barbeque and Rooftop open 6–10 PM.
AE, DC, MC, V. Moderate to Expensive ($5–$15).*

★ **Chotiwala Restaurant.** Booths and tables are crowded into a
narrow space. While a radio plays Hindi music, diners eat ample portions Indian fashion, with the right hand. Friendly
ambience. *Railway Station Rd., tel. 242. Open 8 AM–10:30 PM.
No credit cards. Closed government and Hindu holidays. Inexpensive (under $5).*

Lodging Highly recommended lodgings are indicated by a star ★.
Prices are for a standard double room, including taxes and excluding service charges.

★ **Hotel Natraj.** This new luxury hotel is a three-story stucco-and-
marble structure. It is quiet, with all amenities, but it's in
Rishikesh, 24 kilometers (15 miles) from Haridwar. *Dehradun
Rd., U.P., tel. 1099. 75 rooms with bath. Facilities: TV, air-
conditioning, 24-hour coffee shop and restaurants (vegetarian), health club, shopping arcade, pool, free airport transfer,
travel agency, foreign exchange counter. AE, DC. Inexpensive–Moderate (under $60).*
Hotel Surprise. This little high rise just outside Haridwar has
the upscale traveler in mind. It has a garish lobby, but pleas-
antly unpretentious rooms. It is 1½ kilometers (1 mile) from
Haridwar (to get beyond the vegetarian limits). *Haridwar-
Delhi Rd., Jwala Pur, U.P., tel: 1146 or 1148. 55 rooms with
bath. Deluxe rooms have TV and air-conditioning. Facilities:
foreign exchange desk, travel agency, car rental, pool, shop-*

*ping arcade, doctor on call, nonvegetarian restaurants. AE,
DC, MC, V. Inexpensive–Moderate (under $60).*

Tourist Bungalow. A government facility currently under renovation, it's within walking distance of the center of Haridwar
and faces the Ganga Canal. Rooms have minimal furnishings;
ask for an air-cooled one. *Reservations: Office of the Manager,
Uttar Pradesh State Tourism Development Corporation, U.P.,
tel. 379. 22 rooms with bath (shower). Facilities: restaurant.
No credit cards. Inexpensive (under $25).*

Mussoorie

➍ At first glance, **Mussoorie,** 2,005 meters (6,576 feet) above sea
level, seems a hill-station-turned-honeymoon-retreat where
the emphasis is on short walks, relaxation, and indoor sports.
Along the 100-kilometer (62-mile) drive from Haridwar, you're
bombarded with billboards advertising hotels and pass cars
loaded with young couples. But once you arrive, something unexpected happens. Numerous stalwart reminders of the grand
old elegance welcome you, especially the Savoy Hotel, a
French-style chateau on its own hill. Then there's the moody
weather, which changes at whim.

Getting Around   **Mussoorie** is a walker's town with pedestrian malls. Taxis are
unmetered. Bargain using Delhi rates: Rs. 3.30 for the first kilometer, Rs. 2.40 per additional kilometer. You can hire a
rickshaw pulled by one or two men. Fares are negotiable and
cheaper than taxis. Have sympathy, the routes they cover are
steep.

Addresses and   Visit the **U.P. Tourist Office** (The Mall, tel. 2863), open Mon-
Numbers   day–Saturday 10–5. To rent a car with driver or make travel
Tourist Information   arrangements, contact **Kulwant Travels** (Masonic Lodge Bus
Stand, tel. 2717) or **GMVN** (Tourist Complex, The Mall, tel.
2863); both are open Monday–Saturday 10–5. To cash traveler's checks, visit the **State Bank of India** in Kulri Bazar, open
weekdays 10–2, Saturday 10–noon. The **General Post & Telegraph Office** is in Kulri Bazar; branch offices are at Landour
Bazar and the Savoy Hotel; they're open Monday–Saturday
10–4.

Guided Tours   GMVN (Tourist Complex, The Mall, tel. 2863) offers conducted
car tours to Kempty Falls and Dhanolti. **Kulwant Travels** (Masonic Lodge Bus Stand, tel. 2717) also arranges tours via taxi
for higher prices.

Exploring   Head west from the Savoy on Charleville Road to **Happy Valley.**
Mussoorie's   Here Buddhist prayer flags mark a religious transition. When
Happy Valley   the Dalai Lama fled the Chinese in 1959, he and many of his followers came to Mussoorie. On the highest pinnacle, where
prayer flags bristle the length of the summit and a sacred stupa
points the way to enlightenment, His Holiness preached to the
citizens of this new Tibetan township. Beneath the summit is a
new community monastery with *thang-kas* (religious scrolls),
contemporary frescoes, and that customary peaceful aura.
Nearby is the **Tibetan Homes Foundation** (an orphanage that
extends a home and hope to uprooted Tibetan children). Donations are welcome and put to good use.

Off the   If you're staying in Mussoorie 48 hours (the time it takes to
Beaten Track   develop a photo), stop at Doon Studio (The Mall) for a "photo
opportunity." Dress up in "hilly" clothes and the photographer

will pose you before a Himalayan backdrop. *Open Thurs.–
Tues. 8AM to 10 PM.*

Shopping Tourist souvenirs crowd every shop. For good handcarved
walking sticks or canes, go to **Star Walking Sticks** (London
House, The Mall). Prices range from Rs. 15 to 150. It's open all
the time; the owner lives there. For silk from Varanasi, head to
Banaras House (The Mall, near the Police Outpost); it's open
daily 10–7 and does not accept credit cards. For an old treasure,
visit **Vinod Kumar Objets of Art & Antiquity** (Clock Tower, tel.
2801); it's open March–December, daily 9–8; the rest of the
year, it's closed on Sunday. It does not accept credit cards.

**Outdoor
Adventures** Get a **fishing** permit from the Divisional Forest Officer in
Mussoorie and head 27 kilometers (17 miles) northwest to
Yamuna Bridge and try for trout or *mahseer* (Himalayan river
fish). Plan a 3-kilometer (2-mile) **hike** up Camel's Back Road
through forest glades to arrive on the mountaintop at sunset.
Swim at Kempty Falls's natural pool, 15 kilometers (9 miles)
north of Mussoorie. Go by taxi or horse—arranged through
your hotel.

Dining Highly recommended restaurants are indicated by a star ★.
Prices are per person, including taxes and excluding drinks and
service charges. Reservations are required. Dress is casual.

★ **The Savoy.** Whether you eat inside, in the enclosed front terrace, or outside gazing at the mountains, the Savoy is definitely
for epicureans. You might even get a bottle of good wine—rare
in India. The menu includes good Chinese, Continental, and Indian cuisine. *Tel. 2510 or 2601. Open 7:30–10, 12:30–2:45, 7:30–
10. AE, DC, MC, V. Expensive ($10–$15).*

★ **Carlton's Hotel Plaisance.** Meals are served in a family dining
room or on the enclosed porch of this elegant inn. Tasty Indian
(including nonvegetarian) and Continental cuisine. *Happy Valley Rd., tel. 2800. Open 1–2:30, 8–10. No credit cards.
Inexpensive–Moderate (under $10).*

Lodging Highly recommended lodgings are indicated by a star ★. Prices
are for a standard double room, including taxes and excluding
service charges. Make your reservations early.

★ **Carlton's Hotel Plaisance.** If cozy elegance appeals to you, stay
in a small memorabilia-filled bungalow built by an English barrister in the early 1900s. Gracious hosts cater to your needs. No
Himalayan views; you're nestled in an orchard. Discounts offered mid-November–March. *Reservations: Happy Valley
Rd., U.P., tel. 2800. 10 rooms with bath. No credit cards. Moderate ($25–$60).*

★ **Savoy.** The chateau-style Savoy on a hill overlooking the mountains opened in 1902 when no road led to Mussoorie. The first
guests arrived on horseback or in palanquins that bearers had
carried for miles. Queen Mary stayed in these grand rooms
when she was Princess of Wales; Nehru and the Dalai Lama
have also been guests. Tarnished edges are part of the charm.
Request a deluxe suite or an upstairs double off the veranda.
Meals are included. *Mussoorie, U.P., tel. 2510 or 2601. 121
rooms with bath. Facilities: room service, restaurants, beer
garden, bar, laundry, travel counter, doctor on call, foreign
exchange counter, post office. AE, DC, MC, V. Moderate
($25–$60).*

From Mussoorie to the Char Dhams

Before the construction of roads, the *yatra* (pilgrimage) to the Char Dham temples—Yamunotri, Gangotri, Kedarnath, and Badrinath—was arduous and lengthy, yet this never stopped the pilgrim, no matter his or her age or health. If he couldn't walk, a coolie carried him or he'd go by animal. First he visited Haridwar and bathed in the Ganga. Spiritually ready, he headed north into the Garhwal Himalayas to pray at Yamunotri, then made his way east to the other temples, saving Badrinath—the holiest—for last.

Once you reach Garhwal, you've entered the realm of the sadhu, *sannyasi* (elderly Brahman who has renounced his family and the material world), and swami. Sadhus, sannyasi, and swamis live at the Char Dhams and in nearby cities and villages. Some live in huts; others have air-conditioning, television, and autos.

Many of these holy men speak English and will talk to visitors about their beliefs and customs. They'll tell you that they wear saffron, yellow, or red because these are the colors of fire before it turns to ash. Each smears ash on his forehead to honor the gods—three horizontal stripes for Shiva, vertical stripes for Vishnu. Some of the famous swamis and sadhus may still live at Gangotri.

The route described here will take you to Yamunotri and Gangotri, temples dedicated to the holy Rivers Yamuna and Ganga and to the goddesses of the same names who are revered as divine mother figures. To get directly from Mussoorie to the temples at Kedarnath and Badrinath, go straight to Tehri, a 76-kilometer (47-mile) trip. This trip is less scenic. Dedicated to Shiva and Vishnu, the two most important gods in the Hindu pantheon, Kedarnath and Badrinath are the most ornate temples; but Gangotri is the temple to visit if you're curious about sadhus and swamis.

All roads are usually open only from May to mid-October. In winter, once you get within 50 kilometers (31 miles) of the temples, the roads are subject to heavy snow. In any season, the trip is a long one. The monsoon season (July and August) can cause landslides, which are usually removed in a few days or sometimes hours.

To see all the shrines by car takes 10–12 days—with no lengthy stays, no glitches, no overnight side trips, no detours. Hire a car with driver from a recommended travel agency in Mussoorie. Figure Rs. 4 per kilometer and halt charges of Rs. 50–100 per night.

A visit to Kedarnath or Yamunotri requires an additional 14-kilometer (9-mile) trek each way via foot or pony (available at the start of the trek, along with food and lodging).

Bring sufficient rupees. There are banks, but only in the few cities, like Uttarkashi or Joshimath. Carry lots of small change; numerous shrines expect small offerings.

Dining and Lodging Meals are vegetarian—a religious stricture. On the road, your options are Tourist Rest Houses run by the government; stalls; or, best, Indian-style diners. Your driver will know the latest "in" spot. For beverages, stick to tea or bottled carbonated drinks. Bring snacks, especially if you plan to take walks. Bring bottled water or a canteen and water-purification tablets. *All meals are inexpensive (under $5 per person, excluding drinks, service, and taxes). No credit cards. Eating establishments are generally open sunrise–about 8 PM.*

Most lodging are government run with few amenities—not dirty, but humble. For an attached bathroom, request a "deluxe" or "executive" room with two twin beds or a family suite with four beds. Other options are "ordinary double" or a dormitory with a shared bath. Most bathrooms have an Indian-style toilet and simple shower, most often with hot water available by bucket. The *chawkidar* (caretaker) will fix you a simple vegetarian meal (called catering). Bring a sleeping bag or a sleeping bag sheet, a flashlight with ample batteries, a towel, a bar of soap, mosquito repellent, and a roll of toilet paper. *Reserve all lodgings on this excursion in advance through the manager (if listed) or through the Assistant General Manager (Tourism), GMVN, Munikireti, Rishikesh, U.P., tel. 372 or 357. No credit cards. Inexpensive (under $15 per double room; dormitories are under $5 per bed).*

On to Yamunotri

Since the Yamunotri Temple, 140 kilometers (87 miles) from Mussoorie, is modest and involves a trek, omit it if you're short on time. The trip, however, is beautiful, with green valleys and distant snow-capped mountains like sentries guarding the shrine. Once you cross **Yamuna Bridge** 27 kilometers (17 miles) from Mussoorie and pass through **Barkot,** an aura of sanctity hangs in the air. Hindu shrines dot the roadside. Pine-covered mountains close in, waterfalls shoot across the road, the holy Yamuna rages in the gorge below. At Hanumanchatti, 32 kilometers (20 miles) from Mussoorie, you reach the end of the car-worthy road and the start of a 14-kilometer (9-mile) trek on foot or by mule.

At the village of **Markkandiya,** enjoy **sulfur springs** before heading to **Jankibaichatti's Tourist Rest House,** 7 kilometers (4 miles) farther. **Yamunotri** is another steep 6-kilometer (4-mile) walk. Start early in the morning to get back to the Tourist Rest House by night.

Yamunotri According to legend, an ancient sage, Asit, built a hermitage on a ridge by the banks of the Yamuna in the foothills of Banderpunch Mountain. When old age prevented him from traveling to Gangotri, the source of the Ganga, a tiny tributary of the river emerged from nearby rocks. In the 19th century, the wife of the maharajah of Jaipur built the Yamunotri Temple on the site of Asit's tiny house. Destroyed in 1923, it was then rebuilt. The actual source of the Yamuna is 1 kilometer (a half mile) up, at the top of a steep and difficult climb.

The goddess Yamuna is represented by a black marble idol in the temple's inner sanctum. Outside the temple, hot springs bubble in *kunds* (tanks). Surya Kund is considered the most sacred kund. Here, devotees immerse cloth filled with rice and potatoes, which cook quickly in the near-boiling water. Called *prasad*, these gifts are offered to the goddess. In the warm water of Bai Kund, which spills into the Yamuna, devotees take a ritual dip. The Divya Shila is a sacred rock worshipped by all Hindus before the *puja* (prayer service) in the temple. *Daily puja is early morning and evening; the temple is open 6–noon and 2–9.*

Dining In Barkot, Hanumanchatti, and Jankibaichatti, the government-run **Tourist Rest Houses** sell simple, inexpensive meals. **Stalls** at Yamunotri offer safe-to-eat snacks.

Lodging **Tourist Rest Houses.** In Barkot, Hanumanchatti, and Jankibaichatti, they have unadorned, clean rooms: executive, ordinary double, or dormitory, with hot water available by bucket. *Barkot reservations: Manager, Tourist Rest House, tel. 36. Hanumanchatti and Jankibaichatti reservations: GMVN, Munikireti, Rishikesh, U.P., tel. 372 or 357. Under 10 rooms each.*

On to Gangotri

To get to the Gangotri Temple, 235 kilometers (146 miles) from Yamunotri, head south to **Dharasu,** 100 kilometers (62 miles) from Yamunotri, and follow the Bhagirathi River north. The pace is slow until you reach **Uttarkashi** after 28 kilometers (17 miles). Though this city is ancient and honors Shiva, it is no beauty.

Anglers and trekkers take note: This is the departure point for the short trek to **Dodital Lake.** *For fishing licenses, visit the Uttarkashi Tourist Bureau (tel. 190), near the bus station.*

When you head north, the Himalayas close in on the narrow valley. Boulders hang over the road. The Bhagirathi River, often deep in a gorge, rushes by. Near **Gangnani,** 56 kilometers (35 miles) along, stop at **Parashar Kund** (Rishikund). Visit the shrine midway up the slope and enjoy the clean temple bathing tanks, fed by hot springs.

The simple shrine perched above the sacred water tanks is reputedly 500 years old and honors the *Rishi* (Saint) Parashar who came here 2,000 years ago searching for god. After Rishi did penance for 12 years, he realized his goal, and sulfur springs emerged from a rock behind the temple. Women should use the temple bath behind the wall that is on the right of the open tank reserved for men. Bathing attire required. *Admission free. Open sunrise–sunset.* The nearby U. P. government canteen serves tea.

The journey to **Gangotri** turns rugged. The road snakes and cuts through forests. The river churns. Mountains draw closer. Until 1984 the car-worthy road ended at Bhaironghati. The final 10 kilometers (6 miles) required a trek that included crossing the highest rope bridge in the world, now replaced by a towering bridge for vehicles. No photographs are allowed.

Gangotri The road ends at the bottom of the path to the temple. You step outside the car and join ongoing festivities. Stalls sell sacred beads and religious souvenirs. Sadhus, camped out in crude tents, display personalized shrines with framed pictures of Shiva. Some sadhus do penance—sitting on a bed of thorns or wrapped in coils of barbed wire.

Hindus believe that when this entire area was covered with glaciers, the goddess Ganga was brought down to earth by the mythological King Bhagirath who had prayed 5,000 years to have the ashes of his relatives purified. Shiva caught the goddess in his matted locks, and she divided into four or seven rivers, depending on the version you hear. This event occurred at Gangotri, and the river, believed to contain *amrit* (holy nectar), is said to cleanse one of all sins. Even scientists agree that the water at Gangotri contains no impurities.

The Gangotri Temple itself, set on a plinth, is a modest granite structure first built in the early 18th century, then rebuilt by the maharajah of Jaipur. In the temple courtyard, pilgrims who have traveled from every corner of India congregate, waiting to get inside the inner sanctum. When the temple door opens, they rush the entrance and heave their offerings at the sacred statue of the goddess Ganga. Nearby, the Bhagirathi River thrashes over jutting rocks into a gorge. *Daily puja is 6–noon and 2–9.*

To meet the following swamis, just mention their names; they're well known. Swami Hansa Nand Tirith, who lives with his young disciple and an elderly woman he calls Mother, says he's 103 years old. He lives with no creature comforts. A family man until he turned 50, he lived in the forest as a sannyasi for 25 years before he moved to the mountains and entered a life of meditation, wearing his holy *rudraksha* (Himalayan berry) beads around his scantily clad body. Swami Hansa Nand Tirith lives in a hut near the banks of the river from April to October, then lives at the Gaumukh Glacier, the source of the Ganga, from October to April.

Or, look up Swami Sundaranan, the "Clicking Swami," who lives in whimsy—his hut across the river from the temple is surrounded by trees and rocks that he's turned into art objects. In his early 60s, Swami Sundaranan is a mountaineer and photographer whose published photos of Uttarakhand reveal his spirituality and express a wish to save the Himalayas from environmental damage. A mountain resident since 1948, he has a dim view of most of his neighbors, claiming they cut down trees, pollute the river, and ruin the beauty of Gangotri.

Dining **Stalls** on the way to the temple serve good cheap snacks. The **Gangotri Tourist Rest House,** under renovation, will have inexpensive catered food on demand.

In Uttarkashi, eat at **Hotel Satyam,** a small, crowded restaurant with piped-in Hindi music. You'll have good Indian vegetarian dishes—which you eat with your right hand.

Lodging **Tourist Rest House.** At Gangotri, it is under renovation and will have a spruced-up rustic look, with hot water on request. Choose rooms from deluxe to dormitory. *About 20 rooms with bath or shared bath. Reservations: See Tourist Information, above.*
Tourist Rest House. In Uttarkashi, it needs a face-lift; but the simple rooms are clean with Western-style toilet and Indian shower. *Reservations: Manager, Tourist Rest House, GMVN, Uttarkashi, tel. 36. 33 rooms with bath.*

On to Kedarnath

12 Head about 239 kilometers (148 miles) south to **Srinagar,** a 14th-century city with crumbling old ashrams and neglected temples, overshadowed by a new market already coated in dust from the stream of buses taking pilgrims to the shrines. This is the first leg of your 350-kilometer (217-mile) trip. From Srinagar, it's northeast 34 kilometers (21 miles) to Rudraprayag, at the confluence of the Mandakini River (originating at Kedar-nath) and the Alakananda River (originating at Badrinath). Once you cross the Alakananda, you enter Chamoli (District of God).

At Kund, 35 kilometers (22 miles) on, your vehicle will chug up a circuitous road chiseled into the sides of a river gorge. Snow-capped mountains surround you. Then, after 19 kilometers (12 miles), you see **Guptakashi,** Hidden Shiva, a small city of legendary importance to the Hindus. ⓭

After the Great Battle recounted in the Mahabharata, the Pandavas, who had killed their own kin, the Kauravas, sought forgiveness from Shiva, who continually eluded them. They chased him to what is now Varanasi, to Uttarkashi, to the site of Guptakashi, and finally to Kedarnath.

From Guptakashi today, police monitor the flow of traffic to the temple, 45 kilometers (28 miles) away. The wait's never long. At **Soneprayag,** 26 kilometers (16 miles) along, stop if you have time and take the 16-kilometer (10-mile) round-trip hike to **Trijuginarayan,** a Vishnu temple where Shiva married Parvati. ⓮

The village of Gaurikund, 4 kilometers (2½ miles) later, signals the end of the car-worthy road. You must trek or go by pony 14 kilometers (9 miles) to the Kedarnath Temple—a journey that passes by deep ravines, waterfalls, tiny shrines, and tea shops and through forests.

Kedarnath Temple ⓯ About 2 kilometers (1 mile) from **Kedarnath,** you see the temple on a granite plinth at the head of the Mandakini Valley with the Mahapanth and Kedarnath mountains towering above.

Kedarnath also originates from events that occurred in the Mahabharata's Great Battle. Bhim, one of the Pandavas, finally caught hold of Shiva, who had turned himself into a bull. He grabbed Shiva's hump, preventing his escape. The determination of the Pandavas so moved the god that he forgave them. They constructed a temple for him at Kedarnath, which Shiva told them must venerate the hump by which he had been caught. Historians say the temple with its golden pinnacle is 1,000 years old.

The temple, with its carved exterior, sits in a courtyard protected by Nandi, Shiva's mount. Inside the *mandapa* (pavilion) small Nandi faces the Garbha-Griha (inner sanctum). Here, the rock formation, deified as Shiva, is also called a *jyotorlinga*—one of India's 12 naturally formed lingams. The interior has carvings of the Pandavas and their communal wife, Draupadi. Sacred tanks and small temples surround the main shrine. During morning puja, the lingam is shown in its unadorned natural form—called Nirwan Darshan—bathed in *ghee* (butter) and water. In the evening it's dressed—covered with ornaments and flowers, protected by a gold umbrella, and named Sringar Darshan. *Morning puja starts about 6; evening puja begins after 6.*

Dining Stalls sell snacks along the trek and at the temple.

Lodging **Chandra Puri Tent Camp.** North of Rudraprayag, it is a riverside cluster of walk-in, safari-style tents, each with four beds. Bring your own sleeping bag. *About 10 tents with shared bath. Reservations: See Tourist Information, above.*
Tourist Rest House. At Gaurikund, it has rooms from deluxe to

dormitory, and hot water is available on demand. *Reservations: Manager, Tourist Rest House, Gaurikund, U.P., tel. 2. About 10 rooms with bath or shared bath.*

Tourist Rest House. In Guptakashi, it has family suites or dormitories. *Reservations: Manager, Tourist Rest House, Guptakashi, U.P., tel. 21. About 6 rooms with bath or shared bath.*

Tourist Rest House. In Kedarnath, it offers ordinary rooms or a dormitory. *About 16 rooms with bath or shared bath. Reservations: See Tourist Information, above.*

Tourist Rest House. In Rudraprayag, on a hill overlooking the river, it has executive and deluxe rooms and a dormitory. *Reservations: Manager, Tourist Rest House, Rudraprayag, U.P., tel. 46. About 25 rooms with bath or shared bath.*

Tourist Rest House. At Srinagar, it is unattractive but quiet, a miracle given its main street location. The rooms are clean. The super-deluxe and deluxe rooms have Western-style bathrooms with hot and cold showers, though water is intermittent. You can also stay in an ordinary double or dormitory. *Reservations: Manager, Tourist Rest House, Srinagar, U.P., tel. 99. About 70 rooms with bath or shared bath. Facilities: tiny gift shop, tourist bureau.*

On to Badrinath

16 Return the 51 kilometers (32 miles) to **Kund,** the first leg of a 235-kilometer (145-mile) trip to Badrinath. In Kund, take the road to the left that leads to Ukhimath, the winter home of the Kedarnath priests. The first stop is Chopta, 37 kilometers (23 miles) to the southeast. The narrow road passes through hamlets where women, bodies stooped, cut grass in open fields or trudge along with baskets of fodder. Water buffalo huddle under thatched sheds. Gentle tree-covered hills invite walks and inspire picnics, but you should wait for Chopta.

The road climbs to Dogalbhitta, the forest ends, and the horizon extends along alpine meadows filled with rhododendron. **17** At last you reach **Chopta,** an idyllic "must stop." Eat at a thatched-covered tea stall as a tinny radio wails out Garhwali songs, woolly dogs hover at your feet, and once you say *"Namaste"* (hello), curious villagers treat you like a long-lost friend.

From Chopta, climb to **Tungnath Temple,** the highest shrine in Garhwal, atop Chandrashila Mountain, 3,680 meters (12,070 feet) high. At the conclusion of the *Mahabharata*, when the Pandavas had caught Shiva, his bull manifestation shattered into five sections called Panch Kedar (Five Shivas). The hump stayed at Kedarnath, the face turned up at Rudranath, the stomach at Madmaheshwar (temples near Chopta), the hair in Kalpeshwar near Joshimath, and the arms fell here.

On a clear day, just the view from Tungnath is worth the steep climb. On the slopes, sheep graze the fields, Garhwali life unfolds, and in the distance are the spiritually famous Himalayan giants, Nanda Devi, Kedarnath, and Neelkanth. This 7-kilometer (4-mile) walk takes about four hours. Stone benches appear periodically; good food waits at the top.

18 From Chopta, head north to **Joshimath,** about 100 kilometers (62 miles) farther—the destination for skiers setting off for **Auli,** 16 kilometers (10 miles) away; for serious mountaineers heading for the **Nanda Devi** summit; and for hot springs aficionados eager to relax at **Tapovan**, 17 kilometers (10½ miles) away. If you're in Joshimath during the **Trimundiya Festival** (April or May), then this conjested city, an army base and popular pilgrim halt, is worth an overnight stay. Other times of the year, just visit the **Narsingh Temple** (winter home of the priests at Badrinath and the festival location) and see its idol, which reflects the state of the world.

Legend claims an 8th-century king constructed the Narsingh Temple for Vishnu in his Narsingh manifestation. In its inner sanctum, the sacred idol (made of Shaligram, a semiprecious black stone) has an arm that is said to be shrinking each year. The devout say that when *Kaliyug* (Evil Time) arrives, the arm will shatter, a flood will occur, and the present world will be destroyed. A new world will begin with the shrine of Badrinath emerging in a new location, Bhawishya Badri in the Tapovan Valley.

The festival of Trimundiya, imbued with a sense of the miraculous, occurs about a week before the spring opening of Badrinath. Trimundiya means "God with Three Heads"—a three-headed spirit that lives in an individual from a particular family in Joshimath, passed on from father to son. The festival begins with beating drums and the sound of pipes. A crude image of the goddess Durga—a long stick of bamboo with black hair on one end—is carried to the Matha Angana (Holy Courtyard).

The priest prays over the Durga, then over the present-day incarnation of Trimundiya, who proceeds to eat 60 pounds of rice and to down water from a large clay pot filled 8–10 times. A goat's throat is slit. The incarnation sucks the blood, peels off the skin, and eats most of the animal raw; then he drinks more water. Circling the Durga, he throws the remaining rice and goat meat to those at the festival—his gift to them. The food he has eaten is his gift to the god. Those who catch a bit of the goat say it will heal all wounds. They also swear that medical tests done before and after the festival show that nothing is ever inside Trimundiya's stomach. Once the festival is over, the spirit departs from the individual's body—supposedly well fed and pleased.

From Pandukeshwar, 29 kilometers (18 miles) north of Joshimath, police control the flow of traffic to Badrinath, 23 kilometers (14 miles) farther. **Govindghat** village is the start of the trek into the **Valley of Flowers** and **Hemkund Lake.** Once again, the closer you get to a shrine, the more pronounced the landscape. The road winds in a gorge with sheer cliffs dropping down to the Alakananda River. Evidence of landslides lingers on either side of the road. Streams splash off boulders. Sadhus, walking to the shrine, fill you with respect—their journey is rough. Finally, you reach **Hanuman Chatti** where your driver stops at a roadside temple dedicated to Hanuman (the monkey god). For one rupee, the priest blesses the vehicle and you—a spiritual tollgate.

Badrinath Temple
⑲

From Hanuman Chatti, the road climbs above the tree line. You see the snow-covered Mt. Neelkanth, like an arrowhead piercing the sky; then finally you reach Badrinath, a village sprawled in a valley divided by the Alakananda. This most important Char Dham is brightly painted.

Badrinath also figures in Buddhist lore. Hindus claim that eons ago, a sage named Narad chastised Vishnu for indulging in an earthly pleasure—allowing his consort, Lakshmi, to rub his feet. Vishnu sent Lakshmi away and fled to this valley. Here, he meditated in what Hindus call the *yogdhyani* posture, which is associated with the Buddha, who also happens to be the ninth incarnation of this Hindu deity. Over time, Lakshmi found Vishnu and begged him to give up this un-Vishnu-like pose. He agreed, but only if Badrinath remained a valley of meditation.

Buddhism also figures historically. Under the influence of Emperor Ashoka, 274–232 BC, Badrinath became a Buddhist shrine, and the idol of Vishnu was tossed into the Narad Kund, a nearby pond named after the sage who had berated Vishnu. Centuries later, Adiguru, a Hindu saint, dove in and recovered the idol, reestablishing the Badrinath shrine as the premier Hindu temple.

Because of the increase of pilgrims, much of the temple has been enlarged. Only the ancient inner sanctum has escaped alteration. All day long, devotees climb the stairs to the shrine, jumping up to ring a brass bell that hangs from the portico leading into the temple courtyard. The main shrine has a mandapa and inner sanctum with a black stone idol of Vishnu sitting under a gold canopy.

In one of the small shrines that surround the temple, Hanuman holds the Himalayas in his palm. When Ramayana hero Rama (Vishnu) told Hanuman to get medicinal herbs from the Himalayas, the monkey god, not knowing which herbs to bring, carried back the entire mountain range. Another shrine is dedicated to Lakshmi. And another honors Adiguru, who recovered the idol.

Before the start of evening Arti and *darshan* (viewing of the idol), pilgrims gather in a room off the temple courtyard and listen to a priest tell stories of Vishnu. Clanging bells signal arti. The devotees rush into the mandapa and brush their hand over a brass plate with burning oil to get its blessing. Then they file into the inner sanctum where the High Priest sits by Vishnu, who is dressed in flowers. After the crowd has passed before the idol, beating drums announce the end of Arti. The idol goes back to bed. *Open daily 4:30 AM–1 PM, 3–9 PM. Evening Arti 6–7 PM.*

Dining   In Badrinath and Joshimath, head for the most crowded restaurant, your assurance of reasonably good food. *Eateries generally open 8 AM–9 PM.*

Lodging   **Hotel Devlok.** In Badrinath, it is government-run and offers the best accommodations in the Char Dham region. Deluxe and executive rooms are spacious, and beds have clean comforters. You can also stay in an ordinary double. *Reservations: Manager, Hotel Devlok, Badrinath, U.P., tel. 12. About 30 rooms with bath (shower). Facilities: lounge and restaurant.*
Tourist Rest House. At Joshimath, it sits on a hill, which offers an escape from this noisy town. Three choices of rooms—executive, ordinary, or dormitory. Hot and cold water are usually available. *Reservations: Manager, Tourist Rest House, Joshimath, U.P., tel. 81. About 15 rooms with bath or shared bath.*

Deoprayag

㉑ If you plan to end your trip in Garhwal by returning to Dehradun, stop at **Deoprayag** (God's Place), a city of *pandits* (Hindu scholars). It's about 400 kilometers (248 miles) from Badrinath, set where the Alakananda and Bhagirathi merge to form the Ganga. Cross a swaying pedestrian bridge to get to the hamlet. It's a town built into a cliff wall; walk through narrow lanes with stalls on either side and vine-draped boulders hanging overhead.

Exploring Deoprayag is tranquil, a place to walk. Visit the modest **shrine** on the edge of the Ganga, then climb steep steps to the renovated **Raghunath Temple,** honoring the spot where Rama (an avatar of Vishnu) meditated. Plan for an hour-long walk.

Dining Eat at a stall or roadside eatery by the suspension bridge that leads into town. *Inexpensive (under $5 per person).*

Lodging **Tourist Rest House.** This is the only option, on a quiet hilltop a short drive from the village. Executive and ordinary rooms are clean and have twin beds and Indian-style bathrooms with hot water by bucket. *Reservations: Manager, Tourist Rest House, Deoprayag, U.P., tel. 33. 4 rooms with bath (Indian). Facilities: catering. No credit cards. Inexpensive (under $25).*

Corbett National Park

Founded in 1935, India's oldest wildlife sanctuary is named after the fearless hunter and conservationist Edward James Corbett, author of *Man-Eaters of Kumaon.* Corbett grew up in these hills, and the local people, a number of whom he saved from tigers at the risk of his own life, revered him.

㉑ Corbett hunted his share of tigers, then regretted the sport as he saw the turn-of-the-century population of 20,000–40,000 tigers reduced to 1,800. In 1973 **Corbett National Park** was designated a tiger preserve.

Arriving and Departing
By Plane **Vayudoot** makes four weekly flights from Delhi's **National Airport** to **Pantnagar Airport,** the approach to Corbett, 135 kilometers (83 miles) away. Flights take about an hour. For fares and schedules, call, in Delhi (tel. 3312587). Try to book your ticket before you depart. From Pantnagar Airport, a two-hour taxi ride takes you to Corbett for Rs. 300–Rs. 400.

By Hired Car with Driver To drive from Delhi to **Dhikala,** the entrance to Corbett, about 300 kilometers (186 miles), plan for a seven-hour trip on decent roads. You must arrive before sunset when the park closes. Hire a car from a travel agency listed in the Delhi section, above.

By Train Two daily trains go from the **New Delhi Railway Station** to **Ramnagar,** 51 kilometers (37 miles) from Corbett National Park—the afternoon *Kashi Vishiwanath Express* and the inconvenient, late-night *Lucknow Mail.* Journey time is about three hours, which is faster than by car and much cheaper. If you book an overnight journey, reserve a sleeper *and* berth, or you risk being put off the train. Get your ticket well in advance in first (air-conditioned or nonair-conditioned) or second (air-conditioned) class. For train information in Delhi, call 3313535.

Exploring You must enter the park before sunset. Bring binoculars and bug repellent. Only daylight photography is allowed. Fishing is currently banned. Contact the Reception Center at Dhikhala to arrange for a wildlife guide, jeep, or elephant ride. While searching for animals, don't wear bright clothes, don't talk, and don't roam through the park alone. *Admission: 3 days, Rs. 35 (4th day, Rs. 6; 5th day, Rs. 12); students: Rs. 2. Vehicle fee: Rs. 10.*

Dining **Dhikhala Forest Rest House Complex.** In the park, this is your only choice for prepared meals (Continental and Indian) if you're staying in the complex. *No credit cards. Inexpensive (under $5 per person, excluding drinks, service, and taxes).*

Lodging Prices are for a standard double room, cottage, or tent, including taxes and excluding service charges.

Camp Corbett. In a forest an hour outside the actual park, this new, privately run "luxury camp" offers a choice of accommodations—deluxe cabins with thatched roof and modern attached bathroom or a safari-style tent (sleeping bag suggested). A rustic rooftop restaurant allows you to spot animals while eating good food (meals included). *Kaladhungi, U.P., no phone at press time. Reservations advised. 30 cabins; numerous tents. Facilities: fishing, jungle guides, natural pools, restaurant, bar. No credit cards. Moderate to Expensive ($25–$100).*

Dhikhala Forest Rest House Complex. This facility is in the park. The rooms are simple and clean. The old lodge has better ambience than the new one. Rent a cabin for more privacy or a tent (bring a sleeping bag). *Reservations: Field Director, Project Tiger, Ramnagar, tel. 189, or the Chief Wildlife Warden, Lucknow, U.P., tel. 46140. Numerous rooms with bath (Indian shower). Facilities: restaurant, reception center. No credit cards. Inexpensive (under $25).*

Bijrani, Khinanauli, and Sarpduli Rest Houses. Set farther into the forest and not convenient to the complex's restaurant, they offer rustic rooms, no-frills kitchens, and privacy. Bring a sleeping bag and provisions. *Each has about 6 rooms with Indian bath and hot water by bucket. Facilities: kitchen. Reservations: See Dhikhala Forest Rest House Complex. No credit cards. Very Inexpensive (under $5).*

Section 2
Northeast India & Calcutta

Calcutta is much maligned and much misunderstood. If you have an obligatory stop in Calcutta, don't book into the airport hotel unless your stay allows just time enough to sleep. Go into Calcutta with an open mind. Dominique Lapierre chose an apt title for his book on Calcutta: *City of Joy*. Calcutta is, above all, a celebration of life.

Arriving and Departing by Plane

There are few convenient international flights to Calcutta. Arrive in the region in Delhi (*see* Delhi, above) and take one of Indian Airline's three daily flights to Calcutta.

To get to the eastern Himalayas from Calcutta, the gateway to that area, go by plane. Other forms of transportation—train or car— require a Restricted Area Permit (*see* Before You Go to North India, above).

Airlines and Airport All international and domestic airlines use **Dum Dum Airport.** From here, **Indian Airlines** (tel. 260730) makes the following flights: one hour to Bagdogra for Sikkim and Darjeeling (daily); two hours to Dehli (three daily flights); one hour to Guwahati in Assam and the gateway to Meghalaya (four daily flights); 90 minutes to Kathmandu in Nepal (daily). **Vayudoot** (tel. 447062) flies daily to Shillong in Meghalaya, 90 minutes. **Druk Airlines** (tel. 442649) makes four weekly one-hour flights to Paro in Bhutan.

Between Airport and City Dum Dum is 15 kilometers (9 miles) from Calcutta. Only the **Hotel Airport Ashok** offers free pickup service. The **airport coach** goes to most of the better hotels and the city center; its counter is near the baggage claim area; or go by **taxi** for about Rs. 70.

Getting Around

Taxi drivers don't use their meters. Ask your hotel for the appropriate fare so you can negotiate. Auto rickshaws are cheaper; follow the same procedure.

Addresses and Numbers

Tourist Information The **West Bengal Tourist Department** (3/2 Benoy Badal Dinesh Bagh–East, tel. 288271) is open Monday–Saturday 10–5. It also has a counter at the airport and the railroad station. Tourist offices of the various eastern states include **Assam** (8 Russell St., tel. 298329), **Meghalaya** (9 Russell St., tel. 213310), and **Sikkim** (Poonam Bldg., 5/2 Russell St., tel. 295476).

Emergencies If you have a medical emergency, ask your **hotel** to recommend a physician or contact your consulate: **American** (5/1 Ho Chi Minh Sarani, tel. 443611) or **British** (1 Ho Chi Minh Sarani, tel. 445171). There is no Canadian consulate.

Bookstore The best English-language bookstore is **Oxford Booksellers** (Park St.), open Monday–Saturday 10–6.

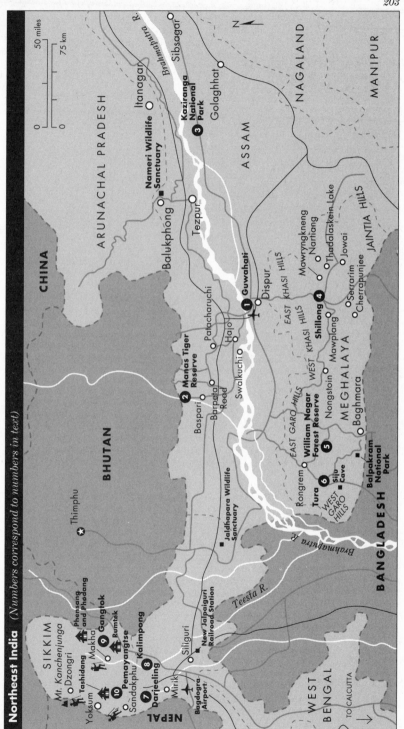

Northeast India (Numbers correspond to numbers in text)

Travel Agencies   **ITDC** (c/o Government of India Tourist Office, 4 Shakespeare Sarani, tel. 440901), **American Express** (21 Old Court House St., tel. 286281), **Mercury Travels** (46-C J. L. Nehru Rd., tel. 443555), or **Travel Corporation of India** (46-C J. L. Nehru Rd., tel. 445469).

Banks   Banks are open weekdays 10–2, Saturday 10–noon. Branches include **American Express** (*see* above), **Bank of America** (8 India Exchange Pl.), **Citibank** (Tata Ctr., 43 J. L. Nehru Rd.), **Grindlays Bank** (19 N.S. Rd., tel. 228346), and **State Bank of India** (33 J. L. Nehru Rd.).

Post Offices   The **General Post Office** (B.B.D. Bagh Rd. and 8 Red Cross Sarani) is open Monday–Saturday 10–4:30.

Exploring Calcutta

Walk northwest from the Great Eastern Hotel on Old Court House Street. At Lal Bazar, just after the West Bengal Tourist Office, turn right, then left onto **Rabindra Sarani.** Soon you enter an Islamic world and a shopper's paradise. Women walk by in *burkas* (long tent-shape robes), their eyes barely visible behind weblike veils. Men sit on elevated platforms selling Bengali kurtas, colorful *lungis* (wraps worn by men), and white dhotis. Stands sell vials of perfume created from the essence of flowers.

At Chitpur Road, turn right. On the left is the white marble and red sandstone **Nakoda Mosque,** a 20th-century copy of the Moghul Emperor Akbar's tomb in Agra. Each floor has a prayer hall, and from the top you have a good view of Calcutta. *Open sunrise–sunset.*

Return to Rabindra Sarani, turn right and cross the intersection with M. M. Burman Street to enter a Hindu community. Turn right on Muktaram Babu Street, lined with British buildings lavished with rococo. Charming old homes with elaborate iron grillwork crowd tiny lanes. Up ahead is the **Marble Palace.**

The inspiration of a former Bengali raja, who constructed the palace in 1840, it is set behind a spacious lawn littered with sculptures of Christopher Columbus, the Buddha, Jesus Christ, the Virgin Mary, Hindu gods, and various animals. A large tank near a small granite bungalow where the descendents of the raja still live is home to ducks, peacocks, and ostriches.

The palace interior is equally lavish. A peacock struts in the throne room. Enormous paintings and mirrors cover walls. Gigantic chandeliers hang from ceilings. The hundreds of statues include copies of famous works and a few extraordinary originals. Lamps include gargantuan metal women entwined in trees with a lightbulb on each branch. Ravi Shankar once played music all night here. Movie producers use the palace as a setting for Hindi films. *Plan 3–5 hours for this walk. Admission free; tip your guide. The palace is open Mon.–Wed., Fri., and Sat. 10–6; closed Sun. and Thurs.*

Dining

Calcutta has fabulous food, including Bengali cuisine, with its accent on fish and prawn dishes. Dress is always casual. Reservations are advised unless noted. Thursday is both dry and meatless (no red meat). The following are the best restaurants. Prices are per person, including taxes and excluding drinks and service charges.

Amber. An upstairs restaurant with subdued lighting, this Calcutta landmark serves excellent north Indian food. It has an attached bar. *11 Waterloo St., tel. 286520. No credit cards. Open 10 AM–11 PM. Moderate ($5–$10).*

Saruchi. A popular restaurant with low-key decor, this is the best place for Bengali fish and prawns. *89 Elliot Rd., tel. 293292. No credit cards. Open 11–10. Moderate ($5–$10).*

Sky Room. Extremely pretty, with upholstered chairs, crisp table linen, a ceiling with twinkling stars, and handsome murals, the Sky Room serves reliably good Continental, Indian, and Bengali dishes. Try lobster thermidor, smoked *hilsa* (river fish), or tandoori prawns. *57 Park St., tel. 294362. No credit cards. Open 10:30–midnight; closed Tues. Moderate ($5–$10).*

Aminia. This restaurant has a gigantic front room with overhead fans and taped Hindi music echoing off the walls; family rooms in the back have curtained booths. Delicious tandoori chicken, biryani dishes, kebabs, and great snacks are the draws. *6A S. N. Banerjee Rd., no phone. Reservations not necessary. No credit cards. Open 10–10. Inexpensive (under $5).*

Lodging

Except for the Hotel Airport Ashok, all accommodations are centrally located and about 15 kilometers (9 miles) from the airport. These are the best lodgings. Prices are for a standard double room, including taxes and excluding service charges.

Oberoi Grand. Super posh and newly refurbished, this spiffy Victorian landmark has spacious modern rooms; the best ones overlook the courtyard and pool. *15 J. L. Nehru Rd., tel. 292323. 250 rooms with bath. Facilities: room service, restaurants, bar, TV, air-conditioning, pool, health club, shops, foreign-exchange and travel counter. AE, DC, MC, V. Very Expensive (over $100).*

Hotel Airport Ashok. This fancy, modern hotel with pleasant rooms is for the traveler with just an overnight stop. *Calcutta Airport, tel. 575111. Facilities: room service, restaurants, bar, TV, air-conditioning, pool, shopping arcade, foreign-exchange and travel counter. AE, DC, MC, V. Expensive ($60–$100).*

New Kenilworth. Popular with repeat visitors to Calcutta, this hotel has two attractive wings—one new and the other refurbished—surrounded by gardens. The rooms are comfortable and spacious. *1 and 2 Little Russell St., tel. 448394. Facilities: room service, restaurants, TV, air-conditioning, travel counter, bookshop. AE, DC, MC, V. Expensive ($60–$100).*

Fairlawn Hotel. If you want old-fashioned charm, stay here. Another Calcutta landmark, it was built in 1801 on a side street. The rooms are furnished with chintz and memorabilia. In the hot months, ask for air-conditioning. Meals are included. *13/A Sudder St., tel. 244460. 20 rooms with bath. Facilities: restaurant, TV. AE, MC, V. Moderate ($25–$60).*

Great Eastern. Once Kipling's favorite hotel, it is now run by the government. Though the management is wonderful, the hotel has lost its grandeur. The rooms are spacious and clean; the location is ideal for a fast look at Calcutta. *1 Old Court House St., tel. 282331. 200 rooms with bath. Facilities: room service,* *restaurants, bar, TV, air-conditioning, foreign-exchange and travel counter. AE, DC, MC, V. Moderate ($25–$60).*

Assam

In Assam, in the southern foothills of the eastern Himalayas, a bright sun pours down onto rice paddies, coconut and banana groves, and canals, creating a landscape you'd think was in India's sultry south. Assamese village life is tranquil; rural customs prevail. You find little urbanization except in Guwahati, the biggest city and former capital that's suddenly become a concrete boomtown.

Everywhere else, ducks, cows, water buffalo, chickens, and goats wander along the road or in fields. Bicycles and animal-drawn carts outnumber cars. Men wear bright lungis or crisp dhotis—just as they do in India's south. But draped around the shoulder or turbanlike around the head is a red-and-white hand-loomed cotton *gamoucha* (scarf)—the traditional Assamese gift. Women, unless they belong to a tribe, wear the Assamese two-piece sari—the *mekhela* (skirt) with a *chadar* (upper body portion) wrapped over a short-sleeve blouse.

Villages in Assam are a photographer's dream. After a devastating earthquake in 1897, the British brought in the Japanese to construct the dwellings you see today, which are designed to withstand tremors. Each home is a cluster of one-room dwellings made of thatch and bamboo that have been plastered with a mixture of lime, sand, and dung. The exterior is often washed a sky-blue or aqua and has dark laquered trim. Each cluster of homes, often belonging to an extended family, sits behind a bamboo or jute fence and is surrounded by a rice paddy.

Assam is home to numerous tribes, such as the Karbi, Mishing, and Boro; all along the road you see tribal peoples—faces tatooed, wearing distinctive garments that set them apart from the Hindu or Moslem Assamese. The most ethnically pure traditional villages are in secluded areas. The people here are welcoming; foreigners are as intriguing to them as they are to us.

Assam has abundant wildlife, protected in the grasslands and tropical forests of 12 preserves, including two of India's finest—Manas and Kaziranga. You don't have to be on a safari to come across a wild beast. Elephants and rhinos often wander beyond the parks.

Travel Restrictions

To visit Assam, you must have a Restricted Area Permit, which takes up to 12 weeks to process. (*See* Before You Go to North India, above, and follow the instructions carefully.) When you fill out the permit, list as destinations Guwahati and the two game parks, Manas and Kaziranga. The trip length is currently limited to a week; this is also under review. Ask the Government of India Tourist Office for the latest information.

Travelers can also visit Assam as part of a tour group. (*See* Before You Go to North India, above, for a list of indigenous tour operators, including **Travel Corporation,** which offer trips in Assam.) Another especially good outfit is **Sheba Travels** (*See* below).

Addresses and Numbers

Tourist Information Contact the **Assam Directorate of Tourism** (Station Rd., Guwahati, tel. 27102), open Monday–Saturday 10–5. It has a counter at the airport and the railroad station, plus branch offices in important destinations.

Emergencies For all emergencies, turn to your hotel or the tourist department. The nearest consulates are in Calcutta. **American** (5/1 Ho Chi Minh Sarani, tel. 443611) and **British** (1 Ho Chi Minh Sarani, tel. 445171).

Travel Agencies **Sheba Travels** (G. N. Bordoloi Rd., Ambari, Guwahati, Assam, tel. 23280) is open Monday–Saturday 10–6.

Arriving and Departing

By Plane
Airport and Airline To Guwahati, **Indian Airlines** makes four daily one-hour flights from Calcutta, two daily three-hour flights from Delhi, and one daily 45-minute flight from Bagdogra, and the **Meghalaya Tourist Development Corporation helicopter** flies daily except Sunday from Shillong in Meghalaya (one hour). For fares and schedules, call, in Delhi (tel. 3312587), in Calcutta (tel. 260730), in Bagdogra (tel. 20692), in Shillong (tel. 23206), or in Guwahati (tel. 23128). Book your seat before you depart from home and reconfirm all tickets 72 hours before flight time.

Between Airport and City Assam's national airport is 21 kilometers (13 miles) from Guwahati. If you come from Calcutta in the airbus (currently the afternoon flight), a bus meets the plane and goes to Guwahati for Rs. 10. A taxi costs about Rs. 60. On arrival and departure, all foreigners must show their permit to airport police.

By Hired Car with Driver Unless you're traveling between Guwahati and Shillong in Meghalaya, 103 kilometers (64 miles) away, arrive by plane. To hire a car with driver, use a recommended travel agency in Shillong (*see* Meghalaya, below). The three-hour trip costs about Rs. 400.

By Train Trains are impractical and take a long time.

Getting Around

By Hired Car with Driver Because of the current trip-length restrictions, you should hire a car with driver. You'll make better time and can design your own trips, such as to remote tribal villages. Through a **private agency**, the cost is about Rs. 400 per day (unlimited kilometers) plus a halt charge of Rs. 100 per night. If you hire a car with driver through the **Assam Directorate of Tourism,** the cost is about Rs. 3.75 per kilometer and Rs. 50 per night halt (*see* Guwahati, below, for details).

Guided Tours

The **Directorate of Tourism** (Station Rd., tel. 27102) offers three overnight tours by minibus from Guwahati: Kaziranga, Manas, and Sibsagar. It also has a day trip to Shillong. **Blue Hills Travels** (tel. 31427) and **Assam Valley Tours and Travels** (tel. 26133) offer these trips at higher prices.

Outdoor Adventures

Highly recommended adventures are indicated by a star ★ .

Fishing: *Manas Tiger Reserve:* There's good fishing here, especially in February and March. Bring your own rod and reel.

★ **Wildlife Sanctuaries:** *Manas Tiger Reserve:* Open October to May, its best viewing time is from January to April.

Kaziranga National Sanctuary: Open mid-October to mid-April, its best viewing time is November to March.

---

❶ Guwahati

Numbers in the margin correspond with points of interest on the Northeast India map.

In ancient times, **Guwahati** was called Light of the East and City of Astrology. Today, it's a modern city wrestling with traffic problems and a construction boom.

Getting Around
By Taxi or Hired Car
For short excursions, hire one of the nonmetered taxis (about Rs. 3 per kilometer) or arrange for a car with driver (*see* agencies, below.

By Rickshaw
For trips in the city, take an auto rickshaw (about Rs. 2 per kilometer) or use a bicycle rickshaw (Rs. 1.50 per kilometer).

Addresses and Numbers
Visit the **Assam Tourist Department** (Station Rd., tel. 27102), open Monday–Saturday 10–5, for information or travel and tour arrangements.

Tourist Information Travel Agencies
Two good travel agencies are **Blue Hills Travels** (at Ashok Hotel or at Blue Hills Complex, Brahmachari Rd., Paltan Bazaar, tel. 31427) and **Assam Valley Tours and Travels** (G. S. Rd., Paltan Bazaar, tel. 26133). Both are open daily 7–7.

Bookstores
Two good English-language bookstores (on the main street of Pan Bazaar) are open Monday–Saturday 10–7.

Banks
The **State Bank of India** (M. G. Rd.) and **Grindlays Bank** (Fancy Bazaar) are open weekdays 10–2, Saturday 10–noon.

Post Office
The **General Post Office** and **Telegraph Office** are open Monday–Saturday 10–4:30.

Guided Tours
The **Assam Directorate of Tourism** runs a Sunday river cruise on the Brahmaputra. Contact the Tourist Information Officer (tel. 24475).

Exploring
Assam's most important shrine is **Kamakhya Temple,** dedicated to the goddess Sati (also known as Kali or Shakti). When the father of Shiva's consort, Sati, insulted Shiva, Sati was so humiliated she threw herself on a funeral pyre. Shiva took her body and circled the world causing so much destruction that Vishnu, the Hindu god of preservation, trailed after him and slowly hacked Sati's body into 51 pieces, which fell over the Indian subcontinent. Her yoni (vagina), considered the source of all creation, fell on Nilachal Hill, which is said to represent Shiva's lingam. Kamakhya Temple commemorates their union. In time, Sati reappeared in a new manifestation, Parvati, who became Shiva's new consort.

The temple complex you see today—an assortment of beehive-shape shrines commemorating the various manifestations of the Mother Goddess—represents renovations and remaining bits of temples first constructed in the 13th century by the Ahom dynasty, which ruled northeast India from the 12th to the 18th century.

Long ago, kings sacrificed humans at this most sacred tantric temple. When this practice was banned, Durga and Kali had to make do with a goat—representing lust—or buffalo—bestial passion. Tantrics believe that the act of sacrifice destroys these base instincts and gives the sacrificed animal an opportunity for rebirth at a higher station.

Although non-Hindus may not enter the main shrine with its revered yoni, they can witness the purifications and sacrifices performed in the extensive complex. A door to the left of an old pavilion leads into the temple; a set of stairs descend to the sacred cave. The hallowed stone yoni, which is always dressed (covered with a cloth), is under a gold canopy inside the cave. Not even the special class of people allowed to clean the temple and purify the yoni set their eyes on the stone, but perform their tasks blindfolded.

Once you've circled the main complex, drive to the **temple of Bhubaneswari Devi** on a nearby foothill. Here the goddess Bhubaneswari, a manifestation of the Mother Goddess, is represented by a red slab of rock located under a canopy in a sunken dark chamber. Hindus say that the rock represents the abdomen of the goddess and that to protect her modesty, it's purposely difficult to see. *Plan 5 to 6 hours. Kamakhya is 10 km (6 mi) west of Guwahati. Temples open sunrise–sunset.*

Time Out   **The Orbit,** a tiny circular restaurant, revolves on the top of a hotel in a busy market in central Guwahati and serves tasty multicuisine snacks and good ice cream. *Hotel Kuber International, Hem Barua Rd. in Fancy Bazaar. Open 7 AM–11 PM.*

Shopping   Assam has beautiful hand-woven cottons and rare silks: *endi* (raw silk), *pat* (soft hand-dyed silk), and *muga* (naturally golden heavy silk). You can also buy good tea and honey and products of bamboo, cane, jute, and brass. The following shops are open Monday–Saturday and do not accept credit cards.

Visit the **Government of Assam Emporium** (G. N. B. Rd.), open April to September, 10–7; October–March, 10–6, for excellent handicrafts and hand looms at reasonable fixed prices. **Jagaran Artfed Handloom House** (G. N. B. Rd.), open 10–7, also government-run, offers a similar selection. **Purbashree Northeastern Handicrafts and Handlooms Development Corporation** (G. N. B. Rd.), open April to September, 10–2 and 3–7; October–March, 10–6, has handicrafts and hand looms from the northeastern states.

For Assamese tea, try **Kamrupa** (G. S. Rd., Paltan Bazaar) or **Kalpataru** (H. B. Rd., Pan Bazaar), both open 10–7.

Traditional heavy hand-tooled brass products are at the **Assam Cooperative Bell Metal Manufacturing Society** (S.R.C.B. Rd., Fancy Bazaar), open 8–7. This is one of the few shops that sell bell metal teacups, curry bowls, platters, and tumblers.

Dining   Try the Assamese thali—assorted small portions of various moderately spicy local dishes, such as *pabha* (river fish simmered in mustard paste), *moricha* (a spinachlike green cooked in mustard oil), *roho* (fish in lemon or tomato sauce), *dahi* (lentils), and *omita* (fried papaya simmered with baking soda). Dress is casual. Reservations are not necessary unless noted. Highly recommended restaurants are indicated by a star ★. Prices are per person, including taxes and excluding drinks and service charges.

Parag. An enormous restaurant on an upper floor of a hotel, it offers views of Guwahati and a decor that's a blend of coffee shop and Indian ornate. The food is equally eclectic and is excellent. *Hotel Kuber International, Hem Barua Rd., Fancy Bazar, tel. 32601. AE, DC, MC, V. Open 11–3 and 7–11. Moderate ($5–$10).*

Ushaban. This cozy restaurant is modern Assamese, with white ceilings and lots of laquered lattice. The chef cooks excellent multicuisine dishes. *Hotel Brahmaputra Ashok, M. G. Rd., tel. 32632. Reservations advised. AE, DC, MC, V. Open 12:30–2:30 and 7:30–10. Moderate ($5–$10).*

★ **Paradise.** Guwahati's most popular eatery, with upscale chain-restaurant decor, serves the best Assamese cuisine in town. Try the delicious thali. *G.N.B. Rd., no phone. No credit cards. Open 10–3:30 and 6:30–10. Serves beer until 7:30. Inexpensive (under $5).*

Lodging   Highly recommended lodgings are indicated by a star ★. Prices are for a standard double room, including taxes and excluding service charges. All lodgings are moderate ($25–60).

★ **Hotel Belle Vue.** Guwahati's oldest hotel is away from the bustle on a hill overlooking the Brahmaputra. The interior is whimsical and lovely—an elevator done up with a blue sky and fluffy clouds. Carpeted rooms are spacious. Corner rooms offer the best river views. *M. G. Rd., Reservations: Box 75, Guwahati, Assam, tel. 28291. 45 rooms with bath. Facilities: restaurant, bar, room service, air-conditioning, TV, house doctor, car rental, foreign-exchange counter. AE, DC, MC, V.*

★ **Hotel Brahmaputra Ashok.** Guwahati's stylish new hotel is on the Brahmaputra River near the center of town. The rooms are centrally air-conditioned and spacious, with contemporary Assamese decor. The best rooms have a river view. *M. G. Rd., Guwahati, Assam, tel. 32632. 50 rooms with bath. Facilities: restaurant, bar, coffee shop, room service, TV, foreign-exchange and travel counter, house doctor. AE, DC, MC, V.*

Hotel Chilarai Regency. A reasonably modern hotel near Pan Bazar, its rooms are carpeted and clean with a subdued decor. In the hot months, request an air-conditioned room. *H. P. Brahmachari Rd., Guwahati, Assam, tel. 26877. 44 rooms with bath. Facilities: restaurant, room service, house doctor, TV, car-rental and travel counter. No credit cards.*

Nightlife   With rare exceptions, you can only drink beer and only in hotel bars, which are open 11–11. Dry days are Thursdays and the first and last days of the month.

Excursion from Guwahati to Swalkuchi and Hajo

Once you cross the Brahmaputra, the pace of life slows down. Men tend rice paddies, wending their way among the shallow pools. Children fish with bamboo poles or nets from the banks and from long narrow dugouts. Banana-tree rafts ply the river banks. Bridges cross canals and connect to paths on elevated bunds that, in turn, lead to isolated dwellings or small villages.

Farmers heading to the market along the road carry *boras* (poles) that have dangling from either end fresh coconut or bamboo baskets filled with mustard greens or eggplants. Jute is hung to dry over bamboo fences.

About 25 kilometers (15 miles) from Guwahati, you enter the tiny village of **Bonkhar,** home of the Boros, a patriarchal tribal group with Mongolian features. The Boros migrated here from Tibet. Just beyond Bonkhar, you turn left and head to **Swalkuchi,** a village of silk weavers where hand looms click rhythmically on every street. Ask to visit the home of Bogaram Baishya; he'll show you his cottage industry and take you to others. Muga or pat is 30% cheaper here than in retail shops. Mr. Baishya can also make on order and ship.

About 6 kilometers (4 miles) north of Swalkuchi, you come to **Hajo,** a village where you can shop for bell-metal work. Follow the sound of tapping, and you'll come to a shed where an artisan sits over goatskin bellows, heating a piece of brass that is then shaped, hand-tooled, and polished to create an urn, plate, bowl, or tumbler.

A festive spirit takes hold of people on the dirt track at one end of Hajo that leads to the **Hayagriba Madhab Temple.** Buddhists from Sikkim and Bhutan flock here in the belief that the Lord Buddha once visited this site and that the sacred idol is created in his image. Hindus come to honor Vishnu (in his ninth incarnation, he's the Buddha).

Plan 5 hours for this 68-km (42-mi) tour. Go by hired car with driver.

---

❷ Manas Tiger Reserve

Extending into southern Bhutan, the **Manas Tiger Reserve** stretches over 2,837 square kilometers (1,095 square miles) of forests and tall elephant grass that abut the Lower Himalayan foothills. This is one of India's most appealing sanctuaries and an angler's paradise, 176 kilometers (109 miles) northeast of Guwahati.

Declared a sanctuary in 1928, Manas is home to tigers and 20 other endangered species, including the golden cat, sloth bear, Indian elephant, one-horned rhinoceros, water buffalo, golden langur (a monkey that lives only in Manas), swamp deer, and pygmy hog. You also have a good chance of spotting the panther, leopard, Himalayan black bear, wild boar, and a host of slithering reptiles—flying snake, python, cobra, cat snake viper—plus 300 species of bird—stork, pelican, egret, kingfish, and parakeet.

The road to Manas passes through tropical lowlands and Assamese villages where nearly everyone travels on foot, by bicycle, or in a wood cart drawn by a bullock, horse, water buffalo, or even by men. Rice paddies and plots of jute are kept under water by wide canals where villagers fish. The journey presents an opportunity to see a local industry: the creation of *morapat* (jute). After the long stalks, which grow in clusters in the water, are harvested, they're laid out on the water to soften for about 15 days. Then the outer skin is stripped by hand and hung to dry. It becomes rope. The remaining stalk is dried for fencing.

In the town of Barpeta Road, 135 kilometers (84 miles) from Guwahati, stop and buy food to eat in the park because there are no restaurants there. If you need to change money, stop at the **State Bank of India,** open weekdays 10–2, Saturday 10–noon.

From Barpeta Road, you pass the tiny hamlet of Basbari and Assamese tea gardens. Though Darjeeling's tea is more famous, Assam has the largest number of tea plantations in India and over 1 million people working in the industry.

When you see the outline of the Lower Himalayas, you're near the entrance to Manas. Foreigners must show their permits at the **Foreigner's Check Gate.** You must reach the park before sunset, when it closes.

Staying in Manas

Getting Around The best way to get around the park is on the back of an elephant. The park has 90-minute morning and afternoon safaris. You can also rent a boat to explore the river. For all arrangements, contact the Field Office (*see* below). Under no circumstances roam the park alone. Don't leave your bungalow after dark, except to race back and forth to the bathroom.

Addresses and Numbers Visit the local Forest Officer in the **Field Office** (near the Interior Bungalow) to pay park fees and make arrangements for excursions or fishing.

Dining You'll rely on food you have brought with you.

Lodging *Reservations: Reservation Authority, Deputy Field Director, Project Tiger, Barpeta Rd., Assam, tel. 153 or 19. Reserve your room at least 2 months in advance. No credit cards.* The caretaker at each lodge will make your meals for a small fee. Highly recommended lodgings are indicated by a star ★ . Prices are for a standard double room, including taxes and excluding service charges. All lodgings are inexpensive (under $25). All bathrooms have Western-style toilets and showers with hot water by the bucket.

★ **The Upper Bungalow.** This lodge, on a hill overlooking the river, is typically Assamese and offers the best location. The interior rooms are spacious, with simple furniture and an overhead fan. The upper rooms open onto a veranda with great views. *7 rooms with bath.*

Lower Bungalow. From the Lower Bungalow, also an Assamese design, you can hear the river. The rooms are spacious and comfortable, but have little furniture and no overhead fan. There's a private front porch. *2 rooms with bath.*

Cottages. They're near the lower bungalow. The rooms are small and sparse, but the linen is clean. Decent bathrooms are nearby. *3 cottages with nearby bath.*

❸ Kaziranga National Park

While Manas specializes in the tiger, **Kaziranga** protects India's one-horned rhinoceros. Kaziranga was established in 1977 and covers 430 square kilometers (166 square miles) of forests and grasslands in an area of central Assam bordered on the north by the Brahmaputra River. It's 220 kilometers (136 miles) east of Guwahati. Numerous animals live here: elephants, swamp deer, bison, wild buffalo, sloth bears, tigers, leopards, jungle cats, langurs. So do reptiles. Birds include the stork, pelican, ibis, and eagle. See these creatures from the back of an elephant, from a jeep, or while waiting quietly in a watchtower.

Getting Around The best way to get around Kaziranga is on the back of an elephant. The park offers early morning 90-minute rides. You can also travel 45 kilometers (28 miles) into the park in a jeep at 8 AM and 2:30 PM. Make all arrangements at the Mihimukh Forest Range Office (*see* below). Don't roam through the forest or tall grass alone. Don't wear bright clothes.

Addresses and Numbers Stop at the **Mihimukh Forest Range Office** to pay fees and to make arrangements for jeep and elephant rides or excursions to a Karbi tribal village or a tea plantation.

Dining There are three lodges in Kaziranga at the Mihimukh entrance. They all serve the same decent inexpensive food and are noted below.

Lodging Reservations: *Deputy Director of Tourism, Kaziranga National Park, Post Office Kaziranga Sanctuary, District Jorhat, Assam, tel. 23 or 29. No credit cards. Write at least 2 months in advance.* Highly recommended lodgings are indicated by a star ★ . Prices are for a standard double room, including taxes and excluding service charges.

Kaziranga Forest Lodge. The rooms in this nondescript new hotel are clean, adequately furnished, and comfortable and have balconies. There's a mid-April to mid-October discount. *24 rooms with bath (shower). Facilities: bar, shop, fans, multicuisine restaurant (open 7–10, noon–2, 7–9). Discount when park is closed. Moderate ($25–$60).*

★ **Tourist Lodge I.** This attractive Assamese-style bungalow has cozy, simply furnished rooms with mosquito netting. Upstairs rooms open onto a veranda. *5 rooms with bath. Facilities: fans, dining room serving Indian and Continental food (open 7:30–10, 12:30–2, 8:30–10). Inexpensive (under $25).*

★ **Tourist Lodge II.** The rooms in this Assamese bungalow with a front veranda are simply furnished. The beds are clean with mosquito netting. There's also a dormitory with clean bed linen supplied. *8 rooms with Western- or Indian-style bath (shower); dormitory with shared Indian-style bath. Facilities: fans. Inexpensive. (under $10).*

Excursion from Kaziranga to a Karbi Village

Near Kaziranga and throughout the Nowgaon District, small villages are populated by the Karbi, tribal peoples of Mongolian descent. When you arrange your visit through the tourist office at the park, they'll suggest a village accustomed to visitors. Instead, pay extra for the additional mileage to see a more distant village where the Karbi lifestyle remains pure.

Older Karbi women are easy to recognize: a thin dark line is tatooed from the forehead to the bridge of the nose or down to the lips—the traditional mark received at puberty. Though the younger women no longer adhere to this custom, every female at the time of death is tatooed prior to cremation. The older women also have holes in their ears nearly the size of the lobe. Ordinarily they wear bone plugs, but on festive occasions they adorn themselves with heavy silver earplugs.

The Karbi village is constructed in compounds, each belonging to an extended family presided over by the eldest male. Single-story thatched homes with bamboo walls plastered with cow dung and mud surround each courtyard. In flood-prone areas, homes are elevated on pillars. The Karbi are farmers of rice, mustard, and vegetables. Numerous chickens, goats, and pigs wander around the courtyards. Cows are kept in separate sheds.

Hindus who worship no idols, the Karbi celebrate their Sarak festival whenever they feel the need to receive a blessing or protection. In the courtyard, they construct a three-foot mud shrine, then sacrifice three or four pigs and chickens. They conclude with dancing, singing, and much drinking of beer.

Under *all* circumstances, ask before you take photographs. The women are very proud and will want to dress in their best—exchanging their bone earplugs for silver.

Meghalaya

Introduction

Except for Shillong, the capital, and Cherrapunjee, the wettest place on Earth, few foreigners have seen much of Meghalaya, between Assam and Bangladesh and home to isolated hill tribes. Since independence, this state has been off-limits to foreigners. At press time, however, the tight restrictions were under review.

Choosing the Bible as their weapon, the British, during the Raj divvied up this area among missionaries of various Christian faiths; then the crusades to subdue the headhunting tribals began. Today, the Western missionaries are gone, booted out by India at independence, but native itinerant preachers still spread the Word among non-Christians. Meghalaya—India's Bible Belt—is at a precarious crossroads, with traditional culture facing extinction. In no other Indian state currently open to foreigners do travelers cross such cultural extremes. There's the capital, Shillong, very Western, with Western music, Western clothes, and Western problems like drugs and divorce. Travel one day to the east and you're in remote hill country, where many of the people have never seen foreigners, where borangs jut above the fields, where women are apt to be bare-breasted. The only statewide common symbol is the Christian cross. The British chose a powerful weapon.

Meghalaya has three racially distinct hill tribes, all of them matrilineal societies: the Khasis, who live primarily in the central Khasi Hills and trace their ancestry back to the Khmer of Cambodia; the Jaintias of Indo-Chinese descent, who live in the western Jaintia Hills; and the Garos, who migrated from Tibet to the Garo Hills. All three show greater physical affinity with their original ancestors than with the rest of India.

Throughout the state, educated tribal women hold important positions in the government and business community. Bara Bazar, the popular tribal market in Shillong, is run by women. Though many marriages are still arranged, dowries don't exist, and the husband, not the wife, moves in with the spouse's family—which sets Meghalaya apart from Hindu and Moslem India.

Travel Restrictions

Currently, individual travelers are not permitted into Meghalaya. You must arrive in a group of four or more with a government-approved agency, and your trip is limited to seven days. (*See* Tour Groups, below, and in Before You Go to North India, above, for a list of appropriate tour operators.) If your plans are flexible or geared to a major festival, chances are you'll get in. Your tour operator can help you procure the obligatory Restricted Area Permit.

You must plan your trip months in advance. Contact the Government of India Tourist Office for the status on individual travel. If the ban has been removed, follow the instructions in Before You Go to North India, above, for obtaining the Restricted Area Permit. Allow 12 weeks for clearance and specify these destinations: Shillong, Tura in the Garo Hills, Jowai in the Jaintia Hills, and Nongstoin in the West Khasi Hills.

Addresses and Numbers

Tourist Information Contact the **Tourist Information Center** (Police Bazar, Shillong, Meghalaya, tel. 6220), the **Meghalaya Tourism Development Corporation** (Shillong Tourist Hotel, Polo Rd., Shillong, Meghalaya, tel. 22129), or the **Government of India Tourist Office** (G. S. Rd., Police Bazar, Shillong, Meghalaya, tel. 25632). Each is open Monday–Saturday 10–5. The **Meghalaya Tourist Department** also has an office in Tura in Garo Hills.

Emergencies For all emergencies, turn to your hotel or the tourist department. The nearest consulates are in Calcutta: **American** (5/1 Ho Chi Minh Sarani, tel. 443611) and **British** (1 Ho Chi Minh Sarani, tel. 445171). There is no Canadian consulate.

Travel Agencies Contact **Sheba Travels** (Crowborough Bldg., Police Bazar, Shillong, Meghalaya, tel. 23015 or 26222) or **A. S. Sen** (Shillong Club, Shillong, Meghalaya, tel. 23354 or 25454). They are open Monday–Saturday 10–6.

Arriving and Departing

By Plane On arrival and departure in Guwahati and Shillong, foreigners must show their permit to the police.

Airport and Airline **Vayudoot** makes one daily 90-minute flight into Shillong from Calcutta's Dum Dum Airport. **Indian Airlines** makes four daily one-hour flights to Guwahati from Calcutta, two daily two-hour flights from Delhi's National Airport, and one 45-minute daily flight from Bagdogra Airport, and the Meghalaya Tourism Development Corporation helicopter flies from Guwahati to Shillong daily except Sunday (one hour). Call, in Delhi (tel. 3312587), Calcutta (tel. 260730), Bagdogra (tel. 20692), Shillong (tel. 23206), Guwahati (tel. 23128).

Between Airport and City Shillong's airport is 127 kilometers (79 miles) from the city. A taxi (about Rs. 400) takes about three hours. You can also take a **Meghalaya Road Transport Corporation (MTRC)** bus, a four-hour trip every hour from the airport (Rs. 45).

By Hired Car
with Driver
Flying is the only realistic approach to Meghalaya unless you're coming from Assam. In Assam, hire a car with driver from a travel agency in Guwahati (*see* Assam, above).

Highlights for First-time Visitors

A trip to Meghalaya must include a trip to the Garo Hills, one of the most interesting destinations in eastern India. Accommodations are rustic, but the scenery is fabulous and the inhabitants fascinating. Clomping along the roads are domesticated elephants ridden by handsome Garo tribesmen. Tangled forests of bamboo stretch for miles, interrupted by rice fields and banana groves. The mountains are low, with narrow valleys threaded by streams. If you time your trip to coincide with the exuberant Wangala festival in November or December, you'll have an exciting vacation.

Getting Around

By Hired Car
with Driver
Given travel-time restrictions in Meghalaya, visitors should hire a car with driver. You'll travel at your own pace and design stops according to your interests. If you hire a car with driver through a private agency, the cost is determined by the destination. From Shillong due south, the round-trip to Jowai in the Jaintia Hills or due south to Cherrapunjee is Rs. 400; to Nongstoin in the West Khasi Hills, Rs. 600; to Tura in the Garo Hills, Rs. 1,500. For overnights, add Rs. 100 per halt. Hire a car from a travel agency listed in the Shillong section, below.

By Helicopter
The **Meghalaya Tourism Development Corporation (MTDC)** (Shillong Tourist Hotel, Polo Rd., tel. 22129) has a helicopter service from Shillong to Tura (Rs. 350), which currently makes the trip three times a week.

Guided Tours

MTDC sponsors daily tours by non-air-conditioned deluxe bus: local sightseeing around Shillong as well as to Cherrapunjee, the Jaintia Hills, Thadlaskein Lake, and the town of Jowai. Tours depart from the Shillong Tourist Hotel and Bus Station on Jail Road. For reservations, contact MTDC (*see* above). The private travel agencies (*see* Shillong, below) also run similar tours by taxi.

Outdoor Adventures

Since Meghalaya is just opening to foreigners, numerous adventures were under development at press time. Few details are available. Highly recommended adventures are indicated by a star ★.

★ **Caving:** Meghalaya has a vast network of limestone caves: Syndia in the Jaintia Hills, Siju in the Garo Hills, and Mawsmai near Cherrapunjee. Contact the Tourist Information Center for details.

★ **Fishing:** At present, no license is required, and you must bring your own rod and reel. The best fishing is from February to November, with numerous good locations, especially in and near William Nagar Forest Reserve and Balpakram National Park in the Garo Hills.

Golfing: Shillong has one of India's prettiest golf courses. In 1990 you'll be able to rent clubs.

Rafting: Runs are currently under study. Contact the Tourist Information Center for latest information.

Trekking: As with rafting, routes haven't been finalized.

Wildlife Sanctuaries: *Balpakram National Park and Biosphere:* This new park in Garo Hills is on a vast plateau on the Bangladesh border (*see* Excursions from Shillong to the Garo Hills, below). Park fees aren't established yet. The best time to visit is from November to February.

❹ Shillong

Set on a series of rolling hills, **Shillong** is unlike any other former British hill station. You won't find the usual Pedestrian Mall on an upper ridge; you won't see billboards promoting the ideal honeymoon retreat. You will see evidence of Christianity. More pictures of Jesus than Shiva are placed in homes and shops. Church spires are everywhere.

Getting Around Shillong is a walker's town. Taxis (Rs. 5 per kilometer) are available but often get stuck in traffic jams.

Addresses and Numbers
Tourist Information Visit the **Tourist Information Center** (Police Bazaar, tel. 6220), **MTDC** (Shillong Tourist Hotel, Polo Rd., tel. 22129), **Government of India Tourist Office** (G. S. Rd., Police Bazaar, tel. 25632). All are open Monday–Saturday 10–5.

Travel Agents Contact **Sheba Travels** (Crowborough Bldg., Police Bazaar, tel. 23015 or 26222) or **A. S. Sen** (Shillong Club, tel. 23354 or 25454). They are open Monday–Saturday 10–6.

Bookstores Visit **Modern Book Depot** (Police Bazaar), which is open Monday–Saturday 9:30–12:30 and 3–6:30 and sells English-language publications.

Banks **State Bank of India** (G. S. Rd.) is open weekdays 10–2, Saturday 10–noon.

Post Office The **Post Office** (G. B. Rd., Police Bazaar) is open Monday–Saturday 10–4:30.

Exploring Walk through the **Bara Bazar,** a produce market run by tribal women. The market is open from sunrise to sunset. Then get away from the bustle and explore reminders of the Raj. Walk through the quiet, well-kept grounds of the **Botanical Garden.** Then stroll around or go boating on the adjacent **Wards Lake.** *Garden and boating facilities open daily 9–5. Plan 3 hours for this tour.*

Outdoor Adventures Except Sunday, you can watch **archery contests** in the polo ground; it's a popular sport of the Khasi tribe. Play **golf** at the Shillong Golf Club (tel. 3071); equipment is available at nominal cost. **Fish** at Umiam Lake, 16 kilometers (10 miles) north of Shillong; bring your own equipment—no license is necessary. **Hike** the three-hour round-trip up to Shillong Peak, 1,960 meters (6,428 feet), for a good view of Shillong and, right after the monsoon, of the distant Himalayas. **Picnic** at Beadon and Biship falls, 5 kilometers (3 miles) north of Shillong, or at Elephant Falls, 12 kilometers (7 miles) to the south.

Dining Dress is casual. Reservations are not necessary unless noted. Highly recommended restaurants are indicated by a star ★.

Prices are per person, including taxes and excluding drinks and service charges.

★ **Pinecone Restaurant.** This restaurant, with a handsome rustic ambience, serves the best food in Shillong: Chinese, Indian, Continental. *Hotel Pinewood Ashok, tel. 23116. AE, DC, MC, V. Open 1–2:30 and 8–10. Moderate ($5–$10).*

Orchid Restaurant. Overlooking a bazaar, this informal restaurant pipes in hit tunes from the West and serves decent multicuisine food. *Shillong Tourist Hotel, no phone. No credit cards. Open 6:30 AM–9:30 PM. Inexpensive (under $5).*

Jadoh Stall. Try Khasi food at the simple Jadoh Stall: *jadoh* (Khasi rice), *turembah* (fermented soy), or chicken dishes. *Police Bazar, no phone. No credit cards. Open 8 AM–9 PM. Inexpensive (under $5).*

Lodging Highly recommended lodgings are indicated by a star ★. Prices are for a standard double room, including taxes and excluding service charges.

★ **Hotel Pinewood Ashok.** On a hill above the center of Shillong, this is a charming 100-year-old bamboo-and-wood bungalow with cottages. The rooms are carpeted and comfortable, with fireplaces. The best ones (deluxe doubles) open onto a veranda. Cottages, divided into suites, are less well appointed, yet nicely located on the extensive grounds. *Shillong, Meghalaya, tel. 23116. 70 rooms with bath. Facilities: restaurant, coffee shop, bar, room service, TV, house doctor. AE, DC, MC, V. Moderate ($25–$60).*

Crowborough Hotel. This new MTDC hotel is scheduled to open in 1990. It will be modern with 117 rooms and numerous amenities. Rooms could not be inspected at press time. *Contact MTDC (see Getting Around, above) Credit card arrangements will be announced.*

Nightlife The best bar is in **Hotel Pinewood,** with a quiet ambience and rustic decor. *Open 10–2 and 6–10.*

Excursion from Shillong

Contact the MTDC or recommended travel agencies (*see* Important Addresses and Numbers, above) for information on excursions to historic monoliths in Nartiang village in the Jaintia Hills

Excursion from Shillong to Cherrapunjee

A trip south to **Cherrapunjee** will delight the cave buff or waterfall fancier. Every year almost 450 inches of rain are dumped on the Cherrapunjee area. As the road winds through gently rolling hills and cuts through plateaus just south of Shillong, look for isolated monoliths set back in fields.

To get to the **Nohkalikai Falls,** the fourth highest in the world, turn into the village of Serrarim, about 5 kilometers (3 miles) from Cherrapunjee. The falls plummet into an aquamarine pool. They're named after Ka Likai, whose husband, a jealous stepfather, cooked her child and served it to her as an unnamed delicacy. He had hidden the child's fingers in a basket of betel nut, which Ka Likai soon discovered. She leapt over the falls that now bear her name.

Just beyond Cherrapunjee, you come to the **Nohsngithiang,** or **Mawsmai Falls** (Falls Kissed by Sunset). Gaze into the Bangladesh plains to see a rainbow. In Mawsmai, you can also explore limestones caves, such as the **Lum Lawbah** under Mawlong Syiem Peak. Bring a flashlight. *Without spending much time at the caves, this excursion takes about 5 hours. Round-trip distance is 110 km (68 mi).*

Excursion from Shillong to the Garo Hills

After you leave Meghalaya's capital and enter the West Khasi Hills, stop at **Mawplang,** about 25 kilometers (15 miles) from Shillong, and visit a Khasi **sacred grove,** one of the few that still exist. Once a year, local Khasis invoke here the blessings of spirits that govern their life. Remember, the area is sacred—don't remove anything.

After Nongstoin, about 100 kilometers (62 miles) from Shillong, the road narrows. Homes are constructed of handsome bamboo and thatch, typically Garo. An occasional domesticated elephant, used for logging, lumbers by.

Once you enter the East Garo Hills, you see evidence of *jhuming* (the Garo and Khasi slash-and-burn method of clearing land for cultivation).

5 The **William Nagar Forest Reserve,** about 220 kilometers (136 miles) from Shillong, is the home of wild elephants and, with the Simsang River meandering through its borders, an angler's treat. At the reserve, you can also arrange to visit a typical Garo village—a work of art made of bamboo.

Usually the entrance to the village is through a grove of jackfruit trees, which produce an important food staple. In the compound, even chickens have their own miniature bamboo homes—coops complete with ladders for easy access. Pigs are kept in tidy bamboo pens. In the middle of the courtyard, look for the *nokpante,* a thatch-covered pavilion, crowded with men who live here from age 12 until they marry. It's also the meeting place for male elders.

The standard Garo house is set on a woven bamboo platform and takes about three months to build. Traditionally, a string of eggshells is hung over the entrance—an auspicious talisman for the animist Garos. To enter, you pass through bamboo sliding doors (no nails are used in the entire construction) and enter a ground-level storage and sitting area. A ledge leads to an elevated portion.

The front portion of the oblong house has two stoves: one against the front wall for cooking; another used in the winter for heating. Bamboo baskets and containers are stacked on shelves or hung from bamboo hooks. You may see hung on a wall a *melam* (traditional sword), hand-forged and dangerously sharp. Village elders will proudly explain that long ago, the favorite head they hunted was British. Now the melam is used as an important accessory during colorful celebrations. Behind the kitchen is the sleeping area, with bamboo mats, then a storage room and an elevated outhouse with a ready supply of lime to mask odor.

In front of many homes, long stakes, frequently notched and decorated, are dug into the ground. After the cremation of a family member, the stake *(kima)* is placed as a memorial. A cow is sacrificed and its blood rubbed on the stake. Corn is often draped across the top—food for the departed's spirit, which they say resides in Balpakram, the Garo heaven located in the southern Garo Hills near the border of Bangladesh.

To this day, most villages have a borang from which villagers watch for animals, wild or domesticated, wandering into precious crops.

These villages have seen few foreigners. Expect most older women to be bare breasted, wearing just a *sengki* (wrapped skirt). Many of the men wear a *gandomakal* (loin cloth) and wrap their long hair in a turban.

❻ From the William Nagar Forest Reserve, continue on to **Tura,** the district headquarters of the West Garo Hills, about 70 kilometers (43 miles) away. If it's Monday, stop at the village of **Chinabat,** at about 14 kilometers (9 miles), and walk through the festive weekly market. If it's Friday, stop in **Rongrem,** 50 kilometers (31 miles) from the reserve. You see Rajastanis, Punjabis, and northeastern tribal peoples selling everything from locally grown tobacco to exotic medicinal potions. If you see Western-style bread—some is coated with sugar and raisins—buy a loaf. It's delicious.

Dining Bring a packed lunch and snacks to eat along the way.

Lodging From Shillong, it's a long drive to Tura—320 kilometers (198 miles). Travelers should break their trips at the Circuit House in William Nagar Forest Reserve, about 240 kilometers (149 miles) from Shillong and then spend the next night at Tura.

Circuit House. Perched on a hill, this Assamese bungalow has simple, clean rooms. Food is available on demand. *Reservations: Deputy Commissioner, East Garo Hills, William Nagar Forest Reserve, Meghalaya. 10 rooms with bath (shower). No credit cards. Inexpensive (under $10).*
Orchid Lodge. This new bungalow has simple clean rooms with overhead fans. It is managed by MTDC. *Tura, West Garo, Meghalaya, no phone. 9 rooms witih bath (shower). Facilities: multicuisine restaurant, tourist office. No credit cards. Inexpensive (under $10).*

Excursion from Tura to Balpakram National Park and Siju Cave

The **Balpakram National Park,** straddling the Bangladesh border, features prominently in Garo mythology as the land of their dead. The park, inaugurated in 1987, is a biosphere with an array of herbs that blossom during the monsoon. It is surrounded by a vast canyon that is the stomping ground of wild elephants. The park itself sits on a high plateau of thick jungle and forest threaded with rivers feeding into small lakes. You may see wild buffalo, bears, leopards, and tigers, plus a large number of migrating birds—hornbills, peacocks, Siberian ducks.

The **Siju Cave,** on the banks of the Simsang River, is one of the biggest caves in Meghalaya. Its interior, filled with stalactites, stalagmites, and bats, awaits thorough exploration. The Simsang River provides excellent fishing from November to April.

Bring walking shoes, a packed lunch, and a flashlight. For permission to enter the park, stop at the **Field Director's office** at Baghmara, 65 kilometers (40 miles) from the park.

To spend the night, arrange to stay at the **Baghmara Circuit House,** a simple new building with clean rooms. *Reservations: Sub-Divisional Officer (Civil), Baghmara, East Garo Hills, Meghalaya. 5 rooms with bath (shower). Facilities: simple Indian meals available on demand. No credit cards. Inexpensive (under $10).*

This excursion, attempted in one day, takes 14 hours. The park is 170 km (105 mi) from Tura.

Northern West Bengal

In the northern stretch of West Bengal, the Himalayas dominate the landscape, towering above the waterfalls that thunder down ravines, the deep gorges sliced by fast-flowing rivers, and the terraced slopes of tea plantations. On clear days, Kanchenjunga, the world's third tallest mountain, draws your eyes to its snow-clad pinnacles. No one may climb this peak, the abode of Indra, the Hindu god of rain.

In this state, you find the former British hill station of Darjeeling, called the Queen of the Himalayas. Few billboards point the way and few concrete high rises mar its skyline; old hotels like the Windamere still evoke the Raj, with pampering part of the experience. The British also established a hill station at Kalimpong, a destination south of Darjeeling that was the family seat of a governor of Bhutan and is still popular with Bhutan's royal family.

Travel Restrictions

Foreign nationals who fly to Bagdogra Airport, then take the Toy Train, taxi, or bus to Darjeeling for a stay of fewer than 15 days don't require a Restricted Area Permit. They must, however, register at the Foreigner's Registration Office at the airport on arrival and at departure.

A Restricted Area Permit is necessary for a visit to Kalimpong that exceeds 48 hours. (*See* Before You Go to North India, above, and follow the instructions for getting this permit. Allow 12 weeks for clearance.) If you plan just a two-day visit to Kalimpong, you can obtain a permit in Darjeeling at the Foreigner's Registration Office.

Trekkers must register with the Foreigner's Registration Office in Darjeeling before setting off to hike more than two days. They must also report their arrival at the checkpoint at any destination. Treks may not exceed 15 days starting from arrival at Bagdogra Airport or the railway station.

Addresses and Numbers

Tourist Information Contact the **Government of India Tourist Office** ("Embassy," 2 Shakespeare Sarani, Calcutta, West Bengal) or the **Directorate of Tourism, West Bengal Tourist Department** (Government of West Bengal, 2 Brabourne Rd., 4th floor, Calcutta, West Bengal) for information before you depart. Offices are also located in major destinations.

Emergencies For all emergencies, turn to your hotel or the tourist department. The nearest consulates are in Calcutta: **American** (5/1 Ho Chi Minh Sarani, tel. 443611) and **British** (1 Ho Chi Minh Sarani, tel. 445171). There is no Canadian consulate.

Travel Agencies **Nawang Gombu Sherpa** (Himalayan Mountaineering Institute, Jawahar Parbhat, Darjeeling, West Bengal) sponsors the best treks in West Bengal and Sikkim. **Himal Venture** (H. D. Lama Rd., Darjeeling, West Bengal, tel. 2710) can put together a rafting trip in West Bengal and Sikkim. The **West Bengal Tourist Department** can arrange for excursions, trekking and rafting trips, and car and jeep rentals (*see* Tourist Information, above).

Arriving and Departing

By Plane The best way to reach northern West Bengal is by plane.

Airport and Airline **Indian Airlines** makes a one-hour flight to the **Bagdogra Airport,** 90 kilometers (56 miles) south of Darjeeling, from Calcutta's Dum Dum Airport and from Assam's Guwahati Airport. You can also make a two-hour flight into Bagdogra from Delhi's National Airport. Call, in Calcutta (tel. 572031), in Guwahati (tel. 82279), or in Delhi (tel. 3014433). Book your seat before you depart and reconfirm your ticket 72 hours before flight time. On arrival and departure in Bagdogra, foreigners must register at the **Foreigner's Registration Office.**

Between Airport and City To get from Bagdogra to Darjeeling, you can take the delightful narrow-gauge **Toy Train** from the nearby **New Jalpaiguri Railroad Station.** The train departs at 9:30 AM and arrives at 5 PM. It's a memorable day-long trip. You can also take the **West Bengal Tourist Department's Tourist Coach,** which has departures and arrivals coinciding with all flights (Rs. 30 for the four-hour drive), arrange for a hired car with driver, or take a taxi. The taxi or hired car with driver will cost about Rs. 300 and takes about three hours.

By Hired Car with Driver Travelers can drive from Gangtok to Darjeeling, a six-hour excursion through the tropical Himalayas, past cultivated rice fields, waterfalls, and streams. Hire a car for about Rs. 600 from a recommended travel agency. Obtain a Restricted Area permit.

Getting Around

By Hired Car with Driver Outside Darjeeling, travel by hired car with driver so you can be sure to meet the 48-hour visiting limit for Kalimpong and its surrounding area. Hire a car through a recommended Darjeeling travel agency. Fares are usually determined by destination.

Guided Tours

The **Darjeeling Tourist Bureau** (1 Nehru Rd., tel. 2050) offers tours by jeep or bus round Darjeeling, to Kalimpong, or to Gangtok via Kalimpong.

Outdoor Adventures

Highly recommended adventures are indicated by a star ★.

Climbing and Mountaineering: Outward Bound–style courses for teenagers combine climbing, rafting, canoeing, trekking, cross-country running, and solo camping. Courses run 15 to 32 days. Arrange months in advance through the Principal, Himalayan Mountaineering Institute (Darjeeling, West Bengal).

Fishing: Currently banned to increase the stocks.

Rafting: *Teesta and Rangit rivers:* Make a one- or two-day run September–May on the Teesta and Rangit rivers. Arrange in advance through Himal Venture (H. D. Lama Rd., Darjeeling, West Bengal, tel. 2710) or the Darjeeling Tourist Bureau (*see* address, below).

Trekking: All treks, except for the two-day Tiger Hill hike, should be arranged in advance. Contact the Darjeeling Tourist Department or any of the recommended travel agencies (*see* Important Addresses and Numbers, above). Rustic trekker's huts are available at Manaybhanjang, Sandakphu, and Phalut. Bring a sleeping bag. The cost is Rs. 10 per bed.

Trekking (up to a week): *Tiger Hill:* Take an overnight trek from Darjeeling to Tiger Hill, camp the night, wake up at sunrise, and watch Mt. Kanchenjunga show off its early morning colors; then walk back to Darjeeling via the Ghoom Monastery. Good except during the monsoon.

★ *Sandakphu:* If you have four or five days, take a 118-kilometer (73-mile) round-trip trek from Manaybhanjang, 26 kilometers (16 miles) from Darjeeling, to Sandakphu, altitude 3,636 meters (11,929 feet), returning by the same route. You walk through a lovely hamlet with a monastery; traverse rhododendron forests filled with Himalayan birds; descend into tropical valleys; then climb to Sandakphu on the border of Nepal for great views of Mt. Kanchenjunga and, if you're lucky, Mt. Everest. If you have six days to trek, continue from Sandakphu to Phalut for more forests and another good look at Kanchenjunga, Everest, and the mountainous juncture of Sikkim, West Bengal, and Bhutan. The best time for these treks is April–May and October–mid-December, with the best visibility in November.

❼ Darjeeling

In 1835 Britain's General Lloyd settled a war between the kingdoms of Nepal and Sikkim with a treaty that gave the East India Company control of **Darjeeling,** then a part of Sikkim.

The simple huts of the original inhabitants gave way to manor houses, bungalows, and cottages with gingerbread trim. English-style gardens flowered everywhere. Tea gardens thrived in the perfect climate. By 1881, when the narrow-gauge Toy Train began to zigzag up the mountains to Darjeeling, the hill station was completely anglicized. The British lived on the town's top ridge, and their workers lived on the hills below—a social and geographic stratification that exists today, with the Indian upper classes taking the place of the British.

Getting Around Darjeeling is a walker's town. For short excursions around Darjeeling, hire a car with driver from an agency listed below.

Addresses and Visit the **Darjeeling Tourist Bureau** (1 Nehru Rd., tel. 2050).
Numbers It's open April–mid-June and mid-September–November,
Tourist Information Monday–Saturday 9:30–5:30, Sunday 9–1; mid-June–mid-
September and December–March, Monday–Saturday 10–4:30,
closed Sunday.

Travel Agencies To hire a car with driver or arrange excursions, contact the
Darjeeling Tourist Bureau, Travel Corporation of India (Rm. 5,
Bellavista Apartments, Gandhi Rd., tel. 2694), **Clubside Mo-
tors** (Robertson Rd., tel. 2123), or **Greenland Travels** (21
Beechwood, Laden La Rd., tel. 2976). They are open April–
mid-June and mid-September–November daily 10–6; June–
mid-September and December–March, Monday–Saturday.
10–6.

Bookstores Visit **Oxford Book and Stationery Company** (Chowrasta),
which is open weekdays 9:30–5:30, Saturday 9:30–2:30 and
sells English-language publications.

Banks **Grindlays Bank** and the **State Bank of India** (Laden La Rd.) are
open weekdays 10–2, Saturday 10–noon.

Post Office The **Post Office** (Laden La Rd.) is open Monday–Saturday 10–
4:30.

Exploring From **Chowrasta (The Mall)**, walk to **Observatory Hill.** A winding path leads by hordes of pesky monkeys. Atop the tiny
summit is the **Mahakali Temple,** a cave sacred to Shiva. Shiva's
faithful bull, Nandi, guards the shrine along with two stone
temple lions, your clue that this is also a solemn site for Buddhists. Indeed, it is the site of a former monastery, Dorje Ling,
which was destroyed in the 19th century by Nepalese Gorkhas.
You see Buddhist prayer wheels, chortens, and prayer flags
alongside bells for Hindus to clang, announcing their arrival to
Shiva. Pilgrims to the shrine first get a blessing from the
Hindu priest who sits in the inner sanctum, then they receive a
blessing from a Sikkimese Buddhist lama. Then devotees of
both religions circle the structure three times, spinning the
prayer wheels, ringing the bells, and burning incense in the
chortens. *Open sunrise–sunset.*

From Chowrasta, walk down C. R. Das Road and visit the
Bhutia Busty Monastery, which belongs to a Buddhist Red Hat
Sect and was built in 1934 by a former king of Sikkim. On the
way to the monastery you pass **Step Aside,** a modest museum
commemorating the Indian nationalist leader Chittaranjan
Das. *Admission to both free. Monastery open sunrise–sunset.
Museum open daily 10–4.*

Jawahar Parbhat (formerly Birch Hill), on a lower ridge northeast of the monastery, is dominated by the handsome blue-
domed **Raj Bhawan** (Governor's Palace), built in 1879 (not open
to the public). Behind the Raj Bhawan is **The Shrubbery,** a garden planted by a former British governor of West Bengal. From
here, you get a magnificent view of the Mt. Kanchenjunga and
the Singla Valley. *Admission free. Open sunrise–sunset.*

Head south to **Lloyds Botanical Garden,** which is set on
Darjeeling's lowest ridge, with examples of flora from the Him-
alayas as well as plants from Australia, Africa, and the
Americas. The garden has 2,000 species of orchids in its Orchid

House. *Admission free. Open daily 6 AM–5 PM. Plan 6 hrs for this tour.*

Time Out **Penang Restaurant** on Laden La Road, north of the Dhirdham Temple, is a hole in the wall with four curtained booths that serves the best Tibetan *momo* in Darjeeling. (Order beef; pork can be risky if it's undercooked.) *Open daily 11–7.*

On Nehru Road, head to **Glenary's Pastry Shop** and try good lemon tarts, cookies, cakes, even fresh cheese. *Open daily 7–6.*

The Himalayan Mountaineering Institute was established by Prime Minister Nehru after Sir Edmund Hillary and Tenzing Norgay climbed Mt. Everest in 1953. England rewarded Hillary with knighthood; India built the Sherpa Norgay this institute. Its museum re-creates with photos and artifacts the thrills of Himalayan expeditions dating back to 1857. *Jawahar Rd. 2 km (1½ mi) north of Darjeeling. Admission: Rs. 1 Open summer, Wed.–Mon. 9–1 and 2–5; winter, Wed.–Mon. 9–2 and 2–4.*

Shopping Visit the following shops for Tibetan curios: **Habeen Mulliek and Son** (The Mall, tel. 2399), open daily 9–6:30, accepts American Express, Master Card, and Visa credit cards; and **Nepal Curio House** (16 Nehru Rd., tel. 2410), open daily 9:30–7, no credit cards. Two good fixed-price shops sell handmade Tibetan carpets, woolen sweaters, socks, and handicrafts: the **Tibetan Refugee Self-Help Center** (Lebong), open Monday–Saturday 8–5; and **N.P.A.A. Functional Literacy Shoppe** (Hayden Hall, Market Rd.), open Monday–Saturday 9–12:30, 1:30–5. Neither shop accepts credit cards.

On Saturday or Sunday, visit **Chowk Bazar** (on the lowest ridge). It's a typical Indian market jammed with villagers selling produce.

Outdoor Adventures Take an enjoyable half-hour **hike** south from the railway station along a trail that passes through a glade with orchids and cherry trees to Victoria Falls. This walk is best after the late summer monsoon. At press time, **fishing** around Darjeeling was banned; check with the Divisional Forest Officer in Darjeeling or the Tourist Bureau for the status at the time of your trip. If fishing is allowed, the Tourist Bureau will rent equipment.

Dining Most restaurants stop serving dinner by 9:30 PM. Dress is casual. Highly recommended restaurants are indicated by a star ★. Prices are per person, including taxes and excluding drinks and service charges.

★ **Glenary's.** Darjeeling's most famous restaurant—dating back to the British—is under renovation. A large upstairs establishment with banks of windows, its tin ceiling and fireplaces will be spruced up, lace curtains replaced, and bar polished. It offers good multicuisine choices. *Nehru Rd. Reservations not necessary. Open 8 AM–9 PM. AE, DC.*

Kanchan. This cheery hotel restaurant is in an old Raj-style bungalow. Fixed-menu meals are Continental, Indian, Tibetan, or Nepalese. *Hotel New Elgin, tel. 2182. Reservations advised. Open 7–9:30, 1–2, 7–9. AE, DC. Moderate ($5–$10).*

Shangrila Restaurant. This attractive restaurant, with tile floor, fireplaces, and sleek decor, serves tasty Szechuan food. *Nehru Rd., no phone. No reservations necessary. No credit* *cards. Open mid-Mar.–mid-Nov., daily 7:30 AM–10 PM; otherwise 7:30–7:30. Moderate ($5–$10).*

★ **Windamere Hotel.** A lovely old restaurant with wonderful views, the gracious service matches the ambience— tablecloths, fresh flowers. The fixed menu includes mildly spiced Indian and Continental cuisine. Upper Ridge, *tel. 2841. Reservations required. No credit cards. Open 8–9, 1–2, 7–8:30. Moderate ($5–$10).*

★ **Hotel Alice Villa.** This dining room is cozy, with crockery set up on sideboards, and a few small wood tables. The fixed menu has Indian and Continental dishes. *Upper Ridge, tel. 2381. Reservations advised. No credit cards. Open 7–9:30, 1–2, 7–9.*

Lodging Highly recommended lodgings are indicated by a star ★. Prices are for a standard double room, including taxes and excluding service charges.

Hotel New Elgin. This rambling 100-year-old bungalow is set on a ridge near the Mall. New rooms have been added, but the older rooms are still the most pleasing and comfortable. Meals are included. There's a mid-Nov.–mid-Mar. discount. *Darjeeling, West Bengal, tel. 2182. 25 rooms with bath. Facilities: restaurant, bar, room service, garden, travel counter, car rental, doctor on call, baby-sitters, library, cultural programs on request. AE, DC. Moderate ($25–$60).*

★ **Windamere Hotel.** Set near the uppermost ridge, this bungalow with cottages is surrounded by gardens. It's owned by an elegant Tibetan woman in her 80s. In its cozy drawing room, Hope Cook met her future husband, the king of Sikkim. Cottages and upper-floor rooms are spacious, with lots of chintz and a fireplace blazing by the time you slip into bed, your feet warmed by a hot-water bottle. Meals are included. *Darjeeling, West Bengal, tel. 2841. Reserve well in advance. 27 rooms with bath. Facilities: restaurant, bar, travel counter, dens, foreign-exchange counter. No credit cards. Moderate ($25–$60).*

Hotel Alice Villa. Each room in this small bungalow opens onto an enclosed veranda. The decor is simple, with clean furnishings and fireplaces. There's a mid-June–mid-September and mid-November–April discount. *West Bengal, Darjeeling, tel. 2381. 10 rooms with bath (hot water by bucket). Facilities: restaurant, bar. No credit cards. Inexpensive (under $25).*

Nightlife For intimacy, you can't beat the bar at the **Windamere Hotel,** where 10 people mean a crowd. The homey ambience creates good conversation. **Glenary's** restaurant, under renovation, has an attached bar that is popular with the year-round population.

Excursion from Darjeeling

Contact the Darjeeling Tourist Bureau or recommended travel agencies (*see* Important Addresses and Numbers, above) for information on excursions to watch tea cultivation at the Happy Valley Tea Estate, to the handicraft and carpet factories at the Tibetan Refugee Self-Help Center, to Tiger Hill and a sunrise view of Mt. Kanehenjunga, and to the nearby Yiga-Choling Buddhist Monastery, which was established in 1850 by Lama Sherap Gyansto, a famous Tibetan astrologer.

⑧ Kalimpong

Kalimpong is tiny, with a central street lined by buildings built in the 1920s. Walks offer views of the Deola Hills to the north; the Durbindara Hills to the south; and, on a clear day, the plains of Nepal's Terai and the lofty summits of Kanchenjunga.

Travel Restrictions Foreigners must register at the **Foreigner's Check Post** in Teesta, 22 kilometers (14 miles) from Darjeeling, and with Kalimpong's **National Registration Officer for Foreigners,** located on Rishi Road.

Exploring Head to the Tripai Hills, 3 kilometers (2 miles) from the center of town, and visit the **Tharpa Chholing Monastery,** built in 1922 and belonging to the Gelug. A pavilion with a gigantic prayer wheel and walls covered with old frescoes leads to a prayer hall filled with more old frescoes and statues. On the left side of the front wall is a statue of Guru Padmasambhava. To his right is a statue of Nowang Kegang, the founder of the monastery. Behind the altar is a statue of Sakyamuni surrounded by photos of the gurus of His Holiness, the Dalai Lama. To his right is a bronze statue of the Avalokitesvara. Exquisite thang-kas, brought from Tibet, hang in the center of the hall along with prayer drums. During the Tibetan New Year, lamas perform sacred chaams. A few days after Durga Puja (usually October), the lamas also offer a special puja and dance during a celebration called Chhogya Luper Lejo. Bring a flashlight. *Admission free. Prayer ceremonies at about 5 AM and 2 PM. Open sunrise–sunset.*

The new **Zangdogpalrifodang Monastery,** on Durpin Dara Hill at the other end of Kalimpong, also belongs to the Gelug. Stairs to the side of the monastery lead to the Cherisi (Prayer Chamber), which is covered with brightly painted frescoes. Here, a replica of a celestial chorten that was destroyed by the Chinese in Lhasa dominates the room. It took the lamas two years to construct at a cost of Rs. 50,000. The statue of the Buddha to its right was originally in Lhasa. On the top floor is a tiny chamber containing 1,000 small statues of the Buddha. The walls of the main hall on the ground floor, where the daily prayer services are held, are covered with frescoes, and the front altar enshrines a large statue of the Buddha.

Time Out An **unnamed bar** above Sonny Video Parlour on Rishi Road serves great chang and momo. Sit in the tiny dark room crowded with tables. Let your chang sit 10 minutes after hot water is poured in, then sip it through the straw. *Open 9 AM and into the night.*

Shopping **Kalimpong Arts and Crafts Cooperative Society** (off Main Rd.) sells fixed-price Bhutanese, Lepcha, and Sikkimese handicrafts, including embroidered bags, purses, and placemats. It's open 8:30–3:30; closed Sunday and the second and fourth Saturday of the month. No credit cards are accepted. **Book Depot Shop** (Main Rd.) sells not books, but fixed-price inexpensive handicrafts and handmade sweaters, socks, baby clothes, Nepali caps. It's open Monday–Saturday 9:30–4:30. No credit cards are accepted. **Kazi Ratna Sakya & Bros.** (Main Rd.) has a good selection of Tibetan and Bhutanese curios, jewelry, and thang-kas. It's open Monday–Saturday 9–6. No credit cards are accepted.

Dining Dress is casual. No reservations are necessary. Highly recommended restaurants are indicated by a star ★. Prices are per person, including taxes and excluding drinks and service charges.

Kalimpong Park Hotel Restaurant. This simple restaurant, with Buddhist symbols painted on the walls, serves excellent Chinese and good Indian or Tibetan food. *Tel. 304. No credit cards. Open 7 AM–9 PM. Inexpensive (under $5).*

★ **Mandarin Restaurant.** Lace curtains, family booths, a slightly Chinese look, and subdued lighting add up to a pleasant ambience. The menu is multicuisine. *Taxi Stand, no phone. No credit cards. Open 7–7. Inexpensive (under $5).*

★ **Gompo's Restaurant and Bar.** Set in the back of Gompo's Hotel, this casual restaurant offers views of the valley and good Chinese, Tibetan, and Indian food. *Just off Main Rd., No credit cards. Open 9–9. Inexpensive (under $5).*

Lodging Highly recommended lodgings are indicated by a star ★. Prices are for a standard double room, including taxes and excluding service charges.

★ **Himalayan Hotel.** A short walk from the center of town, this secluded hotel is a former British family residence, built in the 1920s. The hotel features a mixture of East and West—thangkas share the walls with family memorabilia. Ask for an upstairs bedroom for views and a veranda. The dining room has an attached sitting room. Meals are included. *Kalimpong, tel. 248. 9 rooms with bath (hot water by bucket). Reserve well in advance. Facilities: restaurant, beer available. No credit cards. Moderate ($25–$60).*

Hotel Silver Oaks. This modern hotel, close to the main market, has an attractive lobby, beautiful gardens, and rooms with a subdued decor. Ask for a room with a view of the Kanchenjunga range. Meals are included. *Kalimpong, tel. 296. 25 rooms with bath. Facilities: restaurant, bar, room service, foreign exchange, travel counter and car rental, baby-sitters, doctor on call. AE, DC. Moderate ($25–$60).*

Kalimpong Tourist Lodge. Government run and located about 3 kilometers (2 miles) from the heart of Kalimpong, this hotel was converted from a granite manor house built in the 1930s. The building is set on seven acres of lawns and gardens. The best views from any hotel in the area are from the upper-floor rooms. The rooms are simple and spacious, with mosquito netting and working fireplaces. *Reservations: West Bengal Tourism Development Corporation, Reservation Counter, 3/2 Benoy-Badal-Dinesh Bagh (East), 1st fl., Calcutta, West Bengal. 7 rooms with bath. Facilities: bar, restaurant. No credit cards. Inexpensive (under $25).*

Sikkim

Lepchas, the first known inhabitants of Sikkim, called their mountain home paradise—a description that holds true today. The last *chogyal* (king), who ruled Sikkim until it became India's 22nd state in 1975, was an avid conservationist who protected the environment of his beautiful Buddhist land. Today, tropical forests are still rich with hundreds of species of orchids and rhododendron. Waterfalls pour down mountains and are channeled to power prayer wheels. Valleys have tidy hamlets bristling with prayer flags and surrounded by terraced fields. Sikkim's guardian diety, Mt. Kanchenjunga—the world's third-highest peak, altitude 8,598 meters (28,208 feet)—is revered by all who live in her shadow.

Distinct ethnic groups share Sikkim. The Lepchas, or Rongkup (Children of Rong), originally lived in seclusion in northern Sikkim. Although many have converted to Buddhism, most still worship aspects of their physical surroundings—rainbows, clouds, rivers, and trees. Village priests preside over elaborate rituals, including animal sacrifices, to appease animist deities.

Tibetan Bhutias came into Sikkim in the 17th century with the first chogyal and were members of a three-tiered hierarchy: the aristocracy, the landholding Kazi, and the commoners. Buddhism governs Bhutia daily life. Every village has its prayer flags and chortens; most families have a relative who has joined a monastery or nunnery. Every home has an altar room.

The Bhutias' culture dominates Sikkim. The national dress for women is the traditional Bhutia *kho* or *bhoku*, a slim-fitting sleeveless robe—the epitome of elegance. It's worn over a *wanju* (blouse), with the *pangden* (apron) a colorful touch restricted to married women and formal occasions.

Nepalese immigrants are responsible for the introduction of terrace farming to Sikkim. Although most Nepalese are Hindu, you see few Hindu temples in Sikkim; often their faith incorporates Buddhist beliefs and practices as it does in Nepal.

Travel Restrictions

Because of Sikkim's sensitive border location, you need a Restricted Area Permit to travel there (*see* Before You Go to North India, above). Parties of four may apply for a trekking permit, no matter what they plan to do. This gives them a 15-day stay and access to the western area of the state. However, because of the poor roads, visitors will travel through much of the west by jeep. If you're going with fewer than four people, you can get only a seven-day permit, with a three-day extension available in Gangtok for areas around there. Be specific about your destinations.

For a seven-day permit, list Gangtok, Phodang, and the Rumtek and Pemayangtse monasteries. For a trekking permit, list the above locations and Dzongri. Make three photostats of the completed form. Send the original to the Ministry of Home Affairs, Government of India (Lok Nayak Bhavan, Khan Market, New Delhi). Send a copy to Sikkim Tourism (New Sikkim House, 14 Panchsheel Marg, Chanakyapuri, New Delhi), which will expedite the process. Keep the third copy for your records. Allow a minimum of 12 weeks for clearance.

You can also visit Sikkim with a tour group (*see* Before You Go to North India, above, and the northerrn West Bengal section, above, for a list of tour operators). Your tour operator will secure any necessary permits.

Addresses and Numbers

Tourist Information
Contact the **Sikkim Tourist Information Center** (Mahatama Gandhi Marg, Gangtok, Sikkim, tel. 2064), which is open mid-September–mid-November, daily 9–5:30; mid-November–mid-September, Monday–Saturday 10–4, closed the second Saturday of the month. There's also a counter at Bagdogra Airport.

Emergencies
For all emergencies, turn to your hotel or the Sikkim Tourist Information Center. The nearest consulates are in Calcutta: **American** (5/1 Ho Chi Minh Sarani, tel. 443611) and **British** (1 Ho Chi Minh Sarani, tel. 445171).

Travel Agencies
Get in touch with the **Sikkim Tourist Information Center** (*see* above) for details about treks, new tours, yak safaris, fishing, and rafting. It can arrange car or jeep rentals. For good privately run treks, contact **Nawang Gombu Sherpa** (c/o Himalayan Mountaineering Institute, Jawahar Parbhat, Darjeeling, West Bengal). Most of the hotels in Gangtok have travel counters that arrange car rentals or excursions.

Arriving and Departing

By Plane
Unless you're planning to visit from Darjeeling or Kalimpong, flying is your best bet. If you go by car or train from Calcutta, you need a separate Restricted Area Permit to cross northern West Bengal.

Airport and Airline
Indian Airlines makes a daily flight from Calcutta's Dum Dum Airport, Assam's Guwahati Airport, and Delhi's National Airport to West Bengal's **Bagdogra Airport,** the gateway to Sikkim. Flights from Calcutta and Assam take about an hour, from Delhi about two hours. Book well in advance and reconfirm your ticket 72 hours before flight time. Call, in Calcutta (tel. 572031), Guwahati (tel. 82279), or Delhi (tel. 3014433). At Bagdogra, foreigners must register at the **Foreigner's Registration Office.**

Between Airport and City
You can take an enjoyable 30-minute helicopter flight from the Bagdogra Airport to Gangtok. Tickets are available at the Tourist Information Center, Bagdogra Airport. Cost is Rs. 375 per person. Reserve in advance through your travel agent or the Sikkim Tourist Information Office in Gangtok (Mahatma Gandhi Marg, tel. 2064). You can also go by taxi or hired car with driver to Gangtok, 124 kilometers (77 miles) away, a five-hour journey through beautiful valleys and mountains. Taxis are plentiful at the airport. Hire a car from the Sikkim Tourist Department; write in advance, with a 50% deposit (about Rs. 300) to Manager, Transport (Tourist Department, Gangtok, Sikkim).

By Hired Car with Driver
You can also drive to Gangtok from Darjeeling or Kalimpong in northern West Bengal. The journey takes about five hours and costs about Rs. 600 per vehicle. Hire a car from a recommended northern West Bengal travel agency.

Getting Around

By Hired Car or Jeep with Driver
From Gangtok, hire a car with driver from the **Sikkim Information Center** for about Rs. 400 per day (gasoline not included); also figure on a Rs. 200 per night halt charge. Contact in ad-

vance with a 50% deposit: Manager of Transport (Tourist Department, Gangtok, Sikkim). Some hotels also arrange car rentals. The Sikkim Tourist Information Center plans to make jeeps available. Contact the Manager of Transport for details.

Outdoor Adventures

In Sikkim, adventure tourism is just developing. Options increase each year. Highly recommended adventures are indicated by a star ★.

★ **Climbing and Mountaineering:** Climbers can attempt Rathong Peak, 6,707 meters (22,000 feet), and Kothang Peak, 6,148 meters (20,167 feet). All expeditions must be planned well in advance and approved by the Indian Mountaineering Foundation (Benito Juarez Rd., New Delhi, tel. 671211).

Fishing: Contact the Tourist Information Center in Gangtok for information regarding permits and locations. The season runs from mid-October until March. Bring your own equipment.

Hot Springs: Good hot springs await the trekker to Dzongri in western Sikkim.

Rafting: *Teesta River.* One- or two-day rafting trips in September to May are under review. Contact the Tourist Information Center in Gangtok for the latest details.

Trekking: The best treks are in western Sikkim, with the most popular season from mid-September to June. A highly recommended trek in the winter means cold nights and snow, but the temperature warms up by day, and you see numerous orchids at this time of year. Trekkers should also get in touch with the Sikkim Tourist Information Center for specifics about new culture- and nature-oriented treks. Details weren't ready at press time. The Tourist Information Center rents sleeping bags and good tents.

★ **Trekking (up to a week):** *Makha to Maenam:* This four-day trek goes to Maenam, once the center of the Sikkim kingdom, and on to Ragbagla. You walk through rhododendron forests filled with orchids, past streams and quiet villages.

★ **Trekking (over a week):** *Yoksum to Dzongri:* This seven- to 10-day trek isn't exceptionally difficult, but because it has a lot of up- and downhill walking, you should be physically fit. You hike from Yoksum in western Sikkim through forests of rhododendron, orchids, pine, and magnolia to Bakhim village. The next day's tough walk passes through valleys and their villages populated by the gentle yak-herding Lepchas to Dzongri outpost with its views of Kanchenjunga. At Dzongri, altitude 4,030 meters (13,218 feet), you can ride a yak, relax in sulfur springs, hike up to Thangsing, altitude 3,930 meters (12,890 feet), at the base of Jopine Peak, and climb to Zimathang, altitude 4,500 meters (14,760 feet). This excellent trek, rarely made by foreigners, offers terrific eastern Himalayan vistas.

★ **Sightseeing Flights** (*see* Guided Tours, below.)

❾ Gangtok

Gangtok, at 1,676 meters (5,497 feet), always bustles, especially when the military is on the move north to watch over India's sensitive border. The ongoing construction of concrete high rises is ending the air of enchantment that still hangs over the rest of Sikkim.

Getting Around Taxis are unmetered and frequently pick up extra passengers. Rates are always cheap: figure Rs. 3 per kilometer.

Addresses and Numbers
Tourist Information Visit the **Tourist Information Center** (Mahatma Gandhi Marg, tel. 2064). From mid-September to mid-November, it's open daily 9–5:30; mid-November–mid-September, Monday–Saturday 10–4, except the second Saturday of the month.

Travel Agencies Many hotels have travel agencies that arrange excursions and car rentals.

Bank The **State Bank of India** (Mahatma Gandhi Marg) is open weekdays 10–2, Saturday 10–noon.

Post Office The **Post and Telegraph Office** (Paljor Namgyal Stadium Rd.) is open Monday–Saturday 9–5.

Guided Tours From Gangtok, the **Sikkim Tourist Information Center** runs a 35-minute helicopter flight around Kanchenjunga from mid-September to mid-November, weather permitting.

The **Sikkim Tourist Information Center** also offers two daily local sightseeing tours with guides to the sights in Exploring, below, and more. You can also make these tours with a hired car. No private guides are available in Gangtok.

Exploring Travelers interested in Buddhism should visit the **Research Institute of Tibetology,** founded by the Dalai Lama in 1957 and the most important Buddhist study center in India. It has a vast collection of rare Lepcha, Tibetan, and Sanskrit manuscripts, many donated by the Dalai Lama; numerous priceless statues, including a seven-foot statue of Manjushri, a 10″ copper image of Avalokitesvara; and rare thang-kas, some created on tapestry. Lamas are on hand to help any reader analyze a text. *On a hill above the center of Gangtok. Admission free. Open Mon.–Sat. 10–4; closed Sun. and government holidays.*

Walk through the **Orchid Sanctuary,** with numerous species in bloom during the winter months. *Below Research Institute of Tibetology. Admission free. Open sunrise–sunset.*

See the **Do-Drul Chorten**, built in 1945 by the Venerable Trulsi Rimpoche, head of the Nyingmapa (Red) sect. Surrounded by 108 prayer wheels, this chorten commemorates the Buddha's victory over evil. Nearby are two statues of Guru Padmasambhava. *Down from the Research Institute of Tibetology near the Deorali Bazaar.*

You have to time your visit right to get into **Tsuklakhang,** the royal gompa of the former chogyal of Sikkim. On a ridge above Gangtok, it's constructed in typical pagoda style. It was the most important monastery in Sikkim. The main hall has exquisitely carved and painted woodwork, frescoes, and precious Buddhist icons. Here kings were crowned and royal marriages were consecrated. The most important festivals were performed in its courtyard. Across the meadow sits the **Royal Palace**—also closed to the public. *Gompa open only during Pang Lhabsol (Aug. or Sept.) and Kagyat (Nov. or Dec.). Allow 5 hours for this walk.*

On Sunday, walk through **Lal Bazaar.** Bhutias and Lepchas in traditional clothes come from nearby villages to sell vegetables, spices, chickens, clothing, and trinkets. *Begins around 8 AM. Plan for 1 hour.*

Time Out   **Risur Hotel & Bakery**, on the National Highway in Deorali Bazaar, serves great momo in its popular restaurant. *Open daily 8–8; closed Tibetan holidays.*

Shopping   The fixed-price **Government Institute of Cottage Industries** (on the northern edge of Gangtok) sells excellent wool carpets; new thang-kas; hand looms in wool, silk, and cotton; traditional clothes; jewelry; handbags; handknit sweaters; masks; wood carvings; and furniture. It's open Monday–Saturday 9:30–12:30 and 1–3:30. No credit cards are accepted. The **Tourist Department Gift Shop** (Mahatma Gandhi Marg) also sells good fixed-price handicrafts. It's open mid-September–mid-November, daily 8:30–6:30; mid-November–mid-September, Wednesday–Monday 10–5, closed Tuesday and government holidays. No credit cards are accepted. **Babu Kazi Sakya** (Mahatma Gandhi Marg) sells new and old traditional jewelry, curios, and handicrafts at fixed prices. It's open 8–7; closed Hindu holidays. No credit cards are accepted.

Two good tailors can make handsome traditional costumes. **Pema Seyden, Tibetan Tailor** (Lall Market Rd.) is open Wednesday–Monday 7 AM–8 PM; closed Tuesday. Ms. Seyden will help you pick out fabric in a nearby shop. **Lhasa Tailors** (Wangdi Children Park, near Market Taxi Stand) is open 7 AM–8 PM. Both are reliable, inexpensive, and will complete your order in two days. They don't accept credit cards.

Dining   Expect good eating in Gangtok. The cuisine is diversified—Tibetan, Indian, Chinese, Continental, and Sikkimese. You have to request Sikkimese dishes. Try, in particular, Sikkimese sautéed ferns (in season), sautéed bamboo shoots, nettle soup, and roast pork. If you like momo, order the beef or vegetable variety—pork is risky if undercooked. Sikkim also makes good local brews: cherry or musk brandy, wine, Teesta River white rum, juniper gin, *pan* (mixed nuts and leaves) liquor, and chang. All hotel restaurants are open to the public except for Norkhill, which you should call first to see if it can accommodate you. Many restaurants close by 9 PM. Dress is casual and reservations are not necessary unless noted. Highly recommended restaurants are indicated by a star ★. Prices are per person, including taxes and excluding drinks and service charges.

★   **Blue Poppy.** This delightful Sikkimese-style restaurant, with star cutouts on its blue ceiling, pastiche all over the place, and views of the mountains, serves good steaks, as well as Chinese, Indian, Sikkimese, and Continental fare. *Hotel Tashi Delek, Mahatma Gandhi Marg, tel. 2038. Reservations advised. Open 8 AM–10 PM. AE, DC, MC, V. Moderate ($5–$10).*

Shapi Restaurant. A modern hotel dining room with a bank of windows that provides great views. The food is extremely good: Chinese, Indian, and Continental. There's an attached bar. *Hotel Mayur, Paljor Namgyal Stadium Rd., tel. 2752. Open 7 AM–9 PM. No credit cards. Moderate ($5–$10).*

Blue Sheep. This informal upstairs restaurant is done up in modern Sikkimese style. You can choose Continental, Tibetan, or Indian food. There's an attached bar. *Next to the Tourist Information Center, Mahatma Gandhi Marg, no phone. Open Mon.–Sat. 9–9. No credit cards. Inexpensive (under $5).*

House of Bamboo. Another upstairs restaurant, it's very informal, very Tibetan, and very cheap. You can also choose Chinese dishes. There's an attached bar. *Mahatma Gandhi Marg, no phone. Open 8–8; closed on full moon, half moon, and the Tibetan New Year. No credit cards. Inexpensive (under $5).*

★ **Snow Lion.** This peaceful restaurant is run by the Dalai Lama's staff. Expect soft lighting, Tibetan decor, and good views of Mt. Kanchenjunga. Popular and informal, it serves excellent Tibetan, Japanese, Chinese, and Indian food. *Hotel Tibet, Paljor Namgyal Stadium Rd., tel. 2523. Open 7 AM–9:30 PM. DC, MC. Inexpensive (under $5).*

Lodging Most hotels in Gangtok have appealing Buddhist touches. Highly recommended lodgings are indicated by a star ★. Prices are for a standard double room, including taxes and excluding service charges.

Hotel Norkhill. Gangtok's oldest hotel, once owned by the king, is on a quiet ridge below the city. It has a lovely garden and lawn and excellent views. Its exterior and public rooms are in a sedate Sikkimese style. The rooms are simple and clean, but they lack elegance. Ask for a room with a view and a tub if that's important to you. Meals are included. *Gangtok, tel. 2386. 25 rooms with bath. Facilities: restaurant, bar, room service, gift shop, library, baby-sitters, house doctor, gardens, travel and foreign-exchange service, Sikkimese dances on request. AE, DC, MC. Moderate ($25–$60).*

★ **Hotel Mayur.** Centrally located, this spiffy hotel has nicely furnished rooms and pine ceilings and trim. Modern bathrooms have tubs (in super deluxe rooms) and showers (in deluxe rooms). Standard rooms are smaller. For mountain views, ask for a super deluxe or deluxe room. *Paljor Namgyal Stadium Rd., Gangtok, tel. 2752 or 2825. 25 rooms with bath. Facilities: restaurant, bar, room service, house doctor, gift shop, car rental, TV. No credit cards. Inexpensive (under $25).*

★ **Hotel Tibet.** Run by the Dalai Lama Charitable Trust, this hotel is also centrally located and has wonderful Tibetan ambience and decor. The rooms are clean and simple. The best views are to be had from super deluxe rooms (tubs) or deluxe rooms (showers). *Paljor Namgyal Stadium Rd., Gangtok, tel. 2523 or 21568. 28 rooms with bath. Facilities: restaurant, bar, room service, car rental, foreign-exchange counter. DC, MC. Inexpensive (under $25).*

Hotel Tashi Delek. Also centrally located, this hotel's public rooms feature Sikkimese decor in colors bright enough for sunglasses. The bedrooms are small and simple with partial views of the mountains. *Mahatma Gandhi Marg, Gangtok, tel. 2038 or 2991. 45 rooms with bath. Facilities: restaurant, bar, rooftop garden, baby-sitters, travel and foreign-exchange counter, shopping arcade. AE, DC, MC, V. Inexpensive (under $25).*

Nightlife Gangtok shuts down early unless there's a festival or chaam underway. Hotels and most restaurants have bars. Try the local brandies or chang—just remember they're potent. **Snow Lion Bar** in the Hotel Tibet is cozy, with good views (open 10–10). **Yak Bar** in the Hotel Tashi Delek is jazzy Sikkimese, with red brocade-draped booths and good views (open 10–9).

Excursion from Gangtok

Contact the Tourist Information Center (*see* Important Addresses and Numbers, above) for information on excursions to three nearby monasteries: Enchey, Phodang, and Phensang.

Excursion from Gangtok to Rumtek Monastery

When the Chinese occupied Tibet, His Holiness Gyalwa Karmapa, the 16th incarnation of the founder of the Karmapa sect of Tibet, took refuge in Sikkim. The chogyal of Sikkim gave him 75 acres to set up the **Rumtek Monastery**—a replica of the gompa at Chhofuk in Tibet. Following the custom, before Gyalwa Karmapa died in 1982, he wrote and hid a lengthy prophesy that described the 17th incarnation. In May 1988, the four head rimpoches of the monastery discovered the document. At an auspicious time, they will reveal its contents, locate the child it describes, and bring him to Rumtek for his enthronement.

Rumtek contains numerous chambers (some not open to non-Buddhists). A courtyard leads to the entrance of the ornate main prayer hall. The throne, facing the assembly hall, is for His Holiness and has a photo of the 16th incarnation to its right. Reincarnated lamas sit on raised seats near the throne, with the chant leaders on the next highest platforms. The other lamas sit on rows of low cushions. The Head Disciplinarian sits on the high cushioned platform by a pillar near the entrance. From here, he keeps his eyes on young novices and controls the departures of lamas during all ceremonies.

Steps behind the right of the exterior lead to the prestigious **Nalanda Institute for Higher Studies** and the **Great Golden Reliquary,** which contains the relics (bones and remnants of the cremated body) of the 16th Gyalwa Karmapa and a gold-plated chorten surrounded by 16 statues of former Gyalwa Karmapas. *24 km (15 mi) southwest of Gangtok. Admission: Rs. 10 donation. Prayer services usually 4 AM and 6 PM; check with the Tourist Information Center.* See also *Festivals and Seasonal Events, above.*

Excursion from Gangtok to Tashidang and Pemayangtse Monasteries

The town of **Rabangla,** 65 kilometers (40 miles) from Gangtok, is the gateway to western Sikkim. The road begins to climb and hug the mountains. Jagged rocks are covered with fern. You traverse dark tropical forests with moss hanging from trees. Shafts of sunlight dart through clearings. The road winds, then descends, taking you past a small monastery, **Yung Drum,** studded with flags. Moments later, you round a sharp bend, and on a distant peak you see the **Tashidang Monastery,** its golden pinnacle catching the sun. Behind it looms the spectacular Mt. Kanchenjunga, with clouds swirling around its crest.

In **Legship,** about 91 kilometers (56 miles) from Gangtok, take the road to the right; stop the car and walk up the path to Tashidang, atop a hill between the Rangit and Ratong rivers. It's an active monastery with about 60 monks from the Nyingmapa order. According to legend, Guru Padmasambhava shot an arrow in the air, and where it fell (here) he vowed to pray. In 1642 one of the three lamas who consecrated the first chogyal built a *lhakhang* (shrine) venerating this sacred spot. In 1716 the main monastery was constructed.

Tashidang's exterior remains a lovely example of Sikkimese temple architecture, but its interior, including the old frescoes, needs repair. See the Thongwa Rangdol chorten, said to contain the holy relics of Manjushri. Just the sight of it cleanses the devotee of sin. Guru Padmasambhava is also credited with the creation of the bumchu, which you can see during the Bumchu Celebration in February. At this time, the sacred bumchu, which has a perpetual sweet aroma and has never been refilled since its discovery, is emptied of its holy contents. The amount of water determines Sikkim's prosperity in the new year. Bring a flashlight. *Plan for a 30-minute walk to the monastery. Admission: Rs. 10 donation. Open sunrise–sunset.*

Return to Legship and head west to Geysing, 10 kilometers (6 miles) away. Here, a jeep-worthy shortcut leads to **Pemayangtse,** Sikkim's most important monastery, with 200 Nyingmapa lamas. The original lhakhang, constructed in the mid-1600s is the second-oldest monastery in Sikkim. The monastery has been renovated several times since then.

A gaily decorated entrance leads into the main assembly hall. Old frescoes cover the walls; prayer cushions for the lamas and higher platforms for the head monks are set between red pillars. Behind the front altar stands a large gold-covered clay statue of Guru Padmasambhava flanked by his two consorts— all of them protected by an arch of wood nagas (sacred serpents). To the right is Avalokitesvara with his disciples; a statue of the Buddha is to the left.

Steps on the right lead to upper floors. The first chamber, Guru Lhakhang, has frescoes and statues depicting Guru Padmasambhava. On the right wall near the statues, a fresco portrays the consecration of the first chogyal of Sikkim (he's on the left).

Interior walls of the other chamber on this floor are covered with 1,000 images of the Buddha; the room contains the holy scriptures and the main statue of Lord Buddha. A 20 by 30 foot thang-ka depicting the Buddha is also kept in this room and unfurled only during the annual festival (usually in February).

On the third floor is the "must-see" chamber, with its astonishing chorten. About 30 years ago, Dungzin Rimpoche, now deceased, spent five years reconstructing a description of a vision of Sangthokpalri, the celestial palace of Guru Padmasambhava. The miniature palace takes into account the tiniest details: a combination of the whimsical and the serene. *This entire journey should be made by jeep. With an early morning start and a stop at Tashidang, you should arrive at Geysing by nightfall. Pemayangtse is 140 km (87 mi) west of Gangtok. Admission: Rs. 10 donation. See the Pemayangtse Monastery in daylight. No photographs allowed inside. Check with the Sikkim Tourist Information Center for times of services.*

Lodging Only one hotel currently exists in this part of Sikkim. Reserve well in advance. Prices are for a standard double room or cottage, including taxes and excluding service charges.

Hotel Mt. Pandim. This government-run bungalow is lovely, set on a hill with great views and an attractive garden. The restaurant serves reasonably good multicuisine food, and meals are included in the room cost. The modestly furnished rooms are large; ask for one with a view. *Pemayangtse, Pelling, West Sikkim, Sikkim, tel. 56. 25 rooms with bath. Facilities: restaurant, bar, room service, laundry, tour guide hire and car rental, doctor on call, library, gift shop. No credit cards. Inexpensive (under $25).*

Trekker's Huts. In west Sikkim, the government has put simple huts with rustic rooms or dormitories in delightful locations. Bring a sleeping bag and bug repellent. A caretaker will prepare simple meals. At present, trekker's huts are at Pemayangtse, Barshey, Yoksum, Tsokha, and Dzongri. *Reservations: Assistant Manager, Hotel Mt. Pandim, Pemayangtse, Post Office Pelling, West Sikkim, Sikkim, tel. 56. Indian-style bath (hot water by bucket). Inexpensive (under $10).*

Excursion from Pemayangtse to Yoksum

Yoksum hamlet is about 43 kilometers (26 miles) to the north. You must go by jeep. This is the start for the trek to Dzongri. Once you arrive at Yoksum, a plateau set in a pine forest amid mountain lakes, you understand why the three lamas who consecrated the first chogyal of Sikkim chose this spot for the ceremony. The simple outdoor wood throne with a painted altar still exists. The quiet is pervasive; even the air feels holy.

Dhubdi Monastery, or the **Hermit's Cell,** is an hour's climb from Yoksum. At Dhubdi, only visiting chanting lamas and chattering birds break the quiet. Set on a summit, this is Sikkim's oldest monastery—the sanctuary is nothing more than wood steps leading up to a painted altar and exalted views. *Leave early in the morning and bring a packed lunch. Round-trip from Pemayangtse is about 100 km (62 miles).*

6 North Pakistan

Introduction

Pakistan is a late arrival on the tourist's map. For years, this Moslem land has been left to anthropologists, mountain climbers, and the occasional trekker. They all knew this was one of the least spoiled and most beautiful areas on Earth. Here, you're never far from towering mountains and intriguing tribal people—gun-toting Pathans, animist Kafir-Kalash, and the seminomadic Gujjar. Nor are you ever far from the sounds of the call to prayer. Five times a day people stop their work, face Mecca, and praise Allah. The typical greetings are *Assalam-O-Alaikum* and *Salam* (May God be with you).

In the extreme north, the Federally Administered Northern Areas (FANA) is dominated by the Great Himalayas and Karakorams—a 322-kilometer (200-mile) string of peaks that converge in the Pamir Range, the offshoots of which form Pakistan's northwestern border with Afghanistan. In the Karakorams, you find Mt. Godwin Austin, called K-2 (K is for Karakoram) and the rival of Everest. Just recently, scientists settled the issue of which was taller, giving Everest an 840-foot edge.

Still, FANA can claim the world's greatest proliferation of king mountains, with over 35 peaks that rise 7,000 meters (22,960 feet) and four peaks pushing 8,000 meters (26,240 feet). Here, you find the world's longest glaciers outside the polar region and the world's newest wonder—the rugged Karakoram Highway, blasted through a stretch of rock that extends all the way to China. The publicity showered on this late arrival has let it upstage the equally impressive Gilgit-Skardu Road, a skinny east–west thoroughfare that hugs a gorge above the raging Skardu River, and the Punial Highway, which takes you through wild glaciers in the Karakorams to the Hindu Kush and the North West Frontier Province (NWFP).

In NWFP, west of FANA, the Hindu Kush are a jumble of red-hued peaks crossed by the legendary Khyber Pass, the route traversed by Marco Polo, defended centuries later by the British, and now lorded over by Afghan guerrillas and Pathans. In these mountains, you find places immortalized by Rudyard Kipling—the romantic Swat and Chitral valleys; numerous tribal areas where ancient laws prevail; and the frontier city, Peshawar, a Pathan stronghold.

Northern Pakistan's exotic villages and bazaars are dominated by men; most women are strict observers of *purdah* (self-imposed isolation) and are confined to the home. Roads have more goats, donkeys, and horses than vehicles. Vehicles are primarily buses and trucks—each one a traveling folk-art show. Exteriors are elaborately painted with pictures of animals, the Taj Mahal, lotus flowers, eagles, Pakistan's heroes, bits of Urdu poetry, and warnings to drive safely. Doors are intricately carved in wood or constructed of hand-tooled, decorated tin. Each owner spends almost $4,000 for the artwork and truck's body alone.

To visit northern Pakistan and not take a ride in a Disco Bus is to miss a memorable adventure. Inside, you're surrounded by tinsel streamers, painted chrome panels, and blinking lights. A sign in Urdu warns: No smoking; all parts of body must remain in bus; cooperate with the driver and conductor; don't be noisy;

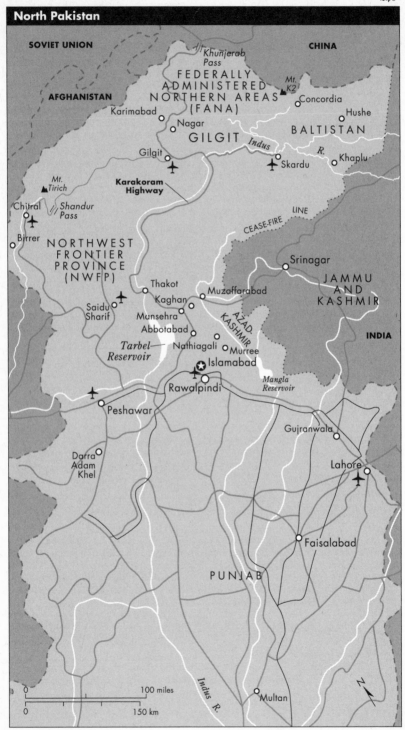

North Pakistan

SOVIET UNION

CHINA

AFGHANISTAN

Khunjerab Pass

FEDERALLY
ADMINISTERED
NORTHERN AREAS
(FANA)

Mt.
K2

Concordia

Hushe

Karimabad

Nagar

GILGIT

BALTISTAN

Gilgit

Indus

Skardu

R.

Khaplu

Mt.
Tirich

Karakoram
Highway

*Shandur
Pass*

Chitral

Birrer

NORTHWEST
FRONTIER
PROVINCE
(NWFP)

CEASE-FIRE LINE

Srinagar

JAMMU
AND
KASHMIR

Thakot

Kaghan

Muzaffarabad

INDIA

Saidu
Sharif

Munsehra

AZAD.
KASHMIR

Abbotabad

*Tarbel
Reservoir*

Nathiagali

Murree

★ Islamabad

Rawalpindi

*Mangla
Reservoir*

Peshawar

Gujranwala

Darra
Adam
Khel

Lahore

Faisalabad

PUNJAB

100 miles

0

150 km

Indus R.

Multan

N

children cannot have a seat, but must pay half-fare; keep the bus clean; when you enter the bus, please say the name of Allah; please ask for God's forgiveness, this may be your last journey.

Don't worry, it won't be your last trip, nor will it be somber. Once the Disco Bus rolls, music blares; cigarettes light up; hands, arms, and feet hang out windows; and people pile on the roof. The drivers are good and love every inch of their vehicles (washing them in a river at day's end).

History Pakistan had a shared past with India until the time of independence and partitioning (*see* the Introduction in North India, Chapter 5). In 1947 the new nation of Pakistan had a geographic challenge. A thousand-mile stretch of India separated East Pakistan from West Pakistan. Over time, the two territories developed separate goals. Just after Zulfikar Ali Bhutto took control of Pakistan, war broke out in East Pakistan. India intervened, and Bangladesh became a reality in December 1971.

Pakistan at its formation also had to contend with its indigenous tribes and feudal states, which remained fiercely independent. Though they ultimately ceded their sovereignty to Pakistan, they still retain certain local jurisdiction.

Subsequent decades haven't been easier on Pakistan, with political intrigue and twists of fate shaping her history right up to press time. In 1977 Zia-ul-Haq, a general under Bhutto, staged a successful coup. Bhutto was arrested, tried on charges of murder and corruption, and finally hanged on April 4, 1979.

Zia's 11 years in power resulted in military rule and an increasingly strict interpretation of the concept of an Islamic state. Elections were continually postponed until 1985, when military rule was finally ended. At the polls, the outcome was never in doubt. Zia won. But bending to the will of the people, he opted for civilian rule and named a prime minister to head the cabinet.

In August 1988 a plane crash took Zia's life. Later that year, free elections were held. Benazir Bhutto, the daughter of Zulfikar Ali Bhutto, had put an end to self-imposed exile and returned to Pakistan. She triumphed as the candidate of the People's Party of Pakistan, the party her father had created. The civilian democratic state was reborn. The challenge is great for this young woman, born in 1953, now the prime minister of an important Islamic nation.

Before You Go

Government Tourist Offices

Limited information is available through the Pakistan's embassies and consulates (*see* Visas, below) and the overseas offices of the **Pakistan Tourism Development Corporation (PTDC),** a government undertaking affiliated with the following companies.

In the U.S. **Lan-Si-Air Travel** (303 Fifth Ave., Suite 508, New York, NY 10016, tel. 212/889–5478).

In Canada **Best Way Tours and Safaris** (West Broadway, Suite 202-2678, Vancouver, B.C., V6K 2G3, tel. 604/732–4686 or, in British Columbia and Alberta, 800/663–0844).

In the U.K. **PTDC,** Marketing Services, Tourism and Travel (Suite 433, High Holborn House, 52–54 High Holborn, London, WC1V 6R1, tel. 01/242–3131).

Tour Groups

The following private companies in Pakistan, with offices in the United States, offer terrific tours and outdoor adventures. Their guides are excellent, service is tops, and prices are competitive. You can join a fixed-departure trip or let them custom design a vacation for you. (*See* also Before You Go to the Himalayas, Chapter 1, for a list of agencies that handle trips in Pakistan.)

Indus Guides (7-E Egerton Rd., Lahore, Pakistan, tel. 304190); in the United States, contact **World Associates in Travel** (29 Birch Brook Rd., Bronxville, NY 10708, tel. 914/793–7310 or 800/624–5659). This new company offers excellent treks, horseback and bike rides, fishing and rafting trips, and excursions in the north by jeep or car. Indus can also arrange for car and jeep rental with driver and private guide.

Travel Walji's (Walji's Bldg., 10 Khyaban Suhrawardy, Box 1088, Islamabad, tel. 828324; In the U.S.: 6 Pond Rd., Box 15464, Stamford, CT 06901, tel. 203/356–0027 or 800/255–7181). The granddaddy of the travel industry in Pakistan, Walji's offers cultural excursions, excellent treks, pony treks, jeep safaris, bicycle tours, photo safaris, trout fishing, and rafting. Walji's also rents cars and jeeps with driver and can arrange for a guide.

Pakistan Tours, a subsidiary of PTDC for budget travelers (in Pakistan: General Manager, Rm. 10, Flashman's Hotel, Rawalpindi, tel. 65449; *see* above for overseas offices). It offers jeep tours, fishing excursions, and trekking in all the best regions and arranges for cars and jeeps with drivers.

When to Go

The best times to visit North Pakistan are generally April and May and from mid-August to mid-October. The weather is at its best; roads over passes are free of snow. During June and July, the monsoon can bring heavy showers.

In NWFP—even though Peshawar gets extremely hot—the best time to visit is from May to October. Winter months are cold; some valleys are inaccessible. Gilgit and Skardu in FANA are year-round destinations; October to February, expect cold days and nights and some passes closed. Murree, a former British hill station, is open year-round. You can also plan a vacation around an exciting festival, such as a Kafir-Kalash celebration or a ferocious polo match in FANA (*see* Skardu or Gilgit destination sections, below) or in NWFP (*see* Chitral section, below).

Festivals and Seasonal Events

Many festivals are timed with the lunar calendar; dates change each year. Check with an embassy or consulate of Pakistan or your travel agent before you depart.

Mar.: Nauroze is celebrated in Gilgit, Skardu, Hunza, and Chitral with polo matches and folk dances.

Mar. 23: Pakistan Day marks the date in 1940 when Moslems decided to campaign for a separate state.

Mar.: With night-long prayers and feasts, **Shab-E-Mairaj** celebrates the night of Mohammed's ascent to heaven.

Mar. or Apr.: During **Jashn-E-Khyber,** tribal peoples in Peshawar put on a cattle fair and sporting events.

Apr.: Shab-I-Barat remembers the dead. Mosques are illuminated and fireworks light up the sky.

Apr.: Ramadan commemorates the descent of the Quran from heaven with a month-long period of obligatory daytime fasting for Moslems.

May: Eid-ul-Fitr, a two-day celebration and feast, concludes Ramadan.

May: After Kafir-Kalash girls pick the first blooms of the year, the villages celebrate **Joshi** or **Chilimjusht** with traditional dances, songs, and a feast.

Mid-July: Utchal is a two-day Kafir-Kalash harvest festival with traditional dancing and singing.

July or Aug.: Eid-ul-Azha honors with sacrifices and feasts the sacrifice of Harrat Ibrahim who willingly agreed to kill his son, Ismail, at the behest of God. This is also the time for the pilgrimage to Mecca.

Aug. 14: Independence Day celebrates the birth of Pakistan.

Aug. or Sept.: On **Ashura (Muharram)** Moslems pay tribute to the martyrdom of Mohammed's grandson, Hussain, with all-night chanting and self-flagellation.

Sept. 6: Defense of Pakistan Day commemorates the 1965 war with India over Kashmir.

Sept. 11: On this day, the country remembers the **death of Mohammed Ali Jinnah,** the Father of Pakistan.

Sept.: Chitral holds a gigantic **festival,** including dancing, songs, and polo matches.

Mid-Sept.: Phool, another Kafir-Kalash event, celebrates the walnut and grape harvests with dancing and music.

Oct.: Eid-Milad-un-Nabi marks the birthday of the Prophet Mohammed.

Nov. 1: Polo matches and folk dances in Skardu and Gilgit celebrate the **Independence Day** of the Northern Territories.

Nov.: The **Gilgit Festival** is a time of traditional dances and more thrilling polo.

Dec. 25: Pakistan celebrates **Mohammed Ali Jinnah's birthday.**

Taking Money Abroad

Pakistan has no restrictions on the amount of foreign currency and traveler's checks allowed into the country; bring checks in small denominations and cash them only when necessary, saving all official exchange receipts. Change money only with government-authorized institutions. Many hotels have foreign exchange counters but offer a poorer rate. When you leave Pakistan, banks will reconvert only up to Rs. 500 (about $30) upon presentation of an official exchange receipt. If you need to exchange a larger amount, prepare for a time-consuming hassle: You'll fill out an application form from an authorized exchange bank, which is then forwarded to an office of the State Bank of Pakistan.

The units of Pakistani currency are the rupee and paisa (100 paisas equal 1 rupee). Paper money comes in Rs. 1, 2, 5, 10, 50, and 100 denominations; coins come in Rs. 1, 2, 5, 10 denominations; and paisas come in 25, 50, and 100 denominations. At press time, the rate of exchange was US $1 = Rs. 17; f1 = Rs. 30.

What It Will Cost

Except for fancy hotels in Lahore, Pakistan is a bargain destination. Once you leave Lahore, the few high-priced accommodations you encounter cost about $50 per double, often with meals included. Most lodging is extremely inexpensive. Transportation by jeep with driver—often the only way to travel in remote areas—costs about Rs. 160 per day, plus Rs. 6 per kilometer. A car with driver is about Rs. 850 per day and a Rs. 100 halt charge per night.

Foreigners must pay Rs. 250 departure tax when they leave Pakistan. They must also pay either a Rs. 100 international airport tax or a Rs. 10 domestic airport tax for each flight.

Visas

Travelers need a tourist visa, available through their local Pakistani consulate or embassy. Visas, good for a three-month stay, are free for Americans and Canadians. Britons must pay the equivalent of $73. To get the visa, you must have two passport photos and a valid passport. If you apply in person, the visa is ready in three working days. Offices normally accept visa applications weekdays 9:30–1:30. If you apply by mail, allow a month for processing. Foreigners who plan to stay in Pakistan more than a month must register with the Foreigners Registration Office located in each city.

Americans Contact **Embassy of Pakistan** (2315 Massachusetts Ave. NW, Washington, DC 20008, tel. 202/939–6200) or **Consulate General of Pakistan** (12 E. 65th St., New York, NY 10021, tel. 212/879–5800).

Canadians Contact **Embassy of Pakistan** (151 Slater St., Suite 608, Ottawa, Ont. K1P 5H3, tel. 613/238–7881) or **Consulate General of Pakistan** (3421 Peel St., Montreal, Que. H3A 1W7, tel. 514/845–2297; 4881 Younge St., Shepherd's Ctr., Suite 810, Toronto, Ont. M2N 5X3, tel. 416/250–1255).

Britons Contact **Embassy of Pakistan** (35/36 Lowndes Sq., London, SW1X 9JN, tel. 01/235–2044).

Travel Permits

Permits are required for travel to certain areas of NWFP: Darra-Adam Khel and the Khyber Pass near Peshawar, Garam Chasma (hot springs), and the Kafir-Kalash villages near Chitral. Permits are either free or available at nominal charge. They take about two days to process and can be acquired on arrival.

Customs and Duties

On Arrival Don't bring liquor or illegal drugs into Pakistan. The following items are permitted: a watch, a travel clock, two still cameras, a movie camera, a pair of binoculars, 200 cigarettes or a half pound of tobacco, a portable radio or cassette player, a typewriter, sporting equipment (including camping gear) for personal use, and gifts and souvenirs not exceeding $50 in value.

On Departure Antiques (over 100 years old) are not allowed out of the country. No other purchase restrictions apply.

Time Zone

Pakistan standard time is five hours ahead of Greenwich mean time and nine hours ahead of the U.S. eastern standard time.

Staying Healthy

See Before You Go to the Himalayas, Chapter 1. You need a yellow-fever vaccination if you arrive from yellow-fever-infected areas and, at press time, a cholera vaccination if you arrive from India. No other innoculations are required.

Renting Car or Jeep with Driver

Though self-drive cars and jeeps are available, travelers are advised to hire a car or jeep with driver from our recommended agencies. Roads are unpredictable; signs are not in English. Don't hire a tourist taxi or car with driver from unapproved or unlicensed operators.

Arriving and Departing

To reach Lahore, the gateway to the north, fly in from Karachi or Delhi. (*See* Arriving and Departing North India, Chapter 5, if you're coming via Delhi; via Karachi, *see* below.)

From North America by Plane

Airports and Airlines **Pan American** (tel. 800/221–1111) and **Pakistan International Airlines (PIA)** (tel. 212/370–9157) offer direct flights from New York to Karachi International Airport. Most other international carriers have flights that require a change of planes in Europe or the Middle East.

Flying Time Plan on about 18 hours flying time from New York to Karachi, not including stops.

Discount Flights *See* Before You Go to the Himalayas, Chapter 1. Check with **PIA** for package tours.

From the U.K. by Plane

Airports and Airlines **British Airways, Philippine Airlines,** and **PIA** offer direct flights from London to Karachi. Other international carriers have flights that require a change of planes in Europe or the Middle East.

Flying Time Plan on eight hours flying time to Karachi from the United Kingdom.

Discount Flights *See* Before You Go to the Himalayas, Chapter 1. Check with **PIA** for package tours.

Staying in North Pakistan

Behavioral Dos and Don'ts

Never put a book about Pakistan on the floor or ground; it's considered a sacrilege. *See* also the Behavioral Dos and Don'ts in Staying in the Himalayas, Chapter 1.

Getting Around

By Plane **PIA,** your only choice of airline in Pakistan, covers the following destinations: Karachi, Lahore, Peshawar, Islamabad, Gilgit, Chitral, Skardu, and Saidu Sharif. Get your tickets in advance, preferably when you purchase your initial international-travel ticket to the subcontinent. Reconfirm each ticket at least 72 hours before departure, and arrive at the airport an hour before your flight.

Weather can affect flights into remote regions. Scheduled flights to and from the extreme north frequently run late; some even get canceled. Never schedule back-to-back flights; plan for unexpected delays. If your schedule is tight, fly into a dependable destination like Peshawar or Islamabad, then proceed by car or jeep, the best way to see Pakistan.

By Car or Jeep with Driver Some of the best destinations are approachable only by jeep or on foot. Use a recommended travel agency and make all arrangements before you depart (*see* What It Will Cost, above).

By Train Few tracks run through the mountains. You can go by train from Lahore to Peshawar; Murree (via Rawalpindi); and Dir, Chitral, Swat, and Kaghan (via the Jungshahi station). Foreign tourists are allowed a 25% discount for non-air-conditioned classes; apply through the Office of Chief Marketing Manager of Pakistan Railways at the Headquarters Office in Lahore, Rawalpindi, or Peshawar. Bring your passport. If you want an air-conditioned seat (recommended), ask a recommended tour operator to get your ticket or go to the reservation counter at a railway station. Once you have your ticket, your seat is guaranteed.

Telephones

Local and International Calls Most major cities provide direct-dial facilities for local and international calls. In cities without international direct dialing, the call will be booked for you. If you call from your hotel, the cost will include a service charge. Except in Western-style hotels that accept credit cards, expect to pay for all phone calls in local currency.

Operators and Information In the major cities, dial 17 for assistance or information; speak slowly. In other areas, ask a Pakistani to assist you.

Telegrams and Telex Telegrams and telex messages can be sent from local post or telegraph offices in reasonably large cities.

Mail

Receiving Mail For the traveler on the move, the easiest way to receive mail in Pakistan is through a local branch office of **American Express** (in Peshawar and Lahore). Mail is held for 30 days before it's returned to the sender. It can also be forwarded for a nominal fee. It's a free service if you have an American Express credit card or traveler's checks; otherwise, there's a small charge.

Postal Rates The cost of an airmail letter (weighing 10 grams) to Great Britain, Europe, Canada, and the United States is Rs. 7.50; aerograms cost Rs. 5.

Tipping

See Tipping in Staying in North India, Chapter 5.

Opening and Closing Times

Pakistan has numerous government holidays, when the commercial world shuts down. Obtain relevant dates from government tourist offices or your travel agent. Hours of various establishments are listed. Most businesses are closed Friday, the holy day.

Shopping

Pakistan has great bazaars selling gold and silver jewelry, precious and semiprecious stones, brasswork, clothes, and handicrafts. Though the price of gold by weight is what you'd pay almost anywhere else, the cost of the labor is remarkably low. Silverwork may not be 100% silver; ask when you negotiate the price. In the bazaars and in many shops, bargain.

Dining

Except for a couple of hotels in Lahore, alcohol may be consumed only in your room. Tuesday and Wednesday are meatless days—no red meat, only fish and chicken. The cuisine of Pakistan varies from region to region, so specialties are noted in each destination section.

Mealtimes In Lahore and Peshawar, restaurants usually stay open until 11 PM or midnight. In remote areas, expect an early dinner unless you're staying in a Western-style hotel.

Precautions *See* Staying Healthy in Before You Go to the Himalayas, Chapter 1.

Ratings Highly recommended restaurants are indicated by a star ★.

Category	Cost*
Very Expensive	(over $15)
Expensive	($10–$15)
Moderate	($5–$10)
Inexpensive	(under $5)

per person, including taxes and excluding drinks and service charges

Lodging

The tourist infrastructure is just developing in Pakistan. In Lahore, you'll find a wide range of accommodations. In some destinations, you won't have much choice. In Western-style hotels, rupees are accepted only if you have an official slip proving you've changed foreign currency or traveler's checks with an authorized money changer; otherwise foreign nationals must pay their hotel bills with foreign currency, traveler's checks, or credit cards.

Western-style Hotels When it comes to amenities, Western-style hotels are top-of-the-line. They are most costly; most accept credit cards and traveler's checks.

The **Pearl-Continental Hotel Chain,** with hotels in Karachi, Lahore, Rawalpindi, and Peshawar, has reservation offices overseas as well as within Pakistan. Call Utell International (in the U.S., tel. 800/448–8355; in Vancouver, tel. 800/663–9582; in Toronto, tel. 800/268–7227; in Quebec, tel. 800/268–7041; in London, tel. 01/741–1588).

Pakistani-style Hotels A Pakistani-style hotel is less fancy and less costly. The bathroom is often not Western-style. Many of these hotels offer amenities, but very few accept credit cards. Some take traveler's checks; all take rupees.

Government Lodging PTDC provides inexpensive accommodations, often called rest houses or motels, throughout northern Pakistan. Various government departments of Pakistan also have simple lodgings. The quality varies. Some rooms are fine, others are shabby and provide a dreary ambience, and some are rustic and wonderful —just bring a sleeping bag. Except in Peshawar and Lahore, the rooms are very inexpensive (under $10).

Camping Camping is possible throughout most of northern Pakistan.

Ratings Highly recommended hotels are indicated by a star ★ .

Category	Cost*
Very Expensive	(over $100)
Expensive	($60–$100)
Moderate	($25–$60)
Inexpensive	(under $25)

Prices are for a standard double room, including taxes and excluding service charges.

Credit Cards

Western-style hotels, travel agencies, and fixed-price shops usually accept American Express, Diners Club, MasterCard, and Visa credit cards.

Lahore

Lahore reached its zenith under the rule of the Moghul Emperor Akbar, who made the city his capital in 1584. When the British arrived in 1849 in this city on the Ravi River, they added handsome Victorian structures to the skyline. Today, Lahore's title belongs to Islamabad, the new capital of Pakistan, and the Moghul's Koh-i-Noor diamond is now on display in England. Well-preserved monuments that rival the Taj Mahal and the Agra Fort in India remind us of that heyday.

Addresses and Numbers

Tourist Information Pakistan Tourism Development Corporation (PTDC) has a 24-hour counter at the Lahore Airport International Arrivals Lounge and an office at Faletti's Hotel (Egerton Rd., tel. 303660) that's open summer, Saturday–Thursday 7:30–2; winter, Saturday–Thursday 9–4.

Emergencies For medical assistance, ask your hotel or the Tourist Department to recommend a physician who is connected to a good private clinic. The embassies are in Islamabad: **American** (Diplomatic Enclave, Ramna 5, tel. 92518261), **Canada** (Diplomatic Enclave, Sector G-5, tel. 92821101), **British** (Diplomatic Enclave, Ramna 5, tel. 92822131).

Bookstores The best English-language bookstore is **Feroze Sons** (60 The Mall), open Saturday–Thursday 10–6. Other bookstores are nearby.

Travel Agencies For travel assistance or a car or jeep with driver, contact **Indus Guides** (7-E Egerton Rd., tel. 304190), **Travel Walji's** (122-A, Tufail Rd., Lahore Cantonment, tel. 374429), **Pakistan Tours,** a division of **PTDC** (*see* above), **American Express** (1121 Rafi Mansion, Box 249, Shahrah-E-Quaid-E-Azam, tel. 312435), or **Thomas Cook** (5 Egerton Rd., tel. 306208). These companies are open Saturday–Thursday 9–5.

Banks Contact **American Express** (*see* above), **Habib Bank** and the **National Bank of Pakistan,** which are on Shahrah-E-Quaid-E-Azam. Banks are open Monday–Thursday 9–1, weekends 9–noon.

Post Offices The **General Post and Telegraph Office** (Shahrah-E-Quaid-E-Azam) is open Saturday–Thursday 9–4.

Arriving and Departing by Plane

Airport and Airlines All international and domestic flights arrive and depart from the **Lahore Airport.** From Lahore, **PIA** makes two daily flights to Peshawar in NWFP and five weekly flights to Saidu Sharif, also in NWFP. PIA flies daily to Gilgit in FANA and makes two daily flights to Skardu, also in FANA. PIA makes six daily flights to Islamabad, the approach to Murree, the Karakoram Highway, and Kaghan Valley. Get your tickets in advance, preferably when you purchase your ticket to the subcontinent. Reconfirm each ticket at least 72 hours before departure and arrive at the airport an hour before your flight. The PIA booking office is in the Shahdin Building (Shahrah-E-Quaid-E-Azam, tel. 306411; flight information, tel. 370061).

Between Airport and City The airport is 8 kilometers (5 miles) from the center of Lahore. A taxi from the airport costs about Rs. 40; you must bargain. (*See* Lodging, below, for hotels offering free pickup service.)

Arriving and Departing by Hired Car or Jeep with Driver

If you plan to visit NWFP, fly from Lahore to Peshawar. Don't waste time driving. If you plan to make the journey up the Karakoram Highway or visit Murree or Kaghan Valley, fly into

Islamabad and proceed by car or jeep, depending on your destination. (*See* What It Will Cost, above, for costs.)

Arriving and Departing by Train and Bus

By Train From **Lahore Railway Station** (tel. 320271 or 325445), you can go by train to Murree (via Rawalpindi) or to Peshawar. The trip to Rawalpindi takes about six hours; to Peshawar, about nine hours. (*See* Getting Around in Staying in North Pakistan, above, for foreign-tourist discounts and procedures for purchasing an air-conditioned seat—recommended.)

Getting Around

By Taxi Taxis cost about Rs. 3 per kilometer.

By Auto or Bicycle Rickshaw Auto rickshaws are the best way to travel. Figure Rs. 2 per kilometer. A bicycle rickshaw should cost Rs. 1 per kilometer.

Guided Tours

PTDC offers tours of Lahore (*see* Tourist Information under Important Addresses and Numbers, above).

Private Guides For an excellent guide, contact **Indus Guides** or **Travel Walji's** (*see* Travel Agencies under Important Addresses and Numbers, above).

Exploring Lahore

Don't miss seeing the **Lahore Fort,** inside a crumbling brick rampart on the edge of the old city. After you pass through the Alamgari Gate, built by the Moghul Emperor Aurangzeb in 1673, you enter a wide thoroughfare that leads to the **Royal Gate,** built in 1631 by Shah Jahan, and the **Elephant Gate,** with steps designed to accommodate an elephant's feet. Here, concubines used to stand on the balconies and shower the royal family with flowers.

Leave the Royal Gates and see the rest of the fort in chronological order. Start at the large **water tank,** constructed by Akbar in the 16th century. Nearby is the spacious **Char Bagh,** a Persian garden (*bagh*) divided into four (*char*) quadrants. Head south to the snack center in front of what was the main gate. When commoners petitioned the emperor, they had to climb broad steps and walk a considerable distance—a humbling experience. It was a serious offense to look at the ruler, who sat on his balcony in the **Diwan-i-Am** (Hall of Public Offices).

The red sandstone and white marble Diwan-i-Am was built by Akbar in the 1630s. Its architecture, which draws on Hindu motifs and design, reflects his religious tolerance. Here, Akbar would dress as a Hindu Brahman and perform Chroca Darshan (Balcony Appearance), blessing his subjects. Note the pillars in the hall. Dragged by camels and elephants 400 miles from Rajasthan in India, their design is Hindu, not Moslem. In the interior rooms, where Akbar relaxed, you see remnants of intricately painted ceilings and delicate mirror-inlaid ornamentation. Near the **Delhi Gate,** to the east, is Akbar's personal palace.

Next, proceed to **Jahangir's quadrangle,** built in the early 1600s. Jahangir, the son of Akbar, loved the fort and spent most of his time here. His red sandstone palaces and private chambers surround an opulently decorated water tank.

Shah Jahan, who came to power in 1627, built the most beautiful quadrangle, dominated by marble. Inside his summer sleeping chamber, fountains cooled the air and, treated with an aromatic plant, added fragrance.

Shah Jahan's winter sleeping chamber has fireplaces built into each wall, and the room was designed without cross-ventilation.

Shah Jahan designed his wife's **Shish Mahal** (Palace of Mirrors) with hundreds of mirrors that flickered like stars on the ceiling when oil lamps were lit. Across from the Shish Mahal is **Nau Lakha** pavilion. Originally, its surface was inlaid with precious and semiprecious stones, removed by the Sikhs when they ruled Lahore.

During the 19th-century civil wars, the complex was severely damaged. The British then used it for barracks, a dispensary, and a chapel; Jahangir's beautiful water tank served as a tennis court. *Lahore Fort complex. Admission: Rs. 2. Open sunrise–sunset. No on-site guides; a guidebook is available at the entrance. Museum admission free. Museum open daily 9–12:30 and 2:30–6.*

After you leave the fort, visit the **Badshahi Mosque,** the world's largest Moslem shrine, constructed by Aurangzeb in 1674. Notice the Tree of Life carved on either side of the entrance and the lotus, a symbol of purity, on the ceiling. Graceful minarets in each corner of the courtyard offer a good view of Lahore. Three marble domes draw your eyes to the inner sanctuary.

Near the mosque is the tomb of Pakistan's spiritual father and poet, Allama Iqbal, who died in 1938. *Non-Moslems are allowed inside; remove your shoes. Attend a call to prayer, usually 5 AM, 2 PM, 4:30 PM, sunset, and 9:30 PM.*

From the mosque, walk into the **old city,** where many buildings are over 300 years old. Faded wood facades with intricately carved verandas and open balconies hang over narrow streets. Alleys twist off in all directions, plied by tonga carts squeezing through the skinny thoroughfares, clomping past stalls. People lumber by with enormous loads of merchandise balanced on their heads.

Search for the following destinations: **Kinari Bazaar** is the street of gold and silver embroidery where glittering bridal shawls hang in windows. Kinari Bazaar leads to **Soha Bazaar** (look for a yellow tile wall). Buy plastic and glass bangles or walk up the enclosed walkway and splurge on 22-karet-gold jewelry.

From Soha, return to Kinari, cross the street and, after walking through a brass, copper, and tin market, look for the **Kasera Bazaar** (secondhand metalware market) with stacks of enormous copper-and tin-plated pots and old household treasures at bargain prices.

Art lovers should head for **Fakir Khana Museum** on Hakiman Bazaar just inside the Bhati Gate. Located inside an exquisite old *haveli* (palace), this is Lahore's best museum. Numerous tiny rooms hold treasures: the exquisite collections of three ministers who served Sikh rulers, including hundreds of miniatures. Ask to be told the story of a miniature related to an artist's self-portrait. Also look for a "pin prick" painting, which can't be seen until it is held up to light. The museum also has the world's smallest Buddha, eggshell teacups, and 1,000 rare handwritten manuscripts. *Tel. 324771. Admission free. Hours by appointment. Closed Sat.*

Hidden in another tangle of alleys near the Delhi Gate Bazaar is the **Wazir Khan Mosque,** built in 1634, and the only mosque in Pakistan that is completely Persian-style, with an exterior covered with mosaics. Inside the mosque, you'll notice an ornately carved wood pulpit, a gift of Lord Curzon, one of the British viceroys. Every inch of the interior is painted with tiny flowers and verses from the Quran. *Mosque open sunrise–sunset.*

Outside the mosque on the far side of the courtyard, a row of shops sells clusters of chains with curved blades (razor sharp) attached to each loose end. Shiites buy these for self-flagellation on Ashura (Muharram). *Shops in these bazaars are open 9 AM–7 PM; closed Fri.*

Dining

Lahore has numerous good restaurants, some with great ambience. Dress is casual. The best restaurants follow. Prices are per person, including taxes and excluding drinks and service charges.

Menage. This Western-style restaurant has high-tech decor, low lighting, and intimate rooms. You can eat Chinese, Pakistani, and Continental cuisines à la carte or enjoy an excellent buffet. Try *karahi* (chicken cooked in a clay pot with tomatoes and chilies) or *Thai goong* (fried shrimp in spicy oyster sauce). *75 D-1, Main Blvd., Gulberg III (in Liberty Market), tel. 870411. Reservations necessary. No credit cards. Open daily 1–3, 7:30–11. Moderate ($5–$10).*

Tabaq. This large modern restaurant with subdued lighting has excellent Pakistani food (buffet available at lunch). Try mutton stew with ginger and garlic, roast marinated chicken, or steamed marinated leg of mutton. *2/K, Main Blvd., Gulberg II, tel. 872136. Reservations advised. AE, V, MC. Open noon–3, 6–11. Moderate ($5–$10).*

Tai Wah. This extremely popular Chinese restaurant has a low-key oriental-style decor. The best dishes are chicken Manchurian (sweet and sour), fried beef with green chili sauce, and duck stuffed with chicken and shrimp. *78-E 1, Gulberg III, tel. 873915. Reservations advised. No credit cards. Open noon–3, 6:30–11. Closed Chinese New Year. Moderate ($5–$10).*

Abbott Road. Have a two-course meal on this street with fabulous roadside stalls. You're in the right area when you hear the sound of "tik-tik," created by cooks pounding meat. Start at **Nishat Restaurant** which has a few tables out front. Choose from beef or goat kidneys, testicles, heart, and brains and marinated ribs, chicken legs, and breasts and watch as your selection is pounded until it's tender and then cooked with onion and spices. It's served with hot *roti* (bread) and rice. Then walk down toward Egerton Road to **Sheesh Mahal,** in front of a tall minaret with glowing green windows. Have Kashmiri tea and *firni* (rice dessert made with rose water and milk) served in a small clay bowl. *Abbott Rd. (near the old cinemas and Mc-Leod Rd.). No credit cards. The best time to go is in the evening. Inexpensive (under $5).*

Lodging

Lahore has a good range of hotels to satisfy all budgets. The best follow. Prices are for a standard double room, including taxes and excluding service charges.

Pearl Continental. This modern high rise has lovely rooms done up in pastels. The best rooms overlook the pool. *The Mall, Lahore, tel. 69931. 200 rooms with bath. Facilities: restaurant, coffee shop, evening barbeque, poolside snack bar, room service, air-conditioning, TV, pool, tennis courts, travel and foreign-exchange counter, car rental, shopping arcade. AE, MC, V. Very Expensive (over $100).*

Hilton International. This Western-style high rise has clean, simply decorated rooms with small balconies. April–September discounts are offered. *87, The Mall, tel. 69971. 190 rooms with bath. Facilities: restaurant, room service, coffee shop, barbecue, pastry shop, TV, air-conditioning, health center, pool, travel and foreign-exchange counter, shopping arcade, courtesy airport pickup. AE, DC, MC, V. Expensive ($60–$100).*

Faletti's Hotel. The best rooms in this old British bungalow are in the old wing with a veranda overlooking the lawn. The decor is PTDC-institutional, but the rooms are clean and spacious. *Egerton Rd., tel. 303660. 66 rooms with bath. Facilities: restaurant, room service, travel and foreign-exchange counter, shops, post office. AE. Moderate ($25–$60).*

Murree and Nathiagali

When the British ruled the Punjab, from the mid-18th century until Independence, the summer heat drove them north to cool villages, called *gallies*, in the Lower Himalayas. Their favorite village was Murree, 60 kilometers (37 miles) north of Rawalpindi. Murree quickly became the premier hill station of the subcontinent and the summer government headquarters. Today, Murree is such a popular destination with domestic tourists that travelers searching for undisturbed tranquility should head to Nathiagali, an idyllic retreat 32 kilometers (20 miles) north of Murree.

Addresses and Numbers

Tourist Information For travel assistance or tourist information, visit Cecil's Hotel, run by the **Pakistan Tourism Development Corporation (PTDC)**, tel. 2247.

Emergencies The nearest embassies are in Islamabad: **American** (Diplomatic Enclave, Ramna 5, tel. 92518261), **Canadian** (Diplomatic Enclave, Section G-5, tel. 92821101), **British** (Diplomatic Enclave, Ramna 5, tel. 92822131). For medical assistance, ask your hotel or the tourist department to recommend a physician who is connected to a good private clinic.

Banks and Banks are open Monday–Thursday 9–1, weekends, 9–noon;
Post Office the Post Office is open Saturday–Thursday 9–4. Both are located on Jinnah (The Mall).

Arriving and Departing

By Plane **PIA** makes six daily hour-long flights from Lahore to **Islama-**
Airport and Airline **bad.** Reconfirm your flight 72 hours before departure (in
Lahore, tel. 306411, and in Islamabad, tel. 25091). Murree is
about a 60-kilometer (37-mile) drive north of Islamabad.

Between Airport From Islamabad, you can drive up to Murree in under three
and City hours. If you're planning to visit just the gallies, you don't need
a jeep; roads are good. But for trips farther north, a jeep is a
must. Hire a car or jeep from a recommended tour operator
listed in the Lahore section, above.

Outdoor Adventures

Fishing: *Nathiagali.* Fish for trout on the Haro River.

Horseback Riding: *Nathiagali.* Ride for hours on beautiful
trails.

Dining and Lodging

The best choice is listed below. The restaurant price is per person, including taxes and excluding drinks and service charges.
The lodging price is for a standard double room, including taxes
and excluding service charges.

Cecil's Hotel. Run by the PTDC, this two-story bungalow, the
oldest British-built residence, has a sweeping upper veranda,
lovely lawns, and great views. Simple spacious rooms have lin-
gering Victorian details. The large restaurant serves decent
Pakistani and Continental food. *Mount View Rd., Murree, tel.
2247. 42 rooms with bath. Facilities: room service; inexpensive
(under $5) restaurant, open 7–9, 12:30–2, 7:30–9:30; coffee
shop; travel and foreign-exchange counter; car rental; tennis
court. AE. Moderate ($25–$60).*

On to Nathiagali

A winding road north of Murree leads to Nathiagali, 32 kilometers (20 miles) away. At about 30 kilometers (19 miles), you
pass a string of stalls. A signpost on the right near a dirt road
advertizes **Hotel Pines (Shadman).** *Shadman* means happy, an
appropriate choice for one of the nicest lodges in north Pakistan. If you can't spend the night, stop and have lunch.

Hotel Pines, on an isolated mountain spur, was built by the
British in 1922. The Victorian bungalow has an extended veranda bordered by cottages, all delightfully painted and facing
an inviting lawn and garden with a stunning Himalayan vista.
The rooms are rustic and clean. The food, a fixed menu of Pakistani or Continental dishes, is excellent. Breakfast is included
in the room rate. The management is wonderful. You can fish or
swim in the nearby Haro River, go horseback riding, or just relax in the splendid surroundings. There's an off-season
discount from November to June. *Nathiagali, tel. 505. 25
rooms with bath (shower, hot water by bucket). Facilities: inexpensive restaurant. No credit cards. Inexpensive (under $25).*

From Nathiagali, travelers can proceed north to Kaghan Valley or the Karakoram Highway (*see* Karakoram Highway, Part I, below).

Karakoram Highway, 1

Mansehra, north of Murree, sits on the old Silk Route, the treacherous path that once carried traders from Central Asia, across the subcontinent, to China. Today, a new road has replaced the dirt track. This chapter will take you along this road with Gujjar nomads on their semiannual migration to or from the southern plains to the Kaghan Valley and will then send you north with buses and carloads of tourists on the Karakoram Highway.

The Moslem Gujjar lived in Gujarat, now a state in India, until Afghans invaded in the 10th century and forced them to flee north, where they adopted a nomadic existence. An individual's appearance reveals his or her status. If a woman's hair is parted in the middle, she's married; along the side, she's single. A girl under age 10 wears bangs, and female babies wear fancy embroidered caps. Married Gujjar women wear heavy silver ornaments; all the women and girls wear elaborate glass-bead necklaces called *motia*. Men wear large turbans and long robes and streak henna on their hair, beards, hands, and feet, believing it has a medicinal property. You also see henna adorning the livestock.

Gujjars are proud, private people. Don't photograph women, girls, or babies; ask before you photograph anyone else.

Addresses and Numbers

There are few tourist facilities in this remote area. For information or travel agents, consult the Important Address and Numbers in large towns in Federally Administered Northern Areas or North West Frontier Province (*see* below). The nearest embassies are in Islamabad: **American** (Diplomatic Enclave, Ramna 5, tel. 92518261), **Canadian** (Diplomatic Enclave, Sector G-5, tel. 92821101), **British** (Diplomatic Enclave, Ramna 5, tel. 92822131).

Arriving and Departing by Plane

Travelers who plan to visit Kaghan Valley or travel up the Karakoram Highway should fly from Lahore to Islamabad, then proceed by car or jeep, depending on the destination.

Airports and Airlines From Lahore, **PIA** makes six daily flights to **Islamabad Airport.** From there, it's a 146-kilometer (91-mile) drive to Mansehra, the approach to the Karakoram Highway, and a 194-kilometer (120-mile) drive to Balakot, the gateway to Kaghan Valley.

Between Airport and Destination Hire a car or jeep with driver in Islamabad from a recommended travel agency. If you plan to travel to the Kaghan Valley, you need a jeep. The trip from Mansehra to the Karakoram Highway can be made by car, but a jeep is required if you plan to do side trips.

Highlights for First-time Visitors

Musts in this region include a visit to Naran village in Kaghan Valley, with its government-run safari-style tents and cottages nestled by a river; the road journey up the Karakoram Highway; and the horseback riding adventures (*see* Outdoor Adventures, below).

Getting Around

By Hired Car or (*See* Before You Go to North Pakistan, above, for approximate
Jeep with Driver jeep and car rental costs.)

Guided Tours

Pakistan Tours offers fishing trips and treks in Kaghan Valley. **Indus Guides** and **Travel Walji's** sponsor numerous high-quality trips, with excellent guides. Arrange in advance. (*See* Before You Go to North Pakistan, above.)

Outdoor Adventures

Highly recommended adventures are indicated by a star ★.

★ **Fishing:** *Kaghan Valley:* In Naran, you can fish for trout along the Kunhar River from May to October. Permits are necessary; details are listed in each destination section. Bring your own gear. The tour operators listed in Before You Go to North Pakistan, above, also arrange fishing excursions in Kaghan Valley.

★ **Horseback Riding** *Kaghan Valley:* Ponies are available in Naran. *Balakot to FANA:* From Balakot in the Kaghan Valley, you ride four days to Naran. After a day's rest, you ride four days to the Babusar Pass (near Chilas on the Karakoram Highway) and on into FANA. Contact Indus Guides or Travel Walji's (*see* Before You Go, above). Make arrangements before you depart.

Trekking (up to a week): *Darrel Valley to Gupis:* The one-week trek, made June to November from Darrel Valley near Chilas to Gupis in Gilgit, is a moderately easy walk commencing in the pine groves of the Pathan village of Tangir. From here, you walk through forests, follow clear streams, head across vivid flower-strewn meadows, pass through shepherd villages, and head north with the great Karakorams rarely out of sight. You spot bears, tigers, and wild sheep. To arrange this trek, rarely made by foreigners, contact Indus Guides or Travel Walji's (*see* Before You Go, above).

Trekking (over a week): *Kaghan Valley to Chilas in FANA:* A moderate eight-day trek through the Himalayas from Naran in the Kaghan Valley, home of the Gujjar nomads, takes you through remote mountain villages, past grazing livestock, into the foothills of the Karakorams. From here, you climb to the Babusar Pass, at 4,065 meters (13,333 feet) with sweeping views of the mountains, and descend into Chilas in FANA.

Dining and Lodging

Eateries and lodgings are suggested for the stops along your route. Dining prices are per person, including taxes and excluding drinks and service charges. Lodging prices are for a standard double room, cottage, or tent, including taxes and excluding service charges.

Excursion through Mansehra to Kaghan Valley

Numbers in the margin correspond with points of interest on the Karakoram Highway map.

❶ Today, **Mansehra**'s nothing more than a transit stop, with a good bazaar to pick up food for trekking or camping and a bank to change money, open Monday–Thursday 9–1, weekdays 9–noon. (There are no banks at Naran village in Kaghan Valley.)

On to Naran

❷ From here, take the Naran Road (Kashmir Road) to **Balakot,** the gateway to the Kaghan Valley, 49 kilometers (31 miles) from Mansehra and another transit town. Camels and donkeys amble around; Afghan refugee camps line the banks of the Kunhar River. If you arrive late in the day, stay the night; after Balakot, the road turns extremely rough.

PTDC Motel. *Reservations: PTDC, Flashman's Hotel, The Mall, Rawalpindi, tel. 66231 or 581480, or in Balakot, tel. 8. 5 rooms with bath (shower). Facilities: plain clean rooms, tourist office, jeep rental, inexpensive restaurant. No credit cards. Inexpensive (under $25).*

Hotel Park. *Tel. 23. 18 rooms with bath. Facilities: clean rooms, room service, inexpensive restaurant, terrace, near the river. No credit cards. Inexpensive (under $25).*

Once you cross the Kunhar River, follow part of the old Silk Route into Kaghan Valley, where waterfalls plunge down low mountains to the river. You pass the Gujjar, with their caravans of donkeys, cows, buffalo, sheep, goats, and dogs. Women carry large metal pots and bags of grain on their heads and babies or chickens in their arms. Men in bright turbans or caps drape lambs, calves, or toddlers across their shoulders or carry vast bundles on their backs. Tiny children with lambs tied onto their laps are, in turn, strapped to the backs of ponies. Chickens sit like kings on stacks of blankets on the backs of donkeys. Some Gujjar amble along with carved walking sticks used to keep their livestock in line. Others carry open black umbrellas to shield them from the strong sun.

You pass through **Kewai,** 19 kilometers (12 miles) from Balakot, a prosperous Syed village. The Syeds, originally from Mecca, claim descendancy from Hussain or Hassan, Mohammed's grandsons. Though they have intermixed with other tribes, they still consider themselves the most sacred of the Islamic people and are accorded tremendous respect.

About 27 kilometers (17 miles) after Balakot, you pass through **Paros,** with tea stalls along the road and groves of walnut trees. Shimmering in the distance, you see the snow-covered Mt. Malka Parbat (Queen Mountain). Massive rock-faced mountains and pine forests descend to the river. Trees bend across the road. Boulders, blasted apart, hang over your jeep. Melting glaciers shoot water across the road, now rutted, with many sharp turns. Packs of goats, buffalo, and donkeys crowd the road. This is tricky, slow driving.

258

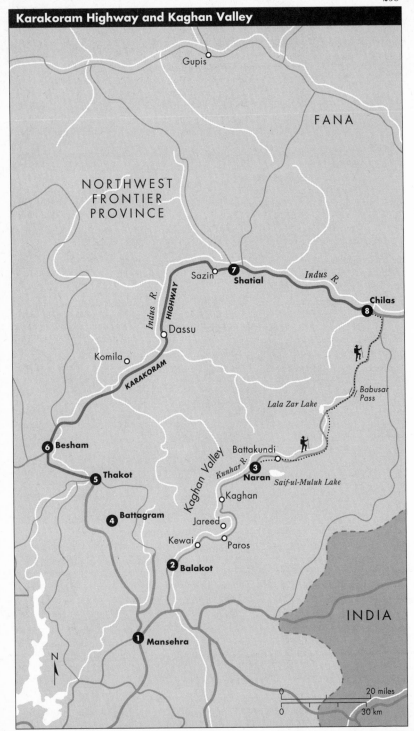

Karakoram Highway and Kaghan Valley

Gupis

FANA

NORTHWEST
FRONTIER
PROVINCE

Indus R.

Sazin 7 **Shatial**

Dassu

Komila

8 Chilas

Babusar
Pass

Lala Zar Lake

KARAKORAM

6 **Besham**

5 **Thakot**

Battakundi

Kunhar R.

3 **Naran**

Saif-ul-Muluk Lake

Kaghan

4 **Battagram**

Jareed

Kewai   Paros

2 **Balakot**

INDIA

1 **Mansehra**

N

0   20 miles

0   30 km

Jareed, 40 kilometers (25 miles) from Balakot and a prosperous Swati village, has a roadside bazaar selling attractive walnut carvings: trays, walking sticks, intricate lamps, delicate boxes. From here, it's about 20 kilometers (12 miles) to **Kaghan village.** If the winter was hard and your trip is in June, the road is often buried under glacier ice or flooded. The trip can take up to three hours. In Kaghan, spend the night at **Lalazar Hotel.** *Kaghan, tel. 22. 24 rooms with bath (shower). Facilities: 4 attractive mountain-view rooms, good inexpensive restaurant (open 6 AM–10 PM). No credit cards. Inexpensive (under $25).*

Naran

From Kaghan village, the road climbs 25 kilometers (16 miles) into the Himalayas to **Naran.** Naran, the last significant town you will pass on your trip through Kaghan Valley, is an idyllic mountain village with a tiny bazaar. It's also the starting point for great outdoor adventures (*see* below).

Getting Around   Your feet or ponies are the best modes of travel.

Addresses and Numbers   For tourist information, emergencies, or arrangements for outdoor adventures, contact the manager of the **PTDC Motel.** There is no bank.

Outdoor Adventures   In Naran, **fish** for trout in the nearby river from May 15 to October 10. Licenses are available in Naran. Rent inexpensive equipment in the bazaar. **Horseback ride** (Rs. 100 per four hours) to Lake Saif-ul-Muluk 9 km (6 mi) or to Lala Zar Lake 56 km (35 mi).

Take a delightful 2-kilometer (1-mile) **walk** to Soach village. Follow the river at the base of the PTDC Campsites and head toward the Babusar Pass. You pass colorful Gujjar campsites, and after about 2 kilometers (1 mile), you come to a suspension bridge that leads to Soach, a Moghul and Swati village with homes nestled beneath snow-covered mountains and glaciers. This is a delightful place to picnic. Plan three hours.

From the Naran Bazaar, **walk** along a road up the mountain to the lovely village of Shabaig, 1½ kilometers (1 mile) away. Plan two hours for this walk. A footpath, 5 kilometers (3 miles) from Naran on the road to Balakot, leads into the mountains to the village of Batlan, set in pine groves in front of a glacier. Batlan is the home of Swatis and Moghuls who migrated here from Turkey in the 16th century.

Naran is also the place to have a great Pakistan **bus adventure.** Take a Rs. 4 ride to beautiful Nera Beki village; it's about 8 kilometers (5 miles) each way.

Naran is also the starting point for the seven-day **trek** over the Babusar Pass to Chilas (*see* Outdoor Adventures, above).

Dining and Lodging   The best place to eat and stay in Naran is listed below. **PTDC Motel and Campsites.** Ask to stay in a charming riverbank cottage or a secluded safari-style tent; both come with clean linen and bedding. The cottages (moderately priced) have a front porch and spacious rooms (some sleep four). The spacious tents (inexpensive) are delightful. *Reservations are a must: PTDC, Flashman's Hotel, The Mall, Rawalpindi, tel. 66231 or 58140. 50 rooms with bath and 29 tents with nearby bath (showers). Facilities: good inexpensive restaurant serving Continental breakfast and Pakistani lunch and dinner,* *travel assistance, lovely grounds. No credit cards. Inexpensive to Moderate (under $60).*

Excursion on the Karakoram Highway

The trip to the Karakoram Highway starts from Mansehra (*see* above) and heads 99 kilometers (61 miles) north to Thakot, the start of the famous new road.

On to Besham

4 After the town of **Battagram,** 70 kilometers (43 miles) from Mansehra, the road hugs the Nidyar River, which races through a wide valley and tiers of mountains—their lower halves covered with terraces and occasional dwellings.

5 At **Thakot,** 26 kilometers (16 miles) from Battagram, the Nidyar intersects with the grand Indus River. Here, in 327 BC, Alexander the Great defeated the Buddhist Udyanas, and here the Karakoram Highway officially begins. When Alexander captured this valley, he renamed it Sinthos, after the cotton clothes worn by the Udyanas. After 400 years, Sinthos turned into Sindo. By the 7th century, Arabs called the area Hindo and added *stan* (country). In the 18th century, the British altered the pronunciation to Indos, then Indus. Hence, the Indus River, the Indus civilization, and India (still called Hindustan by the Indians). Many Pakistani nationalists call their river the Sind, not the Indus.

The **Karakoram Highway,** 656 kilometers (412 miles) long, starts at the bridge that takes you across the Indus River: a cement structure with small Chinese-style lions on the end posts—a reminder that the construction of this road was a collaboration between the two bordering countries.

Started in 1958, the highway proceeded in stages: first a walking path, then a jeep-worthy dirt road that allowed them to transport light machinery to blast away the formidable stretch of rock. The final stage was the metal road on which you now travel.

Every day for 20 years, 5,000 people worked on the road under the aegis of the military. The actual cost of construction remains a secret. Even now, the expense continues, with extensive landslides, torrential glaciers, and the occasional earthquakes obliterating bridges and chunks of the road. The cost in human terms is also a matter of conjecture. The official number of deaths was 408, but some insist the number exceeded 1,000. Along the route, you see inscribed memorials where workers died. At the time of the road's inauguration in 1981, one of the principal engineers wept.

6 As you head up the highway to **Besham,** 132 kilometers (82 miles) away, the Indus River is a roiling gray mass racing through the Himalayas. Besham is a Pathan village (for a description of the Pathans, *see* NWFP, below) with a roadside bazaar where you can stock up on whatever provisions you need until you reach the next destination, Chilas, 209 kilometers (129 miles) away, just inside FANA, or Gilgit, 358 kilometers (222 miles) away (*see* FANA, below). The attractive new two-wing **PTDC Motel,** set by the Indus River, is a good first-night halt. *Reserve in advance: PTDC, Flashman's Hotel, The Mall,*

Rawalpindi, tel. 66231 or 581480. 17 rooms with bath (shower). Facilities: fans, inexpensive restaurant (open 6:30–8:30, 12:30–2:30, 7:30–9:30). No credit cards. Inexpensive (under $25).

On to Chilas

Besham marks the end of Swat Valley and the start of the Kohistan (Country of the Mountains) Valley, inhabited by Pathans and Kohistani Dards, who have distinctly Aryan features. The tribal Dards fought against the intrusion of the highway. Cut off from most of Pakistan, luxury for them meant a wristwatch, even a matchbox, and they took such objects from the bodies of the soldiers, laborers, or engineers who worked on the road. They also hoped a few deaths would put an end to the project.

Now, the Dards are somewhat pacified. They still love their matchboxes; wristwatches; and, above all, their guns, especially the Russian Kalashnikov, which they carry without a permit. They also love the road and tourists. Their bazaars flourish, and they've become the leading domestic supplier of wood.

At **Komila,** 80 kilometers (51 miles) from Besham, the mountains grow desolate, forbidding. You enter the Karakoram watershed, a 50-kilometer (31-mile) stretch of territory that separates the Himalayas from the Karakoram Range. Rugged mountains rise up on the far side of the river. Jagged rocks jut precariously over the road, their fault lines clearly visible. Haze hangs over the valley; distant waterfalls look like ribbons of white paint streaked on the rock. The road bends down to the water, rises up the mountain slope, and crosses streams and glacial torrents.

Sazin, about 60 kilometers (41 miles) from Komila, marks the entrance to the Karakoram (literally, Hard Brown Mountains) Range. Vast barren mountains are packed tight together, dark as lava. About 70 kilometers (43 miles) before Chilas, the river valley widens, exposing beaches of sand created by earthquakes and landslides.

The entire stretch is arid, receiving no more than three or four inches of rain a year. The air is dry, summer days are hot, and winters are extremely cold with heavy snowfall. Gusts of wind sweep down the Indus, blowing sand up the slopes and turning the glacier-filled crevices dusty brown.

On the far side of Shatial, a small village 10 kilometers (6 miles) from Sazin, you see a marker—Shatial Sites—at the point where the highway links up with the original Silk Route. The **➐ Shatial Sites,** a short walk from the road toward the Indus, are a group of boulders covered with white carvings left behind by Mahayana Buddhists who traveled to China from the 3rd to 8th centuries. The strong sun, combined with heavy annual snowfall, oxidized the rock, creating an ideal surface on which to carve. Along with the Standing Buddha and two depictions of stupas, you see Hindu iconography: a sexually graphic Shiva lingam next to a Hindu *swastika* (symbol of good luck and compassion).

Trekkers take note: **Darrel Valley** is just beyond the Shatial Sites. From here, you can make a one-week trek to Gupis in FANA (*see* Outdoor Adventures, above).

After Shatial, barren deep red and brown mountains close up, then occasionally break open to reveal a glimpse of the green Himalayas, hidden behind the Karakorams. Isolated boulders are so black they look charred. Here and there are hamlets with water channels that trap water from glaciers to create remarkably fertile terraces of wheat, fruit trees, and land vegetables. Fifteen kilometers (9 miles) from Chilas, Mt. Nanga Parbat, altitude 8,131 meters (26,660 feet), flies into view, with its sandy base and its crest often hidden in clouds.

Chilas   **Chilas** makes a good second-night halt. Stay in the Shangrila
8   Midway House Hotel, an attractive Western-style hotel with pine-paneled rooms. *Reservations: Shangrila Hotels & Resorts, 143-N Murree Rd., Rawalpindi, tel. 73006, or in Chilas, tel. 69. 100 rooms with bath. Facilities: coffee shop, restaurant serving good Pakistani and Continental food, gardens. AE. Moderate ($25–$60).*

About 3 kilometers (1½ miles) north of Chilas, you see a boulder carved with a depiction of Manjushri (Future Buddha). As you proceed north toward Gilgit, gigantic peaks rise in the distance —Mt. Hara Mosh and Mt. Rakaposhi. The Indus River forks, and you enter the Gilgit Agency, described in Federally Administered Northern Areas and Karakoram Highway, 2.

Federally Administered Northern Areas and Karakoram Highway, 2

The Federally Administered Northern Areas (FANA), which includes the territories of Gilgit and Baltistan in the extreme north of Pakistan, is one of the most beautiful destinations in the subcontinent. More than 100 peaks soar over 7,000 meters (22,960 feet). Sand dunes rise up in river basins. Emerald-green lakes catch the sun. Rivers thrash through wind-eroded gorges. Glaciers hang down crevices and spill for miles across fields.

Though the trekking is sublime and the mountaineering first-rate, just moving around in a jeep, the best way to get around, makes you feel like an explorer. You can travel up to China along the Karakoram Highway, the highest trade route in the world. You can bump and snake along the remarkable Skardu-Gilgit Road or the Punial Highway, where glacier-fed rivers may creep up to the jeep's bumper. You can fish for trout, search for wild animals, refresh yourself in hot springs and cold streams, and camp in mountaintop pastures filled with wild-flowers, grazing donkeys, and yak. You can watch fierce polo matches. You can even scoop up uncut garnets lying at the base of a mountain. And when you long for a few Western amenities, you can stay in a beautiful resort surrounded by breathtaking vistas.

Addresses and Numbers

Tourist   PTDC has offices in Gilgit and Skardu (*see* destination sections,
Information   below).

Federally Administered Northern Areas
(Numbers on map correspond to numbers in text)

AFGHANISTAN

CHINA

Khunjerab Pass **4**

Khunjerab R.

Sost

Passu Glacier

Batura Glacier

Batura Peak ▲

Passu

Shimshal R.

Phandar

Gulmith

Gulking Glacier

Shimshal

HUNZA VALLEY

Karimabad **2**

Hunza R.

Nilt

Murtaza Abad

3 Nagar

Hopar Glacier

Hispar Glacier

Mt. Rakaposhi ▲

Jaglot Springs

Gula Pur

Gilgit R.

Gilgit **1**

PUNIAL VALLEY

Sherqila

Bar

Naltar

Naltar Lake

10

PUNIAL HWY.

Singal

Gakuch

Gupis

GUPIS VALLEY

Phandar Lake **11**

Tero

12

Shandur Lake

Shandur Pass

GILGIT AGENCY

NORTH WEST FRONTIER PROVINCE

Indus R.

Dassu

KARAKORAM HIGHWAY

Mt. Nanga Parbat ▲

Astor R.

Astor

Mt. Haramosh ▲

SKARDU-GILGIT RD.

Indus R.

Baicha **5**

Kachura Lake

Skardu **6**

Shigar

Dassu

Biafo Glacier

Astole

BALTISTAN AGENCY

Lake Satpura

Gol

Kuru

Keris

Shyok R.

Khaplu **9**

Machulu **7**

Thalle La Pass

Hushe Khane

Hushe

8 Hushe

K6 ▲

K7 ▲

Siachin Glacier

Mt. Masherbrum ▲

Saltoro R.

Kondus Glacier

Baltoro Glacier

Concordia

K2 ▲

Broad Peak ▲

Mt. Gasherbrum ▲

Hidden Peak ▲

N

50 miles

75 km

Emergencies For medical emergencies, contact a hotel physician or turn to your guide. The nearest embassies are in Islamabad: **American** (Diplomatic Enclave, Ramna 5, tel. 92518261), **Canadian** (Diplomatic Enclave, Sector G-5, tel. 92821101), **British** (Diplomatic Enclave, Ramna 5, tel. 92822131).

Travel Agencies **Indus Guides** has an office in Karimabad. **Travel Walji's** has an office in Gilgit (*see* destination sections, below).

Highlights for First-time Visitors

The best trip in FANA is the grand tour from Mansehra (*see* Karakoram Highway, Part I, above) following the journey laid out below. This is an epic trip: You travel the Karakoram Highway (go at least to Karimabad, the capital of Hunza Valley), then proceed to Skardu from Gilgit via the Skardu-Gilgit Road; finally, you tackle the rugged Punial Highway from Gilgit to Chitral in NWFP. Without any extensive stops or long outdoor adventures, this trip requires a minimum of two weeks.

If you have more time or want to get off the road, you can combine a jeep safari with a great trek in the alpine Nanga Parbat Fairy Meadows below the moody Mt. Nanga Parbat, with walks through peaceful villages backed by an erosion-pitted landscape. Or you can take five days and go off on a yak or pony or travel down on a river in a kayak or raft. If you want rugged adventure, you can embark on one of the best treks in the subcontinent—the 22- to 30-day Concordia excursion, where a difficult trail takes you through a sea of glaciers close to K2 and other peaks that soar over 8,000 meters (26,240 feet).

Getting Around

By Hired Jeep with Driver Arrange for a jeep with driver/guide through a recommended travel agency.

By Plane **PIA** makes a weekly flight between Skardu and Gilgit, but the bird's-eye view doesn't compare with the road trip.

Outdoor Adventures

Highly recommended adventures are indicated by a star ★.

★ **Biking:** Mountain biking in north Pakistan means rigorous pedaling in high altitude. All cycling trips last 5 to 14 days. The season is July to November, depending on the weather. *Khunjerab Pass:* You can go by mountain bike up the Khunjerab Pass. *Hunza to Swat:* You can pedal from Hunza to Swat in NWFP. For both trips, make arrangements before you depart through Travel Walji's (*see* Before You Go to North Pakistan, above). *Mt. Masherbrum to Mt. Nanga Parbat:* You can bike with a Karakoram Experience tour group from Masherbrum to Nanga Parbat via the Deosau Plains (*see* Before You Go to the Himalayas, Chapter 1).

★ **Climbing and Mountaineering:** Experienced climbers who want to join a fixed-departure expedition in the Karakorams should arrange in advance through recommended private tour operators (*see* Before You Go to the Himalayas, Chapter 1). To organize your own expedition, you need a permit from the Tourism Division, Government of Pakistan (F-7/2, Islamabad, Pakistan). Approval can take more than a year.

Fishing: You can arrange extended fishing expeditions through the tour companies listed in Before You Go to North Pakistan, above. The season usually runs from April to November. Some equipment is available; serious anglers should bring their own gear. *Skardu:* Fish for trout at Kachura and Satpara, two lakes near Skardu in Baltistan. A permit is required, available from the Deputy Commissioner's Office in Skardu. *Gilgit:* Go for trout in numerous streams and lakes around Gilgit. Permits are issued through the Assistant Director of Fisheries, Government of Pakistan (Gilgit).

★ **Horseback Riding:** *Gupis to NWFP:* From May to September, ride five days through mountaintop vistas and beautiful villages from Gupis in the Gilgit Agency to Mastuj in Chitral (NWFP). Arrange in advance through Travel Walji's (*see* Before You Go to North Pakistan, above).

Hot Springs: Delightful springs are scattered throughout FANA—perfect respites after a day's dusty hot ride in a jeep.

★ **Polo:** See great games in Gilgit and, if a game's scheduled, at the world's highest polo arena at Shandur Pass, the gateway to NWFP.

Rafting: Rafting and kayaking are new sports currently under development along the Indus, Gilgit, Hunza, and Astor rivers. At press time, only a couple of runs were scheduled. Check with the recommended travel agencies for the latest trips. *Punial to Gilgit:* Travel Walji's offers a three-day run on the Gilgit River. *Astor Valley:* Travel Walji's is scheduling a 40-kilometer (24-mile) run on the Astor River. It's near Chilas on the lower edge of the Karakoram Highway heading east toward Ayed Kashmir. Arrange in advance (*see* Before You Go to North Pakistan, above).

Trekking: All trekking should include an experienced guide. Glaciers turn streams into dangerous torrents. In addition, some treks are in restricted zones, which means you must have a government-approved guide and a permit. Use a tour operator listed in Before You Go to North Pakistan, above, or Before You Go to the Himalayas, Chapter 1, to simplify the process. Trekking is often strenuous; easy treks exist, but you always cope with high altitude. The season is generally June–October.

★ **Trekking (under a week):** *Naltar to Bar:* Make a five-day moderate–easy trek from the forests of Naltar village, northwest of Gilgit. You pass Naltar Lake; head over the Diantar Pass, altitude 4,800 meters (15,744 feet); and enter a valley—abloom with flowers in August and September—that leads to the remote village of Bar.

Khane to Mt. K6: From Khane village, north of Skardu, take a moderate six-day trek to K6, near the Kondus Glacier. You travel with shepherds through rugged mountains. See wild sheep and perhaps spot a snow leopard or a tiger.

Passu to Shimshal: Culturally rich but extremely difficult, the trek from Passu village to the village of Shimshal in Hunza is a stunner. A tricky path takes you over passes, glaciers, and primitive suspension bridges. Every day, you're rewarded with gorgeous vistas and at Shimshal, a 1,000-year-old village near the Malangudi River, the inhabitants are delightful Wakhis, originally from Wakhain, now a part of Afghanistan.

Upper Hunza to Nanga Parbat: From the mountain village of Ghulkin, traverse a sea of glaciers to the village of Patundas and its mountaintop pastures—a beautiful trek that keeps you off the beaten path.

★ **Trekking (over a week):** *Mt. Nanga Parbat:* Numerous treks, ranging from 7 to 20 days, take you to the Nanga Parbat Base Camp, at 8,126 meters (26,653 feet), and the nearby Fairy Meadows, at 3,500 meters (11,480 feet), which local villagers believe are inhabited by spirits. The Nanga Parbat (Naked Mountain) is an eerie beauty, with barren stretches of sheer rock. It's also one of the most difficult peaks to climb. But this trek is easy–moderate and puts you in glacier country and takes you through lush meadows, past crystal streams, and by grazing livestock. You must be prepared for climbing.

Baltoro to Concordia K2: The 22- to 30-day tough trek from Baltoro Glacier to Concordia K2 is the king of treks in Pakistan. Starting from Folko near Skardu, you walk past hot springs and through villages to Askole, the last outpost before you step into wilderness and a world of glaciers, deserts, and lofty mountains that lead to the base of the Baltoro Glacier, an impressive sight and an experience to cross. From here, you spend time negotiating scree, then arrive at the juncture of the Mustagh and Baltoro Glaciers, which afford astonishing views of the Mustagh Tower, Masherbrum, and Gasherbrum IV peaks. The last destination is Concordia, surrounded by K2, Broad Peak, the Gasherbrum Group, Golden Throne, and Chogolisa, almost all of them towering over 8,000 meters (26,240 feet). This trek, Pakistan's most popular, may bring you in contact with a few trekkers, but you're also in the world of ibex, wild sheep, and migrating shepherds.

★ **Yak Safari:** From July to October, Travel Walji's (*see* Before You Go, above) sponsors a four-day safari by yak—considered the Mercedes-Benz of the animal kingdom—from Passu to Shimshal villages (*see* Trekking—under a week, above).

Gilgit

Numbers in the margin correspond with points of interest on the Federally Administered Northern Areas map.

❶ Set in a narrow valley dominated by the Rakaposhi peak, **Gilgit,** the largest trading center in FANA, was originally called Garagrab (Land of Mountains). The population of Gilgit represents the peoples of central Asia: Hunzas, Nagars, Shinas (people of Tibetan and Aryan ancestry), Gilgitis, and a few refugees from Uighur who fled China during the Communist revolution. Though they all share the Moslem faith, they belong to different sects: Shiites, Sunni, and Ismaeli.

Polo rivals in importance Gilgit's position as a premier trading center. Gilgitis don't play the game according to the reserved rules of the British. They call matches fights and play freestyle with no referee. According to Ahmed Khan, a captain of one of Gilgit's best teams, polo first arrived in this part of Pakistan along with Genghis Khan. At that time, each team had five or six players and whacked a goat's head around the field.

Gilgit holds annual local tournaments in November and during Jachne Bahara, a spring festival held in March or April. An intense rivalry also exists between Gilgit and Chitral. The competition is so fierce that the cities play on the border of the two districts. Their ancient arena is the world's highest polo ground, altitude 3,700 meters (12,136 feet), near Shandur Lake. Here, both men and horses find it difficult to breathe. Is it the horse or the rider that makes for victory? Khan grins, "It's 50/50. Without the horse, you can't play polo."

Arriving and Departing *By Plane*
From **Lahore** and **Islamabad, PIA** makes two daily 90-minute flights to **Gilgit Airport.** Reconfirm at least 72 hours before departure (in Lahore, tel. 306411; in Islamabad, tel. 25091; or in Gilgit, tel. 2417). The **Gilgit Airport** is about 10 kilometers (6 miles) from the city. A taxi (about Rs. 60) is the best way in and out of Gilgit.

By Hired Car or Jeep with Driver
A jeep is your best bet; cars can't get to many remote destinations. Use a recommended travel agency and make all arrangements before you depart. (*see* What It Will Cost in Before You Go to North Pakistan, above, for costs).

Getting Around
Gilgit is a walker's town. Excursions beyond the city require a jeep.

Addresses and Numbers
For tourist information and travel assistance, contact **PTDC** (Chinar Inn, tel. 562), open Saturday–Thursday 9–5, or **Travel Walji's** (Baber Rd., Airport, tel. 3848), open daily 9–5.

Bookstore
For good books in English on Pakistan and the northern areas, visit **Mr. Bagh's Book Store** (Sir Aga Khan Rd.), open Saturday–Thursday 8–1 and 3–7.

Bank
To change money, head to the **National Bank of Pakistan** (Sir Aga Khan Rd.), open Monday–Thursday 9–1, weekends 9–noon).

Post Office
The **General Post Office** (Sir Aga Khan Rd.) is open Saturday–Thursday 9–4.

Exploring
Gilgit is a trading center—a place to stock up on supplies and prepare for a great adventure. Stroll through **Gilgit Bazaar,** which extends the length of Sir Aga Khan Road, the main thoroughfare. Near the middle of town, a side street leads to **Masjid Bazaar,** a narrow road that intersects with Sir Aga Khan Road. Poke around the stalls, and you'll find good handicrafts.

Shopping
The **Northern Areas Traders Corporation** sells merchandise exclusively from China: silk shoes, embroidery, and crockery. It's open Saturday–Thursday 8:30–4 and doesn't accept credit cards.

Outdoor Adventures
Gilgit's **polo** season runs from April to June and September to December. Games are played every other day. The excursions from Gilgit (*see* below) include good **walks.** Head west by jeep from Gilgit about 8 kilometers (5 miles) along the narrow Punial Highway and take a rough road to the right that hugs the Kargha Nala (Cold River) to a hydroelectric station. From here, a path leads past shepherd's huts to perfect spots for a **picnic,** a **swim,** or **trout fishing.** (Fishing permits are available from the Assistant Director of Fisheries, Gilgit.)

Dining and Lodging
The best food is in the hotel restaurants, all inexpensive (under $5 per person, including taxes and excluding drinks and service charges). Dress is casual and reservations are not necessary. All the hotels are equally good. Lodging prices are for a standard double room, including taxes and excluding service charges.

Gilgit Serena. This Western-style hotel is on a hill outside Gilgit and has a good view of Rakaposhi. The rooms are modern with terraces. *Jutial, Gilgit, 3 ki (2 mi) from the bazaar, tel. 2330. 46 rooms with bath (shower). Facilities: courtesy airport pick-up, garden, luggage storage, shops, room service, very good multicuisine restaurant (open 7–9:30, 12:30–2:30, 7:30–9:30; snacks 7 AM–10 PM). AE, MC, V. Moderate ($25–$60).*

Chinar Inn. Though not fancy, this excellently managed PTDC hotel has an inviting ambience and central location. The oldest wing, constructed of stone and wood, has spacious wood-beamed rooms. Two newer wings are also attractive and have a simpler decor. Ground floor rooms are cooler and a few open onto a lovely garden. *Reservations: Flashman's Hotel, The Mall, Rawalpindi, tel. 66231 or 581480, or in Gilgit, tel. 2562. 28 rooms with bath (shower). Facilities: room service, good multicuisine restaurant (open 7 AM–9 PM), fans, garden and lawn, jeep and car rental service, tourist information. No credit cards. Inexpensive (under $25).*

Excursion from Gilgit to Hunza Valley

At press time, no exchange facilities existed in Hunza: bring sufficient rupees. If you smoke, bring sufficient cigarettes, since they are not available locally—smoking is prohibited for the area's Ismaeli Moslems. Also make sure your vehicle has sufficient gas. Hunza Valley is 105 kilometers (65 miles) from Gilgit.

The spiritual leader of the Ismaelis is Prince Karim Aga Khan, called the Hazir Iman (Present Leader), who lives in Europe, but visits his people every few years. Throughout Hunza, Ismaeli mosques—immaculate white or green stone buildings—fly his personal flag. Mountain slopes are covered with the greeting spelled out in white stone, WELCOME OUR BELOVED HAZIR IMAN. The schools, hospitals, and welfare centers he sponsors are ubiquitous—all identified by the initials, AKRSP (Aga Khan Rural Support Project).

When the Hazir Iman visits, his people flock from distant villages to listen to his advice about the importance of education, communal unity, and respect for the government. Then they celebrate with a large feast and dances performed by the men, with the women watching from a respectful distance.

In Hunza, you won't hear the call to prayer. Unlike Sunnis and orthodox Shias, the Ismaeli pray just twice a day—an hour before sunrise and just after sunset. Women and girls here wear flat embroidered caps, called *erage* in Lower Hunza and *skidh* in Upper Hunza. Around the necks of many children, you see a small cloth pouch *(tawaz)*, which contains verses from the Quran to keep the child in good health. You also see dead *ghashep* (black and white birds the size of crows) hanging from houses or poles in fields. They are believed to prevent a reccurance of the plague. Since the last reported case was over 500 years ago, the custom continues.

People in Hunza claim that many men here live over 100 years. Why just men? A villager explained that women work harder, taking care of the home, bearing and raising numerous children, tending the fields. Elders also believe the Karakoram Highway will cost all of them their longevity. Less wholesome food now comes up from the plains, along with farming machinery and motorbikes. The young are growing soft.

To get to Hunza, head north from Gilgit and rejoin the Karakoram Highway. Soon the Hunza River replaces the Gilgit. Midway up the sand-strewn stretch of mountain on the far side of the river, a trace of the ancient Silk Route wends its way along a precarious slope. Before the highway was completed, it took three days to make the trip from Gilgit to Hunza; now it takes three hours. About 28 kilometers (17 miles) after Gilgit, you enter the village of Jotal, a green oasis famous for apricots and wheat.

The Karakorams are now streaked yellow and white. Gorges rip open the mountains, sending glacial water into the Hunza; simple suspension bridges lead across the fast-moving torrent. On the right, a few kilometers beyond Jotal, watch for two pipes that send clean water from the Jaglot Spring into a channel. One pipe gushes hot, the other warm—a refreshing way to remove travel dust.

Just beyond the spring, Nagar Valley begins on the right side of the river and Hunza Valley on the left. The people who live in each valley—the Khajuns of Nagar and Hunzakuts of Hunza—are tall with Aryan features; some have blond or red hair. Young children wave, women smile shyly, and you breathe in the fragrance of sweet grass.

Eighteen kilometers (12 miles) from Jotal, you enter the village of **Jaglot Springs,** a photo opportunity, with fields of wheat, orchards, and snow-topped mountains, including towering Mt. Rakaposhi, just 10 kilometers (6 miles) away.

The village of Nilt, 27 kilometers (17 miles) from Jaglot, marks the end of Nagar Valley. You're now in Hunza. As you approach Thole village, 32 kilometers (20 miles) from Jaglot, you see a **small blue-domed shrine** near the river. It's dedicated to Syed Shah Wali, one of four brothers who came to this region from Iran about 700 years ago. According to village elders, this region was Buddhist when Syed Shah Wali arrived, and he was responsible for converting the people to Islam. The place where he sat, meditated, and spread the word is 200 feet (60 meters) south of the shrine.

Just before the Dadlimal Link Road, 25 kilometers (15 miles) from Thole, stop and check the road at the base of the mountain for rough garnets that fall from this part of the range.

At Murtaza Abad village, 30 kilometers (18 miles) from Thole, the Karakorams look like giant stalagmites eroded by wind and glaciers. Groves of poplars indicate distant villages, with their narrow lanes lined with stone walls and terraced slopes green with fertile crops. Take a steep road on the right, 17 kilometers (10 miles) from Murtaza Abad. It climbs past a string of shops and a couple of hotels into the sprawling village of **Karimabad,** the capital of Hunza Valley. Perched atop a mountain, it's home to the current mir (king) of Hunza.

❷ Karimabad

The mir (king), who ruled over this valley until Pakistan federalized the area in 1974, and his wife, the rani, remain deeply committed to their people. In a society where females often stay in the background, the rani projects a new attitude. In 1985 she started the Northern Area Woman's Organization (NAWO), which revitalized the intricate Hunza art of cross-stitching and turned it into a profitable enterprise for women and girls. Today, NAWO produces the best handicrafts in Hunza; a second branch has been organized in Gilgit. The rani also started the Maternity Center, which teaches family planning and child care. She hopes to open a day-care center and a school.

Getting Around Karimabad is for walkers.

Addresses and Numbers **Indus Guides** (Mountain View Hotel, Karimabad, tel. 17) is open daily 9–5.

Exploring Take a 2-kilometer (1-mile) walk to the top of the village and the 400-year-old, four-story **Baltit Fort and Palace,** the residence of the mir until 1960. The interior is nearly empty, but from the roof (watch out for holes), you can see five peaks with heights over 7,300 meters (23,944 feet). *Go to the gate at the mir's new house nearby. A caretaker has the key to the fort and will accompany you. Admission: Rs. 10. Open sunrise–sunset.*

Shopping The **Woman's Welfare Center** (near the mir's home, tel. 3) sells Hunza handicrafts at reasonable fixed prices with all proceeds benefitting local women. It's open daily 7–6 and doesn't accept credit cards.

Dining and Lodging The best food is in the hotel restaurants, all inexpensive (under $5 per person, including taxes and excluding drinks and service charges). Dress is casual and reservations are not necessary. When you stay in Karimabad, be prepared for power shortages. Highly recommended lodgings are indicated by a star ★. Prices are for a standard double room, including taxes and excluding service charges.

★ **Mir's Compound.** At press time, many of the buildings in the compound were in the early stages of renovation and details were scarce. Rooms on the lower level will have a fireplace and simple attractive furniture. You can also stay in a Victorian bungalow, called Tashmahal, with homey rooms. Specify if you want a room with a fireplace and a private bath. You can also sleep in a *dasi ghar* (typical Hunza house), ideal for a family or party of six. The house is one large open room with elevated sleeping platforms lining the walls, indigenous decorations, and the traditional dance floor. Reserve all rooms well in advance. *Kamran Iqbal, c/o Rani Ghazanfar, Karimabad, Hunza, tel. 1. About 20 rooms, some with bath. Facilities: nearby restaurant. No credit cards. Moderate ($25–$60) rooms; Expensive (about $70) dasi ghar.*
Park Hotel. This hotel offers plain, clean rooms. From a garden with cherry trees, you get good views of the mountains. You can eat in a screened-in restaurant or in a dasi ghar. *Karimabad, Hunza, tel. 45. 6 rooms with bath (shower). Facilities: fixed-menu Pakistani restaurant (open 7 AM–9 PM), trekking and jeep service. No credit cards. Inexpensive (under $25).*

★ **Rakaposhi View Hotel and Restaurant.** Run by the mir, this pleasant single-story motel-bungalow has a front veranda and great vistas. Rooms are clean and cheery. *Karimabad, Hunza, tel. 12. 25 rooms with bath. Facilities: 2 restaurants serving the best food in town (open 7–9:30, 12:30–2, 7–9:30). No credit cards. Inexpensive (under $25).*

Excursion from Karimabad to Gulmith Head north on the Karakoram Highway. At 35 kilometers (22 miles), take the narrow road on the left up to **Gulmith** (Flower Garden), an enchanting traditional village on a mountain slope. It's immortalized in a Persian song: "Every branch is a precious jewel; every high peak is a sugar king." Visit the tiny **Marco Polo Museum of Hunza Culture,** with Hunza artifacts: 300-year-old carved doors, musical instruments, traditional clothing, weapons (including King Killer, a rifle used against the British, and Lord Kitchener's rifle, a gift to a former Gulmith mir). *Admission: Rs. 5. Open by request.*

The museum's owner can also arrange a visit to an 800-year-old dasi ghar, with typical carved interior pillars, small wood doors, hard clay seats and beds (the highest platform reserved for the head of the house), central dancing floor, and the traditional *ikhooto*, a flat roof that is a series of carved squares with a small opening in the center.

From Gulmith, you can see Karon, a mountain that figures in a legend associated with Shams, another of the four brothers who came to Pakistan from Iran. Shams was endowed with great spiritual power. At his death, he was buried 25 kilometers (15 miles) from Gulmith on a track to the village of Shimshal near another mountain named Pir Shams. The villagers believe if you want to go to Shimshal from either Gulmith or Passu, you'll be first opposed by Karon. If this peak doesn't stop you, Pir Shams will. Only when both mountains are willing can a traveler make it across. (These days, the trekker will succeed with a good guide.)

To stay at Gulmith, you have two choices, both inexpensive (under $25). The new **Silk Route Lodge** is on the highway, a steep walk from Gulmith, but it has modern rooms and offers good views. *Gulmith, Hunza, tel. 18. 20 rooms with bath (shower). Facilities: restaurant with Continental and Pakistani food, open 7–9:30, 12:30–2, 7–9:30. No credit cards.*

Marco Polo Inn, run by the local raja, is small and minimal, but it's right in the village and surrounded by terraced fields and mountains. The rooms are extremely simple, but clean. You can also pitch a tent in the raja's fields, stay in a rustic old dasi ghar, or take over a small plain house and enjoy a cozy sitting room with fireplace. *Gulmith, Hunza, tel. 7. 15 rooms with bath (shower). Facilities: good Pakistani restaurant (open 7–9:30, 12:30–2, 7–9:30). No credit cards.*

Excursion from Karimabad to Altit Fort and Duigar Plateau Drive north on the Karakoram Highway about 3 kilometers (2 miles) from Karimabad to Altit, a hillside village on the left. After passing through the village, stop at a gate that leads through part of the village to the **Altit Fort,** which was built in 1409. Once you step inside the intricately carved walnut door, you enter a series of dark stone chambers. One room was the jail and another, a *mel* (winery) where villagers made wine from apricots.

Upstairs, the main room on the left is the kitchen, with carved wood pillars and the typical ikhooto roof. The other room, with a series of clay platforms, was the mir's private bedroom. He slept on the highest tier. The white decorations that cover the ceiling and pillars are created during the Bufo Spring Celebration, which occurs in February. After villagers gather at the palace, about 60 prominent men greet the mir, who puts wheat flour on each man's shoulder, a gesture that symbolizes the wish for a successful harvest. Then, villagers make flour-paste designs (*bufo*) all over the room. While cooks prepare a village feast, the mir plows a small row in a field as his people cheer and music plays. After mixing gold in flour, he tosses it into the crowd, signaling the start of a feast, followed by horseback riding and dancing.

A steep road winds through Altit, past terraced fields, waterfalls, irrigation canals, wildflowers, livestock, playing children, and farmers. Once you reach the village of **Duigar,** walk up a rocky plateau that overlooks the Hunza River, rumbling softly below. From here, you see nine peaks over 7,000 meters (22,960 feet) high. As the sun sets, haze slides over fields in the valley. The peaks shimmer pink, then gold, the colors softening until the sun disappears. If you bring binoculars, search for ibex, which often graze on the distant slopes at dusk. *The Duigar plateau is 6 km (4 mi) from Karimabad. Admission to the fort: Rs. 10. Fort open sunrise–sunset.*

Excursion from Karimabad to Nagar and Hopar Glacier ❸

East from Karimabad, 3 kilometers (2 miles), a jeep track to the right of the Karakoram Highway leads to **Nagar,** the capital of Nagar Valley. The tiny 1,000-year-old village of Nagar is home to about 200 Shiites. Inside every shop hangs a picture of Ayatollah Khomeini and a welcome sign. Nagar Shiites follow a religious leader called the mushtahideen, who gives orders according to the Quran and the recently deceased ayatollah. His representative in Pakistan is Syed Arif Hussain, who lives near Peshawar in Parchinar.

From Nagar, head on to Hopar Glacier. The road climbs past wheat and potato fields, orchards, and villages. Down below, the Hopar Nala River is a silver thread along the valley basin. Stop at the **Hopar Hilton Inn,** an outdoor restaurant serving simple vegetarian food. If you climb to the edge of the cliff, stay *at least* three feet back from the edge; the rocks break away without warning. Just beyond the cliff and backed by three towering peaks is the **Hopar Glacier.** The glacier is filled with hidden soft pockets, and no one knows its depth. Only villagers and shepherds dare move across its fragile surface. *18 km (11 mi) southeast of Karimabad.*

Excursion from Karimabad to Khunjerab Pass

Head north on the Karakoram Highway. About 2 kilometers (1 mile) beyond Gulmith, you see the **Gulking Glacier.** The glacier is in a constant state of flux, and dislodged boulders lie haphazardly on its slopes. After Gulking, you see the extensive **Passu Glacier** behind the village of Passu, 15 kilometers (9 miles) to the north of Karimabad, and the giant Mt. Shish Por. After 10 kilometers (6 miles), you come to the Batura Bridge. On the left is the mouth of the 45-kilometer (28-mile) **Batura Glacier.** In 1982 melting snow from this glacier crashed down with such force, it washed away the road and bridge without a trace.

Sost is the **military customs checkpoint** for travelers heading into China. Clearance takes 15–20 minutes. From here, the valley narrows as you head to the pass, which was once such a dangerous journey that travelers named it Khunjerab (Valley of Blood). **Deh,** 40 kilometers (25 miles) from Sost, is another **police checkpoint** where you will register. It also is the southern border of the projected Khunjerab National Park, a protected area for game. Until the 1950s, this area was filled with Marco Polo sheep, ibex, wild yak, gray wolf, fox, brown bear, mountains cats, snow leopards, and even camels. When blasting for the highway began in 1955, the animals fled. Only now are they beginning to return.

About 15 kilometers (9 miles) after Deh, you begin the actual ascent to the pass, traveling between two stretches of mountains with the Khunjerab River thrashing below. Once you reach the pass, at 4,878 meters (16,000 feet), you enter a plateau that extends across the Chinese border and is home to wild ❹ yak and wild cats. **Khunjerab Pass** is 115 km (71 mi) from Karimabad. To visit the pass (open May–Nov., daily, to international tourists), you don't need a Chinese visa. The Sost border checkpoint is open until 11 PM. From Gilgit, travelers can take a Pakistan Tours coach or a private **NATCO** bus. Contact the **PTDC** (Chinar Inn, Gilgit, tel. 562) for departure times. Or rent a jeep from Hunza or a van from Sost. Carry drinking water beyond Sost. To make this journey by jeep in one day, start at daybreak. Otherwise, plan to spend the night at the **Sost Tourist Lodge.** *Rooms are clean and plain. Sost Gojal, Northern Areas, tel. 9. 12 rooms with bath (shower) and 6 with shared bath (shower) dorms. Facilities: inexpensive restaurant serving good Pakistani food (open 5 AM–midnight). No credit cards. Inexpensive (under $5); dorms very inexpensive (Rs. 25 per person).*

Excursion from Gilgit to Baltistan

The Baltistan Agency bordering the Chinese province of Sinkiang and the disputed area of Kashmir to the east was once known as Tibet-i-Khurd (Little Tibet). Here you find K2, the world's second-highest mountain, and the 60-kilometer (36-mile) Baltoro Glacier, set amid a field of huge glaciers. Baltistan is also the gateway to the Indus River. Here you see the black flag of the Shiites. The Shiites, especially the Noor Bukashia sect in the Khaplu Valley, dominate this territory. You also notice a new touch added to the decorated trucks, tractors, and jeeps: a black yak tail, which protects the driver from the evil eye.

Descendants of the Prophet Mohammed who left Iran and settled in Kashmir brought Islam to Baltistan 250 years ago. At the time, Syed Hamdini came to Keris, a Buddhist village near Skardu. There, he began the difficult mission of converting the Buddhists. At the time of his death, 75% of the people had adopted his faith.

While Shiites follow the Ayatollah Khomeini and two mushtahideens (Aga Khoi in Iraq and Srazi in Iran), the Noor Bukashia are followers of a religious leader called the pir. The current pir is Syed Aon Ali Shan Almosivi who resides at Khaplu and he, in turn, adheres to the teachings of Khomeini. In almost every respect, the two sects are identical. When you speak with these people, you realize that their deep faith fosters generosity and respect that are extended to everyone they meet.

In Upper Baltistan and the Khaplu area, some men and women follow a local tradition that dates back to the time of the rajas: marrying for a five-year trial period (*mutah*). If the parents are happy and the couple has produced children at the end of mutah, the couple remarry. Men are free to have additional wives; they rarely marry outside their clan.

Women in Baltistan wear a black wool cap (*nateen*) under a rough wool shawl. Before marriage, nateens are fairly simple. After marriage, a woman's nateen is a fancy work of art, decorated with precious stones and silver and costing up to Rs. 2,500. Some nateens show off bits of "found art": a remnant of a flexible watchband, a plastic flower, a discarded bottle cap.

Young girls have short hair until the age of nine; then, following the example of the older women, they wear braids. Their pieces of jewelry—silver embedded with decorated glass or stone— are coveted treasures, but you'll discover they're always willing to make a trade for your ring or necklace.

In Baltistan, though everyone works side by side in the fields, the sexes separate when it's time to relax. Only the youngsters openly intermix. You also notice that the men spin wool, not the women, who are far too busy taking care of the home and family and working in the fields. Finally, though everyone is extremely friendly, especially the children, always ask before you take a photo. The women observe a form of purdah and will want to conceal the lower halves of their faces.

PIA flies into Skardu, but the best way to visit Skardu is to drive by jeep from Gilgit. The trip on the Skardu–Gilgit road is unforgettable. If you do choose to fly, refer to flight details under Skardu.

The Skardu–Gilgit Road, constructed from 1977 to 1985, starts about 38 kilometers (24 miles) east of Gilgit. In 1987 an enormous landslide after record rainfall destroyed large chunks of the road. Along the entire stretch, you see wreckage—huge, precariously wedged boulders. A rock canopy juts out over your jeep. About a foot away from the other side of the vehicle, a steep gorge drops down to the thundering Indus River. Waterfalls shoot across the road. Crude pedestrian bridges crisscross the Indus and lead to delightful Balti villages. The villages are surrounded by lush fields that are irrigated by ingenious canals drawing water from glaciers and snowcapped peaks.

⑤ Baicha village, about 149 kilometers (92 miles) from Gilgit, is a good place to stop for tea while admiring the distant view of snow-covered peaks. The people here look distinctly Tibetan. From Baicha, the valley opens up. The Indus turns placid. Ahead lies Skardu, the headquarters of Baltistan, at an altitude of 2,438 meters (7,996 feet), set against the great peaks of the Karakorams.

⑥ Skardu

Skardu is a military town, the base for troops moving to and from the Siachin Glacier in disputed Kashmir. Soldiers are everywhere, guns stand ready, and helicopters fly overhead. A monument in the middle of the dusty city is a memorial to those who died liberating Skardu from India in 1948. Skardu is also Baltistan's main trading center, with a busy bazaar.

Arriving and Departing *By Plane* From **Lahore** and **Islamabad, PIA** makes a daily flight to **Skardu Airport.** Reconfirm at least 72 hours before departure. Call, in Lahore (tel. 306411), in Islamabad (tel. 25091), or in Skardu (tel. 30).

Between Airport and City	The airport is about 10 kilometers (6 miles) from the city. A taxi (about Rs. 60) is the best way in and out of Skardu.
By Hired Car or Jeep with Driver	A jeep is your best bet. Rent a vehicle from a recommended travel agency and make all arrangements before you depart. (*See* Before You Go to North Pakistan, above, for costs.)
Getting Around	Skardu is a walker's town, but for excursions, you need a jeep.
Addresses and Numbers	For tourist information and travel assistance, contact **PTDC** (K2 Motel, Skardu, tel. 104), open Sunday–Thursday 9–5; closed Friday, or **Travel Walji's** (Main Rd., tel. 7), open daily 9–5. The **PIA office** (New Bazaar, tel. 30) is open Sunday–Thursday 9–5; closed Friday.
Banks	**National Bank of Pakistan** and the **Habib Bank** (center of town) are open weekday 9–1, weekends 9–noon.
Post Office	This is also the location of the **General Post Office,** open Saturday–Thursday 9–4.
Exploring	Walk down the **Old Bazaar,** which intersects with the main street, and look at the merchandise in the shops—clues to Balti life. Dental clinics have paintings of teeth over their doors, barrels display all kinds of tobacco, Chinese crockery is heaped on floors, beautiful brass and silver samovars line shelves, and men sew in miniature covered wagons.
Outdoor Adventures	From the Shangrila Tourist Resort, you can take an hour-long **walk** through small villages and orchards to Katchura Lake, set in a valley and ideal for **picnics, swimming,** and **fishing.** Drive by jeep 8 kilometers (5 miles) from Skardu to Satpara Lake, great for trout **fishing** and perfect for **picnics, boating,** and **camping.** A restaurant serves good Pakistani food. (Fishing permits are available from the Deputy Commissioner in Skardu.) From the Skardu New Bazaar, take a two-hour steep **walk** up to the historic Mindoz Khar (Castle-fort of Queen Mindoz), which offers a good view of the Indus River and Skardu Valley.
Dining and Lodging	The best food is in the hotel restaurants. Dress is casual and reservations are not necessary. Prices are per person, including taxes and excluding drinks and service charges. Be prepared for power shortages. The two recommended hotels have distinctly different ambiences. Let your budget and preference guide you. Prices are for a standard double room or cottage, including taxes and excluding service charges.

Shangrila Tourist Resort. This resort, 20 kilometers (12 miles) from Skardu, offers the height of luxury: an attractive cluster of cottages surrounding a lake, complete with boats for hire and squawking ducks. The cottages have pleasant front verandas and handsome rooms. And there's the novel Dakota Cottage, a salvaged DC 3 that landed 20 miles away in the Indus River in the late 1940s. The owner of Shangrila bought the aircraft and hired 100 men with mules to drag it here. Every time he yelled, "Ya Allah," they moved it an inch. If you want liquor, bring your own from Skardu. *Reservations: Shangrila Hotels & Resorts, 143–N Murree Rd., Rawalpindi, tel. 73006, or in Skardu, tel. GAMBA 19. 95 rooms with bath. Facilities: lovely lakeside restaurant serving delicious multicuisine food (open 8–10, noon–2, 7–9), shops, post office, jeeps for hire, foreign-exchange and travel counter, fishing, horseback rid-*

ing, tennis, swimming, library, gift shop. AE and traveler's checks. Expensive ($60–$100).

K2. This PTDC hotel, set in Skardu, is popular with serious climbers and trekkers. The rooms are simple but clean. You can tent on the spacious lawn. *Reservations: PTDC, Flashman's Hotel, The Mall, Rawalpindi, tel. 66231 or 581480, or in Skardu, tel. 104. 20 rooms with bath (showers). Facilities: jeep rentals, tourist office, excellent multicuisine restaurant serving hearty food (open 7–9, noon–2, 7–9). No credit cards. Inexpensive (under $25).*

Excursion from Skardu to Hushe and Khaplu
East of Skardu, the Indus River hugs the road. The mountains close in as the road climbs and the jeep kicks up dust. Nineteen kilometers (12 miles) from Skardu, a large **boulder** on the left side of the road is chiseled with carvings. The boulder was formerly located along the ancient route from Skardu to Ladakh in India, and the carved depictions of stupas probably date back to the 3rd to 7th centuries. Near the top of the rock, you see a Shiva lingam and a human figure reminiscent of pictographs from before the time of Christ.

Just after the village of Gol, 22 kilometers (14 miles) from Skardu, you cross a wood suspension bridge, with the Indus raging below. The road leaves the Indus to follow the Shyok River. A stone wall marks the entrance to **Keris** village, 5 kilometers (3 miles) beyond Gol, nestled in a valley with baked-mud homes. Yak trod through wheat fields. Everyone works, even children, who carry enormous bundles of wheat and barley on their backs. If you stop here, stay in the **Keris NAWO Resthouse.** *At this spartan lodging, the caretaker will prepare simple meals. Reservations: PTDC, Skardu, tel. 104. 2 rooms with crude Asian-style bath. No credit cards. Inexpensive (under $10).*

Beyond Keris, only occasional trees break up the desert vista. Broken boulders, the result of continual landslides, lay in tumbled heaps. Rock ledges hang over the skinny thoroughfare. The Shyok River, never far from the road, rises so much each day as the sun melts nearby glaciers that you must pass through Kuru village, 12 kilometers (7 miles) from Keris, before mid-afternoon.

Just beyond the Kharfak Bridge, not far from Kuru, a **boulder** on the right has 7th-century inscriptions left by Hindus who had converted to Buddhism—two stupas, the umbrella of enlightenment, and the Hindu swastika.

Up ahead, the road leaves the Shyok River. You see no green and only rare touches of snow on jagged peaks that span the horizon. After the Hushe River links up to the road, you cross a rickety wood bridge and enter the village of **Machulu,** 35 kilometers (22 miles) from Kuru, your first night halt. **Machulu NAWO Rest House.** *At this rustic lodging, the caretaker will prepare a simple meal. Reservations: PTDC, Skardu, tel. 104. 4 rooms with Asian-style bath. No credit cards. Very inexpensive (under $10).*

Three kilometers (2 miles) north of Machulu, you cross another precarious bridge and pass through another small village before you reach the Belegun Suspension Bridge, which crosses the Hushe River and leads to the Siachin Glacier and to Khaplu. Don't take the bridge, but continue north.

Up ahead, if the sky is clear, you get your first glimpse of Masherbrum, altitude 7,821 meters (25,652 feet). A stream shoots water across the narrow road. Beware: by mid-afternoon, melting glaciers turn it into a dangerous cascade that can sweep away the jeep. Roses, bluebells, other blooms grow in profusion. You rumble over a suspension bridge with the Hushe River racing a few feet below, then enter a shady grove that leads to **Khane** village, the starting point for the six-day trek to K6 (*see* Outdoor Adventures, above).

After Khane, peaks crowd the horizon. Wild roses, in every shade of pink, add color to the barren landscape. You cross another suspension bridge and pass shepherds' huts. Then the road ends. You reach **Hushe,** 27 kilometers (17 miles) from Machulu, home to about 500 Baltis.

The people of Hushe are Shiites, who pray five times daily— men at the mosque, women at home. Their most revered leader, called a tom, was Syed Asskar Shan, who was originally from Hushe and died about 80 years ago. Considered a saint, he is said to have been endowed with miraculous powers that enabled him to cross any river without a bridge, any glacier without difficulty. The current tom lives in Surmo village near Khaplu.

Balti homes withstand the heat of summer and the cold of winter. Step inside a typical dwelling, and you see the stone walls are plastered with a rock-hard mixture of mud and sand. Thick wood pillars support a dense clay ceiling, which adds more insulation, as well as protection from the weight of winter's snow.

There may be a handwoven rug on the clay floor; you see few other luxuries: a samovar, a few cooking utensils, a metal trunk containing meager possessions. Walls are decorated with newspapers, election posters, and pictures of the revered Ayatollah Khomeini.

To go from Hushe to Khaplu, return along the Hushe River to the Belegun Suspension Bridge. Directly across the bridge is a **roadside hotel/restaurant.** Sit on a bench or *charpoi* (bed) and enjoy good simple food and the spectacular views.

Back on the road, the terrain again turns dusty; mountains tower. Stop at the village of **Haldi,** 6 kilometers (3 miles) from the bridge, and register at the army **checkpoint.**

The road to the left leads to the Siachin Glacier (off-limits to foreigners). The road to the right takes you to a suspension bridge across the Saltoro River. Watch for a flag-festooned, cloth-draped tomb, near a Moslem graveyard. Across the road is an approximately 400-year-old stone and clay **Nor Bukashia mosque** with a wood railing across the veranda. Stop and look at the ceiling decorations painted in soft colors, the intricately carved door frame with verses from the Quran, and the interior of the main hall, closed to non-Moslems.

As you proceed to Khaplu, the Shyok replaces the Saltoro River. You travel through a sand basin, complete with dunes. Stone walls define the boundaries of barren fields. You pass over a suspension bridge, traversed one vehicle at a time. At Sarma village, 32 kilometers (20 miles) from the Belegun Suspension Bridge, stop at an inviting **truck stop** on a raised terrace by the road and have tea.

About 2 kilometers (1 mile) before Khaplu, you usually see a group of men sitting by the road with an odd yet seaworthy craft of inflated goat and buffalo skins and a few inner tubes attached to a crude square frame. With the aid of long poles, they ferry up to 10 people on a half-hour journey across the river to a village near Machulu. It's a memorable trip—highly recommended to the adventurous. You'll make it both ways; just expect to get wet.

❾ Khaplu, 39 kilometers (24 miles) from Belegun Suspension Bridge, is a prosperous village with a good-size bazaar leading up the mountain to the heart of the village. Kaphlu is a Shiite stronghold, with frequent signs reminding the faithful: "Live like Ali, die like Hussain."

Near the top of the village sits the Khaplu Palace, built about 600 years ago and the current home of the surviving family members of the Raja Fatah Ali Khan, who died in 1983, 11 years after Pakistan abolished his kingdom.

You enter through a gate that the raja's ancestors took from a fort in Skardu. Formerly the stable, this passageway leads to the front lawn where the royal band played during festive celebrations. Behind the lawn stands the four-story palace, which looks much like a fort. Notice the upper-story ceilings above the corner verandas. They're intricately chiseled, then painted—an architectural touch called Hatum Batin. Not a single nail was used to construct the house. *Admission free to grounds and some rooms. Open 9–5 when the raja's family is available.*

There is a **Khaplu NAWO Rest House.** The main house has simple rooms with attached bathrooms. The unattached structure by the stream is less inviting. At press time, the existing management was extremely unpleasant. *Reservations: PTDC, Skardu, tel. 104. In main house, 9 rooms with bath. Inexpensive (under $10).*

Make this journey by jeep. Bring sufficient gasoline, a good sleeping bag, simple food, and candles. Also pay strict attention to the warnings about flooding rivers.

Excursion from Gilgit to the Shandur Pass

Start this 230-kilometer (143-mile) journey, which is feasible *only* by jeep, *early* in the morning. Small streams that splash across the road at 10 AM are torrents by mid-afternoon. Before you set off, make sure your driver has a good spare tire, extra gasoline, and a tool kit. Bring a sleeping bag, candles, toilet paper, soap, towel, quart container to fill with purified water, and all your food supplies. If you don't plan to camp, make arrangements for a room in one of the NAWO rest houses through PTDC (Gilgit, tel. 562). Each rest house has two or three rooms with spartan furnishings and damp, musty, but serviceable bathrooms. Usually the staff of the resthouse will let you pitch a tent on the lawn and a caretaker will fix simple meals for a small price. This trip is rough, but it's also one of the greatest road adventures in Pakistan.

From Skardu, return to Gilgit and head west on the Punial Highway. You follow the Gilgit River. Donkeys wander along the road; cows graze down by the river. Then suddenly, the mountains turn chaotic, with crumbled rock in unstable piles tossed over the slopes. This is landslide country.

After 29 kilometers (18 miles) you come to a pedestrian bridge with no side rails that leads to the village of Barko. If you walk across, stay in the middle. As you continue toward the pass, hukaro trees, with willowy pink branches in June, stand out against the drab rock and the muddied Gilgit River. Just after Gula Pur village, 34 kilometers (21 miles) from Gilgit, a crude bridge leads across a stream. The road turns as rocky as the mountains. Stone houses blend into the hillside.

Then, 44 kilometers (27 miles) from Gilgit, you enter a wide verdant stretch—the start of the Punial Valley, which extends to towering mountains swirled with grays and browns like a giant finger painting. To the right, a suspension bridge leads to the village of **Sherqila,** bordered by a beautiful stream shooting down the mountain. If you have time, walk across the bridge and head up a lane to the **palace** of the former raja, who's still alive, and the ruins of his old fort called Sherqila (Fort of the Tiger).

The road climbs, then sweeps down to a village. Livestock outnumber the people you see. The sound of rushing water is everywhere—from water canals cutting through fields and from the river, not far from your jeep.

As the road climbs, the mountains move in, and clouds hang over a distant chain of peaks. You enter **Singal** village, 57 kilometers (35 miles) from Gilgit. Singal is set in a wide valley with lush fields of wheat. It has a modern Aga Khan Medical Center and a **NAWO resthouse.** The latter is used by the army, which is building the new highway. You can't use the rooms, but you may be able to tent on the lawn.

Gakuch village, 8 kilometers (5 miles) from Singal, also has a simple **rest house** where you can spend the night. Fields are resplendent with maize, wheat, and pink-tipped hukaro. Cattle and donkeys graze by the river that sneaks up by day to the middle of the trunks of the trees along the edge. By mid-afternoon, the river is swollen and treacherous.

Again the road climbs. You travel under a rock canopy and cross more suspension bridges that sway and rumble under the weight of the jeep. Gushing torrents race down gorges. Men, with goatskin bags filled with milk, yogurt, or grain slung over their shoulders, trudge along the roadway carrying walking sticks and umbrellas to block out the hot sun. You pass caravans of donkeys with goatskin saddlebags. Expect interesting confrontations along the entire journey. The road is so narrow that vehicles cannot pass from opposite directions. One must back up and pull into a field or drive within an inch of the sheer cliff of the mountain on one side or the river on the other so the passing vehicle can squeeze by.

Gupis Valley begins 32 kilometers (20 miles) from Singal at an old suspension bridge that crosses the Gilgit River and leads to the village of Huppar. Stay on the highway and continue toward Gupis.

At the end of the charming small village of Rausan, 17 kilometers (10 miles) from the Huppar Bridge, the Rausan Nala River tumbles down from the mountain, a delightful place for a picnic or quick dip before you continue on toward Gupis and Phandar Lake. You must walk over the next suspension bridge; your jeep traverses separately. The risky structure shakes and sways underfoot.

Yet another suspension bridge crosses the Gupis and leads into the nearby village of **Yassin,** home to various tribes, including Gujjar nomads who now live permanently in the far end of the Yassin Valley. Here, you find the **NAWO Rest House,** another reasonable night halt.

At **Gupis,** 11 kilometers (7 miles) from Rausan, you must stop and register with the police before moving on to Phandar Lake. About 20 kilometers (12 miles) from Gupis, the road climbs onto a plateau strewn with enormous rocks and bordered by parched mountain slopes coated in sand. You come to another green stream, the Bathyeat Nala, 25 kilometers (15 miles) from Gupis, which empties into the Gupis River.

After crossing a suspension bridge, the road narrows severely. A rock ledge nearly shoves you into the river, which is never more than a foot to the right. Again, watch the time. By mid-afternoon, the road floods. You journey across more crude bridges, through numerous tiny villages—so perfectly integrated into the rocky mountains that they're nearly concealed.

In the village of Pengan, 42 kilometers (26 miles) from Gupis, simple stone houses no longer have completely flat roofs. An elevated mound (*ghisurkum*) with a square opening for ventilation sits in the center. The Phandar Valley receives up to four feet of snow each year. The ghisurkum keeps the snow from falling in as it collects on the roof. The windowless houses also have an L-shape wall in front of the door, another barrier against the cold.

After the village of Shamaran, 53 kilometers (33 miles) from Gupis, climb toward the Shandur Pass. The Phandar River is on the left, and mountains rise up on the right. Numerous graves on either side of the road pose a tricky problem for the army as they widen the highway. The villagers don't want them removed or disturbed.

⑪ The village of Phandar is idyllic, shaded by trees, with ducks wandering along water canals and donkeys grazing everywhere. Still the road climbs. Suddenly, you see the **Phandar Lake**—placid and green as an emerald. Just ahead is a quaint **NAWO Rest House,** with three rooms, dining room, sitting room, and picture-book vistas. This is the ideal overnight stop. You need a sleeping bag, since the accommodations are rustic. From here, you can take delightful walks past braying donkeys and fields of wildflowers. You can fish or just gaze at a paradise on top of the world.

Once you leave the lake, you wind your way toward the pass. Beware of the Phandar River near the village of Shahiman, 15 kilometers (9 miles) from the lake. The road can be a mud pit, sucking in your jeep up to the tire rims. Be prepared to push the vehicle through. Once you're beyond this hazard, you cross a shaky suspension bridge.

The road winds through tiny villages into Upper Phandar Valley. Mountain slopes, the color of brick, create canyons with wide green valleys where the river sneaks in and out of view. Up ahead to the left, you see Nogarchal Mountain, which means Place Where You Bring Cattle, exactly what the locals did long ago. Now they don't take the animals so far.

Twenty-one kilometers (13 miles) from Phandar, you reach **Tero** village, where you can spend the night in the minimal **NAWO Rest House,** set back from the road. Beyond Tero, a crude bridge passes a powerful stream. You travel through wide plateaus surrounded by mountains; houses sit in small tight clusters strewn across the plateau. Men walk by with goatskin blankets draped across their backs. The road dips down to the Phandar Nala on your left, just beyond Bersot village, 32 kilometers (20 miles) from Phandar. The road turns into a gravel bed leading into a plateau and the placid **Shandur Lake,** 61 kilometers (38 miles) from Phandar Lake. To the left of the lake is the world's highest polo ground, bordered by stone bleachers and the setting of the contest between Chitral and Gilgit.

It costs millions of rupees to mount this game, which is usually played in July or August and is a national event attended by the prime minister and president. The last match was in 1986. Traditionally, once the date is fixed, the Gilgit and Chitral teams set out for the pass with their ponies. As they move along, they stop in villages and have practice matches that turn into festive occasions, with the beating of drums and men dancing to regional tunes. These trial games help the ponies and men acclimatize to the increasingly high altitude; they also rev up the people in the district so they'll flock to the big match.

During winter, the entire 8-mile plateau and polo field lie under nine feet of snow. This is the habitat of wolves, bear, and wild sheep. When the area is quiet in summer, the vista and surroundings are sublime. You see no one, just yaks, sheep, and cattle. Not even the herdsmen stay here. You could camp for days. (For the road trip from here to Chitral, *see* Excursion from Chitral to Shandur Pass in North West Frontier Province, below.)

North West Frontier Province

Introduction

The North West Frontier Province—Pakistan's Federally Administered Tribal Areas—is small, about the size of Maryland, and packed with Buddhist antiquities, extraordinary tribal peoples, and spectacular adventures. You can raft, trek, set out for days on a horse or a bike, and go on memorable jeep rides through an everchanging terrain. In the north, which abuts the Hindu Kush on the west and the Federally Administered Northern Areas (FANA) on the north and east, a rugged landscape is dominated by the chaos of closely packed, dark, jagged mountains. In the south, barren hills replace peaks; fertile farmlands fade into the parched stretches of Baluchistan.

Two thousand five hundred years ago, this area was called Gandhara. In 327 BC, Alexander the Great added it to his empire. It was the Emperor Ashoka who made NWPF an important Buddhist center. Buddhism continued to flourish after his death around 235 BC until AD 660–670, when White Huns invaded from China. They destroyed the monasteries and forced the monks to

North West Frontier Province (Numbers on map correspond to numbers in text)

FANA

KOHISTAN

Mastuj

13 Shandur Pass

Lasput R.

PUNIAL HWY.

Laspur

Kachikhanni Pass

12 Reshun

Mastuj R.

Khogozi

Madaklasht

Ushu

Kalam

▲ Mt. Falakser

Indus R.

KARAKORAM HWY.

▲ Mt. Tirich Mir

CHITRAL

Lotkuh R.

10 Chitral

Ghareet

Birmoghalasht

Drosh

Mir Khani

Lowari Pass

Dir

9

8

SWAT VALLEY

7 Madyan

Miandam

DIR AGENCY

Garam Chasma

Rampur

Ayun

Bumburet

11 Birrer

AFGHANISTAN

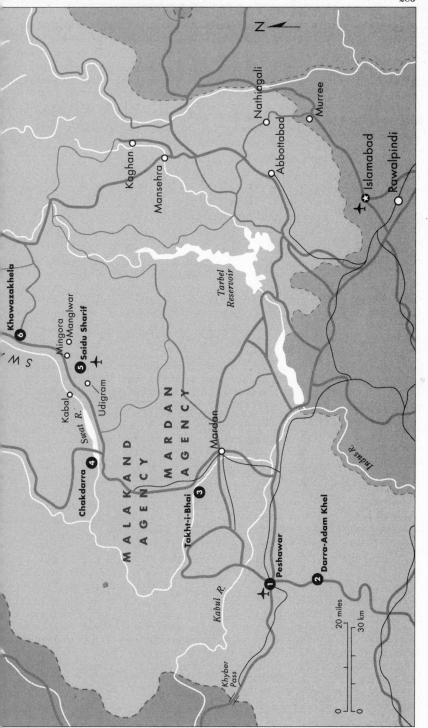

N

Nathiagali

Murree

Abbottabad

Islamabad

Rawalpindi

Kaghan

Mansehra

Tarbel
Reservoir

Khawazakhela

❻

S W A T

Mingora

Manglwar

❺ Saidu Sharif

Kabal

Udigram

Swat R.

Chakdarra ❹

M A L A K A N D
A G E N C Y

M A R D A N
A G E N C Y

Mardan

Indus R.

Takht-i-Bhai

❸

❷ Darra-Adam Khel

❶ Peshawar

Kabul R.

Khyber
Pass

20 miles

30 km

0

0

flee. From the 8th to the 10th century, Hinduism enjoyed a brief reign. Then the Mahmud of Ghazni swept down from Afghanistan and converted the populace to Islam before he moved on to conquer Delhi.

Except for a brief interval of Sikh rule in the 19th century, NWFP remained an Islamic stronghold, with Peshawar, the capital city near the head of the Khyber Pass, a powerful Moghul center. Even the British couldn't exert much influence when they seized control in 1849. On August 14th, 1947, the frontier officially became a part of the new nation of Pakistan. But no one completely rules the great Pathans.

Who are the Pathans? Statistically, they represent 12 million Pushtu-speaking Pakistanis, more than half of whom live in NWFP. Claiming descendency from the "Children of Israel," the Pathans first settled in Afghanistan where a messenger of the Prophet Mohammed converted them to Islam and called them *Batan* (base). They were the Base of Islam—a title that holds true today. Pathans are willing to die to maintain their culture and laws.

Pathan tribes include the Afridis, considered the bravest, and the Wasidi and Mashud, who have a reputation for ongoing antagonism. The tribes, in turn, have subsects. All Pathans, irrespective of their clan, live by a strict code of honor that often leads to clashes over property, money, and women.

This code is called *pakhtunwali*, with the primary concept—*badal*—a reminder to the Pathan male that he must revenge any insult or harm to himself, his family, or his friends. Next in importance is *melmastia*, which calls for hospitality and protection to anyone who seeks shelter. Non-Pathans will receive a warm welcome provided they have been invited. Visitors welcome guests but not strangers, so be sure you have an invitation. The strength of this concept explains the presence of over 3 million Afghan refugees—mainly Pathans—on Pakistan's soil; it also explains the support the Afghan Pathan guerrillas have received from their Pakistani Pathan brethren.

Women are accorded tremendous respect. The few times they venture outside to attend a wedding or a funeral, they're concealed in their burkas and accompanied by the family's best marksman. Should a woman suffer any dishonor, this serious crime demands revenge. In the past, an affront led to war.

Today, the Pathan arsenal includes machine guns and rockets. This has increased the importance of the *jerga*, an assembly of tribal elders who arbitrate feuds. Now many jergas enforce a preliminary seven-day cooling-off period. The modern age has also brought financial success and education, which make mediation a more meaningful route.

Each village belongs to a clan, and residents often are related. The traditional design—a cluster of houses huddled behind a mud wall two feet thick and 15 feet high with a watchtower in one corner studded with gun slits—was made to withstand attack and has usually survived 100 years. Today, with warfare on the wane, many watchtowers have been converted to water tanks.

Once you step through the gate, you enter a large courtyard with a *hujra*—open-sided guest room filled with charpois—set against the interior rampart. Here, men gather after working the fields. You see no women.

The hujra leads to narrow lanes and rows of small clay rooms set behind a wall, with a courtyard surrounded by rooms that are havens of peace—a sharp contrast to the fierce Pathan spirit. A common room contains crockery and kitchen utensils. The walls of each sleeping room are covered with wedding veils or *sera* (paper wedding ornaments decorated with rupees). Metal trunks hold clothing, wedding dresses, jewelry, and often a prayer rug. The floor space is filled with charpois or a carved walnut bed.

Other rooms are for cattle, goats, or donkeys. Cow dung, used for cooking fuel, dries on an outer wall near handsome clay ovens. Chickens, hens, and young children patter around the courtyard. Large clay pots hold water or grain. A wicker birdcage holds a partridge. If bad luck, such as disease, descends on the village, the people believe the bird will die, not the Pathans.

Travel Restrictions

You need a government permit to travel to Darra-Adam Khel and the Khyber Pass near Peshawar, Garam Chasma (hot springs), and the Kafir-Kalash villages near Chitral. Permits, free or at a nominal cost, take up to two days to process and are acquired on arrival. (*See* destination sections, below.) Also heed the advice about travel in tribal areas, which have a delicate relationship with the central government. Pakistan's authority ends when you step off the road. This doesn't mean you travel at risk; just don't stray from the excursions or routes suggested and avoid traveling at night. Foreigners must stop and show their passports and visas at checkpoints, which are noted. Visitors to Chitral must register with the police.

Addresses and Numbers

Tourist Information The central office of the **PTDC** in NWFP (Dean's Hotel, Islamia Road, Peshawar, tel. 79781) is open Sunday–Thursday 9–5; closed Friday. Other offices are noted in each destination section, below.

Emergencies For medical emergencies, turn to your hotel or guide. The nearest embassies are in Islamabad: **American** (Diplomatic Enclave, Ramna 5, tel. 92518261), **Canadian** (Diplomatic Enclave, Sector G-5, tel. 92821101), **British** (Diplomatic Enclave, Ramna 5, tel. 92822131).

Travel Agencies **Indus Guides** has an office in Peshawar and in Swat Valley. **Travel Walji's** has offices in Peshawar and in Chitral. (*See* destination sections, below.) **Pakistan Tours,** a government undertaking, is located at the PTDC office listed above. For tours, treks, and car or jeep rentals, arrange in advance through the home offices of these three companies (*see* Before You Go to North Pakistan, above).

Arriving and Departing

By Plane This chapter describes a road trip starting from Peshawar. Travelers can fly from Lahore to Peshawar. You can also fly into

Chitral or Saidu Sharif. Or, you can continue a trip in FANA
and enter this province in the north by road.

Airports From **Lahore, PIA** makes six daily one-hour flights to Islama-
and Airlines bad and four daily 90-minute flights to Peshawar. Plan for tight
security at the Peshawar Airport. PIA makes five weekly one-
hour flights between Islamabad and Saidu Sharif and two daily
four-hour flights between Islamabad and Chitral. Call, in Lahore (tel. 306411), in Peshawar (tel. 75461), in Chitral (tel. 546),
in Saidu Sharif (tel. 4624), in Islamabad (tel. 825031). Remember to reconfirm each ticket.

By Hired Car or To start your journey from Peshawar, hire a car or jeep with
Jeep with Driver driver from a recommended private tour operator. Jeeps are in
limited supply; make all arrangements before you depart. (*See*
Before You Go to North Pakistan, above, for costs.)

By Train Tracks run only to Lahore, Rawalpindi (near Islamabad), and
Peshawar. Call in Lahore (tel. 74436 or 727308).

Highlights for First-time Visitors

Must-sees include Peshawar, frontier home of the Pathans; the
rugged jeep trip from Gilgit in FANA along the Punial Highway to Chitral in NWFP; and excursions from Chitral to the
Kafir-Kalash villages. Without extensive stops or an outdoor
adventure, the trip through NWFP described here takes about
two weeks by jeep.

Getting Around

By Plane Weather permitting, **PIA** makes up to three daily flights between Peshawar and Chitral and one daily flight between
Peshawar and Saidu Sharif. Get all tickets in advance, and reconfirm each ticket.

By Hired Car or If you plan to travel between Gilgit and Chitral, note that roads
Jeep with Driver are packed dirt tracks and are often flooded with water from
melting glaciers. You *must* go by jeep. For other destinations,
you can travel by car. Hire a jeep or car with driver from a recommended tour operator.

Guided Tours

Pakistan Tours offers cultural excursions, jeep safaris, fishing
trips, and treks in Swat Valley, Peshawar, and Chitral. **Indus
Guides** and **Travel Walji's** offer numerous high-quality trips
with excellent guides. Arrange in advance through their central offices (*see* Before You Go to North Pakistan, above,).

Private Guides If you travel in a jeep or car, hire a guide from a recommended
private tour operator. These guides are knowledgeable and can
act as interpreters.

Outdoor Adventures

Highly recommended adventures are indicated by a star ★.

★ **Biking:** *Khunjerab Pass:* From June to mid-November, you can
go 14 days by mountain bike from Swat Valley (in NWFP) up
the Karakoram Highway to the Khunjerab Pass on the border
of China and back to Islamabad. Contact Travel Walji's (*see*

Tour Groups in Before You Go to North Pakistan, above). Make all arrangements before you depart.

★ **Climbing and Mountaineering:** Experienced climbers who wish to attempt Tirich Mir, 7,700 meters (25,264 feet), or other peaks in the Hindu Kush should contact the private tour operators listed in Before You Go to North Pakistan, above. If you want to organize your own expedition, you need a permit, available through the Tourism Division, Government of Pakistan (F-7/2, Islamabad). Approval can take more than a year.

★ **Fishing:** *Swat Valley:* You can fish in the Swat River from April to September. The tour operators listed in Before You Go to North Pakistan, above, also arrange fishing excursions here. *Chitral:* You can fish from April to September on the Lotkuh River near Garam Chasma and near Bumburet in the Kafir-Kalash valleys. Permits are necessary for all fishing (*see* each destination section). Bring your own gear.

Golfing: You can golf at Peshawar and Saidu Sharif. Bring your own clubs.

★ **Horseback Riding:** *Gupis to Mastuj:* You can ride five days through mountaintop vistas and beautiful villages from Gupis in the Gilgit Agency to Mastuj in Chitral (NWFP). Arrange through Travel Walji's before you depart.

Hot Springs: *Garam Chasma:* Enjoy a private pool replenished with hot spring water in this village about 30 km (18mi) Chitral.

★ **Polo:** You can watch great games in Chitral from April to July and September to October. If a match is scheduled, you can also see the play-off between Gilgit and Chitral at the world's highest arena in Shandur, the gateway to FANA. (*See* Gilgit in Federally Administered Northern Areas and Karakoram Highway, Part II, above, for details.)

Rafting: *Swat:* From November to March, you can do a two-day run in bamboo or rubber rafts and five days of trekking. From the mountain village of Kasoona near Saidu Sharif, you walk to Madyan village in a narrow gorge—the starting point for rafting south on the Swat River to the Mingora Bridge. Contact Travel Walji's (*see* Before You Go to North Pakistan, above). Make all arrangements before you depart.

★ **Trekking:** *Do not* set off into tribal territory without an experienced guide. Some trekking areas are also in restricted zones that require a guide and special permit. Contact a recommended tour operator before you depart, and it will supply a guide and get the permit for you. The trekking season is generally from May to October. NWFP offers so many treks, we can list only the best. If an area interests you, ask a recommended tour operator for more options.

Trekking (up to a week): *Mahodand Lake:* A moderately difficult five-day trek from the alpine Ushu Valley in Upper Swat takes you along a river, through meadows surrounded by waterfalls, and up to the snowy wilderness of the Kachikhanni Pass, altitude 4,756 meters (15,600 feet), which is the gateway to Chitral. You descend along the Kachikhanni Glacier to Laspur village, then swing northwest to the Chitrali village of Mastuj, set in a lush valley. In Mastuj, you can go by jeep to Chitral or extend your trek by a week and arrive on foot.

Drosh to Koghozi: A moderate four- to six-day trek from the village of Drosh in Chitral heads through pine groves and steep gorges to the village of Madaklasht. From here, you walk through the forest and meadow-strewn Shishi Valley, surrounded by white peaks, over the Dok Pass, altitude 4,500 meters (14,760 feet), then descend through the Hindu Kush to the village of Koghozi.

Trekking (over a week): *Kafir-Kalash:* An eight-day moderate–difficult trek from Birrer, a Kafir-Kalash village, heads over the Chumbai Pass, at 3,500 meters (11,480 feet) and into the Bumburet Valley, which has the largest number of Kafir-Kalash. You walk in narrow valleys through forests and meadows and by streams and get a good look at this vanishing animist culture. From here, you follow a narrow river up over a pass, altitude 4,647 meters (15,242 feet), which leads to Birmoghalasht hamlet above Chitral and great views of Mt. Tirich Mir. Here, you can visit the palace of the former *mehter* (ruler) of Chitral before heading on to the village of Garam Chasma, close to the Afghanistan border. At Garam Chasma, you can recuperate in a private hot spring.

Peshawar

Numbers in the margin correspond with points of interest on the North West Frontier Province map.

❶ Peshawar, 56 kilometers (35 miles) from the entry to the Khyber Pass, is a dusty sprawl of antiquity now wrestling with the modern age and a flood of Afghan refugees. Lowell Thomas called it, "Paris of the Pathans, city of a 1,001 sins." For centuries, travelers have lingered here—caught up in its rough-and-tumble intrigue. Inside the old quarter, hidden behind a crumbling wall, *kalifas* (camel caravans) and donkey carts outnumber cars. The obligatory gun worn by the Pathan remains a symbol of frontier law.

Getting Around **By Auto Rickshaws:** These, Rs. 3 per kilometer, are the best way to travel.

By Taxi: For excursions, you can hire a private taxi for Rs. 500 per day.

Addresses and Numbers For tourist information and travel assistance, contact **PTDC** (Dean's Hotel, Islamia Rd., tel. 79781), open Sunday–Thursday 9–5, closed Friday; **Indus Guides** (213 Sunehry Masjid Rd., Saddar Rd., tel. 72588), open Sunday–Thursday 9–5, closed Friday; and **Travel Walji's** (Doctor's Plaza, Rm. 14, 12 Saddar Rd., tel. 72093), open daily 9–5.

Banks **Habib Bank** (Chowk Yaadgar) and **Grindlays Bank** (Shahrah-e-Quaid-e-Azam) are open Monday–Thursday 9–1; weekends 9–noon.

Post Office The **Post Office** (Shahrah-Pehlavi, Saddar Rd.) is open Saturday–Thursday 9–4.

Exploring Start your tour of the old city at **Khyber Bazaar** and stroll up **Qissa Khawani Bazaar** (Street of Storytellers), where raconteurs once regaled audiences with tales and the latest news. Today, storytellers have been replaced by dentists who display false teeth on tables. Pathans, travelers, Afghans, and livestock crowd the sidewalk on their way to market.

Watch for a lane on the left, with finely worked copper or brass kitchenware spilling out of narrow stalls. This is the **Bazaar of Coppersmiths,** where craftsmen sit cross-legged on cushions and pound out handsome plates, samovars, teapots, and vases. From here, it's a short walk to **Chowk Yaadar** (central square of Old Peshawar) and the nearby **Bazaar of Goldsmiths and Silversmiths,** a narrow street hemmed in by tall buildings. Inside tiny cubicles, jewelers sell stacks of bangles and create ornate earrings, necklaces, and pendants with pearls, rubies, and emeralds. Money changers crouch over piles of currency, computing figures on pocket calculators. In courtyards off the main bazaar, Afghan refugees sell old tribal jewelry and curios.

The next stop is the nearby **Mahabat Khan Mosque,** Peshawar's finest Moghul monument, built in the 1670s during the reign of Emperor Aurangzeb. Ravaged by fire in 1898, much of the interior has been replaced, including the decorative paintings. Still, it's a good example of Islamic architecture, with three bulbous domes over the central prayer hall and a graceful minaret in each corner. There are also many clocks and chandeliers. The devout are encouraged to make donations, and the mosque keeps whatever they give, including the Coca Cola clock.

Head to **Bazaar Kalan.** As you walk, narrow lanes lead to more bazaars set up according to trade. The henna market has stalls piled with black powder for the hair and a green powder that turns orange when applied to the skin. Nearby is the bustling produce market crowded into a narrow street still lined with old stucco or wood balconies—bits of old Peshawar.

On a lane across from the market are the century-old **Sethi Mansions,** a row of gracious old *havelis* (palaces) with arched windows and carved wood balconies. They're owned by a prominent old business family. The men of the house hold keys to the more opulent upper-floor rooms; if they're out, the women can show you the interior courtyard and the lower floors.

Time Out   Stop at the **Dilrubba Restaurant** across from the entrance to the Mohabit Khan Mosque. Don't be put off by the greasy-spoon decor, the crowds, or the noise of this typical Afghan eatery. The food is delicious and inexpensive—Rs. 15 for Kabuli (rice), cooked vegetables, mutton kebabs, and Afghan bread. *Open 10:30–2 and 6:30–11.*

Shopping   This is the best shopping in Pakistan. If you like old kilims and carpets from Iran, Turkey, Russia, Afghanistan, and tribal areas of Pakistan, head to **Afghan Handicraft House** (Rm. 9, 1st floor, i.e., 2nd floor to Americans, Saddat Market opposite the Galaxie Hotel in the Khyber Bazaar, tel. 64856), run by knowledgeable Mohammed Raheem, an Afghan refugee. Raheem also sells tribal jewelry, old furniture, and other interesting curios and accepts American Express and Visa credit cards. The shop is open all the time; he lives here. Be sure to bargain. Also visit three shops opposite the General Post Office on Shahrah-Pehlavi (Saddar Rd.): **Bukhara House, Kabul House,** and **Carpet House.** They're open Sunday–Thursday, closed Friday; Bukhara 10–8:30, Kabul 8–8, and Carpet 9–8:30. They accept American Express, Diners Club, MasterCard, and Visa credit cards. Bargain. Another good shop is **Kashmir Victory House** (near Grindlays Bank), open 9–8:30. Bargain.

Pathan Handicrafts sells great Afghan and Kafir-Kalash jewelry, lovely hand-beaded purses, Afghan silk coats, tribal clothing, some kilims. *Qissa Khawani, Shop No. 2580, tel. 63538. Open Sun.–Thurs. 7:30 AM–8 PM; closed Fri. No credit cards. Bargain.*

In **Sarafa Bazaar** and **Shinwary Market** (Andar Sher), you find entire buildings filled with interesting Afghan and tribal jewelry. They're open daily, 9–6; no credit cards. Bargain.

Outdoor Adventures You can play **golf** at the Peshawar 18-hole golf course. Contact PTDC for details. Bring your own equipment.

Dining Try robust Afghan or good Pakistani and Chinese food. Dress is always casual and reservations are not necessary unless noted. Highly recommended restaurants are indicated by a star ★. Prices are per person, including taxes and excluding drinks and service charges.

Lala's Grill. This Moghul-style restaurant has excellent Pakistani food. Try the local favorite: lamb joints with mutton *tikka tandoori* (barbequed mutton) and Kabul *pillau* (rice). *Greens Hotel, Saddar Rd. tel. 76035., Open 6:30–11, 12:30–3:30, 7:30–10:30. No credit cards. Moderate ($5–$10).*

Melmakore. Enjoy good Pakistani, regional, and Continental food in a quiet frontier-style decor with good service. *Pearl Continental Hotel, Khyber Rd., tel. 76361. Reservations advised. Open 7–9:30, 12:30–3, 7:30–11. AE, DC, MC, V. Moderate ($5–$10).*

★ **Salateen Restaurant.** This raucous upstairs restaurant serves the best Pathan meal in Peshawar and is always filled with Pathans, Peshawaris, and Afghans. Curtained booths provide privacy for women in purdah. The talk is spirited, a TV blares. Try *saji* (lamb with tomato), *murk karahi* (frontier-style chicken), mutton tikka, and great *naan* (bread). *Kabul Gate, tel. 73779. Open 11 AM–midnight. No credit cards. Inexpensive (under $5).*

Lodging Highly recommended hotels are indicated by a star ★. Prices are for a standard double room, including taxes and excluding service charges.

★ **Pearl Continental Hotel.** This modern hotel has attractive carpeted rooms done in a low-key decor. Some rooms overlook a golf course and lovely lawns. *Khyber Rd., tel. 76361. 150 rooms with bath. Facilities: 3 restaurants, room service, a Kawa Khana (tearoom), liquor permit room, swimming pool, health club, tennis court, golf course, color TV, car rental, foreign-exchange facilities. AE, DC, MC, V. Expensive ($60–$100).*

Dean's PTDC. This British-era standby has clean, oversize rooms with institutional-type furniture. *Islamia Rd., tel. 76481 or reserve through PTDC, Flashman's Hotel, The Mall, Rawalpindi, tel. 66231 or 581480. 46 rooms with bath. Facilities: mediocre restaurant, room service, air-conditioning and overhead fans, tourist department, liquor permit room, foreign-exchange counter. No credit cards. Moderate ($25–$60).*

Excursion to Darra-Adam Khel As you leave the Peshawar city limits and head south into the foothills of the Hindu Kush, you see the formidable walls concealing Pathan villages. When you hear the sound of gunfire, ❷ you're close to **Darra,** the heart of Pathan country and home of the Afridi sect.

In dusty Darra, 600 shops sell guns; 6,000 people manufacture ballpoint-pen pistols, rifles, machine guns, antiaircraft missiles, and rockets. Before you buy, you *must* have a gun permit— or you'll be stopped at the airport and end up in jail.

The class shop is **Haji Baz Gul** on the main road. Here, men study a weapon with the intensity of a woman analyzing fine silk. Kalashnikovs are the preferred item. Russian originals cost Rs. 20,000; Pakistani knockoffs go for about Rs. 6,000. Though many guns are smuggled in, most of the weapons available are locally made in primitive factories where ingenuity and skill make up for sophisticated tools.

A prospective buyer will test a small gun in the street. Larger weaponry he hauls to a nearby field. With the manufacturer by his side, file in hand and ready to make instant adjustments, the customer blasts a few rounds into a range shared by grazing donkeys and dogs trotting back and forth as if they were deaf.

Foreigners aren't allowed to wander beyond Darra's bazaar. During your trip to and from Darra, don't try to visit a fortified village unless you have a local guide and an invitation. Remember that in Pathan country, there are more guns than family members. *Darra is about 43 km (27 mi) south of Peshawar. To make this excursion, you must get a permit (free) from the Secretary, Office of Home and Tribal Affairs in the Civil Secretariat, open 8:30–1:30. Bring your passport. Explain the nature of your visit: tourist; the permit takes up to 2 days to process. Allow 4 or 5 hours by car.*

Excursion to Khyber Pass Because of the current unstable political climate in Afghanistan, excursions to the **Khyber Pass** are not advised at this time. Contact your travel agent or the State Department for information.

The Arts If you're interested in Gandhara art, the **Peshawar Museum** is a must. Start from the left wall of the central hall, which tells the story of the Buddha's life. Read the inscriptions and study the carved stone panels. Also visit the Hall of Tribes, which contains wood statues removed from Kafir-Kalash gravesites. Unfortunately, the pieces aren't labeled. The grave marker of a woman is identified by slight feminine curves and a hat with two peaks; a man's is distinguished by a pointed peak at the hat's crown. The carving also indicates the stature of the deceased. Low class is represented by a figure standing alone; the next higher class, by a figure on a single horse; and an even higher class, by a man on two horses. An individual in a chair is tribal nobility. Also visit the museum's **Muslim Gallery,** which has Moghul relics and good miniatures from the 18th century. *Admission: Rs. 2. Open summer, Thurs.–Tues. 8–1 and 3–6; winter Thurs.–Tues. 9–1:30 and 3–6.*

On to Swat Valley and Saidu Sharif

A princely kingdom ruled by the Wali of Swat until 1971 when it was federalized, Swat Valley, 85 kilometers (50 miles) northeast of Peshawar, is strewn with monuments, many left behind by Buddhists who called this valley Udyana (Garden) when they took refuge here after the White Hun invasion. They developed the Gandhara School of Sculpture, which was heavily influenced by Greco-Roman aesthetics and dared to show the human form of the Historic Buddha.

Once you leave Peshawar, you leave behind the dust and enter groves of sugarcane and palm trees threaded by irrigation canals where buffalo and children cool themselves. This was once the land of the camel. But today, they're being replaced by the Suzuki—cheaper, faster, and easier to maintain.

The first important village is Takht-i-Bhai (Spring on the Mountain) in the Mardan Agency just below Swat Valley, about 52 kilometers (32 miles) from Peshawar. About 2 kilometers (1 mile) from the bazaar, visit the remains of ancient **Takht-i-Bhai**, a Buddhist village and monastery erected by Kushans in the 1st century. The walk up to the monastery in the barren Himalayan foothills takes about 15 minutes. The sun is intense at midday. Bring a water bottle.

Old Takht-i-Bhai housed about 6,000 people and extended about 5 kilometers (3 miles) around the mountain. Portions of a protective wall still poke up from nearby ridges. Before you enter the monastery, look at the exterior wall with bits of the original plaster. Set in an earthquake belt, the Kushans designed the walls with built-in shock absorbers—big flat stones surrounded by layers of thin stone. They also left about two feet of space between all passageways.

The Court of Many Stupas in typical Gandhara style with square bases is just inside the monastery. Three-quarters of the monastery is original, and all the niches once held statues that are now in the Peshawar Museum. Some archaeologists believe that the main stupa on the elevated courtyard to the left contains relics of the Buddha. On the opposite side of the monastery are the private chambers of the monks who lived here. The meditation center is downstairs: a series of cells off a dark corridor now inhabited by bats. Historic odds and ends from the site, including headless statues that wear Greek costumes, are protected behind a metal fence.

From Takht-i-Bhai, head northwest into the Malakand Agency— the place of the tribal chiefs. Pathans called Malaks and numerous Afghan refugees live here. As the road climbs, bluffs reveal occasional fortlike watchtowers built by the British when they attempted to control the Malaks. Currently, the Pakistan government doesn't control this agency either.

Sakhakot, about 15 kilometers (9 miles) from Takht-i-Bhai, the first sizable village you enter in the Malakand Agency, is another gun town. From Sakhakot, you wind your way up stark mountains over the Malakand Pass into **Chakdarra**. Visit the excellent **Dir Museum** in Chakdarra (2 kilometers, or 1 mile, along on the road to Dir) with a good collection of Gandhara Art dating back to the 4th century. *Admission: Rs. 2. Open Thurs.–Tues. 8:30–noon and 2–6; closed Wed.*

From Chakdarra, the valley widens. At **Landakai** village, 13 kilometers (8 miles) from Chakdarra and the gateway to Swat Valley, foreigners must register at the **checkpoint.** Swat is a region with about 1,000 Aryan and Buddhist remains, all near the Swat River, with numerous streams cutting through pastures populated by donkeys, goats, and cattle. Camels wander along the road. High-grade Virginia tobacco grows in fertile fields surrounded by lotus gardens.

Shingardar Stupa, 27 kilometers (17 miles) from Chakdarra, stands in a field on your right. Legend claims that in 2nd century BC, King Utrasena of Udyana obtained a small portion of the Buddha's holy ashes in India and transported them here by elephant. When the elephant arrived at Shingardar, it refused to budge. The king took it as an omen and built the stupa, with its handsome Greek-style columns on the dome. Behind the stupa, closer to the mountains, are the minimal ruins of a monastery.

At **Gala Gai** village, about 2 kilometers (1 mile) from Shingardar, a headless 5th-century **statue of the Meditating Buddha** is carved into a boulder on the right. More **Buddhist remains** are at **Gogdara** village, about 9 kilometers (6 miles) from Shingardar. Archaeologists assume these carvings of a wheat leaf, deer, and horse cart were created in 1700 BC when people first began to write. **Udigram** (formerly Ora), the capital of Udyana in 4th century BC and divided into Upper and Lower Ora, is just after Gogdara. Few ruins remain today, and all are in dismal condition.

Saidu Sharif and Mingora

⑤ **Saidu Sharif,** about 8 kilometers (5 miles) due north, was the traditional seat of the ruler of Swat. Its neighboring commercial center is Mingora. They're an excellent base for excursions and outdoor adventures.

Getting Around *By Auto Rickshaw*	They are the best way to travel in Saidu Sharif and Mingora. Prices are fixed according to destination; ask PTDC (*see* below) for appropriate rates.
Addresses and **Numbers** *Tourist Information*	For tourist information or travel assistance, contact **PTDC** (Swat Serena Hotel, Saidu Sharif, tel. 2220), open Sunday–Thursday 9–5, closed Friday; and **Indus Guides** (Hotel Pameer, Mingora, tel. 4926), open daily 9–5.
Bank	**Habib Bank** (Mingora) is open Monday–Thursday 9–1, weekends 9–noon.
Post Office	**Post Office** (Mingora) is open Saturday–Thursday 9–4.
Exploring Mingora	Mingora's **main-street bazaar** is worth a quick stroll. Medicine men sell locally made pills and concoctions, including *salajeet* (a black sticky substance found on high-altitude mountains), a remedy for joint ailments and a stopgap against old age and impotence. Women congregate around stalls with barrels of dyes that turn white chaddars bright colors. The veils are dipped in the dye and then given to boys who flap them dry in five minutes. Shops sell intricate old hand-stitched Swati fabrics, elaborate beaded necklaces, old silver jewelry, and semiprecious and precious stones.
Shopping	**Zahib Gul Handicrafts** (Mingora Bazaar, tel. 4212) sells excellent local handicrafts. It's open Sunday–Thursday 8–7; closed Friday. It doesn't accept credit cards. Bargain.
Outdoor **Adventures**	Play **golf** in Kabal, 18 kilometers (11 miles) from Saidu Sharif; equipment is available. Nearby excursions lead to good trout **fishing** from April to September and excellent **horseback riding**. **Skiing** is under development. Contact PTDC for fishing permits and pony information.
Dining and **Lodging**	The best restaurants, inexpensive (under $5), are connected to the two recommended hotels and are noted. Dress is casual and reservations are not necessary. Highly recommended lodgings

are indicated by a star ★. Prices are for a standard double room, including taxes and excluding service charges.

★ **Swat Serena Hotel.** This former guest house of the Wali of Swat was constructed in 1930. New rooms, added in 1962, retain the stately Victorian design. The rooms are attractive; the best ones open onto the upper-floor veranda and interior lawn. *Saidu Sharif, Swat, tel. 4604. 44 rooms with bath. Facilities: courtesy Mingora and airport transport, travel and foreign exchange counter, gift shop, badminton, small golf course, baby-sitters, doctor on call, room service, air-conditioning, fireplaces, coffee shop (open 7 AM–10 PM), excellent restaurant serving Continental and Pakistani cuisine (open 7–9:30, 12:30–2:30, 7:30–10). AE, MC, V. Moderate ($25–$60).*

Hotel Pameer. This good budget hotel has clean carpeted rooms and a terraced garden. *Mingora, Swat, tel. 4926. Facilities: central air-conditioning, free airport transport, car rental, travel and foreign-exchange counter, shopping arcade, good Pakistani restaurant (open 7–9:30, 12:30–3, 8–11). AE. Inexpensive (under $25).*

Excursion from Saidu Sharif to Jehanabad Head north from Mingora to the village of Manglwar. Take the road on the right across the Swat River to the hamlet of Jehanabad. Buddhists say that when Gautama Buddha came to Swat, he preached such a moving sermon that a stone stupa, called the Jehanabad Seated Buddha, emerged where he stood. Though you can see the stupa from the road, the best view requires an hour-long walk. *Jehanabad is 16 km (10 mi) north of Saidu Sharif. If you hike to the stupa, bring a packed lunch and have a picnic.*

Excursion from Saidu Sharif to Madyan ❻ At **Khawazakhela,** 27 kilometers (17 miles) north of Mingora, stop and try a Pathan burger (*chapli kabob*). Men sit on large platforms behind a gigantic vat placed over a clay oven and eat hunks of fresh ground beef mixed with tomatoes, onions, corn flour, and spices and cooked in the vat. This is the most delicious, safest fast food in north Pakistan.

After you leave Khawazakhela village, you see Mt. Falakser, altitude 5,918 meters (19,415 feet), the highest mountain in the area. Just before Madyan, stop at **Madyan Antiquity Center,** 53 kilometers (33 miles) from Mingora. Here you can buy Swati handicrafts, gems, old leather gunpowder bags, beautiful tribal jewelry, coins, guns and lovely stitched and beaded *butwa* (purses). The center is open March–November, daily 7–7; December–February, daily 9–4:30. Prices are fixed and no credit cards are accepted.

❼ The **Madyan Hotel,** your destination, is on the far side of the **Madyan** Bazaar, 52 kilometers (32 miles) from Mingora. One of north Pakistan's best-kept secrets, it's run by an elegant Pathan Ikrumullah Khan. Though the charming bungalow was built in 1957, it feels much older. Its setting is idyllic—in lovely gardens on a hill. The main building with a veranda is perfect for sipping tea. The cheery dining room serves excellent food. The rooms are spacious but not fancy. In those facing the Swat River, the sound of the water lulls you to sleep. *Madyan, Swat, tel. 2. 30 rooms with bath. Facilities: restaurant (open 6:30–10, 12:30–2:30, 7:30–10:30), foreign-exchange counter, fishing equipment available. AE, DC. Inexpensive (under $25).*

From here, travelers can head to Kalam, 49 kilometers (30 miles) from Madyan, a much-touted Pakistani hill station, now overwhelmed by too many hotels. Try visiting instead the charming village of **Miandam** to the northwest. Ringed by snow-covered peaks, Miandam sits in a valley filled with flowers, streams, and orchards. You can spend the night at the **PTDC Motel,** a modest but attractive hotel in a lovely setting. *Reservations: Flashman's Hotel, The Mall, Rawalpindi, tel. 66231 or 581480, or in Miandam, tel. 10A. 10 rooms with bath. Facilities: dining room providing simple good meals. No credit cards. Inexpensive (under $25). The trip from Saidu Sharif to Madyan can be done in 4 hours as a lunch excursion, but try to spend the night. Hire a car with driver in Mingora or Saidu Sharif.*

The Arts The **Swat Museum** in Saidu Sharif has an excellent collection of
Museums artifacts from Swat Valley: Gandhara sculpture from the 1st to 7th centuries; jewelry from the 2nd to 4th centuries; old pottery dating back to 1400 BC; and excellent displays of Swati handicrafts, clothing, jewelry, and instruments. *Admission: Rs. 2. Open Thurs.–Tues. 8:30–12:30 and 2:30–5:30; closed Wed.*

On to Chitral

This trip, about 270 kilometers (168 miles), requires a jeep and can be made only from October to May 15 when the Lowari Pass is open.

To get to Chitral, head south to Chakdarra, 47 kilometers (29 miles) away in the Malakand District. Here, you leave the Swat River and drive north 40 kilometers (25 miles) to the village of Temerghara, the start of the Dir District.

Like Malakand, Dir District is tribal country. Each roadside village has a line of clay-and-wood shops, with at least one selling guns and ammo. Constructed from local materials, each village is a part of the landscape. Nothing in the ambience seems harsh, except for the sight of the usual arsenals and the crowds of donkeys, goats, cars, jeeps, and pickup trucks that fight for the right of way.

8 **Dir,** 70 kilometers (43 miles) from Temerghara, is a crazy city with a must-see frontier bazaar. Stalls sell vegetables, fruit, and spices. A barber has his shop (a chair and table with mirror) set up by a tree. Shoe repairmen sit a few feet away. Medicine men offer a potion made from pelicans brought in from Iran. Near the medicine man sits a bird on a leash. On a blanket tied in a bundle is a pelican's carcass; it's fat has been cooked and sold in various-size bottles as a cure for rheumatic pain. Jars contain pellets, some looking rather like silver bullets, that supposedly increase the sex drive. Shops sell the typical array of armaments. You see few women and they are all hidden in their robes. Have a good Pakistani lunch at the informal **Hotel Al Manzar.** *Dir Bazaar, on the Main Rd. Open daily. No credit cards. Inexpensive (under $5).*

9 The road turns rough as it climbs to **Lowari Pass,** 33 kilometers (20 miles) from Dir. Clouds scuttle between the peaks. Men walk along with rifles slung over their shoulders, an odd counterpoint to the bucolic scenes of grazing livestock. From the pass, you descend through the Hindu Kush into Chitral.

At first, the Hindu Kush are barren, with massive boulders lodged on slopes and stones scattered everywhere. The air is cold, the earth cracked and dry. After 14 kilometers (8.6 miles), you enter Ziarat village. Here, you can take a break at a typical truck stop—a wood building set against the mountain with tables and charpois. Join Pathans and truck drivers to enjoy freshly prepared simple food.

About 13 kilometers (8 miles) later, you reach **Mir Khani** village, 17 kilometers (11 miles) from Afghanistan. Here foreigners must stop and **register at the checkpoint**. Along the road you see Afghan refugee camps pitched by the river or scattered amid the typical Chitrali homes, called *baipash*, made of stone plastered with clay. The flat *ghoraram* (roof) is an attractive design of diminishing squares made from poplar. Not a single nail is used. In the center of the ghoraram is a small opening from which smoke escapes.

Each village has a near-Biblical aura—dusty-hued buildings with sunflowers abloom in lush fields. Donkeys are everywhere. Men, many Afghan refugees, work fields with crude wood plows drawn by oxen. Women in bright Afghan layered skirts and blouses dig up rice with their hands. You're consumed by the tranquility until you reach Chitral, a bustling frontier town. Chitral was formerly a major stop on the ancient Silk Route and an important slave-trading center; it's now home to 30,000 Afghan refugees.

Chitral

10 Shahi Bazaar, the commercial center of **Chitral,** would never win an award for beauty. Donkeys with riders using ski poles, polo mallets, or twigs for prods; strollers (almost all men except for an occasional foreign woman); and open pickups crowd the dusty thoroughfare. But Chitral's melting pot is a great cultural experience.

The main activities in Chitral are trading and polo. If visitors aren't watching a game, they're analyzing Chitral's 30 teams, comparing the horses—either rugged Balkhashi ponies from Afghanistan or the fast Waziri horses from the Punjab—and determining Chitral's ability to overwhelm its great rival, Gilgit.

On arrival, all foreigners must bring their passports to register at the **Chitral Police Station** (Jameh Masjid Rd.). To visit the Kafir-Kalash villages or the hot springs at Garam Chasma, foreigners must bring their passports and register for a permit at the Deputy Commissioner's Office, which is open Saturday–Thursday 7:30–2. Visitors are allowed a two-week permit, renewable for 15 days. Permits are ready in a day. Foreigners planning to fly out of Chitral must reconfirm their seats at the PIA office on Jameh Masjid Road.

Getting Around Chitral is a walker's town.

Addresses and Numbers
Tourist Information For tourist information and travel assistance, contact **PTDC** (PTDC Motel, tel. 683), open Thursday–Tuesday 9–5, closed Friday, and **Travel Walji's** has an office (Mountain Inn, Chitral, tel. 4), open daily 9–5.

Bank The **bank** (off the main bazaar) is open Monday–Thursday 9–1, weekends 9–noon.

Post Office **Post office** (off the main bazaar) is open Saturday–Thursday 9–4.

Exploring Chitral A good place to start a tour of **Shahi Bazaar** is outside the PTDC Hotel, where most stalls are owned by Afghans. You see shopkeepers selling what looks like black stone. Wet your finger and take a taste—it's rock salt. Afghans have introduced a popular new taste treat sold from a cart—fruit syrups, such as pomegranate or mango, poured over a chunk of glacier ice. Along the road, men sit with wood suitcases filled with bottles of essence: rose, musk, sandlewood. Choose a scent, and the seller will pour it into a vial: the purest perfume you can buy for just Rs. 5. Two enormous mallets powered by a generator whack and grind a mixture of local tobacco, ashes, and water creating a wet chewing tobacco *(niswar)*. Chitralis say that if you put niswar in the mouth of a snake, it dies in five minutes. The local users don't swallow it. Stalls sell beads called *tasbih*, used by Moslems to count their obligatory prayers.

The last must-see is a must-do: Walk down **PIA Chauk.** Here you find photo stalls run by Afghan refugees with primitive box cameras carried in from Afghanistan. The camera is a suitcase with a lens fixed on the front, a denim pant leg covering a large hole on the side, and a large screw on the top that allows the photographer to focus. For Rs. 8, you get to hold your pose for an eternity while he first shoots the negative. While you're sitting, notice the Afghan guerrilla emblems plastered over all the box: "By the Grace of Allah, very close to Victory." Five minutes later, you get the negative and finished photo—a great lasting memory.

Walk down Jameh Masjid Road. On your left is the Sunni **Shahi Mosque** and the **School of Islamia and Arabic Teaching Center.** The handsome white stucco building was built in 1936 by the former mehter (king) of Chitral. As you walk along the hallway, stop at a window. Inside the hall, young children sit with elders and learn verses from the Quran.

The mosque has a large courtyard with two minarets on the far corners that honor Mohammed and Ali. All around the courtyard are the tombs of the honored deceased, including the mehter of Chitral, other members of his family, religious dignitaries, and patrons of the mosque.

On a strategic site by the Chitral River and to the right of the mosque is the **Shahi Fort and Palace,** constructed at the end of the 18th century and completely renovated in 1895. Today, however, the fort is in disrepair. But from the veranda by the river, you can get a good view of Mt. Tirich Mir.

Shopping For good *pattu* (Chitrali soft wool) and handwoven *pilask* (goat-hair rugs), visit Sar Faraz Khan, **Shop No. 374.** He's open daily 8–6, but closes for obligatory prayers. Wait 10 minutes, he'll be back. Mohammed Hanif, **Shop No. 78,** sells lovely Chitrali beaded necklaces *(har)*, embroidered *khulta* (purses), old wool saddlebags stitched in Afghanistan, and handsome brass and tin urns. He's open daily 8–6. Neither shop accepts credit cards.

Outdoor Adventures **Fish** for trout from April to September in rivers near Chitral, at the Kafir-Kalash villages, and at Garam Chasma. Fishing permits are available at nominal charge from the Fisheries Department. Excellent treks are described in Outdoor Adventures (*see* North Pakistan, above). In town, the **polo** season runs from March 23 to June 30 and August 14 to November. In Upper Chitral, the season runs from March 21 to November.

Dining and Lodging The best food, inexpensive (under $5), is served in the hotels. Dress is casual. Reservations are not necessary unless noted. Highly recommended lodgings are indicated by a star ★. Prices are for a standard double room, including taxes and excluding service charges.

★ **Chitral Mountain Inn.** The modest exterior leads to a delightful lawn with gardens. The rooms are spacious and clean and have fireplaces. Upper-floor rooms open onto a sweeping veranda. This is a peaceful hotel that also serves excellent fixed-menu meals— Pakistani and Continental. *Chitral, tel. 581. 24 rooms with bath (shower). Facilities: room service, restaurant (open 7–9:30, 12:30–2, 7–9:30), travel and trekking arrangements. Unless you're a hotel guest, you must call 2 hours before mealtime to arrange to eat here. No credit cards. Inexpensive (under $25).*

PTDC Motel. A two-story bungalow, it has spacious rooms with simple furniture. *Main Bazaar, Chitral, tel. 683 or reserve through Flashman's Hotel, The Mall, Rawalpindi, tel. 66231 or 581480. 14 rooms with bath (shower). Facilities: restaurant serving fixed-menu Continental and Pakistani meals (open 7–9:30, 12:30–2, 7–9:30), jeep rental, tourist office. No credit cards. Inexpensive (under $25).*

Excursion to Kafirstan Take the beautiful excursion to Kafirstan (permit required)— the home of the 2,800 Kafir-Kalash (Wearers of the Black Robe) who live west of Chitral in the villages of Birrer, Bumburet, and Rampur. The Kafir-Kalash have been discovered. You'll see the negative effects of tourism; nevertheless, this trip is not to be missed.

Jeep-worthy roads have brought medical care, schools, and other necessary services to the Kafir-Kalash. This change will improve their lives but dilute their culture. The women are now selling their special clothing and beautiful jewelry. Once the Kafir-Kalash danced only at festivals; now they dance for money. Try to respect the traditions that remain and try not to be overly intrusive. Never take a picture without asking and expect to pay for each one.

The handsome Kafir-Kalash claim Greek ancestry. Some have blue eyes and distinctly Aryan features. The women plait their long dark hair by the river (they are forbidden to comb it at home) and keep the comb under a rock. Their foreheads are tatooed with blue dots *(rang)* created with black mulberry and leaves that are boiled, then burnt into the skin.

The women wear *sangatchis* (black dresses of wool or cotton) brightened with red and green embroidery and secured with a wide sash of wool or jute. The quality of the beads and number of strands of their coral-bead necklaces indicate their status. Wrists are nearly hidden under bangles. Long earrings hang from their lobes. Their decorative circular caps *(shuhutto)* are covered with beads of glass; stone; and coral; tiny buttons; large brass military buttons; old coins; cowerie shells; miniature bells; and small plastic flowers. The back of their caps has a three-foot fringed tailpiece that ends in long metal chains that are tucked into the sash. The men used to wear trousers and shirts of goat's wool; now they dress in typical Pakistani clothes.

The religion of the Kafir-Kalash is imbued with elements of animal and nature worship. A pantheon of gods rules over a world of fairies and demons. Mahandeo is the warrior-god who protects the entire Kafir-Kalash territory. Jestak, who has a feminine aspect, protects the realm of the home—love, marriage, pregnancy, birth, and children.

The Kafir-Kalash used to celebrate three important festivals. Joshi, or Chilimjusht (around May 15), marks the start of spring planting. The people put on new clothes, clean their houses, and hang dried flowers from beams and pillars in the home. During Phool, rarely celebrated, the village would select a man to go off into the mountains at the start of winter. When he returned months later, he slept with any woman he chose, and any child he fathered was considered sacred. The third celebration, Chowas, began in December and evoked Mahandeo to protect the Kafir-Kalash from a harsh winter.

All festivals and important events, such as death and marriage, begin with the sacrifice of a goat, whose blood is then sprinkled into a fire. Unlike in most of Pakistan, marriages here are not arranged. When a man and woman decide to marry, they pick a day to celebrate. Villagers congregate in the temple and start a fire with walnut branches. When the couple arrives with the traditional plate of cookies, the villagers wave the burning branches over the couple seven times, then they drink. The couple is now officially married.

Every Kafir-Kalash village has a building called the *beshalene*. When a woman is pregnant or menstruating, she is considered unclean and stays here for the duration. When it's time to eat, another woman from the village brings her food. In the past, this second woman removed her clothes before she entered the beshalene. When she left, she washed completely before she dressed. Now she no longer undresses but does wash thoroughly.

To get to Birrer, the most remote and least visited Kafir-Kalash village, head south from Chitral by jeep along the metal road on the left side of the Chitral River. After about 30 kilometers (19 miles), take the jeep-worthy road on the right and cross a wood bridge. The road narrows, wedged between the mountains and river. You pass tiny villages. After another narrow wood bridge and a **checkpoint**, where you may be asked to show your permit, you head into the mountains following a thin blue river.

⑪ Soon you see the Kafir-Kalash and the village of **Birrer** perched on a slope. A graveyard is to the left of the road. In the past, the Kafir-Kalash never buried corpses, but left them exposed. Then they began to use open coffins. Now, owing to the influence of Islam, they cover the coffin, but continue to leave it above ground; you can see the bones of the deceased inside. Often they bring the dead person's bed to the grave and leave it on the coffin. As protection against evil spirits, the Kafir-Kalash also used to place a wood carving of a man or horse on a grave, especially on the grave of the tribal chief. Carvings of this sort are now in museums (Peshawar has good examples).

Birrer is built in tight tiers of stone and wood homes that have stilts supporting their upper verandas. Small communal food-storage shacks surround the homes. Unlike much of rural Pakistan, the Kafir-Kalash have separate winter dwellings for their livestock. To get from house to house, you climb notched-beam ladders, walk across roofs, and cross narrow front porches where cradles are suspended from ceiling beams.

The interior of the typical Kafir-Kalash house is Bactrian Greek, with wood pillars and a wood ceiling formed by a series of squares that descend in size to a small open ventilation square in the center. Numerous charpois are scattered around clay floors.

On the upper third of a slope above the center of Birrer is **Jestak Aan,** the village temple—a stone building plastered with mud. Two carved horse heads *(stor)* are mounted on each side of the door. Filled with carved walnut pillars, the 300- to 400-year-old temple has been renovated repeatedly; the roof remains pure Bactrian Greek. If you want to spend the night, make arrangements to stay in the **Rest House** when you get your permit. *3 rooms with Asian-style toilet, hot water by bucket. Simple accommodations with plain clean rooms. Nice setting in a garden. Food available. Inexpensive (under $10).*

To reach Bumburet, you return to the wood bridge (again be prepared to show your permit at the **checkpoint**) and take the jeep-worthy road that forks to the left, keeping the Chitral River on your right. The road hugs the Bumburet Nala River. You cross another bridge and traverse a rocky ledge that nearly shoves you off the road before you reach another bridge. On the opposite side, the road to the right leads to an uninteresting Kafir-Kalash village in Rampur Valley. The road to the left leads to **Bumburet,** the most highly populated Kafir-Kalash valley with five villages, including Brun, 27 kilometers (17 miles) from Birrer.

In Brun, look for the **temple** with a wood goat's head mounted on each side of the door. Inside, carvings cover old walnut pillars. Under a grove of trees on the upper left of the slope is a crude altar. This is where the Kafir-Kalash sacrifice a goat before each festival, leaving the head to ward off evil spirits. Women are not allowed to visit this site. For a good minimal meal in Brun, eat at Benazir Hotel and Restaurant, which is enclosed in a garden.

Permit is required for Kafirstan. Birrer is about 39 km (24 mi) from Chitral. Before you start, be sure the suspension bridge at Gahreet is open. Plan a day for this excursion or spend the night in Birrer. A jeep is the best way to go unless you trek.

Excursion to Shandur Pass From Chitral, you head north by jeep with the Hundu Kush on the right. Boulders extend like canopies; the Chitral River churns 30 feet below. In the village of **Rah,** after about 8 kilometers (5 miles), you see an old whitewashed **Sunni Mosque** decorated with wood carvings, delicate paintings, and Babylonian-style arches trimmed with lotus flowers across the front pavilion. If your timing is right, you can stop and watch the men praying—a moving occasion.

Beyond Rah, the road climbs into the mountain. The river races below. Precariously rooted trees brush against the top of the jeep. Then the valley opens into a stretch of cultivated plateaus—terraced yellow and green fields and groves of silver blue to deep green trees. The river roars when you're close, then quiets to a distant rumble when the road climbs. Oxen slosh through rice paddies, men and women work the fields, cattle graze.

Eroded mountains are an unexpected pale green. You wind through fluted peaks, then swing down to a narrow canyon. In time, the road links up with the Mastuj River. Across the way, glaciers tumble down from Tirich Mir and surrounding peaks.

⑫ From here, red-clay villages, such as **Reshun,** 44 kilometers (27 miles) from Rah, are hidden behind high walls. Narrow walkways lead to hidden doors. Trees shade rice paddies. Gigantic haystacks sit on flat roofs, piles of stones, tarpaulins—whatever is handy to keep the hay dry.

At **Kuragh** village, not far from Reshun, foreigners must stop at the **checkpoint,** register, and note their religious persuasions. After Kuragh, the vista opens up on the left revealing the distant green Norkshu Valley. You cross another suspension bridge and enter the village of Chayrun, 56 kilometers (35 miles) from Rah.

Now mountains are as red as the houses. As you enter the village of Boshi, 66 kilometers (41 miles) from Rah, you see Moslem shrines—now usually surrounded by triangular baked-clay outer walls. The valley narrows. The road climbs. Jagged peaks replace the smooth slopes. Rocky ledges hang over the jeep.

About 76 kilometers (47 miles) from Rah, an extensive valley appears on the far side of the river, with narrow cultivated fields and thickets of trees. The mountains behind it look like molten lava. You move away from the river, pass through villages set in groves that become increasingly arid. Above, clean white snow is streaked across the black Hindu Kush, called Shahwuaz (Black Snow Mountain) by local villagers.

At 84 kilometers (52 miles) from Rah, you enter **Parwak,** a dusty village as dry as the landscape and notable for its tea stalls—a good place to take a break. From here, you head toward the Shandur Pass, 108 kilometers (67 miles) from Rah. The Hindu Kush appear tame, rocks firmly in place.

Forty-two kilometers (26 miles) from the pass, the Hindu Kush end, replaced by the Karakorams and the Laspur River. The road climbs, following a parched canyon. In the middle of the canyon is the Laspur, a sullen gray from muddy melting glaciers. Gravel slopes rise up on the left. The mountains, chunks bitten out by wind and erosion, are no longer green, but brown. You climb through sheer desolation, overwhelmed by the **⑬** Karakorams until you get to **Shandur Pass.** The trip from Chitral to Shandur Pass is about 156 kilometers (97 miles) and requires a jeep. Make sure your driver has sufficient gasoline, a spare tire, and a good tool kit. Spend the night at Phandar just beyond Shandur Pass. *See* Excursion from Gilgit to Shandur Pass in Federally Administered Northern Areas and Karakoram Highway, Part II, above. Driving time is two days; add a third day to rest at Phandar—it's beautiful. Bring a sleeping bag and food for Phandar.

7 Tibet

Introduction

In 1950 the People's Liberation Army of Communist China marched into Tibet—a Himalayan kingdom so deeply committed to Buddhism that its kings (Dalai Lamas) are revered as incarnations of the Buddha of Compassion (Avalokitesvara). Simmering discontent led to a national uprising in 1959. Before the Chinese put an end to the fighting, His Holiness the 14th Dalai Lama fled to India.

Since 1950 over a million Tibetans have died in the struggle to regain independence. A profound sadness encircles this eerily beautiful kingdom and its gentle people.

Should foreigners visit Tibet? There's no easy answer. Many insist that if it weren't for our interest, Tibet's culture, remaining religious institutions, even the people themselves, would be destroyed. Only Xizang Autonomous Region—as it is known in China—would remain. Others say that to visit Tibet means providing the occupying force with currency.

In 1989 Tibet was under martial law; individual travel was banned. Because of the June 1989 events in China, it is doubtful that this restriction will be removed. Even if it is, foreigners are *strongly* advised to travel with a recommended tour operator.

Even with group travel, you must accept unwanted surprises. The Chinese keep a sharp eye on both Tibetans and foreigners. Hotel rooms are often searched and trip diaries are often impounded, then returned; you could even be strip-searched.

[Note to the reader: At press time, the U.S. Department of State advised against travel to China and Chinese-controlled areas. Before you plan your trip, check with the appropriate agency in your home country for current advisories.]

Before You Go

Government Tourist Offices

Limited information is available in overseas **China National Tourist Offices** (in the United States and Canada, Suite 3126, 60 E. 42nd St., New York, NY 10165, tel. 212/867–0271, or Suite 201, 333 W. Broadway, Glendale, CA, tel. 818/545–7505; in Britain, 4 Glentworth St., London NW1, tel. 01/935–9427).

Overseas offices of the Tibetan government in exile keep abreast of the current political climate. Americans and Canadians should contact **Office of Tibet** (107 E. 31st St., New York, NY 10016, tel. 212/779–9245). In Britain, also contact **Office of Tibet** (Linburn House, 342 Kilburn High Rd., London NW6 2QJ, tel. 01/328–8422).

Tour Groups

The following companies offer high-quality tours and adventures in Tibet.

Distant Horizons (679 Tremont St., Boston, MA 02118, tel. 617/267–5343 or 800/333–1240) offers scholar-led cultural tours.
EastQuest (32 Pell St., New York, NY 10013, tel. 212/406–2224

304

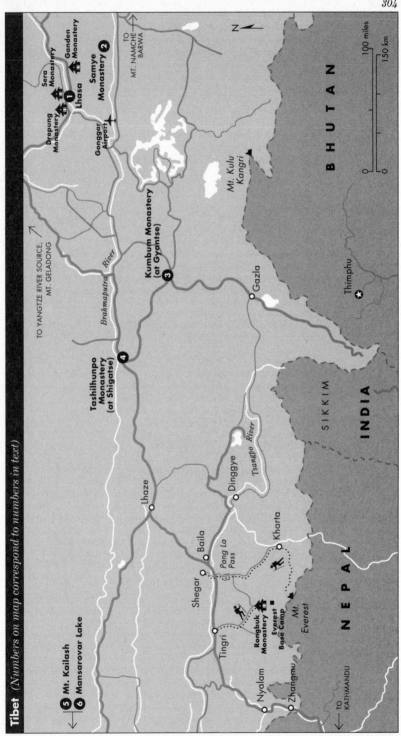

Tibet *(Numbers on map correspond to numbers in text)*

or 800/638–3449) sponsors general- and special-interest tours with flexible itineraries throughout Tibet.

IndoCulture Tours (5601 W. Slauson Ave., Suite 272, Culver City, CA 90230, tel. 213/649–0424 or 800/234–4085) features overland tours to Mt. Kailash and Mansarovar Lake, overland tours from Kathmandu to Lhasa, tours throughout Tibet, and tours planned around Losar (Tibetan New Year).

InnerAsia Expeditions (2627 Lombard St., San Francisco, CA 94123, tel. 415/922–0448 or 800/551–1769) offers overland tours from Kathmandu to Lhasa, treks to the Mt. Everest Base Camp, and treks to eastern Tibet and Mt. Namche Barwa.

Lute Jerstad Adventures (Box 19537, Portland, OR 97219, tel. 503/244–6075) sponsors overland tours from Lhasa to Pakistan and treks to the Mt. Everest Base Camp.

Mountain Travel (6420 Fairmount Ave., El Cerrito, CA 94530, tel. 415/527–8100 or 800/227–2384) operates overland tours from Kathmandu to Lhasa or to Mt. Everest; treks combined with overland tours from Lhasa to the source of the Yangtse River or from Kathmandu to Mt. Kailash; and treks to the Mt. Everest Base Camp, to Mt. Kulu Kangri, and to Mt. Namche Barwa.

Overseas Adventure Travel (349 Broadway, Cambridge, MA 02139, tel. 617/876–0533 or 800/221–0814) sponsors overland tours from Kathmandu to Lhasa with treks to the Mt. Everest Base Camp.

Shelter International Tibet Tours (2230 6th St., Boulder, CO 80302, tel. 303/449–6863 or 800/648–7771) runs theme tours (scheduled-departure or customized) that feature bird-watching, Tibetan medicine, Tibetan art, ecology, and religious pilgrimages. All tours provide close contact with the Tibetan culture, environment, and people.

Tiger Tops Mountain Travel International (2627 Lombard St., San Francisco, CA 94123, tel. 415/346–3402) offers overland tours from Kathmandu to Lhasa, with optional trekking to the Mt. Everest Base Camp and/or Mt. Xixabangma, trekking to Mt. Kailash and Mansarovar Lake, or rafting in yak-skin *coracles* (small round boats) on the Tsangpo River.

Wilderness Travel (801 Allston Way, Berkeley, CA 94710, tel. 415/548–0420 or 800/247–6700) sponsors overland tours from Kathmandu to Lhasa and treks to the Mt. Everest Base Camp.

When to Go

There are no flights into Lhasa from November through March and snow shuts down major passes, so plan to visit Tibet from April through October. From April to August, the temperature climbs. In early autumn dust storms occur, and melting snow often floods the rivers and roads.

Festivals and Seasonal Events

Tibet has two sets of holidays: events observed by the People's Republic of China that shut down businesses and government offices and Tibetan Buddhist festivals that are often shut down by the government. The lunar calendar determines the timing of many events, so check with your travel agent before you depart.

Jan. 1: New Year's Day is a government holiday.
Jan. or Feb.: Chinese New Year celebrates the first day of the Chinese lunar calendar.
Feb. or Mar.: Losar (Tibetan New Year) precedes the celebration of **Monlam;** these two major Buddhist festivals have large processions and are especially important at Lhasa's Jokhang temple.
May 1: Labor Day honors the worker.
May 4: Youth Day honors the student protest against Imperial China in 1911.
May: Temples hold elaborate ceremonies during **Sakadawa** (the birthday, enlightenment, and death of the Historic Buddha).
June: Tibetans gather at **Shigaste** to witness the annual display of an enormous sacred *thang-ka* (religious scroll) and ritual dances.
July 1: This day marks the **creation of the Communist Party.**
Aug. 1: The honoring of the **People's Liberation Army** occurs on this day.
Oct. 1: National Day marks the founding of the People's Republic of China.
Nov.: The **Festival of Lights** honors the death of Tsongkhapa, the founder of the Gelug (Yellow Hat Sect). Butter lamps burn throughout Tibet.

What to Pack

Follow the guidelines in Before You Go to the Himalayas, Chapter 1. Be sure to bring good sun protection, a flashlight, a water bottle and purification tablets, and excellent walking shoes. If you plan to trek, pack light—you're in high altitude. If you plan to stay in budget hotels, bring a sleeping bag. Rooms may not be clean.

Taking Money Abroad

China has no restrictions on the amount of foreign currency and traveler's checks you may import. *Stay away from the black market.* Change money in the **People's Bank of China** or in **hotels** that are allowed to convert foreign currency. To reconvert unspent currency, save your Bank Transaction Receipts. It's illegal to take out the official currency, renminbi.

The official Chinese currency is the renminbi (RMB), which breaks into the yuan, jiao, and fen. Yuan (paper money) come in 1, 2, 5, and 10 notes. One yuan equals 10 jiao (also paper money). Jiao come in 1, 2, and 5 notes. One jiao equals 10 fen (the official coin). Fen come in 1, 2, and 5 denominations. When foreigners change money, they receive instead Foreign Exchange Certificates (FEC), which come in seven denominations that equal 1, 5, 10, 50, and 100 yuan notes and 1 and 5 jiao notes. In private shops, you'll get RMB in change. Once you leave Lhasa or popular destinations, use RMB. Tibetans in remote areas are unfamiliar with FECs. At press time, the rate of exchange was U.S. $1 = RMB 3.10, £1 = RMB 4.91.

Visas

Tourist visas, good for one month, are issued to foreigners after they sign up and pay for a tour. You need a passport and two passport photos. The cost for Americans is $7; Canadians, $36;

Britons, $36. Visas normally take two weeks to process. If your trip extends beyond a month, you can apply for a one-month extension (cost: 5 yuan) at the Public Security Bureau in Lhasa. Previously, some remote destinations required an Alien Travel Permit (ATP), also issued by the Public Security Bureau. Before the June 1989 events, China was relaxing ATP requirements. At press time, the rules were in a state of confusion. Check with your travel agent.

Americans Contact the **Embassy of the People's Republic of China** (2300 Connecticut Ave NW, Washington, DC 20008, tel. 202/328–2517) or a **Consulate General of the People's Republic of China** (520 12th Ave., New York, NY 10036, tel. 212/330–7409; Suite 1200, 104 S. Michigan Ave., Chicago, IL 60603, tel. 312/346–0287; 3417 Montrose Blvd., Houston, TX 77006, tel. 713/524–4311; Suite 300, 502 Shatto Pl., Los Angeles, CA 90020, tel. 213/380–2507; 1450 Laguna St., San Francisco, CA 94115, tel. 415/563–4857).

Canadians Contact the **Embassy of the People's Republic of China** (Suite 415, Andrew St., Ottawa, Ont. K1N 5H3, tel. 613/234–2706) or a **Consulate General of the People's Republic of China** (Suite, 240 George St., Toronto, Ont. M5R 2P4, tel. 416/964–7575; 3380 Granville St., Vancouver, B.C. V6H 3K3, tel. 604/736–3910).

Britons **Embassy of the People's Republic of China** (31 Portland Pl., London W1N 3AG, tel. 01/636–5637).

Customs and Duties

On Arrival Don't bring in fire arms or any articles considered detrimental to Chinese political, economic, cultural, and moral interests (manuscripts, printed matter, tapes, drugs). You may bring in a camera (still, movie, or video) and 20 rolls of film, two cartons of cigarettes, and four bottles of liquor. On arrival, you must declare all valuables.

On Departure Antiques and animal skins can't be exported. Objects created before 1959 are also subject to careful scrutiny and may be seized. Other items can be impounded without notice. Foreigners must pay RMB 20 Foreign Departure Tax when they fly out of Lhasa. If you leave by land for Kathmandu, you need an exit permit (RMB 5).

Time Zone

Tibet observes Beijing standard time, which is eight hours ahead of Greenwich mean time and 13 hours ahead of U.S. eastern standard time.

Staying Healthy

Pay attention to the precautions against high-altitude sickness *(see* also Before You Go to the Himalayas, Chapter 1). No vaccination certificate or inoculation is required for Tibet.

Arriving and Departing

The best approach to Lhasa is from Kathmandu in Nepal (*see* Arriving and Departing, Kathmandu, Chapter 4).

Airlines and Airport **Royal Nepal Airlines (RNAC)** and the official **Chinese Airlines (CAAC)** currently make two weekly flights between Lhasa and Kathmandu. **Gonggar Airport** is 100 kilometers (62 miles) from Lhasa.

Flying Time Plan on about an hour flying time from Kathmandu.

Staying in Tibet

Behavioral Dos and Don'ts

Follow all advice governing proper behavior around Buddhist monuments described in Before You Go to the Himalayas, Chapter 1. Because of indiscriminate photographing by tourists, sky burials, in which the dead are left for vultures, are now off-limits to foreigners. Do not hitch hike; it could be a risk to the driver. He could lose his license. If you're invited inside a Tibetan home, go ahead. The invitation wouldn't have been made unless it was considered safe. When you visit monasteries or important monuments, official entrance and photography fees go to the government. To make a contribution to the monastery itself or to the lamas, put your donation in the offering bowl.

Finally, Tibet is one destination where *you must ask before you take a picture of anyone.* If your film is impounded and developed, the photographs could have serious repercussions for the subjects.

Important Addresses and Numbers

Tourist Information **CITS**, with little useful information, has an office in Lhasa (2nd fl., No. 3 Guest House, tel. 22980); it's open Monday–Saturday 9–12:30 and 3:30–6:30. To extend visas or obtain an overland exit permit to Nepal, visit the **Public Security Bureau** (near Potala, tel. 23170), which is open Monday–Wednesday, Friday, and Saturday 8:30–12:30, 4–7, Thursday 8:30–12:30; closed Sunday. This office also issues Alien Travel Permits if they're required. **CAAC** (the airline) is at 86 Jiejang Lu (tel. 22417).

Embassies No American, Canadian, or British embassies or consulates exist in Lhasa. For a visa to Nepal, contact the **Nepalese Consulate** (13 Norbulinga Lu, tel. 22880) or get your visa when you arrive at the border or land in Kathmandu.

Hospitals **Renmin Municipal Hospital** (Xingfu Lu, tel. 23212) and **Tibetan Hospital** (near the Cultural Park and Jokhang Temple (tel. 24211).

Banks The **People's Bank of China** (on Xingfu Xi Lu) is open Monday–Saturday 8:30–noon and 3:30–6:30; closed Sundays.

Post Offices The central **Post Office** (near the Potala) is open summer, Monday–Saturday 9–6:30; winter, Monday–Saturday 10–5; closed Sunday.

Highlights for First-time Visitors

Numbers in the margin correspond with points of interest on the Tibet map.

1 Most tours in Tibet include **Lhasa** and some of the following important destinations and monuments.

Lhasa **Jokhang:** This is Tibet's holiest temple, with over 25 chapels and countless priceless statues and frescoes. **Barkhor:** This bustling bazaar in Old Lhasa is on the pilgrim's customary circumambulation route around Jokhang. **Potala Palace:** Tibet's resplendent landmark, with over 1,000 rooms and 10,000 shrines, was the home of the Dalai Lamas. **Ramoche Temple:** Lhasa's second-oldest temple has exquisite treasures. **Dralha Lupuk, or Serpent's Cave:** This cave-temple has dieties and historic figures built into rock. **Lukhang or Naga (Snake) King Chapel:** Set in the Dragon King Pool, this monastery has some of Lhasa's finest frescoes. **Norbulinka, or Summer Palace:** From this palace complex, the Dalai Lama fled to India in 1959.

Lhasa Environs **Drepung Monastery:** This is the largest Gelug monastery in Tibet, with the Ganden Palace and several beautiful chapels. *8 km (5 mi) from Lhasa.* **Sera Monastery:** This important Gelug monastery contains numerous chapels, with splendid murals and icons. *5 km (3 mi) from Lhasa.* **Ganden Monastery:** This enormous monastery was established by Tsongkhapa, the founder of the Gelug sect. *40 km (25 mi) from Lhasa.*

Samye **Samye Monastery:** Tibet's first monastery, built in the 700s,
2 has numerous chambers with precious icons and frescoes. *130 km (105 mi) from Lhasa (involves a ferry ride).*

Gyantse **Kumbum Monastery:** One of Tibet's loveliest monasteries, with
3 a golden roof, its chapels house excellent religious art. **Pelkor Chode Monastery:** It has several chapels with memorable interiors. *Gyantse is 264 km (164 mi) from Lhasa.*

Shigatse **Tashilhunpo Monastery:** This vast complex, with dazzling golden
4 roofs and impressive chapels, was the former seat of the Panchen Lama. *About 354 km (219 mi) from Lhasa.*

5 **Mt. Kailash:** The most sacred mountain in the Himalayas for Hindus and Buddhists—to circle it is to achieve salvation.

6 **Mansarovar Lake:** Sacred to Buddhists, this is the world's highest freshwater lake.

Outdoor Adventures

You must be in excellent physical condition to tolerate Tibet's high altitude. Highly recommended adventures are indicated with a star ★.

★ **Jeep Safaris:** *Kathmandu to Lhasa:* The trip length (14–25 days) depends on stops and side trips. From Kathmandu, you head north across the border and follow the Bhote Kosi gorge. You climb through snow-peaked mountains, chug over Nyalam Thong La Pass, altitude 5,000 meters (16,400 feet), and enter the Tibetan plateau: an arid desert with villages huddled at bases of mountains, prayer flags snapping in the wind, and ancient monasteries jutting from craggy perches. If the sky is clear, you see Mt. Everest. You pass nomads with herds of sheep and yak as you continue to Tingri, an old trading town, then visit Shigatse with its famous Sakya (Red Hat Sect) Tashilhunpo Monastery. From here, most tours head to Lhasa via historic Gyantse and a visit to Kumbum. Tiger Mountain includes two days of rafting in coracles on the Tsangpo River.

Trekking: Most treks in Tibet include sightseeing in and around Lhasa, then vehicular travel to the trek's starting point.

★ **Trekking (up to a week):** *Mt. Kailash and Mansarovar Lake:* This trip originates in Kathmandu and starts with an overland journey, first to Lhasa or directly northwest from Kathmandu to the two sacred destinations. Some tours continue west, following the old Silk Route. Trekking time around Mt. Kailash is about three days. Trip time is 28–36 days (June–Sept.).

Mt. Namche Barwa Trek: Mountain Travel and InnerAsia offer a six-day trek in southeastern Tibet near Bhutan, combined with a visit to Lhasa and to the base of Mt. Namche Barwa, altitude 7,758 meters (25,445 feet)—the world's highest unclimbed mountain (Apr. and Oct.).

Yanshiping village to the source of the Yangste River: This seven-day Mountain Travel trek in a remote region north of Lhasa is combined with a tour of Lhasa and Kathmandu (June and July).

Kulu Kangri Valley: Mountain Travel offers another seven-day trek, also combined with visits to Lhasa and Kathmandu, in Kulu Kangri Valley near Bhutan (Sept.–Oct.).

★ **Trekking (over a week):** *Mt. Everest Base Camp or east face overland journey and trek:* Most companies start from Lhasa then proceed to the sacred Rongbuk Monastery, savagely damaged by the Chinese and the starting point for both treks. The Base Camp trek lasts three–eight days round-trip and heads up the Rongbuk Glacier to the Everest Base Camp, altitude 5,182 meters (17,000 feet). Many outfits offer a longer eight-day round-trip trek to the base camp that originates from Tingri and follows the historic route used by the earliest Everest expeditions. This is one of the most beautiful Himalayan treks and the best way to see Mt. Everest (May to Nov.).

Telephones and Telegrams

You can make international phone calls and send telegrams from the **Lhasa Telegraph and Communications Office** and **Lhasa Hotel.**

Mail

Receiving Mail Have letters sent to your hotel in Lhasa; plan on 10 days' delivery time. The sender must address it to you in "Xizang Autonomous Region, People's Republic of China" on the envelope.

Postal Rates An airmail letter (weighing 10 grams) to England, Europe, Canada, and the United States costs RMB .80. Aerograms cost RMB .70.

Tipping

Tipping is strictly prohibited in Tibet.

Opening and Closing Times

The official business day is broken with a long lunch break. Sunday is the official holiday. Some government offices are also closed on Saturday. Banks are open Monday–Saturday 8:30–noon and 3:30–6:30. Post offices are usually open Monday–Saturday 9–6:30. Monasteries are usually open daily sunrise–sunset. Friendship Stores (government department stores) are usually open daily 9:30–4:30.

Shopping

Look for thang-kas, sculptures, prayer wheels, silver *dorjes* (thunderbolts), sacred *khatas* (white scarves), and Tibetan jewelry. Bargaining is customary; aim for a 25% discount. *(See* Customs, above, regarding restrictions on purchases.)

Dining and Lodging

Dining In Lhasa and Shigatse, you can get good Chinese and Tibetan food. Everywhere else, your options are limited.

Mealtimes Most restaurants shut down by 9 or 10 PM.

Precautions *See* Staying Healthy in Before You Go to the Himalayas, Chapter 1.

Ratings Most restaurants are inexpensive (under $5). Hotel restaurants can be moderately priced ($5–$10). Prices are per person, including taxes and excluding drinks and service charges.

Lodging Except in Lhasas, accommodations in Tibet can be bleak. Many tour operators avoid the hotels once they leave this city and camp instead.

Ratings Most hotels are moderate ($25–60) or inexpensive (under $25). Prices are for a standard double room, including taxes and excluding service charges.

Credit Cards

Currently, credit cards are useless.

Index

Personal Itinerary

Departure *Date*

Time

Transportation

Arrival *Date*   *Time*

Departure *Date*   *Time*

Transportation

Accommodations

Arrival *Date*   *Time*

Departure *Date*   *Time*

Transportation

Accommodations

Arrival *Date*   *Time*

Departure *Date*   *Time*

Transportation

Accommodations

Personal Itinerary

Arrival *Date*   *Time*

Departure *Date*   *Time*

Transportation

Accommodations

Arrival *Date*   *Time*

Departure *Date*   *Time*

Transportation

Accommodations

Arrival *Date*   *Time*

Departure *Date*   *Time*

Transportation

Accommodations

Arrival *Date*   *Time*

Departure *Date*   *Time*

Transportation

Accommodations

Personal Itinerary

Arrival *Date*   *Time*

Departure *Date*   *Time*

Transportation

Accommodations

Arrival *Date*   *Time*

Departure *Date*   *Time*

Transportation

Accommodations

Arrival *Date*   *Time*

Departure *Date*   *Time*

Transportation

Accommodations

Arrival *Date*   *Time*

Departure *Date*   *Time*

Transportation

Accommodations

Addresses

Name

Address

Telephone

Name

Address

Telephone

Name

Address

Telephone

Name

Address

Telephone

Name

Address

Telephone

Name

Address

Telephone

Name

Address

Telephone

Name

Address

Telephone

Name

Address

Telephone

Name

Address

Telephone

Name

Address

Telephone

Name

Address

Telephone

Name

Address

Telephone

Name

Address

Telephone

Name

Address

Telephone

Name

Address

Telephone

Notes

Fodor's Travel Guides

U.S. Guides

Alaska
Arizona
Atlantic City & the
  New Jersey Shore
Boston
California
Cape Cod
Carolinas & the
  Georgia Coast
The Chesapeake Region
Chicago
Colorado
Disney World & the
  Orlando Area

Florida
Hawaii
Las Vegas
Los Angeles, Orange
  County, Palm Springs
Maui
Miami,
  Fort Lauderdale,
  Palm Beach
Michigan, Wisconsin,
  Minnesota
New England
New Mexico
New Orleans

New Orleans (Pocket
  Guide)
New York City
New York City (Pocket
  Guide)
New York State
Pacific North Coast
Philadelphia
The Rockies
San Diego
San Francisco
San Francisco (Pocket
  Guide)
The South

Texas
USA
Virgin Islands
Virginia
Waikiki
Washington, DC

Foreign Guides

Acapulco
Amsterdam
Australia, New Zealand,
  The South Pacific
Austria
Bahamas
Bahamas (Pocket
  Guide)
Baja & the Pacific
  Coast Resorts
Barbados
Beijing, Guangzhou &
  Shanghai
Belgium &
  Luxembourg
Bermuda
Brazil
Britain (Great Travel
  Values)
Budget Europe
Canada
Canada (Great Travel
  Values)
Canada's Atlantic
  Provinces
Cancun, Cozumel,
  Yucatan Peninsula

Caribbean
Caribbean (Great
  Travel Values)
Central America
Eastern Europe
Egypt
Europe
Europe's Great
  Cities
France
France (Great Travel
  Values)
Germany
Germany (Great Travel
  Values)
Great Britain
Greece
The Himalayan
  Countries
Holland
Hong Kong
Hungary
India,
  including Nepal
Ireland
Israel
Italy

Italy (Great Travel
  Values)
Jamaica
Japan
Japan (Great Travel
  Values)
Kenya, Tanzania,
  the Seychelles
Korea
Lisbon
Loire Valley
London
London (Great
  Travel Values)
London (Pocket Guide)
Madrid & Barcelona
Mexico
Mexico City
Montreal &
  Quebec City
Munich
New Zealand
North Africa
Paris
Paris (Pocket Guide)
People's Republic of
  China

Portugal
Rio de Janeiro
The Riviera (Fun on)
Rome
Saint Martin &
  Sint Maarten
Scandinavia
Scandinavian Cities
Scotland
Singapore
South America
South Pacific
Southeast Asia
Soviet Union
Spain
Spain (Great Travel
  Values)
Sweden
Switzerland
Sydney
Tokyo
Toronto
Turkey
Vienna
Yugoslavia

Special-Interest Guides

Health & Fitness
  Vacations
Royalty Watching

Selected Hotels of
  Europe

Selected Resorts and
  Hotels of the U.S.
Shopping in Europe

Skiing in North America
Sunday in New York